New Perspectives
on
Encounter Groups

Lawrence N. Solomon

Betty Berzon

Editors

Foreword by Carl R. Rogers

NEW
PERSPECTIVES
ON
ENCOUNTER
GROUPS

Jossey-Bass Inc., Publishers
San Francisco • Washington • London • 1972

NEW PERSPECTIVES ON ENCOUNTER GROUPS
Lawrence N. Solomon and Betty Berzon, Editors

Published in Great Britain by
Jossey-Bass, Inc., Publishers
St. George's House
44 Hatton Garden, London E.C.1

Library of Congress Catalogue Card Number LC 73-186583

International Standard Book Number ISBN 0-87589-128-4

Manufactured in the United States of America

JACKET DESIGN BY WILLI BAUM

FIRST EDITION

Code 7216

The Jossey-Bass
Behavioral Science Series

General Editors

WILLIAM E. HENRY
University of Chicago

NEVITT SANFORD
Wright Institute, Berkeley

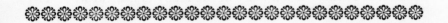

Foreword

This is a solid, comprehensive, and courageous book about various types of encounter groups and their outcomes. I should like to elaborate on those three initial adjectives.

The book is solid because it includes serious and provocative essays by many authors and a number of careful research studies. It contains a summary of the many empirical studies by Betty Berzon and Lawrence Solomon on self-directed groups and describes the effects of groups operating with taped instructions (thus eliminating the need for a leader). An account is given of the remarkable study by Morton Lieberman and others of the effects of differing leadership styles. It contains a carefully documented account of Richard Farson's bold experiment in conducting a group for thirteen weeks on TV, encouraging his viewers to form their own self-directed groups, and following up on the consequences. (Why has this successful experiment never been repeated?)

The book is comprehensive in that it covers everything from research studies to descriptive accounts, by the late Fred Stoller, of marathon groups and the use of videotape feedback. It describes a wide spectrum, from the therapylike group to the educational group, from Gestalt therapy to the task-oriented and team-building groups in industry whose leaders make it very clear that these are *not* therapy. It has accounts of groups for married couples and groups for women only. One need only scan the table of contents to see the riches available—too many to mention here.

The book is courageous in presenting critical and controversial views. The editors include Sigmund Koch's blistering attack on such groups in which he states that they only produce a pseudo openness and pseudospontaneity and impose on the participants a model of conformity, of what man should be. (I cannot resist the comment that any conformity induced by encounter groups is as nothing compared to the conformity absolutely demanded by graduate departments of psychology!) It cites Herbert Marcuse's bitter dislike of groups. I suspect neither Koch nor Marcuse has ever been involved in an encounter group, but it is clear that this probability does not prevent them from being experts.

Many statements by one author directly contradict statements by other authors, so that the reader must think for himself. For example, seven *nevers* are quoted from Everett Shostrom, including "Never participate in a group encounter with close associates, persons with whom you have a professional or competitive social relation." The chapter on group work at TRW Systems is built on exactly the opposite principle. To some extent, so are the chapters on married couples, families, and small children.

I fear I may spoil the book for you by describing it too completely. Let me finish my account by simply saying that anyone who has been in a group, or contemplated joining one, or is interested in using them in education, industry, families, or racial situations, or who is opposed to groups entirely, or who wishes to study them empirically will find rich food for thought in this collection of chapters.

Why all the current interest in the intensive group encounter? For one thing it appears to be a significant part of the cultural attempt to meet the isolation of contemporary life. I am not fond of the often faddish elements in it, but in general the small group experience fills a need. From a social point of view, I believe we are sufficiently affluent that our physical needs are met, and now what would we most like to have? We would like to be free from the alienation that is so much a part of urban life, so much a part of our life in general. We would like somehow to find ourselves in real contact with other per-

sons, and I believe this desire, without question, is one of the
elements that gives much of the magnetism to the intensive
group experience. The person who has come close to experiencing a real I-Thou relationship in a group is no longer an isolated
individual.

Another implication, which is partly expressed in statements by many who have attended encounter groups, is that
the group experience is an avenue to fulfillment. We have
nearly reached the limit of what material things can give the
individual in the way of fulfillment. We are turning more and
more to the psychological world, groping for something that
will give satisfaction, something that will really permit a man
to achieve his potential. I believe this whole development has a
special significance for a culture which appears bent on dehumanizing the individual and dehumanizing our interpersonal
relations. The phenomenon of the group enterprise is an important force in the opposite direction, a direction toward
making relationships more meaningful and more personal.

The intensive group experience has a more general philosophical implication. It is one expression of the existential point
of view which is making itself so pervasively evident in art and
literature and modern life. The implicit goal of the group process seems to be to live life fully in the here-and-now relationship. I think the parallel with an existential point of view is
clear-cut.

One other issue raised by this phenomenon of groups and
the interest in them is expressed in the philosophical questions,
"What is our view of the optimal person?" "What is the goal of
personality development?" "What are we trying to achieve
with the people with whom we work?" Different ages and different cultures would give different answers to these questions.
Those people who are engaged in the group process are reasonably clear that in a climate of freedom, group members move
toward becoming more expressive, more spontaneous, more
flexible, more closely related to their feelings, more open to their
own experience and to that of others. If we value this type of
person and this type of behavior, then clearly the group process
is a valuable process. If, on the other hand, we place value on

the individual who is effective in suppressing his feelings, who operates from a firm set of principles, who does not trust his own reaction and experience but relies on authority, then we would regard the group process as something suspect, something we would oppose. I feel we have to be keenly aware of the fact that there is room for a difference of opinion on this question of the optimal kind of person, the person we are trying to develop, and that we should encourage public and social discussion of that issue.

So I think that information, such as that presented in the great variety of chapters in this book, can do nothing but good. The more we learn about the group process, its theory, techniques, and outcomes, the more able we become to use it for the common good.

La Jolla, California   CARL R. ROGERS
February 1972   *Resident Fellow*
                                  Center for Studies of the Person

Preface

New Perspectives on Encounter Groups had its inception in the years we spent on the staff at the Western Behavioral Sciences Institute (WBSI) in La Jolla, California, for during those first years at WBSI we began our work with small groups. In the early 1960s, they were most often called sensitivity training groups. Several years later, Carl Rogers, by then having transferred his base of operations from the University of Wisconsin to WBSI, gave these groups the name Basic Encounter. The *basic* did not stick. The *encounter* did.

Our inquiry into the small group process was aided and stimulated by the opportunity to work closely with some of the leading social scientists of our time, as they came to WBSI for varying periods as Visiting Fellows. These Fellows were generously supported out of WBSI endowment and had nothing required of them beyond a minimum availability to staff members. We took maximum advantage of the availability of such men as Rogers, Abraham Maslow, Theodore Newcomb, Abraham Kaplan, S. I. Hayakawa, Jack R. Gibb, Alex Bavelas, Sigmund Koch, Herbert Kelman, and others distinguished in their field. Each of these scholars, in his own way, contributed to our growing interest and involvement in the study of the intensive small group.

In the early years we were mainly interested in learning to lead groups. Neither of us had had any formal training in group leadership, despite graduate studies in clinical psychol-

ogy and even, for Solomon, a Ph.D. in that field. In the service
of that interest, we decided to study groups without leaders to
see what was missing. We reasoned that if it were possible to
identify through research those specific functions served by an
encounter group leader, we might then guide our efforts to
develop those skills. We were encouraged to go ahead with this
idea, and the result was the pilot study we did in 1960 on
leaderless groups (Berzon and Solomon, 1964). This study grew
into a series of projects on self-directed groups which, in turn,
evolved into one of the major research programs of WBSI, span-
ning a period of nine years (see Chapter 12 for a report of this
research).

The WBSI training workshops and small group research
efforts grew considerably during the first half of the 1960s. In
those early days, we were groping and toying with this new,
exciting phenomenon called encounter. We learned as we explored. Time and time again we asked ourselves, "What does
this group experience mean?" And we found that only with
further experience and study could we approach the fullness of
understanding evidenced in Jack Gibb's chapter in this volume
(Chapter 1).

We came to understand, for instance, how a kind of
tyranny can develop in the group process, a tyranny which
places the group's needs always before those of the individual
participant. Sigmund Koch addresses this problem in Chapter
3. Sometimes in their fervor to make the process work, group
members innocently enforce that tyranny. They pressure individuals to forego their own needs to meet the need of the group
for complete involvement of all its members.

Of course, careful selection and screening of group participants, as well as proper training programs for group leaders,
can do much to reduce or circumvent this danger. However, in
those days we did not know as much about these two possibilities as is now reflected in Brendan Reddy's Chapter 4 and
Frederick Massarik's Chapter 5. Had we then had the insight
into procedures for introducing small group process into ongoing social systems—an insight which has evolved during the
intervening decade—we might have avoided many errors.

Scholars in the field of small group research are continuing to learn and explore. The chapters by O. S. Farry and S. M. Herman on organizational development groups (Chapter 18) and by Morton Shaevitz and Donald Barr on intensive groups in a small college (Chapter 17) speak directly to these concerns.

Through our engrossing involvement in the beginning encounter culture, we almost relinquished ourselves entirely to the group process. We were excited by the joyfulness and deep emotionality produced by the microlab techniques of fantasy and nonverbal exercises utilized by William Schutz and Charles Seashore (Chapter 10). When marathon groups first began, we invited George Bach to La Jolla to lead part of the WBSI staff (and others) in a weekend encounter. Reading Fred Stoller's chapter on the marathon group (Chapter 9) helps us to conceptualize the affective experiences of that weekend.

As the encounter culture expanded, a wide range of techniques and procedures appeared on the scene. The relatively old procedures of psychodrama began to take on new significance and meaning as they were applied within an encounter group context (see Lewis Yablonsky's Chapter 16). Physical contact, body awareness, and touching found a prominent place in the armamentarium of many encounter group leaders. This departure from traditional therapeutic practices and norms, venturing as it did into tabooed areas, raised many concerns within the professional community. Bertram Forer concentrates on this aspect of encounter group technology in Chapter 11. New technologies generated by the electronic media found application in Richard Farson's bold experiment with encounter groups via public television (see Chapter 13) and Fred Stoller's focused feedback procedure (Chapter 14).

Concurrent with encounter group events centered in and emanating from WBSI was an exciting development on the rugged California coast south of Monterey: Esalen Institute, the first growth center in the nation, opened. Frederick Perls, founder of Gestalt therapy, came to have his major impact on the therapeutic enterprise from his position as psychiatrist-in-residence at Esalen. His influence on encounter groups is de-

scribed by Abraham Levitsky and James Simkin in Chapter 15.
We from WBSI had many opportunities to lead and participate
in programs at Esalen, and there was a lively and enriching
exchange of ideas between the two centers.

Each of our encounter experiences added to our growing
conviction that these group processes were powerful tools for
change and growth. We witnessed the beginning of an encounter culture which held the potential for profound impact on
contemporary society. We developed an equally strong belief in
the need to clarify the limits of group power and to protect the
individual's right to choose his degree of separateness from the
group.

In our joint exploration with others, seeking a personally meaningful balance between separateness and togetherness,
we are aware repeatedly of what might be called the subversive
nature of the encounter culture, as William Blanchard describes
it in Chapter 2. Many values and norms promoted by encounter
groups are opposed to those prevailing in society. The intensive
small group provides a powerful challenge to the status quo and
thus, along with other educative and growth-enhancing procedures, seeks to subvert and modify pathological norms in the
direction of healthy and full functioning.

As a cultural phenomenon, the encounter mode is finding
application today in almost every social institution and subculture of society. From a Magic Circle in elementary school
(see Harold Bessell's Chapter 22) to special group formats for
married couples (Richard Pilder's Chapter 19) and families
(James Sorrells' Chapter 20), the encounter process is having
profound impact on traditional institutions. In harmony with
the liberation movements of this decade, encounter groups are
forming for women only (see Chapter 21 by Betty Meador,
Evelyn Solomon, and Maria Bowen), homosexuals (Don Clark's
Chapter 23), and racial confrontation (Chapter 24 by Price
Cobbs).

The issues raised by the encounter group technologies
are serious and complex. There are practical issues, theoretical
concerns, philosophical problems, and social, economic, and
political considerations, as well as a host of related complexities.

Only a handful of these problems are dealt with in *New Perspectives on Encounter Groups*. But as applications proliferate and technologies are perfected, the need for careful assessment and serious reflection increases. Systematic research is difficult in this area. Three recent attempts are reported in Chapter 6 by James Bebout and Barry Gordon, Chapter 7 by Morton Lieberman, Irvin Yalom, and Matthew Miles, and Chapter 8 by Morton Lieberman.

Much still remains to be done. We hope this book contributes to the continuing dialogue among those informed and concerned individuals who seek, through understanding and study, to refine one of man's most recent inventions for the actualization of his humanity: the encounter group.

La Jolla, California   LAWRENCE N. SOLOMON
April 1972   BETTY BERZON

Contents

Contents

Contributors

DONALD J. BARR, *director of academic services, and professor, College of Human Ecology, Cornell University*

JAMES BEBOUT, *director, T.I.E. Project, and professor of psychology, San Francisco State College*

BETTY BERZON, *consultant and counselor in private practice, Los Angeles*

HAROLD BESSELL, *psychotherapist in private practice, La Jolla*

WILLIAM H. BLANCHARD, *Urban Semester, University of Southern California*

MARIA BOWEN, *clinical psychologist, Center for Studies of the Person, La Jolla*

DON CLARK, *psychotherapist in private practice, San Francisco*

PRICE M. COBBS, *clinical professor, Department of Psychiatry, University of California, San Francisco*

O. S. FARRY, *management and organization consultant in private practice, Manhattan Beach, California*

RICHARD E. FARSON, *School of Design, California Institute of the Arts, Valencia, California*

BERTRAM R. FORER, *clinical psychologist in private practice, Los Angeles*

JACK R. GIBB, *consulting psychologist in private practice, La Jolla*

BARRY GORDON, *research associate, Talent in Interpersonal Explorations Project, Berkeley*

S. M. HERMAN, *director of training and organization development, TRW Systems, Redondo Beach, California*

SIGMUND KOCH, *academic vice-president and university professor, Boston University*

ABRAHAM LEVITSKY, *San Francisco Gestalt Institute; private practice, Berkeley*

MORTON A. LIEBERMAN, *professor of human development and psychiatry, University of Chicago*

FREDERICK MASSARIK, *Graduate School of Management, University of California, Los Angeles*

BETTY MEADOR, *director, Center for Studies of the Person, La Jolla*

MATTHEW B. MILES, *senior research associate, Program in Humanistic Education, State University of New York at Albany*

RICHARD PILDER, *process consultant and psychologist, Community Psychological Consultants East, Riverside, Connecticut*

W. BRENDAN REDDY, *program director, Community Psychology Institute, and professor of psychology, University of Cincinnati*

JEROME REISEL, *private practice, Beverly Hills*

WILLIAM C. SCHUTZ, *Esalen Institute, Big Sur, California*

CHARLES SEASHORE, *organization consultant and consulting psychologist in private practice, Washington, D.C.*

MORTON H. SHAEVITZ, *director of counseling and psychological services, University of California, San Diego*

JAMES S. SIMKIN, *clinical psychologist in private practice, Big Sur, California*

EVELYN SOLOMON, *staff member, Center for Studies of the Person, La Jolla*

LAWRENCE N. SOLOMON, *consulting psychologist in private practice, La Jolla*

JAMES SORRELLS, *professor, Starr King School for Religious Leadership, Berkeley*

FREDERICK H. STOLLER, *deceased, was senior research associate and professor, University of Southern California*

LEWIS YABLONSKY, *Department of Sociology, California State College, Hayward*

IRVIN D. YALOM, *professor of psychiatry, School of Medicine, Stanford University*

New Perspectives
on
Encounter Groups

Meaning of the Small Group Experience

Jack R. Gibb

The expression "Let me tell you about my group experience" has become about as prevalent as "Let me tell you about my operation" or "Let me tell you about my analysis." The supplication has a certain legitimacy. A group experience has a special quality and seems unique to each participant. Observers can pick up commonalities as they study groups, but to the participant the experience often has a dramatic, compelling, and forceful effect that he finds difficult to convey in words to the uninitiated—or even to others who have made the scene.

The small group, like it or not, is with us. It seems to offer something to everyone. Researcher, theorist, trainer-therapist, participant—each is coming to see the small group as a rich source of data. Sociology and psychology are cross-fertilizing each other in the small group arena. Theorists in political science, economics, and all the fields of behavioral science see rich implications in the hard and soft data of small group research. Therapy, vocational rehabilitation, human relations training, organizational development, social work, counseling, education, and executive development have all been touched and have grown through theory and practice in the small group field.

When we speak of *the* small group experience, we greatly oversimplify the situation. There are as many small group experiences as there are groups. We do, however, usually refer to a general experience that stems from the T-group, a method of creating a group experience invented by the staff of the National Training Laboratories in 1947. The definitive nature of this method is that the group spends a large share of its energies focused upon the here and now—the feelings and perceptions generated by the group and the processes of group formation—rather than upon the cognitive content of the discussion. Since the pioneering work in the late forties, many variations and offshoots of this basic method have appeared. These groups have different names: sensitivity, instrumented, marathon, emergent, basic encounter, confrontation, development, and self-directed, to mention a few of the better known. Sometimes, as in the case of the marathon, the name indicates a basic difference in method and theory, but in other instances the name reveals few generic differences. To experienced investigators the most valid way to anticipate the nature of a particular group experience is to learn the name of the group trainer or leader. Yet such prediction is risky, because most major trainers have been experimenting with format, method, and theory.

The literature indicates significant variables on which small group experiences may differ. Groups vary in intimacy and depth of interaction. Depth may be increased by using historical material or by sharing intensely personal feelings engendered in the group. Groups vary in duration, from a few hours in a microlab to several sessions a week for seventeen or eighteen months. The length of time spent in uninterrupted person-contact is shown by marathon experiences to be as critical as any other dimension. Some groups focus primarily on the individual and others focus considerably more upon group and process analysis. The degree of institutional imbedding seems especially critical to workers who are interested in cultural change and in environmental support for change. Other significant variables are amount of prestructuring of the group, group size, homogeneity of its composition, and specificity and nature of the stated goals.

Although theory and practice change rapidly, ten theory-and-practice clusters can be identified as most prevalent. There is great overlap among these categories; most theorists and practitioners are eclectic, opportunistic, and experimental. The group experience interests those in the helping professions mostly because it is a medium for increasing behavior change. The practitioner can find each of these approaches profitable and can choose among a wide range of reputable theories and orientations.

The first cluster may be called sensitivity experiences. The earliest and clearest purpose of the T-group was to help people be more sensitive than they usually are to social reality. I reviewed more than two hundred of the most adequate research studies evaluating the small group experience (Gibb, 1971). The clearest and least controversial finding is that social perceptiveness does improve with T-group experience. A formal and informal body of theory hypothesizes that increased awareness of social reality is correlated with self-actualization and with effectiveness of the rehabilitative processes.

Most theory and innovation in this area are directed toward increasing the validity and reliability of social data (input) entering the cognitive world of the participant. And, significantly, much of the work being reported is directed in part toward increased effectiveness of data processing, particularly on the input side. Stoller's work with focused feedback and videotape, the Western Behavioral Sciences Institute (WBSI) studies, and Yablonsky's work with role playing can all be seen as methods of increasing sensitivity. Role playing, for instance, is one means of presenting reality to the organism in an increasingly processable way.

In the second category are authenticity experiences. The underlying body of theory and practice seems to focus on increasing the validity and reliability of data output. Advocates emphasize openness, authenticity, congruence, transparency, and confrontation. They may describe their group type as basic encounter or confrontation. They try to develop accurate data processing, particularly within the self and in outputs to other selves. These aspects of personal growth and self-development are explored at length in writings in psychology, religion, management, and philosophy. The evidence is fairly good that many group experiences do result in changes in the authenticity of internal data processing.

The third cluster encompasses creativity-release experiences. Some theorists and practitioners believe that a central element in personal growth is an increase in the range and depth of creative output. Creative behavior is increased by reducing inhibitions, reducing fears, increasing spontaneity, practicing expressive-coping behavior, and increasing communication. People are exploring widely varied methods: body movement, sensory awareness, finger painting, free verse, interpretative dance, psychedelic drugs, meditation, the Minerva experience, nude marathons, fight training, Zen, contextual maps, induced aggression, and nonverbal encounters.

The Esalen Institute and the Association for Humanistic Psychology have actively supported experimental methods that explore these theories. Workers in this field talk about such goals as expanding human potentialities, actualizing the self, expanding consciousness, freeing the inner world, or communicating in depth. We have little hard evidence on the effectiveness of these methods. The excitement created in both participants and observers promises enrichment that will come with greater fusion of the sensitivity training methods and the creativity methods.

Programed experiences constitute the fourth category. Promising and diverse groups of people have been experimenting with programed or instrumented learning groups. Solomon and Berzon (1970) describe work done at WBSI in programing the group experience. Robert Morton (1965) and Robert Blake (1966) and their colleagues have been developing what they call instrumented groups, which include programed experiences built into human relations training. Jerome Berlin (1964) and Morton have pioneered in programing the therapeutic group experience. Several empirical field studies have indicated significant behavioral and organizational changes that occur as a direct result of such experiences. When theory can be constructed in detail, any specific experience can be programed.

Imbedded experiences make up the fifth cluster. Because the social environment in which a person is imbedded is so important in determining and sustaining attitudes and behavior, this environment becomes the focus of social change. Proponents of situational support theories work with the home and family, the work team, the management group, the boys' club, and the community committee, and these groups become the training group and have the group experience together. Contextual theories are familiar to people involved in the practice and theory of therapy.

Some experienced workers feel that this approach has the greatest promise of all those described here. Many studies report great dissipation and fall out after the original group experience, no matter how meaningful the experience may be at the time. For instance, measurements made after six months or a year indicate that participants tend to resume the attitudinal coloration of the original home or work environment after they become reimbedded in their former social context. The Gibb experiments (1962) indicate clearly that participants who came to the training groups in pairs or teams tended to retain group learnings longer than participants who came alone. These studies led to attempts to do group training in the institutional setting. Team training has in most instances supplanted stranger groups or heterogeneous groups. The institution becomes the target of change. The group or institution becomes the client for the consultant or organizational development specialist.

The work of Glynn Smith at the California Rehabilitation Center at Corona (1968) is a notable demonstration of the effectiveness of this approach. He is able to create a surprisingly intimate group experience for the sixty members of the ward community who live together in a rehabilitative experience. I have also been working for several years with natural organizational units, creating an intimate experience with as many as five hundred members in one "small" group. All members of the organizational unit meet together in a group to accomplish the aims originally seen as appropriate to twelve-member groups: interpersonal feedback, increased openness, improved problem-solving skills, self-insight, and a climate of trust.

This approach is intended to train and develop teams, as opposed to what inexperienced group leaders often do, namely, to work with individuals who happen to be together in groups. The genius of the historical contribution of group dynamics is that the group *as* group is seen as the significant element in interpersonal learning: group processes become the significant new element in social learning theories; group learning becomes something more than persons learning together in groups; group counseling becomes more than a counselor helping a collection of persons. The group itself is a growing organism.

In the sixth category are religious experiences. Often the person who has a deep experience in a group sees it as having transcendent or mystical meaning. A person may find himself seeing new significance in everyday feelings. He may find new meanings in prayer. His newly deepened feelings of warmth for other group members may seem to transcend in quality his usual feelings of affection. He may see the hand of God or a divine being in his powerful new attitudes toward himself or significant others. Such experiences in depth have caused some people to see the significant element in behavior change as a value shift of some kind. Values become the focus of induced change. The conversion experience takes on new interest.

People writing and studying in this area have taken an interest in mystical and private experiences, meditation and prayer, subconscious and foreconscious content, dream analysis, speaking in tongues, symbol formation, the worship service, nonverbal experiences, and a variety of other phenomena that assume new significance in new contexts.

Motivation shift experiences form the seventh category. Some investigators have been especially interested in personal and group goals and the nature of motivation change. For instance, Weldon Moffitt (personal correspondence) found that group experiences for adults on relief caused deep motivation changes in participants. Participants changed their long-range goals, obtained jobs, retained the jobs, and seemed to make enduring motivational shifts that mediated various behavior changes. I worked with the staff of the JOBS NOW project in Chicago, a program financed jointly by the Chicago YMCA and the Department of Labor. They used and had great success with small group experiences as a core method of creating enduring motivational shifts in illiterate, unemployable inner-city youth, people assumed by other workers to be beyond the reach of available methods of rehabilitation.

Group eight is composed of cognitive shift experiences. Some theorists and practitioners see the significant leverage point in behavior change as a cognitive shift in the participant. Good evidence in available studies indicates that participants do change their assumptions about people and the world, change their theories about themselves, view themselves differently, and think more effectively than they have been about interpersonal problems. Cognitive and perceptual changes do occur. The critical question for us is whether these ideational changes provide impetus for other behavior change or whether they are relatively superficial manifestations of deeper lying, noncognitive elements of the personality or the self.

Depth therapy experiences are classified in the ninth category. Psychoanalytic and other depth group therapy theories tend to focus on individual therapy in group situations rather than on the group experience as we are using the term here. George R. Bach (1954) does perhaps the best available job of integrating the material in group dynamics and the conventional methods of group therapy.

The final cluster centers around emergent or interdependence experiences. Lorraine Gibb and I have developed a theory which relates particularly to the authentic group experience, in which a group emerges into a state of genuine interdependence. We have participated in many groups created without the presence of assigned leaders, therapists, resource persons, or individuals who were given special responsibility for organization or helping the group. These groups differ significantly from the programed or instrumented groups. The programed groups have, in effect, surrogate leaders who provide the experiences in one way or another, by instruments, booklets, guides, instructions, manipulated group composition, or data-collection instruments. In order to achieve an authentic interdependence experience, the emergence group must initiate its own experience, make decisions about its goals, decide on activities that relate to these goals, and create together a group that grows and becomes genuinely interdependent. Our research and experience indicate that these groups are particularly effective in creating conditions for long-lasting behavior change, both in individuals and in organizations.

Several years ago, when we began writing *T-Group Theory and Laboratory Method* (Bradford, Gibb, and Benne, 1964), we were impressed with the fact that the research being done on T-Groups had little to do with the practices used in group training and therapy. My impression is that in the late 1960s this situation changed greatly. A body of fairly respectable theory is growing, and much of the research is relevant to issues central to theory construction. Equally important, much of the innovation in method and practice is directed toward clarification of the theory-produced issues and toward designing tests of the emerging theories.

The meaning of the small group experience, then, is determined in part by the theoretical predilection of the researcher and the practitioner. Meaning is also related to the question: "Why do we use groups instead of some other means to accomplish our aims?" Let me list a few of the reasons people give for choosing to work with groups.

Groups certainly are more economical than other methods of therapy, training, and education. Although there is considerable slippage in the transfer of effects from the group experience to enduring organizational behavior, there is comparable slippage in transfer of learnings from individual therapy and teaching. The evidence is very good that behavior does change in significant ways as a direct result of group experiences.

Therapists and counselors can help a limited number of people in prolonged dyadic situations, but by working with intensive groups, counselors and trainers can multiply the effects of their efforts by perhaps a factor of ten. This needed increase in professional effectiveness is produced even if we do not take into account the much greater potential effects of programed groups and especially of emergent groups.

Many people feel strongly that personal growth is essentially a social process and that the greatest development of human potentialities can be achieved only in truly interdependent relationships in effective groups of people. Thus many experienced psychotherapists are treating some or all of their patients in small groups. Some have gone so far as to limit their practice completely to small groups, and a portion of these feel that almost all patients can benefit more from group therapy than from individual therapy.

Group interaction offers a significant opportunity for social validation of interpersonal reality. The availability of direct, multiple feedback, in appropriate context, can give the participant an immediate assessment of the diversity of perceptual content. He can compare his perceptions with those of others and, to a great degree, can come to see himself as others see him. Most students of human growth agree that contact with social reality is a significant element in achieving growth and personal health.

Groups also provide an opportunity for trying out new behavior in a climate of relative trust where it is possible to progressively alter social behavior in the direction of increased personal effectiveness and satisfaction. This element of growth is often missing in dyadic therapy. There, new behavior must be tried out with the therapist, who has only a limited and special relationship with the client, or in posttherapy and posttraining sessions with relevant others. Provisional behavior with the therapist or leader suffers from a lack of outside people or situations with whom to test the new behavior. Provisional behavior with posttraining groups is limited by a lack of opportunity for direct, immediate, and high-credibility feedback. When I work as a leader or therapist with groups of professional clinicians and therapists, I often find them very capable at diagnosing self and others in terms of personality dynamics but surprisingly weak at diagnosing group dynamics or process problems; and they particularly lack ability to initiate provisional behavior in the group situation. In training predoctoral and postdoctoral therapists in the university setting I have found that good group experiences often induce dramatic gains in the students' ability to do both individual and group therapy. Apparently some relevant learnings come only through T-group experiences, and these learnings are especially important in training persons in the helping professions.

Attaining meaningful membership in a T-group provides a powerful reference group. When making significant social choices long after the termination of the training group, participants often feel the group watching them and providing strength for continuing new behaviors. Members say they are able to display new courage, trust, or openness which would not have been possible without the mnemonic image of the group.

Still another reason for joining a group is that the intensive group experience is "in." People sometimes go into groups, either as leaders or as members, because it is fashionable. People are grouping, so we group.

Helping professionals frequently opt for group therapy because they get so much out of it personally. Each new group is, for the effective leader or professional, a fresh experience that leads to personal enrichment, insight, and satisfaction. As the professional learns to open himself to new experience, joins the group as a co-learner, exposes himself deeply to the group, and enters the group as a person rather than in a protective role, he finds the group experience a medium for continuing personal and professional growth.

In talking about the meaning of the group experience we should be aware that some people do not find the experience satisfying or helpful. Studies show that from 5 to 20 per cent of participants experience no significant change in behavior. A small percentage of people report negative feelings about the group and about the experience. Specific studies (Gibb, 1970) show that negative effects do occur under some conditions:

increased irritability on the job, decreased flexibility, decreased accuracy of self-perception, increased negative reaction to authority on the job, less conformity to rules in the organization, and less consistency in supervisory attitudes and behavior. Some of these effects may be due to the predictable and necessary unfreezing and disequilibrium that occurs in the relearning process. But some group experiences may not be helpful to all members. We must also consider the fact that journal editors are not very receptive to articles showing only negative findings, and probably more studies than we know of found no significant changes in effective behaviors.

A critical question is whether these group experiences cause harm to participants. Several studies (for example, Batchelder and Hardy, 1968) have tried to determine possible detrimental effects of group experiences. Most reports of serious negative side effects have been distortions spread by nonparticipants whose fears caused them to exaggerate. There have been a small number of divorces and psychiatric hospitalizations following group experiences, usually for persons whose residual instabilities were brought to light by the group experience. Yet the number of such instances is surprisingly low considering the number of participants. For instance, more than two hundred thousand people have taken part in groups sponsored by the National Training Laboratories and its affiliates.

I should like to deal briefly with the problem of meaning by telling what the group experience has meant to me. Friends, colleagues, and observers report, in talking with me, that I have changed a great deal in the past several years. I have been working intensively with groups as a therapist, clinician, trainer, and person for the past twenty years, and I feel that my personal growth along significant dimensions is largely a direct result of my group experiences. I see myself as becoming more free and open, happier, and more able to share myself with others.

Four aspects of personal growth I find central and of critical importance. The first is trust—the capacity to trust myself, the world of people, and the processes of nature. The trusting person assumes that the world is a good place to be and is not captive to his fears. He trusts his impulses, his inner feelings, the people with whom he comes in contact, and his own motivations. On this dimension I have grown most.

The second is openness—the capacity to open myself to communication in depth with the persons with whom I live. The open person communicates with his inner self, reveals himself and his feelings to others, and allows the feelings and perceptions of others to touch and to get to him. This dimension has been the most troublesome for me. I have had difficulty in learning to share my negative—and my positive—feelings with others. I am making satisfying headway in this direction. This progress gives me pain at times but also gives my life new enrichment.

The third is self-determination—the capacity to find out what I am like, what I want to become, and to come closer to being the kind of person that I would like to become. The self-determining person is able to take responsibility, to a great degree, for his own life and his own actions. Although I am never completely sure at a given moment how I feel and who I am, I believe I am coming closer to this goal all the time. The quest, shared with many others in many groups, is a satisfying and exhilarating one.

The fourth is interdependence—the capacity to live and work with others, sensing my dependence upon them and achieving freedom and growth with them in overcoming self-defeating overdependence or rebellion. For me, it is in genuine interdependence that a person finds his greatest growth and his deepest experiences of fulfillment. Though I continue to have problems with my own counterdependence, I have been helped in a great many groups to free myself to work and live productively with a wide range of people.

Progressive change in these four aspects of life defines the processes of personal growth. Those who commit themselves to group experience can grow significantly in trust, openness, self-determination, and interdependence. For these people, the small group experience means growth.

2

Encounter Group and Society

William H. Blanchard

Encounter groups today are coming under increasing pressure from social institutions and individuals. The most frequent criticism from a society that believes in form and structure is that growth centers and practitioners of encounter have never defined themselves: "Are you an educational association, a therapeutic organization, a recreation center, a social club, or a business? Who will be responsible for you? Who will regulate you? What are your ethical standards?" The answers, if I were to formulate them myself, go something like this: "We are all these things and more. We are seeking a form of human relationship in which man regulates himself, in which few external controls are required because man is fulfilled within himself. We are evolving a new form of leadership in which no one will bear the full burden of being 'responsible' for others. No one speaks for us. We are educating and leading each other. We are not an institution. We are a way of life." This is my personal vision of the encounter experience. I would not attempt to use these answers before a Congressional investigating committee because they are not valid in our present society—nor are they entirely true.

Today the growth center is already an institution. It is learning the art of grantsmanship, and in some cases it is a successful business enterprise, with an advertising and public relations staff, making a good living for its directors and employees. It is learning to adapt to the society it hopes to change. I would not be surprised to discover that a growth center had begun to sell stock and declare dividends. Profit-making corporations have already begun to organize encounter groups for the general public, hiring professionals to conduct these groups. There is certainly nothing unethical about making a profit—at least not by the standards of our present society—but when the interest in encounter has passed its peak, the large corporation can turn to the manufacture of silver swizzle sticks, maxi-skirts, or whatever seems to be the going thing. An encounter group facilitator who believes he is changing peoples' lives has difficulty accepting the possibility that the whole encounter movement might simply decline from lack of public interest, in large part because he is surrounded by those who believe. It is easy to ride the crest of a fad and imagine that one is changing the world.

Those who believe in the irresistible momentum of the encounter experience have not faced an important fact about its basic philosophy-psychology: that the values of the encounter movement are irrevocably opposed to the highly structured, competitive, capitalistic society in which it has emerged. This opposition produces the let-down which participants in a weekend session so often feel when they go back to their homes and jobs. All the postsession encounters, decompression meetings, and other forms of debriefing will not change this reaction. I am not sure we should be trying to change this aspect of the encounter experience. Perhaps the bad trip that occurs when people return from a marathon or an extended experience at a growth center is a necessary jolt, a way of becoming aware of the striking contrast between the encounter experience and the everyday world in which we live. Instead of easing people back into society I would be inclined to devise negative sensual experiences which heighten their awareness of the artificial food, the pollution, and the uncreative work which is the fare of most of us (see Blanchard, 1970, particularly the incident of the roast beef sandwich). The inability to make the high moments of encounter a part of one's everyday life is, I think, a reflection of the state of our society and not a defect in the encounter experience itself.

Other institutions in our society seem to be islands of contrast to the mores and manners of our culture, but people do not experience a shock or a let-down in moving back and forth from the institution to the social scene. The church preaches brotherly love and protests against selfishness, greed, and injustice in the world, yet most people manage to move in and out of the church experience without any difficulty. They make the transition easily because they do not become involved. I would not like to find people taking the encounter experience in a similar manner. The search for one's self and one's potential is such a deep and meaningful experience that it is difficult for some of us to imagine how this exploration could be taken in a superficial way, but in our optimism we have not considered the potency of the advertising culture. Not long ago I was watching a television commercial in which a girl was dancing through a pastoral setting. She had the hippie look, with long straight blond hair, but she had the cleanliness of the middle class. The background was somewhat blurred and cloudy, giving the whole scene a dreamlike effect. "I like to find out what I really am," the girl said. "I'm searching for myself, and, in everything I do, I want to be me." Then a lipstick container was flashed onto a corner of the screen. Her voice continued, "Blank lipstick helps me to be really me. With its umpteen varieties of shades and colors I can choose the one that is just right for me. It helps me express what I really am."

Some of my colleagues profess to be delighted with this kind of thing. "Don't you see!" they tell me, "we are infiltrating the entire culture in a subtle way. We are using their own methods to get our message across." I would contend that this is not our message. The expression of one's individuality through a series of meaningless choices is the message of American industry. The message becomes, then, not a search for myself but a search for the product which represents me. It is true that we should be trying to infiltrate our society. The encounter group cannot continue as something outside the culture that surrounds it. We must move toward the institutions and the activities of our society or we will become a cult which withdraws from the world and practices strange rituals. But when we begin to involve ourselves in society, it is important to know when we are exerting an influence and when we are being coopted. Co-optation is flattering. It means that someone thinks we are important enough to be coopted. Let's not be seduced by it.

If one takes the encounter movement in its larger perspective, as an aspect of the third force in psychology, it is clear that we are already deeply involved in society—influencing it and being influenced by it. The similarities among the hip culture, the encounter culture, the radical culture, and the humanistic psychology movement are quite striking. The commonalities suggest the extent to which these forces interpenetrate and rub against each other as they move toward a common objective. But all the cultures I have cited are essentially counter-cultures, moving against the dominant theme of the American middle class. The encounter movement can work effectively with these other groups to bring about social change. However, to the extent that we allow ourselves to become coopted by the commercialism of the advertising culture we will find ourselves isolated from our own objectives and from those who might work with us.

Let me give an illustration of what I mean. In an interview with Herbert Marcuse, Keen and Raser (1971) suggested revolutionary implications in the whole movement toward group therapy. Marcuse replied, in part, "I read the catalogs of the Esalen Institute. To me this is sufficient to be horrified. This administration of happiness is nauseating to me." Keen tried to explain that if a competitive society destroys tenderness and intimacy, the awakening of these emotions and the rediscovery of sensuality might have a liberating effect on the individual's political sensibilities. But Marcuse was adamant. He admitted his own lack of direct experience in the encounter movement, but on the basis of the advertising he had read and the reports of others, he was not attracted to it. Clearly Keen and Raser felt Marcuse was turning away from an important area of life that was closely related to his own philosophy. I would have to agree with them, but I would also ask why Marcuse developed the particular misconception that he did—and was it really a misconception? If one has never been to an encounter group, it is easy to get the impression from the brochures (and Esalen is one of the lesser offenders in this regard) that the group leader is going to teach you how to be happy or that he will line you up with a swinging chick and give you a chance to feel her body. A number of facilitators argue that these tactics are necessary to appeal to people who do not know what the experience is all about, to get them there for the first time. But the implication of this view is that we want to get people there, any people, and get them there by any means possible. The advertising of a growth center or an encounter group has a profound influence in setting the atmosphere for the group. It helps to develop the expectations of the participants, regardless of who they are. This process was true in vaudeville and it is equally true in growth centers. The hypnotist who advertised his appearance by billboards, showing his large eyes wide open with sparks of electricity coming from them, was preparing his audience to be hypnotized. The hypnosis had already begun with the pictures and with the information that he was "world renowned." When the hypnotist arrived on stage he merely continued his relationship with the audience, a relationship initiated by billboards. One would assume that most psychologists are well aware of the importance of preparation and expectation in the creation of a particular experience, but these factors do not seem to have been considered in much of the advertising for growth centers. I believe a growth center could evolve into a glorified lonely hearts club, not because the staff set out to create that kind of environment but because they lost their own identity in the effort to become successful. The

ideas that becoming big is becoming successful and that failure
is a reflection of one's personal guilt are dominant attitudes in
the American middle class—hence the urge to spread the
growth gospel and the increasingly messianic zeal of the growth
center operator to expand his business. The idea of personal
growth from within merges with the notion of growth by accre-
tion. Increase in numbers becomes a measure of success, regardless of quality.

It seems to me that the tendency toward commercializa-
tion and superficiality in the encounter movement is a product
of a competitive society. I do not believe the encounter movement can maintain its integrity in our present society if we
learn to adapt to that society and if we decide to become a
financial and business success. I have not come to this conclusion
easily. It is much more comfortable to believe that one can have
one's personal luxuries and change the world at the same time.
My students have made me aware of this problem by confronting me in the classroom with my own living standards and the
effect of these standards on some of my attitudes. If a person is
only talking about social change, if he has not yet committed
his life to bringing about this change, it is easy to imagine that
one only has to change the ideas and attitudes of others and
everything else will take care of itself. With a little touch, a
wink, and a bit of word magic one brings down the whole
system and then drives home in his sports car for a swim in the
family pool. In reality, however, we will find that others will
not become committed to the values of the encounter experience unless we learn to make these values part of a living
environment which includes education and work as well as
leisure and loving.

This discussion raises a fundamental question about the
meaning of personal growth. Are we talking about psychotherapy or social change? In the large sense one could say that
they are the same thing, but in the narrow sense psychotherapy
strives to make people feel better about themselves and to help
them achieve their own desires within the context of the reality
of our present society. Social change may involve the sacrifice of
contentment and happiness, in the narrow sense, in order to

achieve some larger objectives. It may include a great deal of misery and, if one's objectives are not attained, a sense of total disillusionment with life and with oneself. Striving to grow, in this sense, means taking the risk that one will not grow at all. It means exposing the contradictions of a person's life and making him aware of his inability to achieve self-actualization if he functions within the context of our present society. For me, the great value of the encounter movement is its subversive force, its destructive effect on the status quo. I realize that this view is not held by some of my colleagues, but I believe that there is already considerable evidence to support this picture of the encounter movement as a subversive influence in the present American culture (Hampden-Turner, 1970, pp. 97–229). However, unlike many radical movements of the past, the encounter movement does not call on an individual to sacrifice himself for the good of a cause that he does not fully understand. It is subversive precisely because it works directly with the needs of the participant for self-actualization. It just so happens that the sense of community with others which frequently develops from such groups is antithetical to the spirit of competition and the ethic of personal success. The "sacrifice" of personal ambition that may follow such an experience is different from that required by the older notion of duty. It is an admittedly selfish act. Here we come upon one of those peculiar paradoxes of being-cognition described by Maslow (1968), in which a selfish act is, at the same time, a sacrifice of the self (the narrow concept of the self defined by the ego). One of the most significant values that characterize the encounter movement is this decreased emphasis on the ego and the rediscovery of the self through new contact with others.

The effect of the encounter experience on personal ambition is illustrated by the story of John Koehne, a CIA agent, who was well on his way to becoming a successful organization executive when the CIA sent him to an encounter group in 1967 (Anonymous, 1971). It changed Koehne's life. The experience of opening himself up to others was a violation of this new way of being, there was no going back to the old way. everything he had been taught. Once he became involved in

Koehne continued to work at the CIA for a year and a half, but finally he had to leave. "It wasn't right for me," he said. "It wasn't the work. I just couldn't put my needs first there, not in the selfish sense, but in the human one." Leaving the CIA, however, was not a step into paradise. The days directly after he left were the most difficult. He was frightened by his own freedom and the realization that, without his former values, there was as yet no new basis for his life. Koehne's objective was to start a commune with a few friends in an effort to develop a simple life style. He came to believe that man should not be controlled by organizations or competition. Yet he maintained that he was not a political revolutionary. However, as Hampden-Turner (1970, pp. 171–172) suggests, the suspicion that the right-wing individual has exhibited toward encounter groups is probably well founded. Such groups tend to make people aware of the subtle ways in which they have allowed themselves to be oppressed by their culture and their social and occupational roles. This form of awareness is, for Marcuse (1968), the critical first step in liberation: "All liberation depends on the consciousness of servitude, and the emergence of this consciousness is always hampered by the predominance of needs and satisfactions which, to a great extent, have become the individual's own. . . . The optimal goal is the replacement of false needs by true ones, the abandonment of repressive satisfaction." I do not know why the CIA sent Koehne to an encounter group, but I suspect they were trying to know their enemy. The result suggests that a more abstract and symbolic form of knowing might be better for the CIA if one interprets "better" in the narrow sense of enhancing prospects for survival.

In the case of Koehne we are dealing with a new form of politics: the politics of those who reject the values of the existing system but have no desire to overthrow it by force or enter into competition in the traditional political arena. People who are willing and able to encourage others to drop out are changing the system through the indirect method of nonsupport. The renewed interest in communal living is characteristic of this approach. Winthrop's study (1969) of the "intentional community" (the commune) points out that the aims of these communities parallel those of the self-actualizing person as described by Maslow (1968). Although few intentional communities have evolved directly from encounter groups, they are clearly similar in aim and represent logical extensions of the philosophy of the group-community. The major advantage of the intentional community over the encounter group is that it can become a part of the ongoing life of the individual. It is content oriented, directed toward a particular objective. The methods of the group process then facilitate that objective. The group begins to deal with process when there is some difficulty with the content. Conflicts over how to build a workable community or complaints about a lack of participation by some members can be handled by encounter first, rather than by resorting to the development of rules which must be interpreted by those in authority. Winthrop thinks the failure or break-up of these communities is related to a conflict with the host society. "If the mother community becomes frightened enough, it will crush the seedling intentional community by means of the final rationalization of not wanting its children to grow up under the threatening shadow of strange ideas which may be destructive of its own way of life—if one can call the crazy-quilt of cross-purposes by which most of us live a *way of life*. From a political or economic viewpoint it would be easy for a powerful and aroused host community to crush a successful intentional one if it felt this to be necessary." However, if allowed to develop, the intentional community can prove to be the salvation of the host community. If the larger community is heading toward chaos, intentional communities can represent "established success in alternative ways of life to which a world in crisis can turn." In the effort to develop a sense of unity with others on a lasting basis, the intentional community applies encounter group values to a specialized society.

These values can be applied in other ways within the framework of our present culture. Postman and Weingartner (1969) suggest that the whole meaning of the educational experience might be changed by the development of a different psychological climate within the classroom, one which stimulates students to interact with each other, to question authority, and to experience the thrill of personal discovery. Instead of lecturing at students or asking questions followed by a raised hand and a "correct" answer, the teacher learns to stimulate discussion about the meaning of concepts and encourages students to develop evidence for their point of view. The students learn to pay more attention to each other and to rely less on the teacher. This approach breaks down conventional subject categories (history, geography, math), probing areas between subjects and developing a unified knowledge of the world. Here, again, is a situation in which human interaction is content oriented, but the content is handled in such a way as to increase the sense of community and cooperation among the participants. However, the gains from this kind of experience extend beyond the sense of community with one's fellow students. A summary of some research (Blanchard, 1958) suggests that intellectual inhibition may occur when the individual's ego-protecting mechanisms become involved in the learning process. Learning depends on being able to let down one's guard, being open to new experience. The needs to defend one's personal value system, to repress unacceptable sexual impulses, and to demonstrate one's superiority interfere with the urge to learn and discover. To the extent that an educational environment can create an atmosphere of trust and mutual acceptance among the students, it should enhance the creative capacity of the individual.

This approach to learning can be carried a step further by developing encounter groups among students. The experience of personal interaction can be used to complement the process of educational development. At the University of Southern California, Urban Semester, we are attempting to use the group process as an integral aspect of the educational system. In a sixteen-unit program, classes of between thirty and forty students receive concentrated exposure to the processes of urban life. They also receive more direct exposure to each other than they would in a conventional class. Classes are divided into process groups of seven to eight students and one staff member. The purpose of the group is to make individuals aware of their fellow students and their potential contribution to the learning process. The objective is to extend the personal intimacy of the small group to the larger sessions of the full class. On paper this sounds very feasible, but in practice I have found students more critical of the encounter process than are adults at a growth center. There are many reasons for this reaction. Most students do not come to the Urban Semester seeking psychological help. They are aware of some of their conflicts, but some students are not ready to deal with them. However, there is another more constructive source of resistance. Students often find something artificial and phony about a group of people sitting around telling each other how they come on. They are quick to notice another student who appears too skilled and facile in the encounter experience, and they are critical of professional facilitators who visit the group. Students sometimes tell them they are programed or they talk like an encounter textbook. I have reached the point where I am very conscious of this feeling, even when it is expressed as a compliment. My favorite response of this type came after we had all moved around the group telling each person how we felt about him. I was the last to finish, and one student turned to me to say, "Gee, Bill, that was—if you'll pardon the expression—a real professional job. I mean it was just like I always imagined a psychologist would talk." It was, I realized later, just a bit too smooth and professional.

My students have taught me that sincerity is a will-o-the-wisp. The more arduously it is pursued, the more it escapes one's grasp. The same is true of intimacy, honesty, and those other intangibles we seek in the encounter experience. If intimacy is pursued for itself alone, a hothouse atmosphere develops that gets a bit sticky. If it is part of a larger objective, such as education or building a better world, it has greater meaning for me. It is possible to be honest for a few hours or a weekend, but to remake one's profession, one's living standards, and one's life to fit a more humane world requires a different order of commitment. A teacher cannot create such a commitment in the student. He can help to provide a living environment in which such a commitment can be made. Part of this process is to involve the student, by direct experience, in the life of the community he attempts to understand. In the USC program students sometimes spend a week, in part, living on a poverty budget. At the end of the week students pool their funds for a banquet to discover the advantages for low-income people of combining resources. Many ideas for the program come from students. As a result, the program for each semester, while retaining certain regular areas and methods of investigation, also changes in response to the needs and suggestions of students.

This type of program has many advantages. The staff to student ratio is about one to four (although few of the staff are full time). Having at least two or three staff in every class or field session leads to considerable staff interaction as well as staff-student interaction. Staff members feel free to disagree with each other in front of students and this freedom encourages student independence. But in the present university system this new form of education can work against student survival. Follow-up indicates that students often leave the Urban Semester feeling that they can no longer tolerate a traditional educational environment. They are more critical than they previously were of professors in their other classes and begin to offer suggestions to the university faculty on how their courses might be improved. Occasionally they drop out altogether because of increasing conflict with the system, stimulated by their experience in the Urban Semester. I believe these results will be good for the university in the long run, but they are difficult for the student, who may find that his conflict with the university and the industrial state has intensified before he is able to form a coherent image of himself in the world. The Urban Semester lasts only long enough to open up students and make them aware of some things they have been missing through traditional forms of education. It does not begin to resolve their problems. It may leave them hanging, sometimes badly exposed. I generally find that I have just begun to understand some students in my group when it is time for them to leave. What is needed is a two-year or four-year program of this type.

Another big problem of the Urban Semester today is the same one that faces the encounter group. Most faculty, regardless of their mixed ethnic backgrounds, are upper-middle-class liberals who aspire to increase their living standards. We spend part of our time breaking through an older style of education and the remainder competing in the world of commerce or in traditional university lecturing because our Urban Semester salaries do not meet the income standards we have set for ourselves. We have not yet made some of the changes in ourselves that we would like to make in others.

Some institutions for social change have been adventurous in their efforts to break the mold of our present society, but they have also moved into a higher level of personal risk for their participants. I came upon one high-risk organization while helping to plan a field experience for students. We began with a brochure from an institute that advertised a series of weekend seminars devoted to social change. The style of exposition was more content oriented than that of the typical growth center, and there were no implied promises of openness, trust, warmth, joy, or happiness. However, knowing that such weekends could be costly, I decided to contact the institute and see whether the program was something my students could afford. I reached them by phone and asked for the director.

"We don't have a director," was the reply.

"Is there no one in charge?"

"I'm in charge of the office right now. My name is Carol."

I introduced myself and asked the cost of a seminar for the weekend. I was told it was twelve dollars. I was not sure I had heard correctly.

"Is that the total cost? Twelve dollars for everything?"

"Well, you might want to bring about three dollars for food and take along a sleeping bag. We have bunks and mattresses, but no pillows or blankets."

When I arrived on the first day of the seminar I found that the institute headquarters was not a very busy place. People showed up when they had something to do. There was usually someone to answer the phone, and one group provided a potluck dinner on Thursday evening, but there was no regular duty. The informal atmosphere and lack of staff gave me a feeling I might be able to help. I asked what I could do and was told I could vacuum the place. I cleaned the upper and lower floors, emptied the ashtrays, and carried out the wastepaper baskets. Already I felt I was part of the institute. Altogether about thirty people came for the weekend. One of the seminar leaders cooked the meal for the first evening, and a jar was placed on the table in which we were to deposit the food money. Our cook informed us that the evening meal would be her last operation, and it would be up to us to prepare the remaining meals. No one was put in charge of cooking, and no one volunteered that responsibility. In the morning we generally found something for ourselves. At noon a few people got together to prepare lunch and others picked up and washed the dishes. It worked out that way for all the meals. Sleeping arrangements followed a similar pattern. Each person found a cabin and picked out a bunk. No one hesitated in the doorway to ask if the cabin was for men or women. Sexes were mixed, but there was no self-conscious effort to mix them. Everyone dressed or undressed beside his or her bunk or climbed fully clothed into the sleeping bag. Toilet facilities were crowded, but we managed.

People gathered for the seminar in one room of the largest cabin. We sat on chairs, lay on sleeping bags, or perched cross-legged on the floor in various parts of the room. The three discussion leaders sat among us, each leader being separated from the other by several people. We began the discussion without any axioms or definitions and no agenda. If someone asked what was meant by a particular concept, the leader might ask, "What does it mean to you?" The individual was encouraged to try to relate the concept to his own life and personal experience. There was no assumption that a word was some essence that had a true and correct meaning to be uncovered by the discussion leader. Projects of the institute were discussed as examples of ways to bring about social change, but none of the projects seemed to have a leader. Project team members tended to feel that direction must be supplied by themselves and that if they did not make suggestions and show up at project meetings, the project might cease to exist.

Most staff people for the institute were under thirty. One young man had been within a month of his master's degree in mathematics when he dropped out to join the staff of the institute. He did some occasional tutoring, and he slept at the institute, but he received no salary. Another member of the organization had finished two years of graduate work in chemistry. He too had dropped out of the university to work at the institute. By working one day a week as an auto mechanic he was able to buy food and a few other items. He lived on the institute property. One of the young women had been a buyer for a department store. She walked off the job the day her boss told her he had discovered how he was going to sell the hip generation on fashion.

These people had refused to prepare themselves for positions within the current society because they assumed that society was due for a complete change. They lived as though they believed the current system could not last. After the weekend they had no outside world to which they could return. Their lives were a perpetual encounter. There is, in this way of life, a quality of stepping into empty space with nothing for support. A friend of mine asked if I thought these young people would be sorry later that they had passed up so many opportunities. The question assumes that the "later" into which we are moving is the same competitive system in which we exist today. Later is the product of what I do now, and I will not change later unless I change now. If I develop a financially successful institute that pays salaries for the staff, I have already created a different later. If I need twenty thousand a year to get along now, I will probably need more later. If I plan for a position and prepare to fulfill a function in the current society, I will perpetuate that position and the society that treats people as functions.

The fear of failure and the belief that one must compete to survive is based on the Western concept of the ego, which holds that I am separate from others. I am responsible for myself, my family, and for nothing else. I am at war with nature and with other men. It is difficult to break through this way of thinking about the world because any change involves a direct assault on our concept of ourselves. Like the Calvinist fear that certain thoughts were inspired by the devil and must be avoided, the protection of one's ego has been regarded as a mark of one's adequacy as a human being. Such an attitude is basic to Western psychology. "Freud and his followers have persistently confused all ideas of transcending the ego with loss of 'ego strength'" (Watts, 1969, p. 31). There is, then, a mental block at the doorway to a new consciousness. This block comes in the form of the thought: "If you enter here, you will be inadequate." If the individual proceeds further, he may get an intense inner reaction: "You are approaching death! Turn back before it is too late." The limitation of consciousness to the realm of the private ego has several centuries of demonstrable success. It has promoted fear as an incentive for work. It has fired the energy of man and has been a force in the building of civilizations. But, like the heavy armor of the dinosaur, this psychological armor may prove the ruin of man if he cannot discard it or mitigate its influence.

In the past an increased sensitivity to one's surroundings has been a handicap in survival. The good worker was one who stayed at his desk and did not look out the window. The warrior who stopped to appreciate the landscape was slain. A sense of oneness with mankind was bad for anyone who wanted to be successful. For this reason there is something frightening about an expanded awareness. It is not only a letting go of the ego, a merging with others and with nature; it is also a letting go of self-protective mechanisms, a denial of the paramount importance of one's individual existence, a symbolic death. We do not understand many things about the human psyche. The ego appears to be an important mechanism for survival. Like the instinctive startle reaction of the child to a sensation of falling, the fear of ego loss may be a built-in, instinctive response which evolved in man because it protected the organism from danger. For this reason the fear of an expanded awareness may be fully justified, in the individual sense. Awareness could be risky, even dangerous for some. However, it is one of the most powerful means for understanding the forces around us, both the impersonal forces of nature and the energies of living things. Such awareness has not been required in the past in order to provide food, clothing, and shelter. But with the increasing pollution of the environment and the threat of massive intraspecies warfare involving thermonuclear weapons, we face a problem that our species has never encountered. Like two soldiers who hate each other because they see their world in terms of a struggle for certain necessities, we seem to be locked into an attitude that will destroy us if we do not learn how to break its grip. We are afraid because to break that grip would mean letting go of an important human instinct for self-protection which, although it places us at odds with all other living things, nevertheless may be the built-in basis for our survival.

But man has overcome similar instincts for self-protection which were no longer appropriate for a changing world. He has learned to subdue his most primitive response to the sensation of falling. He has, in fact, learned to court it by jumping from a plane, in the confidence that his parachute will open, rather than clinging desperately to a craft that will no longer support him. In like manner he may have to leave this earth for the stars when it can no longer sustain human life or let go of his narrow concept of self to leap into the vault of a larger consciousness if he is to escape the destructive potential of his own ego.

3

An Implicit Image
of Man

Sigmund Koch

Many social critics have been concerned about the tendency of modern man—especially American man—to prize images, pictures, more than the realities for which they "stand." Some fifteen years ago, I had the melancholy accident of falling through a then prevailing picture of psychology—one which contained some of the cant premises of what I now think to be the bad metaphor of "psychological science." Like most images, this one got out of phase with reality, and with its initial intention, almost as soon as it was formed.[1]

Scientific psychology was stipulated into life in the late nineteenth century. That intensely optimistic age, understandably dazzled by the apparent cognitive and technological fruits of the natural sciences, decided to try out a hopeful new

[1] This chapter is adapted from "The Image of Man Implicit in Encounter Group Theory," *Journal of Humanistic Psychology*, 1971, *11*, 109–127.

strategy: that of extending the methods of natural science to all human and social problems. At the very beginning, there was some degree of realism about the magnitude and difficulties of such a task. There was some degree of recognition that the task would require ardent effort over historic time; that the extensibility of natural-science methods to human and social problems is a matter of open hypothesis; that substantial readjustments of the former to the requirements of the latter must be anticipated. But the *image* had been created, and in almost no time at all the ever-autistic character of man under challenge asserted itself. The hypothesis was soon prejudged! The *hope* of a psychological science became indistinguishable from the *fact* of psychological science. The entire subsequent history of psychology can be seen as a ritualistic endeavor to emulate the forms of science in order to sustain the delusion that it already *is* a science.

As a result, the inability of anyone—whether psychologist or his grateful lay victim—to fix the limits of the metaphor known as psychological science has, in my opinion, been close to catastrophic throughout the century. Strange things happen when image is seen as fact! Numbers are assigned to hundreds of millions of people in the line of intelligence, personnel, or educational "measurement" with little regard for their meaning and none for their effects on the dignity, self-image, or practical fate of the victims. Vagrant guesses about the importance of permissiveness, fondling, breastfeeding, and social reinforcement and about the potentialities of teaching machines or computerized instruction are allowed to influence whole eras of parental and educational practice. Dime-a-dozen "breakthroughs" are applied wholesale to the "cure" of the mentally disturbed: exotic little interventions such as partial destruction of the frontal lobes with an ice pick, malarial, insulin, or electroshock. For the less refractory disorders, or just for soul-expanding kicks, psychological "science" has available its endless armamentarium of "psychotherapies," most of them devised with minimal concern for whether the presumably neurosis-free or expanded person who emerges has not also been freed of large areas of his personhood.

But what is perhaps worse than any single symptom of psychological science, as thus far given by history, is something more like an essence: it is the demeaning image of man himself at the basis of its presumably tough-minded conceptualizations, an image which mankind cannot but accept and strive to emulate because of its association with the iconology of science. In its austere form, it depicts man as a stimulus-response mechanism or, worse, a mere mathematical point of intersection between stimulus and response processes, steered by socially "manipulated" rewards and punishments. According to this form of the image, the laws of human and social "behavior" can be derived from rigorous study of the variables controlling the rate at which a hungry rat in a small, dark box presses a lever to obtain tiny pellets of food. The more sophisticated and recent form of the image holds man to be an information processing entity operating on the principles of a binary digital computer programed to conform to payoff criteria which acts much like the rewards of the previous case.

Both of the images of man I have just sketched (and other slightly varied ones) are products of the tradition of *behaviorism*, which for fifty years has maintained hegemony, especially in this country. The first of the images mentioned is representative of what might be called *explicit behaviorism*, while the second—which is now beginning to supplant older forms of behaviorism—might be called *crypto-behaviorism*. The behaviorisms are an especially pure assertion of man's reality-defiling propensities in that they achieve (by arbitrary stipulation) the complete liquidation of psychology's subject matter —the elimination, as legitimate or even meaningful objects of study, of both experience and mind. Even the brain is proscribed, as unclean and somehow fictive, by certain long-influential forms of behaviorism, including Skinner's. The computerized version restores a brain of some sort but tidies it up by insisting that it be reduced wholly to transistors, magnetic "cores," and miles of interstitial wire. I have given much drab effort to the critique of behaviorism. My purpose here is best served by resting the case with these few contumelious remarks, which I hope will suffice as a background to the story I wish to tell.

By the mid-fifties, an appreciable number of psychologists had become restive over the behaviorisms and were searching for more significant professional and human commitments. At about this time, Abraham Maslow, who had long complained about the "means-centeredness" and scientism of psychology and who was discovering existentialism, called for a "third force" in psychology. Fairly soon, such a group—calling themselves "humanistic psychologists"—began to emerge. Initially, it seemed a motley group with heterogeneous interests.

By a process which no one has yet chronicled in a coherent way, the interests of this group soon began to concentrate on various forms of group therapy, a plethora of which were already available. (Approaches to group therapy had been multiplying profusely ever since the early efforts of such people as Trigant Burrow and J. L. Moreno in the twenties and early thirties.) The pre-"humanist" tradition in group therapy took its conceptual inspiration primarily from psychoanalysis and various of the "depth" psychologies. By the mid-fifties, however, a number of group approaches to therapy (or therapy-like changes of individuals and groups), based on principles of "group dynamics" and other nondepth psychological schemes, were in the air. Drawing their ideas from these and other scattered sources (especially a variety of loose interpretations of existential philosophy, but also client-oriented therapy, psychodrama, sensitivity training, dance therapy, Gestalt therapy, relaxation methods), the humanistic psychologists began to experiment lushly and variously with an ever-widening range of eclectic mixes.

Today the group movement has become the most visible manifestation of psychology on the American scene. Carl Rogers has said that "the encounter group may be the most important social invention of the century" (1969). Within psychology, it has captured the interest of an overwhelming majority of students and investigators who wish to maintain contact with a human subject matter. It is tremendously important that we assess its message, impact, meaning, "image of man."

At the risk of displeasing many of you, I will give my assessment right off by saying that the group movement is the most extreme excursion thus far of man's talent for reducing,

distorting, evading, and vulgarizing his own reality. It is also the
most poignant exercise of that talent, for it seeks and promises
to do the very reverse. The movement is adept at the image-
making maneuver of evading human reality in the very process
of seeking to discover and enhance it. It seeks to court spontaneity and authenticity by artifice; to combat instrumentalism
instrumentally; to provide access to experience by reducing it
to a packaged commodity; to engineer autonomy by group pressure; to liberate individuality by group shaping. Within the
lexicon of its concepts and methods, openness becomes transparency; love, caring, and sharing become a barter of "reinforcements" or perhaps mutual ego-titillation; aesthetic receptivity
or immediacy becomes "sensory awareness." It can provide only
a grotesque simulacrum of every noble quality it courts. It provides, in effect, a convenient psychic whorehouse for the purchase of a gamut of well advertised existential "goodies":
authenticity, freedom, wholeness, flexibility, community, love,
joy. One enters for such liberating consummations but inevitably settles for psychic striptease.

Those are strong words, and it will certainly not be easy
to make them plausible to those of you who feel differently.
There is no question of *proof* in relation to such matters. It is
a question of *seeing*, of fidelity of perception of the human condition—and this kind of question is as old as the history of man
and will never be finally resolved. But the history of the humanities has already given us many differentiated, sensitive,
ardent visions of the human condition. All of us, I think, are
capable of significantly sharing in, and even extending, this
noncounterfeit kind of vision—but that only comes the hard
way, the way that involves fear, trembling, loneliness, discipline,
gallantry, humor, and a loving, if ironic, sense of the dimension
of human imperfectibility.

The autisms of those who want it the easy way have put
them out of touch with the differentiated content of the significant visions in man's heritage; worse, they are out of contact
with the intricate and delicately contoured meanings of some
of the best—as well as some of the plainest—words in our language. They nevertheless use these words incessantly, with the

best of intentions, but in debased, vulgarized, schematic ways. For them, such words as openness, honesty, awareness, freedom, trust, growth, feeling, experience form a simplistic conceptual abacus which they manipulate and apply in mechanical, repetitive, incantatory fashion. To convince people who reside within this framework of its impoverished character is like asking for a change of sensibility.

I *could* start with a collection of horror stories about the grave human crises, indeed tragedies, that have been precipitated by membership in one or another kind of "human-potential" group. I do not think this rather horrifying evidence irrelevant, but it is not the main basis of my concern. Group leader Shostrom (1969), in an article entitled "Group Therapy: Let the Buyer Beware" (one of the most reasonable articles about the movement I have seen), presents a roundup of representative suicides, breakdowns, and divorces precipitated by injudicious shopping. He proceeds to develop seven guidelines for the floundering shopper in the form of specific "nos" which should counter-indicate either joining, or remaining in, an encounter group. These "nos" cut a very wide swath indeed and call for exceptional discriminative powers, if not prescience (and omniscience to boot), on the part of the intending grouper. One of the "nos," for instance—"Never join an encounter group on impulse"—explains to the shopper that any "important crisis in your life . . . deserves reflection" and enjoins him to be "doubly cautious" if "you are sanely suspicious of your grasp on reality." To apply such a rule effectively presupposes a remission of the condition that invites its application. Were such a criterion met, I would still doubt that the shopper, or even a committee consisting of his mother, psychiatrist, and priest, could make this discrimination with accuracy.

It is by now no secret that what concerns me about the group movement far more deeply than its toll in human crises of dramatic and identifiable character is the image of man it has purveyed to man. The central horror of the history of psychology is that distorted images of human reality are soon accommodated by the reality which the images distort. Perhaps more frightening than the failures consequent upon participation in groups is the rich reported yield of "successes." The principal toll of the movement is in the reducing and simplifying impact upon the personalities and sensibilities of those who emerge from the group experience with an enthusiastic commitment to its values.

Perhaps the best way for me to explicate this judgment is to present a vignette of my impressions upon accidentally wandering into a national meeting of the American Association for Humanistic Psychology in 1968. I had left psychology for Foundation work some four years before and had not kept in touch with the dramatic strides of the group movement. I included this little vignette as a kind of impressionistic coda to my article on the general plight of psychological science (1969). My strategy will be to give the substance of this vignette and then to enlarge the position by replying to an official rebuttal of it (1969) by Gerard Haigh, president of the Association for Humanistic Psychology. I will quote selectively from the germane part of my article.

I caught up with the "humanistic psychologists" last fall at the annual American Psychological Association meeting in San Francisco. Here scholarly exposition must give way to reportage. . . . A bit of investigation established that these were members of the Society for Humanistic Psychology, which had been holding its own pre-convention for two days. I learned further that the Society now has some 1,500 members and that there are no professional requirements for membership. The humanistic fervor of the group has been channeled into one activity, variously designated as group therapy, T-group therapy, . . .

With curiosity thus reinforced, I attended all the humanists' activities that I could at the APA Convention proper [I had arrived at the very end of the humanists' separate meeting.] It was not easy because every humanistic audience spilled over into the corridors, unlike the sullen, spare audiences at the non-humanistic events.

By far the largest audience showed up at a symposium in which Paul Bindrim, the originator of "nude-marathon group therapy," spoke and showed a film. Reprints of a magazine re-

port on Bindrim's "breakthrough" were made available. Bindrim had wondered whether what he calls a man's "tower of clothes" is not only a safeguard for privacy but a self-imposed constraint to keep out people he fears. If so, a man who disrobed physically might be better able disrobe emotionally. The modest Mr. Bindrim refuses to take sole credit for this hypothesis and wishes to share it with Abraham Maslow. Dr. Maslow had speculated that with nudity in groups, "people would go away more spontaneous, less guarded, less defensive, not only about the shape of their behinds, but freer and more innocent about their minds as well."

Bindrim's methods, for the most part, are the standard devices of group therapy. He was enthusiastic at the symposium, however, about a therapeutic intervention of his own inspired coinage that he calls "crotch-eyeballing." The crotch, he notes, is the focus of many hang-ups. In particular, three classes: (1) aftermath difficulties of toilet training; (2) masturbation guilts; (3) stresses of adult sexuality. Why not blast all this pathology at once! Thus two group members aid in (as Bindrim says) the "spread-eagling" of a third member and the entire company is instructed to stare unrelentingly and for a good long interval at the offending target area. Each group member is given an opportunity to benefit from this refreshing psychic boost. . . .

Admittedly, Bindrim's is only one of many approaches in group therapy. But all these methods are based on one fundamental assumption: that total psychic transparency—total self-exposure—has therapeutic and growth-releasing potential. More generally, they presuppose an ultimate theory of man as socius: man as an undifferentiated and diffused region in a social space inhabited concurrently by all other men thus diffused. Every technique, manipulative gimmick, cherished and wielded by the lovable, shaggy workers in this field is selected for its efficacy for such an end.

This entire, far-flung "human potential" movement is a threat to human dignity. It challenges any conception of the person that would make life worth living, in a degree far in excess of behaviorism. The "human potential" movement ob-

literates the content and boundary of the self by transporting it out of the organism—not merely to its periphery, but right out into public, social space. The force of behaviorism is merely to legislate the inner life out of existence for science, *while allowing the citizen to entertain the illusion, perhaps even the reality, of having one. Even Skinner gallantly acknowledges a world of "private stimulation."*

The "human potentialists," however, are saying in effect that a world of private *stimulations is unhealthy. They generate a militant rhetoric of anti-rigor and are derisive about the "up-tight," whether in scholarship or life. But as fix-it men to the up-hung, they have a passion for the unending collection and elaboration of group engineering* methods. *They have a barrel of them for every type of hang-up. Have hope!*

The moral and logic of the foregoing vignette are too obvious. "Humanistic psychology" started as a revolt against . . . fifty years of reductive behaviorism. In no time at all it achieved a conception of human nature so gross as to make behaviorism seem a form of Victorian sentimentality—which perhaps it was. We have come farther than full circle.

Note that this brief characterization—which I introduced as reportage rather than scholarly exposition—uses a strategy that verges on caricature. But let there be no mistake about what caricature, when responsibly practiced, is: it seeks to reveal essential characters of its subject by selection and even exaggeration. It is not a literal mode; indeed it seeks to be in some sense more "true," more revealing, than literal representation. Dr. Haigh was quite understandably prevented by his framework from perceiving the meaning of my caricature. In his courteous letter of defense (1969), his strategy is to treat it as literal analysis and then rebut certain of the thus misconstrued literal details. He attributes to me three assumptions that I make about the beliefs of the human potentialists and sees in each "a profound distortion." His misconstruals and arguments provide a revealing context for further analysis of the group movement.

Haigh states that my "first assumption is that humanistic

psychologists value total self-exposure for its therapeutic and growth-releasing potential." He "strongly disagrees with such an absolute valuing of openness." He gives the example of a leader who finds "anger toward another participant welling up within" himself. The extent to which this emotion is expressed "will depend upon (a) the intensity with which" it is being experienced, (b) the leader's "personal defenses with regard to such expression," (c) his "concern about the capacity of the other to receive" his "anger," and (d) his "awareness of where the group is in terms of its values and its readiness for effective encounter. . . . There is no consensus among us as to the absolute value of self-exposure."

The issues involved here are indeed fundamental. That there is in the group movement no *explicit* consensus as to the absolute value of self-exposure I am fully willing to acknowledge. But in my brief passage, I was certainly not attempting a *summary* of the mountains of prose generated by groupers about their rationale and practice. As I read that literature, I occasionally run into isolated, *en passant* warnings about "over-exposure." But very seldom. What I do run into, however, on almost every page are recommendations, advertisements, celebrations, hymns, about the cosmic values of openness, disclosure, exposure, honesty, directness, "letting oneself be known," transparency, and so on. The force of most of the theoretical rhetoric, of virtually *all* of the group-engineering devices, of the experience-protocols of group leaders and members, creates an inescapable conclusion that belief in the growth-releasing potential of self-exposure *is* a dominant and pervasive premise of the movement. "Self-exposure" *functions* very much like a therapeutic absolute in the work of the movement.

A recent article by Rogers (1969), which seeks to focus on "certain threads that weave in and out" of "the rich, wild, new tapestry that is the intensive group experience" is an impressive case in point. The threads which he singles out and presents in the rough order of their emergence within the rich, wild tapestry of a group's life (Milling Around, Resistance, Recalled Feelings, Lashing Out, Revealing Self) make it quite clear that in the mind of the thread-unraveler the group process is seen as a kind of Pilgrim's Progress toward the stripping of self. Many other "threads" identified by Rogers either have the character of basic changes which are consequent upon the process of psychic stripping (Cracking Masks, Basic Encounter, Positive Closeness) or facilitate the stripping performance (Here-and-Now Trust, Feedback).

I find this same iterative and echolalic concentration upon self-disclosure as the hub, nub, pivot, and growth-releasing agency of the group process in the writings of other leading encounter theorists such as Frederick Stoller, Jack Gibb, or William Schutz—in fact, in all accounts of encounter rationale, or method, that have come my way. Indeed, if one disregards terminological embroidery and differential turgidity, most accounts of the therapeutic rationale turn out to be remarkably uniform. Growth toward freedom, autonomy, authenticity, spontaneity, expressiveness, flexibility, or realization is released by self-disclosure in a group situation in which all atmospheric variables militate toward mutual self-definition and the "direct" expression of response (whether hostile, loving, or other) by all members to any given member in process of disclosing. When theoretical analysis is attempted, it is customary to point to the joint interplay of reinforcement and feedback in shaping each individual's movement through the group experience. Such variables may be supplemented, in some accounts, by postulating natural healing tendencies which are liberated in individuals by the group process. That is about the size of the rationale, whatever the yardage in which it is conveyed.

Some feeling of the fruits of facilitating these growth-releasing dynamics may be derived from Rogers' description of that tapestry-thread called "Cracking Masks."

In time, the group finds it unbearable that any member should live behind a mask or a front. Polite words, intellectual understanding of each other and of relationships, the smooth coin of tact and cover-up—amply satisfactory for interactions outside—are just not good enough. . . . Gently at times, almost savagely at others, the group demands that the individual be himself, that his current feelings not be hidden and that he remove the mask of ordinary social intercourse. In one group there was a highly intelligent and quite academic man who had been rather perceptive in his understanding of others but who had revealed himself not at all. The attitude of the group was finally expressed sharply by one member when he said, "Come out from behind the lectern, Doc. Stop giving us speeches. Take off your dark glasses—we want to know YOU" *[Rogers, 1969, p. 31].*

Rogers reports that this man looked on the verge of tears during the lunch hour. Then triumphantly: "When the group reconvened the members sensed this and treated him most gently, enabling him to tell us his own tragic personal story which accounted for his aloofness and his intellectual and academic approach to life."

Is it too much to hope that some may see something frightening going on here? Is not the group a bit lecherous in its pursuit of its payoff? Is it not possible that this "perceptive" and contained man was pressured into relinquishing something gallant and proud in his makeup? Is it not conceivable that even if disclosure had made him feel somewhat better, he had become somewhat less? Cracking masks, in Rogers' sense, could be therapy. But it could be brainwashing.

Some profound questions are raised by this example (incidentally, an innocuous one in comparison to many in the group movement literature). Are all so-called facades phony and psychically crippling accretions? Are all surface traits facades? If there is a distinction between a surface trait and a facade, who is to make it? Is every individual or reference group equally competent to do so relative to a given case? Who is qualified to tell Proust to get rid of his fur coat and his hypochondria, Eliot to ditch his reserve, Mann his rather bourgeois surface rigidities, Gide his exhibitionistically asserted homosexuality, Joyce his propensity for occasional fugues of high living, Dylan Thomas his alcoholism and arrogant scrounging? Is the "facilitator," "change agent," "therapist," to be the chap who shouts, "Come out from behind the lectern, Doc"? Is it to be Carl Rogers?

But there are deeper problems here. The concept of *transparency*, as applied by our promoters of human potential, serves grotesquely to mask certain of the most pervasive and potent conditions constitutive of value. Total transparency is constitutive only of nullity, and human beings in process of approximating or sustaining transparency are among the most boring phenomena in creation. We all have run into those bores who want to apprise you of the entire content of their souls, not to mention the consistency of their feces and their taste in deodorants, within five minutes of having met them. We usually feel guilty over such boredom, for we know that they are sick. Or again, what could be more boring, and even sordid and life-denying, than a spouse, lover, or friend who wishes to pass half of each day in salubrious examination of "our" relationship? But the point I am trying to get at is far more subtle and important than such illustrations convey.

We often talk about prizing depth rather than transparency in people and their artifacts, and elsewhere. But depth, too, is a rather coarse-grained and unilluminating concept, as generally used. A little reflection will show that what we tend to prize maximally in our perception of people, or of art, or the natural world, is a special, difficult-to-specify relationship between surface qualities and interior or depth qualities. Really a *class* of such relationships, for there can be all kinds of complementarities, interactions, stresses, distances, degrees of clarity or of ambiguity in the surface-to-interior relations. Whatever the ultimate analysis of such matters, we are so constituted perceptually and affectively as to derive intense and differentiated value from carriers of such relationships. To take a simple perceptual example, most of us differentially value a color which somehow mysteriously emerges from the depths of an exquisite gem (say a fine tourmaline) as against a color of similar spectral properties in the form of a pigmented surface patch. In every form of art what we maximally respond to—when we respond competently—is a set of special and complex relationships between surface and interior properties. The much prized ambiguity that has been a dominant (but inadequately explicated) aesthetic canon over much of the century probably points to a particular subset of such relations.

Until recently, most of us recognized such qualities of human beings as the charm of certain forms of reticence; the grace of certain kinds of containedness (which need not mean stiffness or rigidity but which can be definitive of dignity); the communicative richness of certain forms of understatement, allusiveness, implicativeness; the fetching quality of that kind of modesty which is the outward form of the capacity to prize personhood and to love directionally rather than diffusely. Some of us even used to be charmed by the kind of openness which is not transparency (a quality which renders even glass only utilitarian) nor yet hearty and robust explicitness (which is superficial), but rather a capacity to focus sensitively, precisely, and even vulnerably upon value-laden human and natural objects, and an analogous gift for allowing the self to emerge into focus, but without surrender of dignity or modesty, for valued others.

The encounter groupers I know have a great propensity for saying "that is precisely what we mean" when I attempt such baroque specifications of the ineffable. They will never convince me—for everything they *do* with groups can only obfuscate, belie, and ultimately destroy such distinctions. In this endeavor, they can count on plenty of support from other agencies in our culture.

This easy traffic, on the part of encounter groups, in words and claims which cannot possibly be rendered consistent with their actual practice is illustrated by Haigh in the very passage which initiated this discussion. To prove that he (and presumably other groupers) would not espouse an "absolute valuing of openness," he details a hypothetical complex of considerations that a group leader would bring to bear on the expression of anger toward a participant. You will recall that the extent to which such an emotion is expressed, in his example, will depend upon such matters as its intensity, the leader's "personal defenses," his "concern about the capacity of the other to receive" this anger, and his "awareness of where the group is in terms of its values and its readiness for effective encounter." These are fine words! But they do not help. Such an assemblage of constraints upon a single decision (and of a sort that must be made by a leader at every moment in the life of a group) calls for so exquisite a "weighting" of transitory and subtle circumstances as to place the qualifications for responsible group leadership beyond mortal attainment. Yet, unless these be met, every encounter group must involve grave human risk.

The second misconstrual of which Haigh finds me guilty runs, in part, as follows: "The second assumption you make is that the humanistic model of man is one in which the basic unit is not the individual but the group. Again I strongly disagree." He proceeds to elaborate on this theme for some sentences, but they are irrelevant. For his first sentence is an utter misreading of my words, this time at quite literal level.

In the brief passage to which his criticism refers, I had characterized the human potentialists as holding a theory of man as socius. Haigh, I fear, misunderstood the meaning of socius, a dictionary definition of which is "the individual human organism or person regarded as a participant in social relationships." In the few sentences which developed this contention, I was clearly not maintaining that the encounter movement does not grant ontological legitimacy to the individual or that it espouses some form of a Group Mind position. I was trying to convey that the pursuit of "openness" via self-revelation before an adventitiously assembled group of strangers centers the process of individual self-definition much too heavily upon group response. What is implicit here is a simplistic and crass "solution" to the immensely complex and delicate question of the relation of man and society, one which (despite all loving intentions to the contrary) assigns as much weight to the social shaping of the individual as do most rigid theories of social determinism. I suspect, further, that lurking under all this is a deep misconception of the concept of democracy—a perversion of it which is widespread in the culture at large. This is the sense of the democratic process as an egalitarian merging of happy, well-met, mutually voyeuring "people," rather than a system of agreements guaranteeing maximal dispersion of social control and minimal invasion upon both self-determination and privacy.

The tendency of these cheerful humanists to engineer individuation via "feelingful," "direct," and "honest" feedback has already been illustrated by Rogers' description of the archetypal professor who was savagely denuded of his lectern and then gently restored to "health." As another example, I quote an instructive paragraph from a recent exposition of "Marathon Group Therapy" by Frederick Stoller: "When time is compressed as it is in the marathon, the consequences of one's behavior are placed in greater contiguity to the behavior itself. Both the individual and the other with whom he is involved have the opportunity to specify why he invites his particular fate. The assumption is made that the marathon group represents a sample of the world, and one's behavior within the group represents a sample of one's behavior in the world" (Stoller, 1968).

This differential assessment of the force and value of real life experience as against encounter group experience is frequent in the group literature. Up to a point it is correct, but this constitutes one of the very grave threats of the group movement. What Stoller says about the force and immediacy of group feedback, under the prevailing conditions of member motivation, group-objectives, and the leader's structuring, cannot be denied. But it is a dangerous thing for an adventitiously selected group to have this degree of force in controlling the individual's self-image. As we have already seen, the assumption seems to be that any old kind of feedback is fine—regardless of the degree of sensitivity, general quality of sensibility, and so on, of the feeders. The literature is not encouraging concerning the evidence of such qualifications, whether of the member-feeders or the leader-feeder. The chances for simpleminded, callow, insufficiently considered, or reductive shaping of the individual are high.

The obvious defense against this argument is: "Are the chances any better in actual life?" This is superficial. The chances of winning sensitive feedback (I loathe the word) are probably pretty meager, at best, in any context. But in ordinary life we are most of the time recipients of multiple and disparate feedbacks; we are protected by this very dishomogeneity from the sense that our essence has been caught and fixed by our assessors. Besides, any given assessment is less likely to be perceived as peremptory; we tend more readily to assess our assessors. We do not "enter" ordinary life, as we do an encounter group, with pat and virtuous expectations of self-clarification or improvement; usually we are merely *there*. In life we may pay for our follies, but we do not commit the folly of buying feedback, at so much per yard, from our friends. Indeed the dynamics of friendship are such that people receive much of their feedback from individuals of comparable or higher sensitivity, rather than lower. Most persons need heroes in their lives, and there is at least a faint correlation between admiration and admirability.

However inefficient the ordinary conditions of character formation, it is diabolical to make these contingent on group engineering. Moreover, it is the very "effectiveness" of the group situation which is its great danger. The ambiguities and delays in feedback in normal, nonengineered life are safeguards —guardians of the significant (not nominal) form of authenticity which can only be achieved by allowing intrapersonal factors the fullest possible play in development. The capacity for individual transcendence of the group is perhaps the most value-charged gift of the human station.

Haigh informs me that my third mistaken assumption is that "humanistic psychologists regard the world of private stimulation as unhealthy." He sets me straight by a "few quotes" from the humanistic association's "statement of purpose." I will learn from these that my "assumption is diametrically opposite from" the humanists' "intention." His main quotation from this source is as follows: "[In the humanistic orientation there is . . .] a centering of attention on the experiencing *person*, and thus a focus on experience as the primary phenomenon in the study of man. . . . As a consequence of this orientation, the Association encourages attention to topics having little place in existing systems, such as love, creativity, spontaneity, play, warmth, ego-transcendence, autonomy, responsibility, authenticity, meaning, transcendental experience, courage [Haigh, 1969, p. 4]."

What I actually said, in the course of suggesting certain deeper affinities between the behavioristic model of man and the group movement's model, was: "Even Skinner gallantly acknowledges a world of 'private stimulation.' The 'human potentialists,' however, are saying in effect that a world of *private* stimulation is unhealthy." "Private stimulation" is a technical concept of Skinner's—a ludicrous one, in my estimation, in that it is his only concept bearing on intra-organismic process and experience, and he apparently considers it adequate as the system-language surrogate for that whole domain. Haigh, however, once more attempts to refute me by a straight-faced literal rendition of my perfectly plain metaphor, in this case a minor degree of hyperbole, or exaggeration, having (among other things) a humorous intent.

What *does* merit notice is the character of the evidence that Haigh considers adequate for my re-education: a pompous statement of *intention* drawn from an official document of his association. And as we savor this swollen word-string, we find what?—an iteration of the staple existential "goodies," the names of which preempt half the verbal output of the humanistic literature, and the meanings of which are so uniformly degraded and defeated both in the group's literature and the group practice. We have, in short, another exercise in one of the modes of stripping so dear to this strip-oriented movement: in this application, the stripping away of meanings from words.

I ask you to consider what this mode of stripping involves. The words of our natural language stabilize slowly and hard-won insights—sometimes extraordinarily salient and delicately contoured insights—into the universe, both the inner universe of experience, and the outer universe. The discriminations preserved and transmitted by natural language form the matrix of all the knowledge that we have. Even the technical languages of science have differentiated out of natural language, and their interpretation continues to depend on discriminations within the natural language. From such considerations it follows that if a word has stabilized a salient, delicately bounded, and humanly valuable discrimination with respect to the universe, then a coarsening or degrading of its usage will entail a loss of actual knowledge. An individual's conception of the application conditions for a word is a fact of sensibility.

Coarsening of language means coarsening of knowledge, and a language community that uses language in a coarsened way is a community of coarsened sensibility.

I have repeatedly made reference to the gross and debased ways in which encounter groupers use certain humanly precious words of our language. I hope it can now be appreciated that this deficiency is no mere matter of literary or conversational inelegance. If an image of personhood be specified in coarsened terms, then that image is a coarsened one in comparison to the image that might be specified via more sensitive (thus richer) use of the same terms. When this degraded image now becomes criterial with respect to the desirable directions of personality change, we can anticipate only a degrading of personhood in the course of efforts to move the person toward such "ideal" qualities.

The low-level, mechanical way in which the groupers use glitter-concepts such as authenticity, love, autonomy, and the rest in the inflated rhetoric that passes for their theory, but which nevertheless controls the selection of their methods and practice, at once reveals and promotes a serious impoverishment of sensibility.

I will conclude this chapter with one final example of such crippling uses of language. In encounter group parlance, "trust" is that homogeneous, gelatinous enzyme secreted by a group which catalyzes the process of self-exposure by decreasing the apparent risk-contingencies. The person will "let himself be known" because his share of the collective ambience of trust gives him a sense of safety. And our perspicacious savants have discriminated certain subtle laws of trust: for instance, if X trusts Y, Y is more likely to trust X, or if X trusts Y, Y is more likely to like X, or again if X trusts Y, Y is more likely to please X (whether by services rendered, or in some other way).

I will spare you a serious analysis of trust and merely indicate that it is no simple notion. Even in the sense which our groupers have somewhere in mind (a dictionary form of which is "to do some action, with expectation of safety, or without fear of the consequences"), trust is not an undifferentiated, global matter. I can *trust* someone's good intentions, or his

friendliness, or that he will not steal from me, or poison my
shredded wheat, or that he will not covet his neighbor's wife, or
covet mine, yet *distrust* his capacity to perceive me, or him, or
them or it with clarity, delicacy, or precision. Again, I can trust
X's ability to see me with nicety and in depth, but (perhaps)
not his ability or disposition to respond in a way congruent
with his perception, or to use his perception of *my* trust in
any way that may be congenial, constructive, or safety-en-
gendering from my point of view. Again, I can trust X to be
generally or in the long run or fundamentally decent (or honest), but not that he will not try to work me for all sorts of
short-term and local advantages. Trust, when asserted as between X and Y, is not truly a two-termed relation; when the
word is used sensitively, there is actually a third relatum which
may appear explicitly or be implicitly conveyed by context.
This reflects the human reality that when X trusts Y (and
assuming that X can satisfy some weak criterion of rationality)
he does so with respect to some finite class of Zs.

More revealing, however, than the grouper's general
theory of trust is their understanding of it as signaled by one of
their favorite "nonverbal communication methods." You all
know the device: Trust is presumably instilled by asking a
member of a group to fall backward on the assumption that
another member stationed behind the faller will catch him.
Now, to my febrile mind, this may instructively serve as a
screening device for detecting whether the presumptive catcher
is a psychopath but has nothing to do with trust. Any designated
catcher who played the wry practical joke of allowing the faller
to crack his head on the floor could justly be thought the owner
of a character defect. A catcher, however, who did carry out
the prescribed function of catching could only be thought, by
any intelligent faller, to be a man capable of playing a meaningless game according to prescribed and easily applicable
rules, or one minimally equipped with regard for the survival
of his fellows quite outside the context of those rules, but the
faller would have no warrant for regarding the receiver trust-
worthy as a recipient of psychic confidences.

The operational (or essentially mechanical) definition

of trust conveyed by this example exhibits, in especially witless
fashion, the deficiency of most so-called operational definitions.
These are essentially definitions by symptom and cannot be expected to hold for the relational pattern of symptoms actually
constitutive of any reasonably abstract or general concept. All
other methods in the copious armamentarium of the encounter
groupers have this same garbled relationship to the notions of
which they are the purported realization, and thus to the states
of affairs it is hoped they will bring about.

This "most important social invention of the century"
that we have been considering carries every earmark of a shallow fad. Yet the impetus behind it is poignant and powerful and
permanently embedded in man's condition. Man's search for
egress from the cave, platonic or other, is rendered especially
frantic in such times as ours. However compelling its impetus,
this fad will soon—as historic time is measured—fizzle out. But
its *effects* need not.

When value-charged discriminations drop out of man's
ken, there is no certainty that they will be rediscovered. We
transmit to the future what we are. We may be what we eat,
but we are also what we image. If what we are has been reduced
by shallow or demeaning images, that impoverishment will
persist in the world long after the images that conveyed it have
gone their way.

I have presented these views to several groups—one of
which was an audience (including many of the leaders of the
encounter movement) at the 1970 meeting of the Association
for Humanistic Psychology. I have been treated with great
lenience—even by such people as Drs. Schutz, Shostrom, and
Haigh. In general, the pattern of their response has been: (1)
that I have rendered the movement a service by raising a set
of genuine problems some of which they had begun to consider,
but others of which were new, germane, and troublesome; (2)
that some of these problems point to deficiencies in the efforts
of inexpert, crass, or meretricious group leaders, but *not* of
expert, sensitive and saintly ones; and (3) that, generally speaking, most of my demurs hold only for an indeterminate subset

of the disorderly spectrum of "approaches" within the amplitudinous and fuzzily bounded domain of the "encounter movement."

My rejoinder is that I hope they are right! I sincerely respect the motives, the quality of intent, behind the encounter movement. And I deplore the societal circumstances—whether these be phrased as alienation, dehumanization, depersonalization, emotional anaesthesia, anonymity, existential nausea, or simple loneliness—which have triggered the movement. But I suspect that the votaries of encounter have to be wrong in their belief that my major demurs are applicable only to some but not all of the approaches or that my reservations point to remediable deficiencies. For the essence of my position is that there are generic characters common to all so-called encounter approaches, to all styles and philosophies of leadership, which, when present in some minimal degree, render the group process self-defeating relative to meaningful fulfillment of the stated objectives. (I do not deny, of course, that some approaches and/or some leaders of relatively greater sensitivity accomplish results that are less "bad" than do others.)

Certain entailments (regrettable ones, I think) follow as soon as one isolates such "elements" as: (1) a more or less adventitiously assembled face-to-face group; (2) a leader who, via initial instruction and in other ways, seeks to accelerate the normally slow, tortuous, and painful process of individual self-definition by encouraging frank, direct, and uninhibited feedback of the group members to each other; (3) a presumption that the objective of participation is the enhancement or realization of human potential (as conceptualized in one or another way), and the corollary presumption that self-disclosure as facilitated by trust sets the process of growth toward such an objective into motion; and (4) accessory assumptions which emphasize the importance of centering communication upon the "here and now," of experientially direct rather than "cognitive" or "abstract" communication, of nonverbal as well as verbal expressive fluency, and so on.

One consequence of such presumptions, which I have perhaps not sufficiently traced out, is that the encounter process

becomes an extraordinarily ritualized kind of game. For instance, the attempt to accelerate, in the artificially engineered
ways at issue, what in real life might be the inefficient but
meaningful process of self-definition imposes on leader and
group members alike a tendency to perceive (to interpret and
assess) psychodynamic and internal states in essentially symptomatic modes. The range of evidence afforded by this artificial
situation over its limited time course, and upon which the group
must base its shaping and modulating influences, is so thin as
to enforce the rapid adoption of a crass and simplistic lexicon
of symptom-meaning (or phenotype-genotype) correspon-
dences. The essential complexity, indeed ambiguity, of the
meanings of human actions and expressions, thus of personhood,
is damped out.

    Such simplistic lexicons may vary in content from group
to group, but we are all familiar with a number of rather widely
presumed symptom-meaning equivalence rules. Thus, in many
encounter groups joking or wit may automatically be seen as
evasiveness; sleepiness, boredom or torpor as withdrawal. A
raised voice must mean hostility (rather than, say, passionate
concern) and blocking must be defense (rather than the
stumbling desire to achieve a clear articulation of the complex).
Still more widely, abstract statement must mean a form of intel-
lectualistic concealment or "mind-fucking," despite the fact that
a responsible abstraction can be seen as a perceptual disembed-
ding of a highly specific, if widely instantiated, character from
the concrete—a point recognized in much Western philosophy
and in most of the great Eastern systems of thought. Still more
consequentially, love may be seen as a barter of reinforcements;
honesty as transparency; or trust as a state engendered by being
caught upon falling backward.

Screening and Selection of Participants

W. Brendan Reddy

As the number of encounter groups has increased, the number of problems and adverse reactions reported has grown proportionately. From around the country one hears accounts of suicides, psychotic breaks, and incidents of gross irresponsibility. The sensational press recounts tales of lurid immorality. Newspaper and magazine articles decry this psychological menace that has overtaken the country. Are there real issues and actual dangers, or are the perils merely imagined? This chapter describes the extent of these concerns and explores the related issues of participant selection and screening and group composition. The recommendations offered can reduce the probability of undesirable results.

Two major events in the history of the group movement contributed to its evolution and led to many of its current problems. The first was the shift from a social focus to a clinical focus. The second event was the definition of the encounter group within the framework of psychotherapy. In the early days of the National Training Laboratories, group work focused on improving change-agent concepts and skills. This improvement was the training objective of the social psychologists who originated this type of small group approach and who staffed the first experiential workshops. However, by 1949, most workshop staff were psychiatrists and clinical psychologists. Their Freudian and Rogerian approaches contrasted sharply with those of the Lewinian-oriented staff members. The clinical trend, which affected both trainers and group members and emphasized personal feedback in a here-and-now setting, overcame the basic group-skills approach (Benne, 1964). By 1962, this trend was more clearly articulated by Wechsler, Massarik, and Tannenbaum as "group therapy for normals."

As the focus of the experiential group has changed and as compatible societal values have evolved, so have the number and types of participants. The university campus, the church, and the business setting have provided most participants, but a rapidly increasing number of housewives and other private citizens are now sharing the encounter experience. Currently, and indeed for some time to come, the alienated, the lonely, and the magic-seekers among us will gravitate to encounter groups as a way out of their personal dilemmas.

The reasons for joining encounter groups are varied. Many participants are looking for the quick cure, the illusion of a magical answer for decisions to be made, problems to be solved. Others come to attenuate their alienation; still others to seek out intimacy, sociality, and sexuality. In time past people in psychological trouble would have been inclined to seek out psychotherapy; increasingly, they appear to be looking for simpler and quicker, if less real, solutions. The help-seeker is further enticed to join an encounter group by brochures which promise a week of nirvana or to rid him of his sexual hang-ups in a weekend.

These informed impressions are supported by psychometric data, although such evidence is still meager. A recent study (Yalom and others, 1970) indicates that the self-esteem of college students who enrolled in encounter groups at a California university was significantly lower than that of matched control students. Reddy (1970) found that participants in two encounter groups showed profiles on the Tennessee Self-Concept Scale (Fitts, 1965) in the pathological range.

A related and complicating factor is the assumption that the difference between normality and pathology is one of degree (Schofield, 1964; Burton, 1965) and that many so-called disease entities are really problems of daily human living in our culture. Unfortunately, this view has been interpreted by some group leaders to mean that there are *no* significant differences between the patient and the nonpatient and that all encounter group participants can be dealt with as a single population.

Given these conditions, what is known of the actual incidents of pathology related to the encounter group? Unfortunately, the amount and quality of research in the field has not matched the intensity of reactions against encounter groups. Since humanistic values have been paramount in the movement, it has been read by many as an antiintellectual movement with no or little need for research. Further, as with other group research, methodological problems abound. Control groups are difficult to establish; participants do not want to be placed in an experimental setting, and they resist completing follow-up questionnaires.

Despite these problems, enough valid data have appeared to permit an examination of the dangers of the encounter group. A National Training Laboratories Report (1969) indicated that of 14,200 participants in industrial and summer programs only 33 participants (0.2 per cent) had to leave the program because of disruptive personal reactions. Rogers (1970) reported that of 600 participants seen in some forty groups only 2 (0.3 per cent) developed psychosis. Mintz (1969) did not report any occurrence of psychosis in a follow-up study based upon a sample of 173 respondents and the observation of 279 participants. Nor did Bach (1967) in a study of 400 marathon group participants. In one systematic study, Sata (in Yalom and others, 1970) indicates that, in a two-week residential training laboratory, overt psychosis or need for psychiatric consultation occurred in but 0.5 per cent of the participants.

Yalom and others (1970) report on a university project of nineteen encounter groups composed of 209 students. In a six-month follow-up, only three psychiatric referrals were uncovered. Two of the participants were hospitalized, one with severe depression, the second in a manic state. The third participant had committed suicide. However, a psychological postmortem of the suicide revealed a history of severe disturbance prior to the encounter group experience; he had been in both individual and group psychotherapy.

Batchelder and Hardy (1968) report a follow-up survey of the YMCA's sensitivity training program. Of 1,200 participants, only four "severe psychological disruption" cases came to light. In a study of 73 freshman medical students, Cadden, Flach, Blakeslee, and Charlton (1969) indicate that not only were there no psychiatric casualties, but as a result of the group, psychiatric consultations are down by half.

A few reports suggest a higher incidence of pathology. Yalom and others (1970) indicate that 10 to 15 per cent of all participants in a National Training Laboratories group consulted the laboratory psychiatrist for a wide range of complaints. Fourteen psychiatric disturbances were observed by Gottschalk and Pattison (1969) in three encounter groups with a total population of 32 participants. These psychiatric casualties ranged from mild anxiety to psychosis. Jaffe and Scherl (1969) discuss in detail two cases of psychosis precipitated by an encounter group experience. Reddy (1970), using self-rating scales in a controlled study comparing T-groups, group psychotherapy, and control participants, found that exacerbation of pathology increased significantly following the sensitivity training groups. The psychotherapy group and the control group showed a nonsignificant decrease in self-reported disturbance. In his survey of several groups, Parloff (1970) reports that mild to moderate emotional disturbances occurred during group experiences for 0.5 per cent to 28 per cent of participants. From 0.6 per cent to 6 per cent of group members reported emotional disturbances after the experience.

When the available data are reviewed objectively, one must be impressed by the low incidence of pathology reported. At least when the sponsors of encounter groups are reputable, competent organizations, the cries of gross irresponsibility and high incidence of pathology are simply not warranted.

The reported incidence of psychological disruption in encounter groups has been inferred to be related to the high level of stress generated by the experience. Lubin and Zuckerman (1969) showed the amount of measured stress was well within the normal range. They compared the amount of emotional stress produced in an encounter group setting with that generated by perceptual isolation experiments. The same psychological measures of the degree of emotion aroused were used in both settings. Their research showed that the stress produced in the group was far less than that produced in the perceptual isolation experiments. Moreover, participants in the encounter group did not show anxiety, hostility, or depression beyond a level generally accepted as normal.

However, the fact that some, even a few, participants *do* show pathology during and after an encounter group experience remains an issue that must be addressed. Who are these people, and what are the dynamics with which we are dealing? What types of participants profit least from the encounter experience or are most likely to be hurt by such an experience?

Slater advances the position (1966) that there is a negative correlation between participants' therapeutic need and personal growth they show. In terms of severe and moderate pathology, those potential encounter group participants who would be considered poor candidates for outpatient group psychotherapy are also poor candidates for the encounter group. These include the paranoid, brain-damaged, hypochondriacal, suicidal, psychotic, and sociopathic. Those addicted to alcohol and drugs should not be admitted to general groups but certainly ought to be included in specialized encounter groups designed for those populations. Kuehn and Crinella (1969) recommend that psychotics, hysterics, and individuals in crisis be excluded from encounter groups.

My own experience indicates that extremely narcissistic

individuals are also undesirable, particularly for relatively short encounter groups (three days or less), since they demand and monopolize much of the group time. Consistently, Lundgren and Miller (1965) have shown that individuals who claim a high degree of self-satisfaction overestimate others' opinions of them and tend not to profit from the group experience.

There is also evidence to support the contention that participants who might achieve a deviant role in an encounter group should be deselected. For example, Schachter (1951) shows that communication between the deviant and other group members is initially very high. However, it drops off very rapidly and the deviant is rejected by the group. Most important, in this study, the level of measured rejection is proportional to the degree to which the deviance is relevant to the purpose of the group. Both Asch (1958) and Sherif (1958) demonstrate that an individual will be made highly uncomfortable when he is the deviant group member. Yalom (1970) maintains that certain behaviors—denial, deemphasis of intrapsychic and interpersonal factors, and the tendency to attribute causality to somatic and external environmental factors—readily identify patients who become deviants in group psychotherapy. Yalom further states that these patients can be screened in interviews.

Stone and Tieger (1970) suggest that participants with a history of psychosomatic illness be screened out because exacerbation of those symptoms is likely to occur under the stress of the encounter group. These authors also deselect applicants with histories of difficulty in impulse control, maintaining that they might be pressured into acting destructively or into revealing highly personal material in the encounter setting, where confidentiality is difficult to maintain. Patients in therapy who wish to join an encounter group are recommended to explore that decision with their therapist. These recommendations are consistent with National Training Laboratories standards (1969), which further suggest that those potential participants who do not volunteer for the experience not be accepted. The NTL standards also caution against including people with significant histories of "inadequate coping" with interpersonal stress.

In theory, the deselection of those persons who might be disruptive, harmed, or harmful is not a complex matter; in practice, however, it has become exactly the opposite. A variety of factors contribute to this circumstance. The strong antiintellectual component in the movement has permitted the abandonment of theory and conceptual thinking. Argyris (1967) shows that proponents consistently emphasize expressing emotion for its own sake while lacking theoretical concepts underlying those views. Systematic analysis of the selection process leading to the development of practical guidelines has simply not materialized. It has been, is, and (most disturbingly) may continue to be an area of minimal concern for a large number of encounter group leaders.

A second reason for the establishment of only minimal screening procedures reflects the contention by encounter group leaders that the experience is educational and not therapeutic. Granted, the experience was not designed to alleviate pathological conditions (NTL, 1969). However, encounter group brochures and advertising frequently offer the same gains and outcomes as one might find in long-term, intensive group psychotherapy programs. Indeed, many brochures offer insight and magic that no therapy could approach. Given what is known of personality theory, psychodynamics, and motivation, as well as knowledge of our present society and cultural norms, it is absurd to maintain that encounter groups do not attract persons exhibiting extremes of behavior. Ignoring this problem will not alter its existence.

A third factor has been the controversy over the predictive value of psychiatric diagnosis. The American Psychiatric Association diagnostic manual (1968) has an etiologic and symptomatic format which is at best questionable in terms of its usefulness in predicting interpersonal behavior in a group setting. Moreover, some authors (Burton, 1965; Hendin, Gaylin, and Carr, 1965) have pointed out difficulty in distinguishing between psychiatric and nonpsychiatric populations. Unfortunately, this controversy has been interpreted by some group leaders to mean psychopathology cannot or should not be identified.

A fourth reason screening has not been an integral part

of the encounter group is the inability of leaders to recognize potentially disruptive behavior and pathology. Many are neither clinically trained nor adequately prepared to examine critically those persons whose behavior and dynamics are such that they and their fellow group members would not profit from the experience. Finally, the possible financial gain from encounter groups is so high that sponsors are often profit-motivated rather than humanistically or educationally motivated. Filling group rosters with bodies all too often becomes the norm without consideration for group composition. As might be expected, and consistent with the incidence of pathology, these factors which preclude adequate screening are far less visible in the reputable, competent organizations which have some control over their group leaders.

What is being done to screen potential encounter group participants? In order to remove extremes of behavior a combination of techniques can be used. They are brochure statements, application completion, interviews, psychometrics, and small group sessions. Some, of course, are more feasible than others.

Advertising should clearly indicate that the encounter group is not designed for therapeutic purposes and that individuals in counseling and psychotherapy should discuss the advisability of the experience with their therapist. In light of outcome research on encounter groups, claims of extensive learning and insights are inappropriate, if not false. These claims attract marginal persons who are looking for a "quick cure." It is important to stress volunteerism in brochures in order that highly resistive participants are not included against their own choice.

An application which asks open-ended questions regarding motivation for joining an encounter group and requires a personal and medical history can be invaluable in screening poor candidates. The medical check-off list should include such entities as psychosomatic illnesses. Individual interviews with potential participants, while adding some behavioral and interpersonal data with which to make selection decisions, are expensive and frequently impractical, although they may be useful under some circumstances. Similarly, psychological testing may be helpful in identifying gross pathology but is often impractical because test materials cannot be sent to potential group members. Moreover, standard diagnostic instruments seldom accurately predict interpersonal behavior.

Goldstein, Heller, and Sechrest (1966) argue that prediction of behavior within the group is most accurate when it is based on direct observation of the individual when he is involved in a task closely related to the group experience. This finding suggests that placing prospective group participants in an unstructured small group situation would be most effective for observing and predicting their behavior. Again, expense and impracticality may prohibit a screening group well in advance of the actual group. However, establishing a composition group as the introduction to the encounter group would permit acquaintance between staff and participants, screening for pathology exacerbated by stress, and exploration of interpersonal styles of both participants and staff in order to determine what composition is desirable. Finally, contracts between participants and staff might be established at this time.

Stone and Tieger (1970) describe an elaborate but excellent screening format used in a large religious training program which sponsored week-long intensive encounter groups. Screening was threefold: written application, a battery of psychological tests, and fourteen one-and-one-half-hour small group sessions well in advance of the group and led by one of the author-consultants and one of the encounter group leaders. Of 105 evaluated applicants, 15 (14 per cent) were told they could not attend the encounter group for psychological reasons, 4 for problems with reality testing, 8 for severe symptomatic neurotic problems, 2 for overt homosexuality, and 1 with active chronic ulcerative colitis. Six applicants (6 per cent) screened themselves out.

In a follow-up study of the participants (Stone and Tieger, 1970), two applicants who had been evaluated reported disruptive psychological reactions as a result of the encounter group experience. One was removed from the group after he became overtly psychotic. He received immediate psychiatric consultation, which was available. A second participant became agitated and was removed for a one-day period before returning to the group.

The authors report an unexpected effect of the screening program. The reaction of the encounter group leaders was positive in that they felt more confident in their role as leaders, knew the participants, and felt they could better anticipate initial responses in their groups. The leaders also felt that the probability of disruptive psychological reactions had lessened.

In order to increase feasibility and effectiveness, I propose that as an advance pregroup screening strategy brochures be explicit in their message and that applications be extensive enough to cover psychological and medical history as well as motivations for joining an encounter group. These procedures will permit the immediate elimination of a number of applicants. I suggest that at the immediate start of the encounter group a final pathology and interpersonal behavior screening be initiated in the form of a short, unstructured group session. This session would serve as a final deselection if need be; but more important, it would generate data about interpersonal styles. These data plus a brief measure such as Schutz' (1958) Fundamental Interpersonal Relations Orientation-Behavior (FIRO-B) could be used to precompose groups in order to increase learning by participants. There are data to support this contention (Harrison, 1965; Harrison and Lubin, 1965a and 1965b; Reddy, 1971a).

In group psychotherapy it is often maintained that heterogeneous groups have advantages over homogeneous groups. Homogeneous groups seem to be more cohesive, supportive, and exhibit less conflict. However, heterogeneous groups seem to attain deeper levels of searching interaction which lead to greater learning and insight. In group psychotherapy support for these contentions is primarily anecdotal. In small group research and sensitivity training we find empirical support. Schutz (1958) reports that groups whose members had compatible needs for affection functioned better and were more productive than groups whose members were incompatible on the affection dimension. However, Harrison (1965) and Harrison and Lubin (1965a) indicate that compatible homogeneous groups may inhibit learning. Hoffman and Maier (1966) show that diversity of personality profiles facilitates group problem-solving. Evidence is also presented by Harrison that incompatible persons more readily explore alternative modes of behavior when grouped than do interpersonally compatible people. Harrison further suggests that an effective learning model provides group members with both support and dissonance.

I examined changes in self-actualization in six encounter groups in terms of participants' measured compatibility (1971a). Using Schutz' FIRO-B interchange compatibility measure, I found that both intensive and nonintensive encounter groups made gains on the Personal Orientation Inventory (Shostrom, 1963), a multimeasure of self-actualization. Moreover, greatest gains were made by group members whose affectional compatibility was in opposition to the group compatibility mean. The results support Harrison's contention that incompatibility leads to greater exploration of alternative behavior.

In a second, more controlled study (Reddy, 1971b), forty participants were placed in four encounter groups according to their premeasured compatibility on an affection scale. The hypothesis that participants in the two incompatible groups would gain significantly more on dimensions of self-actualization than would participants in the compatible-affection groups is supported on the predicted scales of the Personal Orientation Inventory.

In light of these data and our knowledge of learning and composition models, we can, as a function of the screening process, enhance the probabilities of encounter group participants' gaining greater learnings, as well as reduce the number of psychiatric casualties.

I have focused on the participants in the screening process. But what about the leaders? As we have seen, the incidence of pathology in groups conducted by competent leaders in reputable organizations such as the National Training Laboratories is relatively low. Bach (1968) points out that incidents of psychological disruption reported to him have occurred in groups conducted by leaders who were incompetent in both the clinical and group dynamics areas.

A study by Lieberman (see Chapter 8) shows that group casualties are not related to the type of encounter group but to the leader's style. "Energizers," as the authors call leaders characterized by aggressive stimulation practices, accounted for seven of the sixteen casualties. These leaders were highly self-disclosing, exhibited high positive caring, were confrontative, and focused on the individual participant rather than the group. Other casualties resulted from attacks in which the leaders rarely intervened. Pregroup psychological tests indicated that casualties had low self-concept, low self-esteem, and high group expectations.

It is unfortunate that criticisms of the encounter group movement have focused on the technique rather than on a specific variable such as the leader. Considerable training and skill are required to maintain a group at an optimal level of regression at which learning can take place emotionally and cognitively. Too many leaders operate on the invalid premise that the more emotion and stress exhibited in the group, the greater the learning. As participants respond to the pressure toward regression, so do group leaders. If the leader is experiencing psychological disruptions in his own life he may develop pathological reactions similar to those of participants. When these reactions occur, and indeed they do, the group leader is all too frequently overprotected by his colleagues at the expense of the client population.

A related but rarely discussed factor is the common practice of co-leading. As in group psychotherapy, the relationship between co-leaders is a significant dimension of the group climate which influences the outcome. The group experience would be more profitable to participants if co-leaders worked out their interpersonal relationships well in advance of the encounter sessions. The dynamics of the encounter group are complex and intricate enough without untrained co-leaders who do not understand their relationship. This relationship is frequently emotionally laden with unresolvable conflicts and reactions. In long-term groups, that is, one-week or two-week residential groups, these conflicts can be worked at and not at the expense of the group members. However, in short weekend groups or marathon encounters, it may be impossible for co-leaders to function adequately and at the same time tend to the needs of participants.

Conversely, the co-leading experience can be an excellent teaching device and does permit leaders to have a check on their perceptions of the dynamics evolving in the group. Factors such as sex, age, and marital status of the co-leaders should be explored before the relationship is formed. These factors often take on a great significance during various stages of the encounter group. Moreover, interpersonal styles as well as personality characteristics of the co-leaders should be considered before they decide to work together.

The male-female co-leading situation approximates the family model and often puts extreme stress on the trainers as well as the participants. Again, if trainers have not worked out their interpersonal difficulties the result can be highly disruptive to the group. Conflicts arising from the co-leading relationship are almost always reflected in the group, but, unfortunately, they are not always explored in postgroup clinicing or in supervision.

I have discussed at length what encounter group leaders can do to protect potential participants as well as themselves from disruptive psychological reactions. However, an equally important issue is what potential participants can do to protect themselves. Shostrom (1969) has given seven timely "never" suggestions for prospective members: (1) Never respond to a newspaper ad; (2) never participate in a group of fewer than a half-dozen members; (3) never join an encounter group on impulse—as fling, binge, or surrender to the unplanned; (4) never participate in a group encounter with close associates, persons with whom you have a professional or competitive social relations; (5) never be overly impressed by beautiful or otherwise class-signaled surroundings or participants; (6) never stay with a group that has a behavioral ax to grind; (7) never participate in a group that lacks formal connection with a professional on whom you can check.

The National Training Laboratories standards manual

(1969) suggests that leaders of long-term residential programs designate a qualified staff member as counselor and recommends they establish a relationship with a local physician for consultation and referral. Potential participants would be wise not to join an encounter group if the above conditions are not met.

Are participants legally protected? While there is little or no licensing of group leaders, Parloff (1970) points out that although group leaders may not offer treatment they are still legally responsible under tort law for any physical or emotional injury sustained by their clients. To further protect the participant, a number of professional organizations have investigated the encounter movement. The American Psychiatric Association has issued a task group report on *Encounter Groups and Psychiatry* (Yalom and others, 1970), and the American Psychological Association Committee on Scientific and Professional Ethics and Conduct has established a task force to propose provisions for encounter-type groups in the *Casebook on Ethical Standards of Psychologists* (1967). The American Group Psychotherapy Association and the Midwest Group for Human Resources are among other organizations which have issued position papers aimed at protecting both participant and competent professional.

Lakin (1969) has raised a number of ethical issues surrounding the use of encounter-type groups and has offered specific recommendations intended to resolve these issues. Likewise, Fred Strassburger, secretary of the APA committee on ethics and conduct, proposed concrete guidelines to help bring encounter groups into the mainstream of professional psychology (Strassburger, 1971).

The National Training Laboratories (1970) developed a proposal for a division of accreditation. Professional members seeking to join the organization are no longer being accepted until the issue is clarified and acted upon. The International Association for Applied Social Scientists (IAASS) was incorporated independent of the NTL in 1971. IAASS will sponsor and engage in activities such as setting standards for competence and ethical performance for practice; developing and applying procedures for admission on the basis of these standards; disciplining; protecting the public interests; and protecting the professional in exercising his professional responsibilities (Drexler, 1971). While this type of accreditation is essential and has been sorely needed, with the already burgeoning movement and its cults, marginal factions and entrepreneurs, it may be too little too late.

In sum, the psychological dangers inherent in encounter groups conducted by competent leaders are relatively low. Some incidents might have been avoided by more careful screening. Systematic screening and follow-up as an integral part of encounter group programs would go far to lessen the probability of marginal and pathological people becoming group participants. This goal would not be particularly difficult to attain. The problem of educating the public to protect themselves from the incompetent is a far greater problem that only legislation and accreditation may solve.

The encounter group experience might be more beneficial if group leaders preselected individuals and placed them in appropriate groups designed specifically to enhance their learning. Certainly the time and sophistication have come when we do not have to refer to all variables as "encounter group." The appropriate questions to ask today are: what kind of encounter group, conducted by leaders with what characteristics and purpose, for what kind of population under what circumstances?

5

Standards for Group Leadership

Frederick Massarik

In the first place, nobody knows what *the* encounter group really is. At least the lack of agreement on definition is very evident as the human potential movement in its multiplex manifestations, the National Training Laboratories and its offspring, variously committed humanistic psychologists, and a wide range of psychotherapists converge from all directions on a suddenly ubiquitous encounter group concept. At a meeting of a newly formed association concerned with the issue of standards in the field (however defined), the following listing of "groups" (a partial one at that—see Gibb, 1970, for a more rigorous typology) was generated in quick order:

T-groups   Gestalt groups
sensitivity training groups   bio-energetic groups
recovery groups   Weight Watchers
Alcoholics Anonymous   integrity groups

survival groups

Synanon

nude encounter groups

human interaction groups

sensory awareness groups

marathons

psychodrama

sociodrama

transactional analysis

inquiry groups

conflict-management labs

life-planning labs

psychosynthesis

meditation

movement groups

alternate life style labs

theatre games

graphic groups

massage experiences

truth groups

psychological karate

personal growth labs

human potential groups

confrontation groups

self-management groups

Primal therapy groups

humanistic 'psychotherapy'

Kräftig Gefühl

Zen

Tai Chi

yoga

This plethora of approaches, each in some sense unique, each reflecting special nuances of goals and styles, strongly suggests that no simple monolithic set of standards will do. Still, some important if abstract strands of concern which link this groupy surfeit give credence to the position that, for the general benefit, some semblance of professional order, whatever the field's chronic clouds of ambiguity, clearly is desirable. "Why now?" one may inquire, "and if it's really so necessary, how come it didn't happen sooner?" And will not standards sap the field of its vitality and destroy willingness to innovate? These questions deserve sensible replies.

In most areas of practice, standard setting is taking place relatively late in their unfolding, and the standard-setting process itself often threatens to be agonizing. In terms of a sociology of knowledge (see Friedrichs, 1970), one may underpin these considerations with a paradigm of professional development, somewhat as follows.

Stage 1: *inchoate origins.* Somebody (the Helper) is doing something for (or with?) somebody that is intended to be helpful ("therapeutic," "adjustive," "growthful") for the latter (the Client). At this point, the Helper's involvement with the Client is experimental: Objectively there is some risk and general uncertainty concerning procedure and outcome. But Client responds affirmatively, even enthusiastically on the basis of generalized faith and/or by attribution of charisma to the Helper. Whatever *it* is, it seems to work. Helper and Client, in their particular relationship at this stage, deviate from a pervasive, accepted model of a helping relationship.[1] But as Helper and Client are a small, perhaps even a tiny minority, the accepted model is little threatened. This leaves Helper and Client with relative freedom "to do their thing," to adapt it, and, indeed, to grow.

Stage 2: *initial, limited expansion.* There are more Helpers and Clients than before. The new model has gained adherents, both Helpers and Clients; become dimly aware of its own identity; become more visible to the "outside." The accepted model takes some note, but the issue's scope is minor.

Stage 3: *the developing struggle.* The expansion of Stage 2—gain of adherents, self-identity formation, and external visibility—continues. Accepted model now manifests more explicit concern with the new model. Accepted model may equate its own purview with the public weal, raising questions about the new model's quality, its efficacy, and its ethics. Further, there are now some defections among Helpers and Clients. Whatever the underlying causality, pockets of disenchantment develop in the ranks of the new model. Among Helpers, this may take the forms of dropping out—leaving the field altogether—or forming a new branch or school, and thus, in this specific sense, iterating to Stage 1 or its equivalent. Among Clients, disaffection may be revealed in private grumbling, with negative impact on localized potential client populations; in more far-reaching but informal public statements, such as a "letter to the editor" or interviews in the media, expressing hostility or reporting pain as putatively related to the new model; in formal

---

[1] The term *model* is used here to denote a general prototypic scheme or closely related cluster of schemes of approach to the helper-client relationship. Typical "models" include, for instance, orthodox psychoanalysis, non-directive counseling, and didactic advice-giving.

actions, such as lawsuits directed toward individual Helpers or organizations associated with the new model; and in manifestations of visible personal damage attributed to exposure to the new model, such as suicide or publicly witnessed psychotic breaks.

Though few, these defections and attacks are sociologically significant in at least three directions. They bring into the arena a variety of persons and organizations (beyond those in the immediate professional sphere within which the early sparring took place), such as social and political groups, that may attribute questionable motives and harmful outcomes to the new model. They provide incentive for the new model, particularly the Helpers' leadership, to reexamine objectives and activities, to review and possibly update and redefine the new model's sense of identity. Finally, they present ammunition for those supporting the accepted model who most ardently seek to maintain it as is and who may achieve this goal in part by pointing to the new model's shortcomings, real or alleged.

Stage 4: *forced maturity*. Stage 3 reflects turbulence. Now, as an object of attention, the new model can no longer be ignored, either by the accepted model or by various significant groups in the general public. Further, the increasing internal fractionization and tension causes the new model to examine itself with heightened attention. The self-identity issue is raised with renewed vigor, particularly by those Helpers who are concerned with the new model's long-range survival. Whatever its inherent energizing and creative forces, the new model is often forced, and forces itself, into defensive postures. Although there is further danger of segmentation, the new model comes to be concerned with normative, self-regulatory issues. In part, these efforts are addressed to actual or potential external constraint, such as public criticism and efforts by governmental or other public bodies to develop and enforce legal or quasi-legal standards. In part they are purposeful systems-maintenance attempts to sort out the tangles of internal tension and reach a renewed sense of coherence and direction and attempts to assume explicit social responsibility, gleaning, both from internal unease and external threat, specific positive lessons for betterment of service. In a way, circumstances associated with Stage 4 have thrust upon the new model, partly against its will, a sense of emerging maturity.

Stage 5: *responsible maturity.* At this point in the profession's life cycle, the new model moves along a gently rising plane, gingerly balancing creativity and self-limiting adaptation (Bühler, 1962; Bühler and Massarik, 1969); innovation and persistently conscious responsibility. There is continuing concern with measures of outcome (including informal observation and systematic research); response to normative issues, such as maintenance of practice standards and qualification levels, is consistent without being defensive or hysterical. The scene is one of relative, growthful equilibrium characterized by strong, articulate internal structure, viable give-and-take with the environment, and hope for the future.

Stage 6: *decline and demise.* As they must come to all that is human—and as professions surely are made of human stuff—so must come decline and demise to what still may be known as the new model. Perhaps a *new* new model now stands in the wings, ready to reopen once more the compelling dialectic; perhaps the basis for the striving by this and alternate methods has been made obsolete by fundamental revisions in people's needs and aspirations. As the slope of action turns downward, the issue of standards moves to yet another aspect: Some Helpers see in strict affirmation of standards a means for assuring orthodoxy and thus, they believe, the new model's survival. To others, this prospect suggests the beginnings of disintegration caused by adherence to standards of little relevance. They may even aver that creative violation of such standards affirms the new model's pending obsolescence and the new day's dawning (Laing, 1967).

Examples of this six-stage paradigm can be found in many fields of practice. Although I do not intend to examine in detail the general fit of the proposed model, suitable new model/accepted model illustrations appear in various constellations, such as mesmerism/established mid-nineteenth–century medicine, Freudian psychoanalysis/turn-of-century medicine and neurology, and humanistic psychotherapy/psychoanalytic therapy, among others. Before elaborating the use of the model in illuminating the development of standards in encounter groups, let me make clear that the definition of encounter groups used here is generic: any association of two or more Clients, together with one or more Helpers (or their surrogates), intended to develop, by means of interpersonal process and/or by means of purposive events mediated through interpersonal process, an enhancement in the Clients' intrapersonal and/or interpersonal functioning.

This definition readily permits inclusion of sensitivity training, encounter, and T-groups, and also, perhaps less obviously, of taped group learning experiences, psychodrama, bioenergetics, conflict-management labs, and even of guided meditation and psychosynthesis if these are tied into or facilitated by group process. One-to-one learning situations (including dyadic therapeutic relations), primarily deficiency oriented (rather than enhancing) therapies, solely individual experiences (methods), physically joining two or more persons but providing essentially dyadic collections of inputs (such as mass classroom lectures)—these are among genres of method excluded from present consideration. Most, though perhaps not all, of the group types cited earlier are in general accord with this definition.

The encounter movement (the term connoting a convenient abstraction imposed upon a spaghetti-like tangle of techniques responding to an emerging hunger for heightened humanness) may probably be placed somewhere along Stages 3 or 4 of the proposed paradigm. The scene shifts quickly, but in 1972, though there necessarily is overlay among stages, Stage 4, forced maturity, appears most descriptive. ·

The encounter movement is no longer easily ignored. Its inchoate origins have been left behind; its period of initial growth is past. It is embodied by a mélange of going concerns, some booming, others "just making it," and a few fading away. There has been sufficient fuss and bother about it—in the public prints (including *The New York Times*), in various legislatures, and, alas, in a few courts of law—that its struggles for identity have not been solely of its own choosing. Lest we forget, *it is* an agglomeration of rather idiosyncratic individuals and institutions, linked by but tenuous mutual awareness and by some unrequited efforts at formal association; whatever the central tendency, particular subelements in the movement will vary considerably in their positions on Stage 4 and the emerging identity crisis. Still, this very heterogeneity remains one viable basis for developing manifest concern for the field's future by key Helpers whose involvements reach beyond their specific specialties.

What, then, are the major earmarks of the encounter group movement's Stage 4? Perhaps most significant among them is the formation of the International Association of Applied Social Scientists or IAASS (known irreverently in the trade as "eyeass"). Current reportage rather than presumed permanence between fixed covers might be the more appropriate style for addressing the issue; still, certain major trends have crystallized. IAASS represents the first full effort to deal, head-on, with the complexities of the field's nascent professional standards.

The preexisting NTL network in some sense performed a circumscribed certifying function. Membership categories of "fellow," "associate," "professional member," and so on, constructed within the National Training Laboratories for Group Development (now the NTL Institute for Applied Behavioral Science), served as prima facie evidence of competence level. The history and concept of NTL, however, have limited the organization's ultimate impact as a far-ranging standards-setting mechanism. Growing from the roots of group dynamics and its applications, reaching to the T-group and its variety of versions, NTL has been essentially a multipurpose operating organization rather than a superordinate certifying agent as it combined the pleasures of association among vaguely kindred spirits, with the administrative functions of running labs—from Bethel to Kings Bay and from Harriman, New York, to Arrowhead, California, (not to mention occasional out-of-country forays)—NTL has had its hands full. Add to this the publication of the *Journal of Applied Behavioral Science*, monographs, and other items, the negotiation of contracts for training ser-

vices, concern with organization development and the voluntary society, the development of trainers . . . by the late
sixties, NTL had emerged as a learning conglomerate in its own
right.

However, like other conglomerates in that decade, on the
stock market and elsewhere, NTL had its troubles. By 1970, a
chronic identity crisis had turned acute, another symptom of
Stage 4 unease. The spark may have had deep-seated causes;
the eruption was not dampened by the last-minute declination
of an apparently committed successor to director Leland P.
Bradford. And a constraining financial squeeze deepened the
dilemma. In the early 1970s NTL's comeback, with the help of
Vlad Dupre's leadership, has been encouraging. Theoretically,
NTL might have chosen to embrace the certification function,
but given realistic resource allocation and the flux of kindred
activity far remote from its accustomed paths, its choice to refrain from doing so appears well-founded.

So fledgling IAASS carries the mantle. Whatever the
concrete outcomes of its future labors, early deliberations and
separate conceptual notions provide some underpinning for the
standards-developing tasks required by encounter group leadership at Stage 4.

The main problem, of course, is that conventional criteria do not really fit. Not formal basic education as such, nor
simply the doctorate, not standard clinical psychological training nor didactic psychoanalysis—none of these nor a simple
combination seems to be quite the answer. For this predicament, we may "blame" at least four co-acting factors. First, the
encounter movement walks a complex path leading variously
from theoretical to applied, and vice versa. Second, it encompasses knowledge from a covey of associated source disciplines
(name them as you will—social psychology, sociology, cultural
anthropology; sometimes philosophy, theology, political science,
economics, physiology—and who knows what others?). Third,
it is internally heterogeneous; its subspecialties cover (phenotypically) vastly differing modalities: "just people talking and
leveling with each other," neatly structured exercises, theatrical
improvisations, massage, body movement, and so on. Last, in

most if not all of its aspects, the encounter movement's strength rests heavily on the essential humanness of trainer, facilitator (or whatever the chosen term), and on his ability to transform this humanness into appropriate person-enhancing behavior.

Now it may be argued that similar circumstances prevail in other professions, such as conventional clinical psychology, medicine, perhaps even law. This position no doubt has some merit. However, the similarity hints that prevailing standards in these professions also leave something to be desired; they, too, need to give greater consideration to the interplay between the applied and theoretic, to their connection with source disciplines, to the varied demands of subspecialties, and to the significance of the human essence, transcending technical know-how. The encounter movement, perhaps more than other clinical professions, is—in the very process of its evolution—superinter-disciplinary and supermodal (wish 'twere also superhuman): Its ways of cross-cutting fields of social knowledge and using this knowledge are legion. While an individual trainer stakes out his particular domain of competence, taken as a whole the profession ranges far and wide. In turn, its impactful expression in the training situation (with the possible exception of highly structured and instrumented labs) demands unusual personal genuineness and authentic interaction; thus the humanness variable is especially important.

Given these circumstances, what are some reasonable standards criteria at this stage in the development of the move-ment? Their general shape has been generally hinted. However, it must be clear, above all, that any criteria proposed here constitute a *gestalt*, a constellation of requirements. In terms of personnel selection methodology, a high score on one dimen-sion does not necessarily compensate for a low score on another. There is undoubtedly a minimum cut-off point for each criterion, though optima may vary among different subspecialties.

Four rubrics of standards criteria emerge: The first is *conceptual knowledge.* There is such a thing as conceptual learning; the effective trainer does know (cognitively, intel-lectually, "with the head") what the field is about. He is aware of relevant theory that underlies practice. Often, his theoretic grasp will extend far beyond the boundaries of his specialty; the appropriateness and the breadth of his conceptual knowledge may be considered.

Further, in seeking yardsticks assessing his conceptual knowledge, one may note the trainer's formal education. But education as such, reflected purely in degrees and course completions, constitutes presumption evidence only. It is necessary to gauge its current relevance in the assessment and its concrete impact on the trainer today. Conversely, non-formal educational experience possibly resulting in conceptual learning (including self-initiated reading, attendance at professional seminars, and so on) needs to be considered in this context.

Surely, the substantive shape of relevant knowledge will vary among subspecialites. Certain basic understandings of human behavior (personality theory? individual differences? motivation? group process?) may be generics, but for some trainers, knowledge of physiology may be urgent (in bioenergetics? massage methods? body movement?), while for others (in conflict resolution or Zen approaches) political science or philosophy may be more relevant.

The second criterion is *training experience*. Leader effectiveness results in large measure from experiential learning. Such learning is derived from a series of experiential involvements, of which those at the lower rungs of a hypothetical ladder are needed prerequisites, though they do not in themselves constitute sufficient bases for certification. Participation as a group member is clearly a starting point for learning, but having "had a group" from, say, Fritz Perls hardly is tantamount to being a Gestalt therapist. Nor does simply repeated exposure in a participant role alter the situation.

Intern or junior trainer roles represent more substantial steps toward qualification. Such experiences constitute the beginning of the professionally responsible relationship. Whatever their particular institutional formats, they are intended to provide supervised and clinical involvements in the relevant subspecialty. Thus, standards assessment must take into account the quality, as well as the extent, of intern or junior trainer activity: Was it an NTL summer intern program? A brief exposure at a growth center? A university-based practicum? Who was responsible for what, and what concept guided feedback from senior trainer to trainee?

Beyond these initial steps into the professional career—still mildly ill-defined and surely searching—the learner eventually receives, if all else has gone well, opportunity for a full trainer role. This may be a co-trainer assignment or a chance to perform the total task in a real-life setting. Colleagues, now as peers, may be there as adjuncts to learning, but the fledgling bird now flies on wings of his own.

The question still remains: How much actual experience (and what kind) has a trainer logged? Determining the answer may require estimating hours or numbers of programs or using similar quantitative yardsticks. These may serve as *rough* indices of some use in standards setting. It is not necessarily true, for example, that after five hundred hours a trainer is much more effective than after, say, three hundred hours; diminishing returns may set in. In another vein, though, direct quantitative measures of this nature do provide an indication of the joint effect of willingness to commit some significant time proportion to practice and of validation within the profession, is the trainer apparently successful enough, according to peer judgment and participant marketplace, to be asked to persist in practice?

The third consideration is *technical skill.* In the group's context, the trainer behaves purposefully, he "intervenes" (*horrible dictu*), falls silent, introduces exercises, does his very special thing: massages, body-moves, reflects, and non-directs—or whatever. Some trainers concentrate on a particular modality; others are more eclectic. All are, in some measure, aware of their intentional use of acquired skills or technique, the systematically created (hopefully not contrived) methodologies that are applied to effect desired outcomes.

In standards setting, the trainer's technical competence should be examined first through his own eyes. The very process of introspection on the skills that he consciously brings to bear is instructive; it creates a didactically helpful grasp of what goes on in the trainer's world of activity. His view may be augmented by the perceptions of others who may have seen him in action.

The final criterion is *humanness*, an ineffable concept. So much to be said about it, and so difficult to deal with it by way of the written word. Basically, it is the trainer's presence-as-a-person, the essence of his existential sense-of-being, interpersonally manifest. An old-fashioned psychologist might have spoken of its pale version as "social stimulus value"; in a valuative sense it might encompass positive (or negative?) charisma. Some might speak of it in terms of the untrained, raw therapeutic emanation of the trainer's personality, particularly as it affects group members. Whatever *it* is, representing spontaneous process rather than fixed state, its impact in group leadership is of paramount importance.

One need not propose mystique to observe that, for the most part, people (including trainers) either have *it* or they haven't. Although technical skill is generally learnable, humanness as such is not readily learnable by usual means in adulthood. Many forces of past and present, over many years of unfolding, have shaped its character. Neither a simple act of the will nor a quick once-over alter its distinct patterning. Major personal upheaval, deep therapy, fundamental reorientation—processes partaking of the self's cataclysm—are required for its reshaping.

Thus—and the view is realistic not fatalistic—what the trainer is, he is (Popeye's "I yam what I yam"?). His total personness is the crucial force in the group situation; in myriad subtle ways and by the essential thrust of image and manner, he communicates significant values and behavior styles. Especially, he communicates the possibilities for change and demonstrates potential change modalities. He acts spontaneously, yet typically he is able to articulate much of what transpires. This dual process—spontaneous (effective) behavior linked to insight and expressed conceptual rationale—constitutes a useful index in trainer assessment.

Tied to the concept of trainer humanness are various factors associated with the trainer's mental health. For instance, does he have adequate capacity for insight into self and for

self-evaluation? Does he possess integrated sensitivity toward
needs and actions of others, as individuals, in dyads, groups,
and organizations? Does he possess sufficient resilience under
stress? Is he able to accept, and indeed to value, differences
among people and among training methods? Is he free of needs
for omnipotence and omniscience; does he view himself in
realistic personal and professional perspective? Can he successfully manage his personal and professional limitations? And
further, what are his values, and how does he translate these
values into training-related behavior?

Finally, in standards setting we must note that the
trainer's humanness is an implicit force for good or evil. If it
fits well with the group's needs, if its impact is growthful and
nonexploitive, then this humanness qualifies well for the training career. If, however, it is unresponsive to group needs, or if
its charismatic aspects and more mundane manifestations are
used to exploit and stunt, then evidently a career as a group
leader is best avoided.

These four criteria, conceptual knowledge, training experience, technical skill, and humanness, are suggested as appropriate standards, yardsticks at this stage of the profession's
development. Their mode of implementation remains a challenge. No doubt the chosen evaluation procedure must draw
on many data sources. These sources include the trainer's own
evaluations, evaluations of his peers, evaluations of participants,
and "objective" inputs, such as information on formal education,
training experience, and the like. IAASS is exploring the concept of constructing a portfolio on each applicant, containing
information obtained from several of the data sources noted
above.

Who decides (and how) the trainer's qualification? In
its initial stages IAASS has created a charter member category,
based on peer nominations, using the following criteria: The
charter member demonstrates outstanding professional competence in the practice of applied social science and devotes a
substantial portion of his time to such practice; his professional
activities reveal, beyond any doubt or question, high standards

of ethical and responsible conduct; and he has taken an active and substantial part in the training of other professionals.

From this group, a standards and admissions committee has been chosen who presumably further embody these characteristics and who possess, it is hoped, a large measure of honest good judgment. Broadening representation to include professionals outside NTL, particularly growth center leaders and trainers outside the United States, seems urgent if standards development in the encounter movement is to become purposefully significant.

Finally, I want to add a cautionary note. I observed earlier that setting standards often is not entirely a free-will process within the profession. Broad social forces—yea, even the shadows of legal authority—have their part in creating concern with standards. Embedded in the encounter movement are certain values that do not exactly cause universal jumping for joy when the standards issue is raised. There is perhaps a bit of counterdependence in this: "If you tell me to watch it, I won't!" (Stomping of feet? Furtive looks the other way?) More positively, these values stress innovation and experimentation. The hidden questions arise: Will standards impede creativity? Will norms become straightjackets, forcing a rigid mold upon all they survey?

At this time, there can be no practical answer based on solid experience; it is too early for that. But, in principle, there is no reason why the development of appropriate standards might not have effects quite opposite to conformity. Here is an opportunity to trace steps taken so far, to assess their creative (or commercial but humdrum) character, and to speculate on lacunae yet to be filled. The very admissions process makes responsible innovation (hand in hand with competence) a major goal. And novelty alone is not, perforce, person-enhancing; the sheer search for different modes does not assure success.

In the seventies, the encounter group graduates. There is little occasion for bland valedictory; too much ferment and action are upon the land. But it is increasingly clear that a new and complex helping profession, drawing sustenance from many roots, is evolving. The journey to maturity continues at reasonable pace; concern with standards is a giant step along this road. Ahead are other miles and other roads. Yet, for the moment it is encouraging that a sense of responsible concern with what is good for people, and how to make it happen, has become truly prominent in the emerging profession's far-flung and ever-searching ranks.

6

The Value of Encounter

James Bebout, Barry Gordon

Since the fall of 1969 we have studied more than one thousand encounter group participants and their one hundred nonprofessional leaders as part of a four-year research investigation into the value of encounter groups for personal and interpersonal growth. [1, 2] The study is organized in four stages; the first entails naturalistic exploratory research (Butler, Rice, and Wagstaff, 1963; Willems and Raush, 1969) and the second consists of refinement and definition of target measures. We have just begun the third phase of the research requiring complete instrumentation and experimental controls. The final step calls for generalization and comparison of our findings to other groups and samples.

The project has ambitious goals—the comprehensive evaluation of outcome, process, and leadership in more than one

[1] The Talent in Interpersonal Exploration (TIE) Project, funded by National Institute of Mental Health grant #RO1-MH17330; sponsoring institution: Stiles Hall, the University YMCA at Berkeley.

[2] We are much indebted to the entire project staff, but especially: Dr. Mimi Silbert, Charles Alexander, Jeff Koon, Carole Marks, Mark Dodson, Chaya Piotrkowski, and Paula Silver.

hundred and fifty nonprofessionally led encounter groups. This paper will report preliminary data on about half of our ultimate sample. The major focus is on description of outcome—significant changes in personal and interpersonal domains reported by members. Leader and group process studies will appear in future reports.

The TIE Project has several distinctive features. The group members are paying volunteers from the university and community. The groups meet in the community, rather than at country sites or professional development institutes. The groups are all led by nonprofessional leaders selected and trained through the program. The average cost for a group per participant is thirty cents an hour. The program itself is community-based, systematic, and almost self-supporting. We thought initially that if tangible outcomes could be observed under this setup we were lucky. No large-scale comprehensive research investigation of the intensive group experience has been carried out and this dearth is our *raison d'etre*.

WHAT IS THE QUESTION?

Does an encounter group experience change people, enable them to self-actualize, or improve their interpersonal relations? Many small-scale studies are available, and most of their findings are positive (Gibb, 1971). Some outcome studies show negative results (Wedel, 1957; Kassarjian, 1965; Kernan, 1963) or negative effects (Yalom and Lieberman, 1971). Most small studies are directed toward one or two specific variables (such as increased sensitivity or self-acceptance), and major faults in research design, such as biased sampling, lack of control groups, and unspecified group process, are more common than not. Are encounter groups worth the trouble if so many hours of emotional stress generate only a few iotas of awareness or self-confidence and cause one to risk being a psychiatric casualty? If this is the case, we should all reconsider.

This was our question, and the following were our major assumptions: (1) significant positive change in terms of self-perception and interpersonal relations will be associated with encounter group participation; (2) talent in encounter group leadership consists of therapeutic attitudes, interpersonal skills, and personality traits; the preliminary assessment of these leader traits will predict success in leading groups as determined by member outcome and satisfaction; (3) regular patterns of group interaction are discernible in encounter groups.

In this chapter we provide evidence on the holistic impact of the group experience in terms of self-perception, values, and relationships. Some explanation is given for the outcome data of our study as far as it goes.

NATURE OF THE EXPERIENCE

There are many types of intensive small groups and many origins of the small group movement. Our groups are called encounter groups and rely on a here-and-now focus on feelings within interpersonal interaction. They are meant to be supportive, exploratory, and to generate more or less intensive experiences furthering people's personal and social growth. To the extent that personal growth is facilitated the groups are therapeutic. We try for a fail-safe approach. Groups are not problem or attack oriented by design, and an individual's right to a defense is respected. Responsibility for change rests most with group members, rather than leaders, and dramatic breakthroughs are valued less than lasting increments in emotional growth and sensitivity to others.

What kinds of activities go on? The term *encounter* implies that the form of interpersonal meeting practiced is uncommon in the formalities of everyday life. In the language of Tierra del Fuego (quoting Martin Buber), the term *far away* translates: "They stare at one another, each waiting for the other to volunteer to do what both wish, but are not able to do" (Buber, 1958). This situation is clearly what encounter is not. Our encounter groups anticipate, and usually obtain, emotional openness, self-disclosure, risk-taking, feedback, trust, intimacy, behavioral enactment, willingness to engage and confront others and perhaps to change. These ingredients are common to many different approaches (Egan, 1971; Gibb, 1971; Rogers, 1970; Schutz, 1971).

Jack Gibb (1970) distinguishes eleven varieties of sensitivity training groups along a continuum from therapylike groups to groups closely resembling educational instruction. In this system our groups fall near the therapeutic pole and are a composite of personal growth and authenticity groups. We stress the theories of Rogers (1970) and Gibb (1970) but use many methods deriving from sensitivity training, Gestalt theory, psychodrama, and sensory awareness.

BACKGROUND OF THE MEMBER SAMPLE

Little is known about who comes to an encounter group. Are they psychological radicals or adventure-seekers? With what personal expectations and problems do they enter a group; should they rather undertake regular psychotherapy? To approach answers to these questions background characteristics and expectations are presented here. In the results section we will describe the initial test characteristics of our sample at some length.

Participants are recruited by local publicity and word of mouth. Groups are composed of about ten members, balanced in sex and generally within a ten-year age span. Each group meets once a week for ten weeks, including a weekend semi-marathon retreat. Meetings last four hours on the average, totalling at least sixty hours in face-to-face interaction over a three-month period.

Background information on a maximum sample of 1,133 participants over seven quarters is given in Table 1.[3] Most members are young (70 per cent between twenty and twenty-nine), single (68 per cent), university students in their third to fifth year in school (58 per cent). Most are unemployed or partly employed (60 per cent); many are housewives. The most frequently reported academic fields of interest are social sciences and humanities. Our sample comes from predominantly small, intact, working white families (78 per cent) in the middle- and

[3] Project quarterly samples are designated alphabetically, as TIE "A" (Fall 1969), TIE "B" (Winter 1970), and so on. Throughout this chapter samples are included or excluded according to the data available. No one test is based on the total sample due to test revisions and design requirements.

upper-middle socioeconomic range. An estimated 1 per cent are black, 1 per cent Latin-American, and 4 per cent "other." Some 12 per cent anticipate occupations in human service professions, 21 per cent of whom expect to become teachers; the remainder are largely undecided.

About half of our sample has had some previous exposure to encounter groups. Forty-five per cent report some previous contact with professional therapy or counseling. There is a 12 per cent dropout rate, almost all of these occurring between the first and fourth meetings and more than half for practical reasons (moving, money).

A procedure was borrowed from Lieberman and others (1971) to elicit members' initial expectations of their encounter group (each rated from 1 to 7 in terms of importance and anticipated opportunity). The large majority (more than 70 per cent) of a sample of five hundred participants taking this questionnaire indicated eleven expectations as highly important (average ratings of five or above), as shown in Table 2.

Table 2

Expectations of Participants

Rank	Expectations	Per cent [a]
1	Increasing my capacity for deeper relationships	88 *
2	Finding out how others really see me	88
3	Being able to express my feelings	87
4	Being sensitive to others' feelings	86
5	Being able to share things with others and get closer	84
6	Experiencing joy and self-fulfillment	83 *
7	Changing some of the ways I relate to people	80
8	Meeting new people and making new friends	78 *
9	Being able to help and support other people	76
10	Understanding my inner self	76
11	Having new experiences	70

[a] Starred percentages are based on a reduced sample of $N = 103$.

These prominent expectations accord generally with the ambitions of our program. Initial test data presented below give a further description of our sample of entering participants.

Table 1

Background Information on Members (TIE A to G)

	N [a]	Per Cent		N [a]	Per Cent		N [a]	Per Cent
Age			**Level of Education**			**Meeting Dropped**		
15–19	135	14.1	Freshman	63	8.3	After 1st	39	32.5
20–24	462	48.3	Sophomore	93	12.2	2nd	13	10.8
25–29	247	25.8	Junior	140	18.4	3rd	25	20.8
30–39	97	10.1	Senior	149	19.6	4th to 10th	43	35.8
40–49	8	.8	Grad. 1–2 yrs.	171	22.5			
50–59	9	.8	Grad. 3–4 yrs.	62	8.2	**PARENTS:**		
			n.r.	82	10.8	**Marital Status**		
Sex						Married	527	67.0
Female	478	49.0	**Field of Interest**			Other (divorced, separated, etc.)	259	33.0
Male	497	51.0	Life Science	65	7.3			
			Physical Science	47	5.3	**Source of Income**		
Marital Status			Social Science	357	40.3	Job	412	83.2
Single	691	72.2	Humanities	174	19.6	Pension/Retire	60	12.1
Married	146	15.3	Education	19	2.1	Welfare	3	.6
Other (divorced, separated, etc.)	122	12.6	Engineering	28	3.2	n.r.	20	4.0
			Arts, Architecture	59	6.7			
Number of Children			Other and n.r.	145	16.4	**Home Ownership**		
None	815	85.5				Under $12,000	21	4.3
One	56	5.9	**Previous Experience [b]**			$12 to $20,000	86	17.7
Two	45	4.7	One group	55	9.7	$20 to $35,000	138	28.5
Three	23	2.4	Two/more	22	3.9	Above $35,000	131	27.0
Four or more	14	1.4	Marathons/weekends	101	17.8			

Table 1 (Continued)

Background Information on Members (TIE A to G)

	N[a]	Per Cent		N[a]	Per Cent		N[a]	Per Cent
School Status			Other encounter	119	20.9	Rental	96	19.8
Nonstudent	277	28.9	Other group/therapy	37	6.5	Other	13	2.7
U.C.	486	50.8	None of above	234	41.2	Religion		
Other school	144	15.0				Protestant	127	25.9
Plan to enroll	49	5.1	Drops			Catholic	82	16.7
			No	903	88.4	Jewish	103	21.0
Plan Grad. Degree/ Teaching Credential			Yes	120	11.7	Other	96	19.6
Yes	614	73.7				No preference	83	16.9
No	156	18.7						
No response (n.r.)	63	7.6						

[a] Less than maximum sample due to missing data.

[b] Overlapping categories: percentages based on total responses.

LEADERS

Since our nonprofessional leaders are selected originally from our own encounter groups, they resemble the member sample in background. Leaders are, however, somewhat older and further along in education than members, and relatively more leaders are or have been married. The typical leader in the TIE Project is a former group member who was interested in encounter groups, applied to lead, and came highly recommended by members of his group. In our first three quarters (TIE ABC) more than two-hundred people applied for our leader training program. About 30 per cent of these became leaders.

The leader selection process has three components: recommendation for leader training from a regular group (occasionally from other programs); self- and other-selection after a weekend marathon evaluation, itself an encounter group; and selection for leadership by self, peers, and staff after ten weeks of training. Most leaders, then, are involved in the program for a minimum of six months before leading a group—three months as a participant and three months as a leader-trainee.[4] Leaders receive continuous feedback during training and leading.

TESTING

Participants and leaders are given a battery of psychological tests before, during, and twice following their group— once immediately after the group and again at a three- to six-month follow-up. Outside friends of participants are tested via the mails. Group observers behind one-way glass keep a running diary of interactions and codify parameters of group behavior. Each meeting is sound-recorded and certain sessions are video-taped.[5] Each test is designed to assess some aspect of our three

[4] A description of the format and content of the training program may be obtained by writing the TIE Project, 2400 Bancroft Way, Berkeley, Calif., 94704.
[5] These are used for leader and observer training and for discrete variable studies.

principal assumptions about the encounter group process and experience. The data reported here will concentrate on outcome.

The first hypothesis of the study is considered in two parts—change in aspects of self-perception and in interpersonal relations. Table 3 shows the target variables and instruments used to measure self-perception and interpersonal relations.

Table 3

Measurement of Self-Perception and Interpersonal Relations

SELF-PERCEPTION

Variables	*Measures*
Self-concept	Q-Sort—63 items describing self
	Q-Sort Self-Factor Scores
Self-esteem	Self and Ideal Q-Sort Concordance
Self-actualization	Personal Orientation Inventory (POI)
Individual problems	Problems Check List
	Problems Change Ratings
Alienation	Social Feeling Index (SFI)
Perception of change	Change Rating Scales
Impact of group	Ranks Test
	Open-End Questionnaire

INTERPERSONAL

Interpersonal values	Survey of Interpersonal Values (SIV)
Relations with friends	Relationship Inventory
Perception of change	Peer Group Change Rating Scales
	Leader Rating of Member Change

The Q-Sort is applied to indicate an important aspect of personality—an individual's concept of himself. The procedure is an adaptation of the work of Butler and Haigh (1954). Item content is altered from the original to conform to our population.[6] As in the original format, items are placed in sets ordered along a continuum from "least like me" to "most like me" with two instructions: "Describe yourself as you are now" (Actual

---

[6] Two forms have been devised: the first seventy-two items form was used in TIE ABC, the second sixty-three items revision was used in TIE EFG.

Self Sort); and b) "Describe how you would ideally like to be" (Ideal Self Sort). The concordance of the resulting two distributions in correlation (Rho) units is our measure of self-esteem. Factor and cluster analysis of items provides self-concept dimension scores.

Shostrom's POI (1966) provides a reliable estimation of reported self-actualizing tendencies or attitudes (defined in terms of subscales of inner-directedness, feeling reactivity, spontaneity, self-acceptance, acceptance of aggression, and so on). This test was pre-factored, and selected subscales were administered. The Social Feeling Index (Srole, 1956; McClosky and Schaar, 1965) has been scaled and standardized on the Berkeley student population as a measure of alienation. Prior factor analysis indicated this measure to have both a socio-emotional and a political-traditional value component. We eliminated the latter dimension.

Gordon's SIV test (1965) gives a quantified profile of common interpersonal values such as support, conformity, recognition (needs), benevolence and (task-oriented) leadership. We guessed that certain interpersonal values or needs would change as a result of an encounter group experience. The Relationship Inventory (Barrett-Lennard, 1970) was given to outside friends of each member before and after the group to indicate changes in qualities of the relationship. The test is scored on parameters of level of regard, empathic understanding, genuineness (congruence), and unconditionality of regard. (Other versions of the test had the group describe its leader and the group as a whole.)

We originated a 165-item Problem Check List to indicate the personal concerns members had entering and leaving their groups.[7] Each specific problem is rated on "improvement" and "change" scales. A count of problems in different areas (such as interpersonal, work-school) gives an overall measure of status and change. A follow-up administration of this test was given three to six months later. Friends of the participants

    [7] This test was piloted by Bebout at San Francisco State College in a study sponsored by the V.R.A., Grant #RD-2047-P-66.

also completed the Problem Check List for each group member.

Each of the above measures was given before and after the group. Many additional measures were given. To examine our second hypothesis (leadership talent) different samples of leaders were administered Selection Ratings, Training Ratings, Self and Ideal Q-Sorts, the SIV, Reactions to Group Situations Test, Short-Form Intelligence Test, the California Psychological Inventory, the POI, the Relationship Inventory, and postquesttionnaires. Data from these sources, and group process measures, will be reported elsewhere.

PREGROUP TEST RESULTS

A profile of participants' typical self-perception prior to their group was obtained by averaging Self-Q-Sort item placements across sex for members in the second-year sample (N=331). Members indicate a generally positive orientation to others ("I am concerned and interested in people's feelings," "I like to get close, to make friends," "I like being touched," "I contribute something to others' lives," "I have warm emotional relationships with people") (see Table 5, p. 97). Positive self-attributes are reported with about equal frequency ("I take responsibility for myself," "I am self-reliant," "I am sexually adequate," "I (do not) feel helpless to deal with my problems"). On the negative side, members indicate they "think a lot about their problems," "are critical," "would like to change many things about themselves," "are less than satisfied with themselves." An earlier Q-Sort version included other negative statements: "I hold myself back," "I am anxious," and "I am often disappointed with myself."

A finer analysis of self-concept is provided by a key cluster analysis of the Self-Q-Sort item correlation matrix of a sample of 406 participants (Tryon, 1970). This multivariate solution yields eleven item clusters or self-concept dimensions with usable reliabilities.[8] The dimensions and sample items are shown in Table 4.

---

[8] Multimethod and cross-sample validation was carried out entailing ten separate analyses to ensure reproducibility.

Table 4

Self-Concept Dimensions

Factor Label	Sample Items
Self-reliance	I am self-reliant I feel I can take care of myself
Expressivity	I express my emotions freely When I'm happy or sad I really show it
Productivity	I work hard I accomplish a lot
Sex	I am not afraid to deal with sex I am sexy
Social Inhibition	I am socially awkward and ill at ease I am insecure with people
Intimacy	I am afraid of getting too close It is hard for me to be intimate
Self-satisfaction	I am often disappointed with myself I am satisfied with myself
Criticality	I like most people right way I am critical I am hard on people at first
Toughness	I can dish it out as well as take it I am often aggressive
Indifference (belle)	Very little bothers me Anything goes with me
Dependence	I am reassured when I know someone is in charge Direction from others is important to me

Scores for each individual member on each dimension of self-concept are generated both pregroup and postgroup. Pregroup means within clusters indicate several male-female differences, mainly predictable from stereotype role definitions —men are higher on self-reliance and social inhibition and lower on intimacy. Comparing self with ideal item placements, all members view themselves as furthest from their ideal in self-satisfaction, social inhibition, and sex. Males report more self-ideal disparity than females in areas of intimacy and expressivity; females more in self-reliance.

Although the members assign to themselves many positive personal and interpersonal traits, they also see themselves (differentially by sex) as lacking in important areas. Self-Ideal (S-I) concordance provides an overall estimate of self-esteem or satisfaction. Before their group experience, a sample of 313 participants (TIE AB) report a median self-ideal correlation of +.35, with a range of —.65 to +.95 [9] (see Figure 1). This average seems within a low-normal range (Shlien, 1961); however, many members enter their groups with an extremely low self-evaluation, and many enter with an extremely positive self-view.

Because self-ideal correlation level may directly affect outcome measurement, we have generally tried to control for this variable in our outcome data analyses. Also, it is impressionistically true that differences in level of self-esteem are significant features of group composition, such that low S-I members tend to be more problem-centered than do high S-I members, creating a possible conflict of interests in a given group of mixed composition. In terms of S-I concordance, it would be reasonable to expect that an encounter group would serve to lower the extremely high self-opinion of some people and heighten the extremely low self-opinion of other people, while showing a generally positive increase for most.

Responses to the Problem Check List for a sample of 574 participants indicate that 50 per cent or more of the members enter the program expressing "feelings of non-belonging, isolation," "inadequate relations with the opposite sex," "depressions," and "uncertainty about future occupation." Thirty per cent or more of first-year participants indicated difficulty in eleven interpersonal problem areas (examples other than above: "lack of confidence in casual social relationships," "lack of confidence in intimate relationships," "difficulty in starting conversations," "difficulty in expressing affection towards others"). They also reported, more than 30 per cent of the time, problems in individualistic areas ("feelings of inferiority," "inadequate sense of identity," "restlessness," "procrastination in

[9] Rho correlation of +1.00 represents a perfect concordance between self and ideal; —1.00 of completely opposite self and ideal.

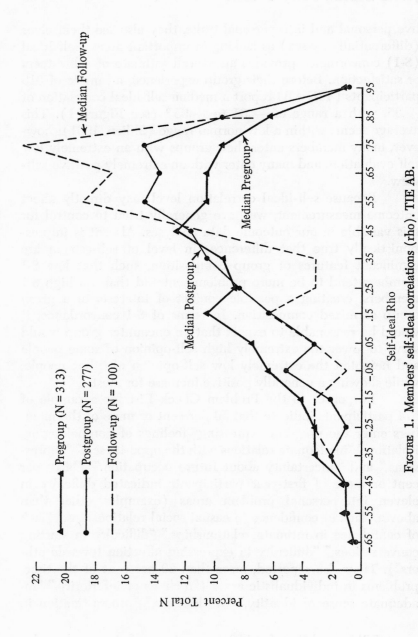

FIGURE 1. Members' self-ideal correlations (rho). TIE AB.

. . . work," "excessive self-criticism," "difficulty in expressing thoughts clearly"). Clinical symptoms, such as phobias and somatizations, are endorsed by less than 10 per cent of this sample.

Mean scores of a sample of 444 group members (TIE ABC) on the Survey of Interpersonal Values indicates that our participants (and leaders) are low on conformity (mean = 4.4) and high on independence (mean = 23.7) and support (mean = 20.5) relative to college student norms. Male participants place a higher than average value on benevolence (mean = 17.1) and less value on task-oriented leadership (mean = 12.8). Leader scores (N = 49) are in the same direction as member scores but more extreme.

The response of members' friends to the Relationship Inventory suggests that in general participants had positive and supportive friendships before their encounter experience. The friends nominated by members (N = 83) indicate highest mean scores on the RI scale of positive regard and lowest scores on conditionality. All scale means are comparable to "good" relationship measures in comparative samples (Van der Veen, 1970; Barrett-Lennard, 1970).

The medium range of self-esteem, characteristic Q-Sort items chosen, expectations, background, and problems and values endorsed all seem to indicate that the people who come to our encounter groups are pretty normal in the context of a modern urban setting. They want to discover deeper relationships and truths about themselves. They are people-oriented and positively motivated toward more supportive, intimate, expressive, and comfortable interactions with others, but not by way of conformity.

IMPACT OF GROUP

Many specific and general changes occur in participants' self-concepts. Table 5 lists the most and least characteristic items, pregroup and postgroup, for a sample of 331 participants. Eighty per cent of these relevant self-descriptive items change significantly from pregroup to postgroup. Nonsignificant changes seem to occur in cognitive-rational traits.

Table 5

Most and Least Characteristic Items of Members'
Actual Self Q-Sorts Pregroup and Postgroup (TIE EFG, N = 331)[a]

Descriptive Items (#)	Pregroup		Postgroup		p[b]<
	Mean	S.D.	Mean	S.D.	
15 Items "Most Like Me"					
I am concerned and interested in people's feelings (28)	7.21	1.94	7.37	1.71	n.s.
I take responsibility for myself (18)	7.02	2.07	7.50	1.85	.01
I feel I can take care of myself (3)	6.82	2.08	7.36	1.94	.01
I think a lot about my problems (30)	6.77	2.31	6.17	2.46	.01
I like to get close, to make friends (7)	6.70	2.18	7.34	1.91	.01
I like being touched (52)	6.59	2.21	7.59	1.72	.01
I am self-reliant (13)	6.43	2.27	6.82	2.18	.01
I am critical (34)	6.23	2.27	5.48	2.23	.01
I am not sexually inadequate (16)	6.15	2.33	6.50	2.24	.05
I contribute something to others' lives (51)	6.14	2.13	6.85	1.85	.01
I take time to figure people out (44)	6.10	2.37	5.95	2.14	n.s.
I have warm relationships with people (35)	6.05	2.38	6.71	2.23	.01
I'd like to change many things about myself (39)	6.02	2.50	5.35	2.43	.01
I am not afraid to deal with sex (9)	5.99	2.42	6.39	2.29	.01
I have a rationale for my behavior (61)	5.83	2.30	5.60	2.29	.10
15 Items "Least Like Me"					
I feel helpless to deal with my problems (19)	3.08	2.19	2.36	1.91	.01
Anything goes with me (58)	3.15	2.09	3.56	2.23	.01
I am hard on people at first (10)	3.48	2.36	3.66	2.38	n.s.
Very little bothers me (40)	3.61	2.33	3.62	2.15	n.s.
I don't believe in pushing myself (36)	3.73	2.28	3.58	2.21	n.s.
I am satisfied with myself (6)	3.83	2.28	4.89	2.39	.01

[a] Sixty-three items are arranged in nine sets of seven statements each along a continuum of Most Like Me (Set 9) to Least Like Me (Set 1) so that mean placements of 5.00 are seen as irrelevant or undecided.

[b] Level of statistical significance for T-test of difference between correlated means.

Table 5 (Continued)

Most and Least Characteristic Items of Members'
Actual Self Q-Sorts Pregroup and Postgroup (TIE EFG, N = 331)[a]

Descriptive Items (#)	Pregroup		Postgroup		p[b]<
	Mean	S.D.	Mean	S.D.	
I am often aggressive (29)	3.89	2.45	4.33	2.45	.01
I am afraid . . . of getting too close with people (22)	3.91	2.47	3.37	2.33	.01
I am lazy (31)	3.91	2.51	3.56	2.44	.01
I am reassured when I know someone is in charge (50)	3.95	2.04	3.81	2.06	n.s.
I am shy and timid (24)	4.08	2.51	3.48	2.27	.01
I am easily irritated (33)	4.12	2.33	3.72	2.30	.01
Direction from others is important to me (45)	4.13	2.22	3.71	2.10	.01
I am not independent enough (25)	4.13	2.80	3.69	2.47	.01
I can dish it out as well as take it (48)	4.14	2.34	5.04	2.21	.01

Does this increased positive perception of oneself last? Figure 1 shows that our most global Q-Sort measure—self-ideal concordance or self-esteem—increases from pregroup to postgroup and from postgroup to follow-up in a total sample of 313 members.[10] The before-group median Rho is +.35, the postgroup median equals +.51, and the follow-up median is +.57.

Members gain in perceiving themselves the way they would ideally like to be. The increment in S-I correlation is substantially greater from pregroup to follow-up than from pregroup to postgroup, suggesting that these gains materialize with time. It should also be noted from Figure 1 that many members still have extremely low scores on this self-esteem measure at postgroup and follow-up, and that there is only a slight reduction in extremely high S-I correlations.

An interesting confirmation of the relevance of our S-I

[10] Pregroup and postgroup medians for the reduced follow-up sample (N = 100) are virtually identical to the total sample medians. Those responding to this test three to six months after their group appear no different test-wise than others.

measure is found in an analysis of a subsample of our first-year members.[11] Two groups of thirty-three members each were distinguished on the basis of their high or low self-ideal correlation (Rho) before their groups. It was found that the low S-I group checked many more problems on the Problem Check List (median=37) than did the high S-I group (median=11). The difference between these two groups in number of problems endorsed is highly significant ($p<.0001$, Mann Whitney "U" Test). When friends of these same members were asked to indicate the members' number of problems on the same check list, friends of the low S-I members indicated significantly more problems than did friends of the high S-I members ($p<.01$).[12] Although both sets of friends' responses regress toward the general mean, they apparently concur in that low S-I members have more concerns than do high S-I members.

In what way does the self-concept change? The self-concept cluster solution provides a more compact analysis of self-perception change. Following our first hypothesis, positive general change was predicted as increased self-reliance, expressivity, productivity, sexual adjustment, intimacy, and self-satisfaction, and decreased social inhibition. No prediction was made for change on clusters of criticality, toughness, indifference, or dependence.

By finding the pregroup and postgroup mean placement for each Q-Sort item contributing to these clusters we examined the direction and significance of change in these self-descriptors for a minimum sample of 156 participants. All predicted changes are significant (Wilcoxon Signed Rank Test) except productivity. The self-concept dimensions that were not hypothesized to show directional change did indicate two significant pregroup to postgroup differences. Criticality decreased for females (not males) and toughness increased for males, not females (both $p<.05$). Other clusters showed no consistent change.

[11] This study was carried out by Chaya Piotrkowski who is presently at the University of Michigan.

[12] One-tail "U" Test; N's were: friends of high S-I members $= 21$; friends of low S-I members $= 19$.

The largest item changes (all significant at or beyond the .01 level) are "I am (more) satisfied with myself," "I am (more) sexy" (females), "I am (less) often disappointed with myself," "I am (less) lonely," "I am (less) insecure with people," "I am (less) critical," "I am (less) often depressed or down in the dumps," "I am (less) uptight about physical contact with people of my own sex," "I can dish it out as well as take it (more)," "I contribute something to others' lives (more)," "I like being touched (more)," "I take criticism (less) hard."

We expected that self-actualizing tendencies would increase as an outcome of encounter group participation. POI scores for a sample of sixty-five females and seventy males (TIE C) are significantly higher postgroup than pregroup on the subscales inner-direction, feeling reactivity, spontaneity, acceptance of aggression, and capacity for intimate contact (Table 6). Only female scores on existentiality show significant change. (These subscales comprise the first factor in previous analysis.) This result corresponds to that of Foulds (1970) (see also Knapp, 1971).

Socioemotional alienation is a commonly reported problem. It is easy to suppose that alienation should lessen with encounter group experience, as the aim and prospect of these groups is to generate a meaningful relatedness between people. The Social Feeling Index is made up of rather antiquated items (such as, "Most people have so much trouble of their own that they aren't concerned about mine," "My life has been barren and meaningless") but does provide a crude index of this variable. A modified version of the Social Feeling Index was completed before- and after-group by 272 participants. The average alienation score at pregroup was 63.1 and at postgroup, 57.3. The difference between the two means is significant at the .01 level. Members subscribe to fewer statements of alienation after their group experience.

The ten most important individual problems selected by each member before the group were re-presented immediately after the group along with three rating scales. Members were asked to rate "change in the way you feel," "change in actual

Table 6

Pregroup and Postgroup Mean POI Scores (Self-Actualization)

Measures	Sex[a]	Pre Mean	Post Mean	Change	p<[b]
Inner-Direction	Male	82.57	86.21	+3.64	.005
	Female	86.31	89.82	+3.51	.001
Existentiality	Male	21.56	22.09	+.53	n.s.
	Female	22.46	23.46	+1.00	.005
Feeling Reactivity	Male	15.73	16.80	+1.07	.005
	Female	16.57	17.32	+.75	.025
Spontaneity	Male	11.17	12.17	+1.00	.001
	Female	12.29	13.37	+1.08	.001
Acceptance of Aggression	Male	15.30	16.17	+.87	.001
	Female	16.11	17.14	+1.03	.001
Capacity for Intimate Contact	Male	18.34	19.17	+.83	.001
	Female	18.75	19.34	+.59	.001

[a] Male N = 70; female N = 65, TIE C.
[b] Sandler's "A" statistic.

behavior," and "how much did the group contribute to helping with this problem" for each of the ten problems.[13] Table 7 shows the mean ratings of the improvement and group help for the nineteen most frequently chosen problems. The largest gains reflect greater self-confidence, understanding, acceptance, and less moodiness, as well as greater ease and emotional satisfaction in relationships. Clearly, the encounter group has least effect on school and work problems. The mean ratings of im-

[13] High and low scale points were defined as "no longer a problem —more of a problem"; "extreme improvement—much worse"; and "helped extremely—hindered extremely," respectively.

Table 7

Members' Average Ratings of Improvement and Group Helpfulness for
Nineteen Most Frequently Chosen Problems (TIE BCD, N = 395)

Problem (#)	Improve-ment[a]	Group Helped[a]	% Endorsing
PERSONAL			
Difficulty in understanding your own feelings (76)	5.28	5.52	37.0
Feelings of inferiority (39)	5.07	5.68	45.1
Difficulty in asserting yourself (86)	5.02	5.40	36.9
Excessive self-criticism (124)	4.90	5.86	39.8
Depressions (21)	4.90	5.72	50.0
Inadequate sense of identity (64)	4.89	5.34	40.6
Moodiness (132)	4.40	4.83	35.4
Difficulty in expressing thoughts clearly (28)	4.22	5.75	36.5
Restlessness (41)	4.07	3.78	39.4
Uncertainty with regard to choice of future occupation (22)	3.72	3.13	48.5
Procrastination in academic work (60)	2.62	2.84	37.8
INTERPERSONAL			
Difficulty in making friends (148)	5.15	5.58	35.6
Feelings of non-belonging, isolation (25)	5.09	5.61	58.8
Difficulty in being comfortable in the presence of others (2)	5.07	5.37	45.1
Difficulty in expressing affection toward others (54)	4.99	5.66	37.0
Difficulty in starting conversations (7)	4.74	5.02	40.7
Inadequate relationships with the opposite sex (121)	4.71	4.95	53.2
Lack of self-confidence in intimate social relationships (66)	4.67	4.84	46.4
Lack of self-confidence in casual social relationships (5)	4.60	5.59	46.5

[a] Scale poles are (1) "much worse" and (9) "extreme improvement"; (1) "group hindered" and (9) "group helped extremely."

provement and group help correlate significantly (Rho = .84), such that those problems seen as most improved are those with which the group was most helpful.

We ask each participant to directly rate himself and each person in his group on "amount of change since coming to the group (regardless of kind or direction)," "degree of change in attitude," and "degree of change in relationships with others" (nine-point scales). With a sample of 406 participants, the average self-rating on "general change" was 4.6; the mean rating on "change in attitude" was 4.9; and on "change in relationships" the mean was 5.0. Each mean is significantly different (.001 level) from the "no change" scale point (1).

Group members rated everyone in their group with the same scales. Averaging these peer ratings group by group also indicates substantial change. Mean peer rating of "general change" is 4.0, of "attitude change" 3.8, and of "relationships change" 4.0. All mean peer ratings are significantly different (.001 level) from the scale zero point. Group members concur in reporting individual changes, but see less of it.

A Survey of Interpersonal Values test, having six variables —support, conformity, recognition, independence, benevolence, leadership—was administered to 356 members. We had no directional hypothesis about this test, and frankly we are surprised at the number of significant changes which emerge. Benevolence decreases significantly for both sexes; males endorse more independence items, and females score higher on support and still lower on conformity. Apparently, there are several "do-goody" items on the benevolence scale which become devalued after an encounter experience. Although significant statistically, most of these changes seem slight, and members' postgroup value profile is very similar to their pregroup profile.

The outside friend relationships we tapped through the Relationship Inventory were of a great variety—husbands, wives, lovers, relatives, roommates, and so on. We know, from following the content of group interactions, that many of these relationships underwent drastic changes. Marriages were dissolved or reassembled, friendships were broken, new love life appeared. It is difficult to expect consistent RI changes from pregroup to postgroup under these circumstances.

Nevertheless, for a sample of eighty-three friends responding on their pregroup and postgroup relationships with group members all four scales changed in the predicted positive direction. Only empathic understanding increased significantly (pregroup mean = 65.6, postgroup mean = 67.6, p<.05, Sandler's A statistic). This seems a striking finding considering that so many relationship changes were going on.

After the group each member was presented a list of seventy possibly significant or meaningful events in his life (the Ranks Test). The events encompassed a first date, an abortion, a trial or legal proceeding, psychotherapy, death of a parent, falling in love, going to Europe, and so on. The items were deliberately diverse and hopefully comprehensive; if not, members were asked to include what they considered significant life-events. These were then ranked on a continuum of 1 to 8 in order of significance or importance in one's life. Following this, members were asked at postgroup to insert their encounter group experience somewhere in this ranking: at rank 1 if it was *the* most meaningful event in their life thus far, in the middle if it was of lesser importance, and at the bottom (rank 9) if it was least important of the eight they chose. This procedure aimed at the particularly idiosyncratic impact of the group experience for each participant.

Distribution of responses by rank and sex for TIE AB reveals a mean rank for males of 7.1 and for females of 6.8. Almost half the participants report the group to be among some of the more meaningful experiences in their lives (rank 5 through 8); about 17 per cent indicate that the group was extremely significant (rank 1 through 4), and 39 per cent rank it lower than all events chosen. The impact of the group experience varies with age, education, and previous experience, such that the greatest effect is felt by the youngest (eighteen to twenty-nine) and those with least group experience (or, best of all, none).

Both negative ratings and comments were solicited at postgroup for each of the ten most important problems members endorsed before their group (Problems Check List). A response was considered potentially negative if there was any indication of a complaint, bad experience, distress, disappointment, continuing or increased concern with a specific problem or if any negative ratings occurred (including "no change" ratings with or without comment). From 20,400 opportunities, we cultivated 112 potentially negative responses.

Three judges, without knowledge of the respondents, sorted these 112 possible negative reactions into four to six sets on a continuum of seriousness. On the average, the judges agreed (blind) on 74 per cent of the statements (defining agreement as when all three placed an item within one rank). Six degrees of seriousness were thus established for potential negative effect.

Twenty-six statements made by 19 members (from a pool of 680) fell in the first two ranks, the most serious category. Following are examples of statements ranked first, on both the personal and interpersonal dimensions.

I don't enjoy life because I don't really live. . . . The problem is much worse because I am painfully aware of much I really don't do in life. (Male, age 23)

I still feel my self-pity is a problem; the group was only a continuation of it and it's getting worse. (F, 22)

My extreme feelings of inadequacy and incompetence are reflected in all aspects of my behavior and feelings. (M, 29)

My guilt feelings over my mother are just as strong. The group did not understand these feelings and now it is harder for me to ask for help in dealing with the guilt. I regret many things. (F, 31)

I'm not willing to trust enough to relax and maintain a friendship. There has been no . . . change in my interaction with people. The problem is still the same but I'm getting more desperate since time has passed and there's no improvement. (F, 20)

I'm more aware of the problem being intolerable but I'm still doing the same things. I played the same tricks in the group . . . and they all worked in the same way. What I wanted was to stop playing tricks. (F, 22)

I still feel distinctly apart from the rest of the world and my experiences in the group helped to emphasize this isolation by showing me how difficult it is for anyone to feel as I do about anything. (F, 19)

I rarely received affection when I needed it; both in and out of the group I probably need it more than ever. (M, 21)

Examples of statements ranked second in seriousness follow.

I still find myself in great depression moods and it affects my relationships. (F)

Still do not have a proper identity, still feel like an exploding atom with fragments flying all about—none connect or make a meaningful whole. (F, 25)

When I get depressed I can't work in school anymore—and I withdraw from personal relationships except with people already close to me. Sometimes the group depressed me and I felt that I couldn't explain why to anyone. (F, 19)

The group made me feel I was achieving something but I really wasn't. I changed but only as long as I was in the group. It was only temporary. I never brought up the problem so it wasn't dealt with. (F, 24)

Many members of the group and the leader especially realized I was being isolated but they offered mostly lip-sympathy without trying to get at the root of some people's rejection of me. (M, 36)

I still have a fear of being hurt. I won't let myself get too close to women in relationships for fear of getting hurt again. (M)

The group gave me a false sense of belonging which was shattered after the group terminated so that I feel a greater sense of nonbelonging presently. Members wouldn't allow me to do the things (like withdrawal) in the group so that I felt I was a part of the group and I belonged. (F, 24)

Examples of statements in the middle category of seriousness are: "Have a greater dislike for casual relationships . . . find it harder to know what to say that is casual"; "I'm now confused about what is appropriate, whereas before I was always tactful; now I'm not sure what to do"; "After the group I started eating foods bad for my skin . . . and my skin is even worse." Examples in the least serious category are: "There is less of a feeling of inertia and stalemate; however the need for satisfying employment has grown, not decreased," "I'm more selective and exclusive in choice of confidante. The group was blah."

A standard procedure is being followed to identify and possibly protect members who appear too unstable to benefit from the group. Applicants are asked at registration to indicate previous psychotherapy experience or hospitalization; group leaders are instructed to notify staff consultants immediately should any member show pyschoticlike or uncontrollable behavior.

In the first twenty-eight months of the project four serious cases of this nature were known to occur. One young male student was undergoing an acute anxiety reaction (associated with an identity crisis) when he applied and was referred elsewhere for psychotherapy. A second individual came to his group's first meeting showing seriously disorganized assaultive behavior and was talked out of continuing (therapy was recommended but not followed up). The two remaining cases were allowed to continue in their groups. Both appeared (to the senior author) to be borderline schizophrenic, and both expressed appreciation for the group experience, although one (male) left voluntarily after five meetings and the other (female) received concomitant psychiatric interviews and was retrieved by her parents following the group because of her bizarre behavior on campus and failure in school. There is no available evidence that the encounter group contributed to these people's disorders; in fact, if anything their groups seemed to serve as a support system during their personal crises.

Many people have serious problems before they come to an encounter group, and they will likely leave with problems. In our sample it is extremely rare that a member indicates his group as the cause of seriously increasing his problems (less than 1 per cent of the time judging from the negative comments). In fact, with the available data, we have not been able to identify a single bona fide clinical casualty resulting from a group, though many egos are bruised and lives changed.

In order to identify participants who might be less obviously disturbed or undergo serious negative reactions from a group, we currently interview each dropout, provide a systematic test-feedback interview to each participant we can contact, and examine extreme negative test changes. We follow-up by telephone and/or interview each individual reporting some clearly negative changes associated with his encounter experience.

After the group, roughly 90 per cent of those answering our open-ended questions (Post Questionnaire) have something good to say. The personal comments of the members give texture and reality to what the experience meant more than does any other source. There are hundreds of these comments. Only a few examples will be given here. Responses are organized below (somewhat arbitrarily because of the amount of overlap) in categories of specific personal learning/awareness, challenge, support, self-actualization, and common humanity—closeness. An estimate of percentage of comments in each category is given. The question asked was: "In your own words, please describe what value your encounter group had for you."

Examples of specific personal learning/awareness (46 per cent) are:

I learned to listen—to recognize that everyone has feelings, fears, personal worth.

I discovered how important it is to express caring for people before they will be willing to open up. I learned how to tune in on my feelings more and to express what I was feeling rather than placating another person by telling them what I thought they wanted to hear.

After being in an encounter group, I realized that in a crowd of people I tend to lose my initiative and identity and play the role of an observer. Now I can begin to attempt to do things in a group.

My encounter group was helpful for me because it helped me sort out my cynical feelings and to see that people reacted to it, leaving me even more cynical. It restored my ability to take a risk in the group.

I have learned to listen to people, I have learned that other people have feelings and that I cannot come through to them without treating them as such. I hope I have won a couple of valuable friends, whose relationship I really appreciate. I am more open, less defensive, because I know that other people are fighting the same things I do.

Two examples of challenge responses (2 per cent) are:

It provided for me an atmosphere where I was encouraged and at times forced to examine my own emotions and face them honestly. Through interacting with others and seeing others interact with each other I was given a valuable model of behavior.

Feeling depressed one week and having to figure out how and why I felt that way and doing something about it.

Participants reported receiving support (14 per cent):

Has been a chance for me to really know what people are thinking of me, and to get a lot of support and friendship. The support is very important because it has given me the confidence to express myself and also to go about my daily life more easily.

Provided important interaction for me with people at a time I needed it—surprised to see my opinion was valued and I was liked—feel a lot better about my self now.

A sanctuary (pause spot) to get perspective on where I'm going, how I'm feeling about myself—from week to week. A place to get feedback and emotional warmth, dump bad feelings, get support, reinforcement, etc.—opportunities I don't normally have on a regularized basis in my everyday life.

This group has exposed me to many different types of people. Even tho they are different from me I accept them; they accept me. This is a new feeling. It has been valuable in that it has helped me confront my personal problems and be much more honest with others and with myself. It has been extremely valuable to me.

Members experience self-actualization (32 per cent):

It has helped open me up again—to experience what it is like to be me, by myself, without always thinking in terms of what my husband and I think together. It has also made me realize more clearly that it is me that has to confront my problems and will sooner or later have to make decisions. This group has brought the richness of close relationships with others and has given me confidence through their acceptance of me that I can make such important decisions.

Once I told the group who I was at the retreat, and saw that they still accepted me, then I felt I could let loose and really say what was bugging me. In this and subsequent sessions, the group was of enormous help in getting me to face difficulties with sex and with my superiors.

I joined this group at a really critical time in my psychic life— and I was attempting to sort out all kinds of feelings about my past, present, and future. The group experience and support has helped me declare my freedom from expectations of family, fear of rejection, of failure. Helped me to see my own power to control my life—love, be loved—to be open and emotionally honest when circumstances indicate it's safe.

I discovered strength in acknowledging my weaknesses. I'm more honest and in touch with myself, but I have more to get into. . . . I need to allow myself time to comprehend the significance of what is happening to me. . . . I'm coming to accept the validity of reality and shared enthusiasm with others in the group. I became especially close with certain group members and will maintain relationships with them. This to me is about the most significant benefit of the group.

Examples of common humanity—closeness responses (4 per cent) are:

Listening to other people's problems and how I felt toward them made me realize the uniformity of human experience . . . feel that I can now talk about my experiences freely without fear of shocking the hell out of anyone—without being "forever" rejected.

I have learned that a group of strangers can become close, which leads me to believe that it isn't so difficult for people to "get together"—but in our society it's something which requires working at. The group has let me see quite clearly what lies in other people's heads and what their personalities are like. I have felt more confident in myself and more of an alive person. I realize my hang-ups more clearly and have something concrete to work on . . . I feel very attached to the group.

GROUP TYPOLOGY

Although our program operates from one theoretical approach (however eclectic), we assumed that leader style, group composition, and other variables [14] would differentially affect outcome. For example, Lieberman, Yalom, and Miles (Chapter 7) find that certain leader approaches are associated with negative effects (casualties) in a sample of university students participating in an encounter group for course credit. To describe and control for differences in leadership and composition, we introduced tests to characterize each group as a whole.

The main instrument used was the Group Q-Sort. Items are designed to indicate relevant descriptors of the group and group process (such as "People have warm emotional relationships in this group"; "The group works hard"; "The group doesn't face things fully").[15] Each group as a whole ordered the

[14] In the spring of 1970, the Berkeley Vietnam moratorium had its impact on the content of group interactions and perhaps process. Field research needs to take into account the larger emotional ecology of its samples.

[15] This analysis is based on the first year's sample—a revised Q-Sort was used in later samples.

seventy-two Group Q-Sort items along a continuum of "most like the group" (9) through "least like the group" (1), arriving at consensus in their own fashion. Factoring this Q-Sort data over fifty groups (with Varimax rotation) generates six dimensions of group self-description.

Other group measures were derived from the group-form Relationship Inventory, from ratings on member helpfulness, activity, and productiveness, and from actuarial data on attendance and drops. These measures generated an additional six dimensions through key cluster analysis. Nine parameters, combining a large number of group-descriptive measures, became elements in constructing a typological analysis (three dimensions were dropped for parsimony because of their smaller variance). Tryon's object cluster analysis was used to locate all similar groups clustered in this nine-dimensional space. Six group types were identified. In effect, a group type is a cluster of groups measurably similar in profile on our prefactored indices.[16]

The dimension labels, basic test instruments, and sample items of this composite solution are shown in Table 8.

Each of the six types contained five, six, or seven groups (fourteen are eliminated as outside the type solution).[17] Group and leader variance contribute differentially to the typology outcome. A summary of each type is as follows:

Type I: Very productive, group-centered; highest on measures associated with a working, expressive encounter and with an atmosphere of acceptance. The leader is seen as positive but not central—group members are active on their own (or perhaps with easy facilitation by the leader).

Type II: Good group, productive, with adequate leadership. Group atmosphere is positive but less so than it is in type I. Leaders are probably more confronting than facilitating and more personally close than are those of type I.

Type III: Leader and group combine in positive climate

[16] Fifty groups is actually a small sample for typological analysis. We anticipate a total sample of 150 groups in the final year of the project.

[17] For a detailed analysis of the scores of the six group types on the nine dimension variables, the reader may contact the authors.

Table 8

Dimensions of Typological Analysis

Dimension Label	Instrument(s)	Sample Scales
Productive-Expressive Group	Group Q-Sort	"This group is active. . . . People express their emotions freely. The group is satisfied with itself."
Active Members	Post Questionnaire	"Group members helped . . . positive atmosphere. The group seems alive."
Warm, Empathic Group Climate	Relationship Inventory (Group)	Positive regard, empathic understanding, genuineness.
"Tough" Group	Group Q-Sort	"This group hurts people's feelings easily. It is tough to be in this group."
Attendance	Actuarial data	Attendance rate for middle and late meetings; drops.
Unconditionality	Relationship Inventory (Group and Leader)	Unconditional regard by group and leader.
Leader Helpful-Accepting	Post Questionnaire Relationship Inventory (Leader)	"Leader helped positive group atmosphere"; empathic understanding.
Leader Close	Post Questionnaire	"Leader is personally involved, 'explores feelings,' is close."
Leader-Centered	Group Q-Sort	"The group needs its leader. The group is organized."

of unconditional regard, empathy, and genuineness without, however, apparent productivity or expressiveness. Type III groups are identifiable love groups; strong negative encounters do not occur. The leaders are important and seen as very positive and close.

Type IV: The leader is prominent and helpful, but the group lacks initiative, movement, and expression. Many of these leaders later went on to lead very successful groups. Our impression of this type is that there is a critical mismatch between the leader and the group so that the distance cannot be bridged. A groupwide ambivalence seems to prevail.

Type V: A tough group tone (conditional, critical, demanding) is probably set by the leader, who is seen as central but less than helpful-accepting. This negativity probably decreases productivity-expression and increases dropouts. The leader's involvement is apparently a negative input.

Type VI: Bad group. No distinguishing leader characteristics emerge, positive or negative, but these groups see themselves as passive, unproductive, inexpressive, and unaccepting more than do other types. In our process of leader evaluation five of these seven leaders were dropped from the program.

In the overall solution certain major features are apparent. Types I and II are active, self-initiating, group-centered groups, and type VI is the opposite. The leader is most prominent in types III, IV and V—positively in III and IV, negatively in V (the tough groups). This typological analysis suggests a pattern of outcome prediction.

OUTCOME BY GROUP TYPE

Arranging group types as conditions, we calculated differences in outcome across nine criterion variables, predicting that, in general, outcome scores would vary according to group type. (Our hunch was that the serial order of types I through VI would correspond to levels of significant positive change.)

The criterion measures were self-rated general change; self-reliance Q-Sort change; the Ranks Test; Interpersonal Problem change; peer-rated general change; peer-rated attitude change; peer-rated relationship change; peer-rated closeness (in the group); and leader-rated (member) change. Results of a one-way analysis of variance for group type by outcome variable are given in Table 9.[18]

[18] Initial Self-Ideal concordance level was found to be a nonsignificant covariate.

Table 9

Analysis of Variance of Group Type by Outcome

Outcome Measure	Group Type Means[a]						F[b]	p<
	I	II	III	IV	V	VI		
Self:								
"General" change	5.46[c]	4.88	4.82	4.57	4.44	3.62	4.16	.001
Self-reliance change	6.11	3.29	0.49	2.65	3.54	2.05	2.29	.05
Ranks Test	5.79	7.50	7.12	6.45	7.18	7.51	4.47	.001
Interpersonal Problem change	4.81	4.10	4.67	4.52	3.85	4.25	2.44	.04
Other:								
Peer rating of "general" change	4.73	4.59	4.63	4.23	4.12	3.69	4.01	.002
Peer rating of "attitude" change	4.65	4.42	4.30	4.17	3.74	3.51	4.87	.001
Peer rating of "relation" change	4.68	4.79	4.70	4.17	4.08	3.65	6.34	.001
Peer rating "close"	4.29	4.45	4.38	3.89	3.82	3.51	3.46	.005
Leader rating change	4.79	4.15	5.29	4.05	4.62	3.80	2.53	.03

         [a] Multivariate F over all variables $= 1.87$, $p < .001$.

         [b] Univariate F-ratio between types; degrees of freedom $= 227$.

         [c] Italicized means are significantly different from grand mean $(< .01)$.

Clearly, outcome does vary by group type (combinations of member composition and leader characteristics). The greatest self-rated change and impact is seen in type I, the least in type VI. Peer ratings are highest for types I, II, and III, lowest for IV, V, and VI. Leader-rated change is highest in type III, lowest in VI. The lowest self-reliance change occurs in type III, where the leader and members join in an atmosphere of warm acceptance without productive energy. Groups in which the leader is the most dominant factor (IV, V) and members are negatively passive are consistently low on relationship measures. Those in type VI are consistently low on everything and could clearly be called failure groups in our sample. The main outcome features of types II, III, IV, and V do not allow a simple linear interpretation. Outcome patterns for these group types are complicated. The findings suggest that the groups generating the most positive change and impact consist of active, self-initiating members and helpful but not overly intrusive leaders. The least positive effect can be expected from groups and leaders who are mutually inactive and insensitive.

DISCUSSION AND PROSPECTS

We have found significant positive changes in members almost wherever we looked. Self-esteem increases, the self-concept changes in many positive directions, self-actualizing tendencies are greater, alienation is reduced, and individual problems are lessened; interpersonal relations become more empathic and improve, and interpersonal values change perhaps toward a more realistic supportiveness; people become close with each other and feel less lonely.

Our encounter groups do little for productivity, work, or school problems. Since the program does not try to affect these areas this result is not surprising. Most of our sample are encounter group beginners—they enter the program positively motivated and with appropriate expectations. Under these circumstances people gain the most. Older members and those with more experience gain less. The generally humanistic orientation of our sample does not change, unless to become more so. Group composition and leader style do make a difference.

Future work will be carried out with larger samples and refinements in method. Multivariate analyses of residual gain scores will be examined with more complete and diverse outcome and process variables. We are now working on a promising approach toward defining a leader style typology and several predictor measures of leadership talent. A dozen studies of the processes involved in more than seventy-five groups have been carried out during 1970 and 1971. From these studies has evolved a systematic and reliable procedure for tracing the naturalistic meeting-by-meeting development of successful and unsuccessful groups which will be used to generate a fuller and more generally applicable group typology.

Our present conclusion is that encounter groups, when

designed to provide a supportive, group-centered climate for personal growth, do produce significant positive changes and have considerable impact. There is good evidence to support the subjective experience of many people—for example, the response of "Jim":

I could write a book about the value this group has had for me. It has . . . affected me totally. . . . My group is the most positive experience . . . I've ever had. It has changed me as a person. I feel for the better—in many ways: it . . . has opened me up to myself, has made me feel that other people can see how I really am, and has alleviated my loneliness enormously. I now feel better able to face life on my own terms and enjoy it. I am less afraid of being hurt in relationships, and can therefore enjoy relationships more and more deeply . . . I am more secure, and consequently able to explore more intense relationships, to myself and others, without constantly feeling that I can't do it. I feel freer of my hang-ups generally, feel free to grow. Thank you, people!

7

Impact on Participants

Morton A. Lieberman, Irvin D. Yalom, Matthew B. Miles

The use of encounter groups for promoting personal growth and the application of encounter techniques in a large variety of settings have mushroomed so rapidly that the gap between what is done and what is known has widened alarmingly.[1] A sense of excitement on the one hand about this bustling and ostensibly highly creative development, and uneasiness on the

Reproduced, with certain modifications, by special permission from *The Journal of Applied Behavioral Science*, Volume 8, Number 1, 1972, from "The Impact of Encounter Groups on Participants: Some Preliminary Findings," by Morton A. Lieberman, Irvin D. Yalom, and Matthew B. Miles. Published and copyrighted © by NTL Institute for Applied Behavioral Science, Washington, D.C.

[1] This chapter is based on the Group Experience Project—a study supported by the Ford Foundation Special Education Fund at Stanford University; The Mary Reynolds Babcock Foundation, Inc.; the National Institute of Mental Health #MH 19212; General Research Funds, Stanford University Medical School; General Research Fund, Division of Biological Sciences, University of Chicago; Social Science Research Committee, University of Chicago; W. Clement and Jessie V. Stone Foundation; Carnegie Corporation of New York; Foundation's Fund for Research in Psychiatry.

other hand, prompted us in the fall of 1968 to launch a comprehensive study of encounter groups.

The questions we attempted to answer are basic and ambitious. How effective are these groups? In which ways and to what degree do they change individuals? What are the risks? What conditions are instrumental in inducing desired or unwanted effects?

Not only did we address basic outcome issues for the encounter experience, but we attempted to describe and compare the many diverse forms and orientations now clustered together under the umbrella of encounter group. This approach offered us the exciting opportunity to develop a taxonomy of leader behavior and group conditions and outcomes associated with those leader behaviors.

Our basic plan consisted of sponsoring a large number of groups on a university campus; the subjects in these groups, as well as the groups themselves, were closely studied. Data on number of outcome variables for each individual were collected prior to the group, immediately after the group, and again six months later. Considerable information about the behavior of the leader and properties and processes of the group as a system was gathered by a team of trained raters who observed each meeting.

This chapter presents an overview of some of our preliminary findings and conclusions stemming from our short-run postgroup outcome measures. A detailed description of the project and measures appears in Lieberman, Yalom, Miles and Golde (1971). A monograph in preparation describes the methodology, the long-term outcomes for individual members, and the conditions related to these outcomes, including pregroup personality variables, leader style, group norms, and a number of such group behavior variables as self-disclosure, level of activity, degree of deviance, cohesiveness, and sociometric status.

DESIGN

Under the auspices of Stanford University, eighteen groups representing ten approaches to personal change were composed of Stanford undergraduates during the winter quarter of 1969. Common to all ten approaches is their attempt to provide an intensive group experience; they focus on the here and now (the behavior of the members as it unfolds in the group); they encourage openness, honesty, interpersonal confrontation, and total self-disclosure; they encourage strong emotional expression. Participants are not labeled patients, and the experience is not ordinarily labeled therapy, but nonetheless the groups strive to increase awareness and to change behavior. Specific goals may vary between groups—occasionally they explicitly try to entertain, to "turn on," to give experience in joy, but overall goals in each case involve some type of personal change of behavior, of values, of life style.

Two groups each represented (1) sensitivity training following a traditional National Training Laboratories approach, (2) NTL-Rogerian ("personal growth") orientation, (3) Synanon, (4) transactional analysis, (5) Gestalt, (6) psychodrama, (7) marathon groups, and (8) leaderless tape groups (using the Bell and Howell tapes). One group represented (9) a sensory awareness approach patterned after groups at Esalen, and one represented (10) psychoanalytically oriented groups.

Most of the typologies are well known, but a few descriptive remarks may be useful. The NTL personal growth style differed from the NTL traditional style by its emphasis on intrapersonal process and a lesser concern about the total group process. The Synanon groups ("games") were held at the Synanon house in Oakland; other groups were conducted on or near the Stanford campus. The leaderless programed groups had no leader other than a tape recorder which issued certain instructions for each meeting. The sensory awareness, Esalen group leader used a large number (an average of eight per session) of structured exercises. The psychoanalytic group, led by an analyst, focused on intrapersonal issues and on personal historical material. To skip ahead for a moment, we must note that these ideological labels convey relatively little information about actual leader behavior; we found it necessary to describe leader styles along totally different dimensions.

The sixteen group leaders were all highly experienced: Most had had approximately ten years' experience leading groups and several had national reputations. They were selected from an initial list of sixty whom a number of knowledgeable persons in the Bay Area had chosen as the two best representatives of each orientation. Very few leaders refused our invitation to participate in the project. They were well paid and many were intrigued by the research design. The research staff did not shackle the leaders; on the contrary we encouraged each leader to "do his thing"—to lead groups in his customary manner. Each group met for approximately thirty hours: some for ten three-hour meetings, others in a massed (marathon) format.

Students were recruited through a course listing in the time schedules of the university, articles in the student newspaper, and posters placed around campus. Those who expressed interest in the groups were invited to a series of meetings in which the research staff discussed the purpose of the research and the nature of the experience to be offered. The students were told that the group experience offered an opportunity to explore a variety of personal learning goals, including racial attitudes and behavior. A microlab technique was used to illustrate the "feel" of encounter groups. For a vast majority of the students, experience or knowledge about encounter groups was readily available, half of them had been in encounter groups, and all but forty-eight (19 per cent) indicated that they did have close friends who had previously been in encounter groups. During the recruitment meeting we indicated that the experience might be emotionally taxing and occasionally upsetting. Students were also informed of the university's concern about potentially harmful effects of encounter group experience, and we described in detail the mental health facilities available to participants if the experience did become emotionally stressful. They were also told that one member of the research team was available to anyone who wished to discuss his feelings or to seek help because of events related to participation in the group. Course credit was given to those who participated in a group and was not dependent upon performance in the group or additional work outside the group. Those who dropped out after initiating participation and desired course credit were asked to write a paper within the general area of encounter groups and attitude change.

Those who expressed interest in participating were assigned to groups according to a stratified random sampling of sex, class year, and previous encounter group experience. Random assignment of participants to groups of varying orientation enabled us to make comparisons of across-treatment conditions. Some students who registered for the course and had completed a series of research questionnaires could not be accommodated in the groups because of schedule conflicts; a few changed their minds—37 of these students served as control subjects, and another 32 control subjects were developed from a random sample of names provided by participants. The final study population consisted of 209 participants assigned to the eighteen groups, and 69 controls. All subjects were undergraduate students evenly distributed among the four undergraduate years. Seventy per cent were male, 30 per cent female; more than 90 per cent were white; most were Protestant; 14 per cent were of Jewish background. Demographically they were entirely representative of the Stanford student population. In comparison to controls, the experimentals had slightly less previous contact with encounter groups and more often majored in social sciences and humanities rather than engineering and physical sciences.

ASSESSMENT PROCEDURES

Problems of what to measure and when and how to measure it, which chronically dog studies of educational and therapeutic outcomes, were magnified in the present case because of the range of leader orientations and of leader and participant goals. We anticipated that some participants, for example, might describe the salience of the encounter experience in religious terms, expressing a deep conviction that it had profound meaning in their lives, although they might report no specific behavioral effects and others would not detect any discrete differences in them. For other participants, the central significance of the experience might be seen to lie in changes in the self-system, while still others might reflect greatest change in their views of or interaction with others. To allow for such variation, outcome was broadly viewed in terms of the impact of the encounter experience on multiple dimensions of personal functioning of differing degrees of specificity.

Change was assessed from three vantage points in addition to participants' own judgments. First, each leader described his view of change in the participants on a set of ten scales anchored to his experience with previous groups. Second, change ratings were obtained from significant people in each participant's social network (Miles, 1965). At the onset of the study, participants and controls were asked to name five to seven individuals who knew them quite well. Six months after termination, letters were sent to these people asking whether they felt the participant had changed over the past six months, and in what ways. Finally, judgments of co-participants on learning achieved and certain group behaviors were obtained on several occasions by means of a questionnaire on which all group members were rank-ordered.

Baseline measures on general attitudes toward encounter groups and on each area of functioning were obtained for all participants and controls several weeks before assignment to the groups; change measures were administered a week or two after the groups terminated, as well as six to eight months later. At the close of the experience, and six months later, participants were asked to evaluate the personal relevance of the groups, as well as to indicate what aspects of the encounter group experience they felt were particularly crucial in their own learning.

Evaluations of a religious character were identified through an instrument in which a peak experience was described. Participants were asked whether they felt they had ever had such an experience and, if so, under what conditions. Inasmuch as the meaning of the experience might be reflected in a reordering or reorienting of beliefs, measures sampled changes in two realms of values—values pertaining to personal behavior, such as spontaneity or expression of feelings, and values reflecting life goals.

Impact on the self-system was assessed through a series of measures of self-ideal discrepancy, self-esteem (Rosenberg,

1965), and congruence of one's own and others' perceptions of self. Kelly's REP Test (Harrison, 1962) was adapted to assess changes in views of other people. Several measures, including self-rating scales, the FIRO-B (Schutz, 1966), and a questionnaire concerning peer relationships, were used to assess various forms of change in interpersonal behavior.

Preliminary explorations had demonstrated that some people join encounter groups because they are considering major personal or occupational changes or undergoing life crises involving major decisions. Since the most salient aspects of the group experience for such people might be related to the resolution of these dilemmas, one questionnaire gathered information on the effect of the groups on decision-making behavior. Encounter groups may also affect styles of coping with personal issues. A person may learn, for example, that paying more attention to his inner life aids coping, or he may utilize the expression of feeling more frequently. A set of coping-strategy scales was developed to assess such changes.

The influence of the group on participants was only one object of inquiry. We were equally interested in developing a meaningful model describing the relations between group characteristics, leader behaviors, and participant learning. At each meeting two observers rated leader behavior and such dimensions of the group as norms, climate, and themes. Observer pairs were randomly changed so that no pair met more than once and no individual saw the same group more than once. From time to time participants also filled out schedules on group norms, level of group cohesion, and their phenomenological experience, focused on critical events.

PRELIMINARY FINDINGS

We learned from all this that it is possible to collect enough data to fill more than sixty thousand IBM cards and to underestimate chronically the financial support required to analyze that amount of information. We have come to appreciate anew the incredible complexity of human beings as they go through what many perceive as a highly meaningful and emotion-laden experience. But the issue before us is the personal growth of the participants, not the investigators. This preliminary report focuses on the general effects of the experience on participants and the particular effects associated with participation in different types of groups. The first issue involves the comparison of participants and controls; the second, the comparison of the various types of encounter groups.

OUTCOMES IN EXPERIMENTAL AND CONTROL POPULATIONS

Seventy-three indices of outcome (see Table 10) data were subjected to linear discriminate analyses (Bio medical series, 07M) to determine which set of change indices differentiated the experimental from the control subjects. This methodology for multiple outcome criteria offers several advantages and one major disadvantage. It provides a method for finding

Table 10

Comparison Between Participant and Controls on
Seventy-Three Change Indices

Indices	Mean Change Scores Participant	Control	Variable Strength
Attitudes Toward Encounter			
1. Safe-Dangerous	1.33	−0.36	1**a
2. Genuine-Phony	0.36	0.23	
3. Socially Beneficial	−0.09	−0.95	
Self-Rating—Behavior			
4. Expressivity	1.00	0.95	
5. Awareness of Others	1.02	0.66	
6. Adequacy of Relationships	1.09	0.63	
7. Intimacy	0.89	0.41	
8. Inner understanding	1.01	0.36	4*
9. Sensitivity	0.94	0.50	
10. Spontaneity	0.75	0.65	
Self-Rating—Environment Opportunity			
11. Feedback	1.58	1.08	
12. Intimacy	0.80	0.46	
13. Openness	1.10	0.61	7*
14. Sharing	0.80	0.62	
15. Novelty	0.63	0.41	
16. Being Direct	0.56	0.39	
17. Trusting	0.57	0.23	
18. Expressing Anger	0.97	0.39	*

Table 10 (Continued)

Comparison Between Participant and Controls on
Seventy-Three Change Indices

Indices	Mean Change Scores Participant	Control	Variable Strength
Interpersonal Values			
19. Directness	0.44	0.29	
20. Feedback	0.09	−0.02	
21. Novelty	0.49	0.81	2
22. Flexibility	0.49	0.69	
23. Expression of Anger	0.78	0.45	11
24. Change	0.25	0.28	
25. Sharing	0.49	0.53	
Interpersonal Behavior—FIRO			
26. Acceptance of control	0.14	−0.33	8
27. Being controlling	0.14	0.17	
28. Acceptance of affect	0.08	0.09	
29. Expression of affect	0.08	0.09	
Perceptions of Significant Others— Interpersonal Constructs			
30. Mental Health	0.11	1.18	
31. Consideration	−0.51	0.67	
32. Honesty	−1.06	−0.77	
33. Permissiveness	−1.98	0.45	5*
34. Total Interpersonal Orientation	−0.93	2.88	
35. Responsibility	−1.68	−0.14	
36. Ability	−1.84	−0.81	
37. Status	−0.65	−0.98	
38. Total Instrumental Orientation	−4.01	−1.94	
39. Activity	−0.70	0.86	
Number of Interpersonal Constructs			
40. Total Interpersonal Orientation	−0.34	0.27	
41. Total Instrumental Orientation	5.37	3.83	
42. Activity	−0.35	0.26	
Friendship Patterns			
43. Extensivity	−0.23	−0.07	15
44. Expansion	−0.51	−0.78	14
45. Intensivity	0.12	−0.11	
46. Constructs—Same Race	−0.52	−0.25	
47. Constructs—Opposite Race	−0.38	0.25	
Self-System			
48. Self-Esteem	0.24	−0.18	12*
Self-Image			
49. Mental Health	1.60	1.34	

Table 10 (Continued)

Comparison Between Participant and Controls on
Seventy-Three Change Indices

Indices	Mean Change Scores Participant	Control	Variable Strength
50. Consideration	0.68	0.07	
51. Honesty	0.22	0.86	10
52. Permissiveness	0.21	−0.54	6
53. Total Interpersonal	2.78	2.77	
54. Responsibility	−0.27	0.18	
55. Ability	−0.05	0.34	
56. Status	−0.22	−0.13	
57. Total Instrumental	−0.47	0.22	
58. Activity	0.50	1.35	
Self-Ideal Discrepancy [b]			
59. Total Interpersonal	−3.25	9.04	9*
60. Total Instrumental	−0.71	−1.16	13
61. Activity	−0.10	0.64	
Coping Styles			
62. Interpersonal Perspective	0.22	−0.73	
63. Interpersonal Problem-Solving	2.96	0.75	
64. Understanding, Empathy	2.98	1.09	*
65. Help from Authority	1.48	−0.69	
66. Spontaneous Action	1.28	1.15	
67. Take Action	1.23	0.79	
68. Planned Alternatives	0.72	0.11	
69. Humor-Minimization	1.89	0.43	3*
70. Tension Reduction Through Flight	1.85	1.13	
71. Escape	1.10	0.63	
72. Expect Worst	0.65	0.72	
73. Denial	1.52	1.00	

Note: Asterisks indicate univariate significance levels.
  * $p \leq .05$.
  ** $p \leq .01$.

[a] Numerals in right hand column indicate relative strength each variable had in discriminating among the experimental and control groups. The first two discriminant variables—#1, Danger of Encounter Groups, and #21, Novelty Value—correctly differentiate 60 per cent of the experimental and control group subjects; each variable in turn adds to increasing discrimination, up to the maximum found at Step 15—74 per cent correct identification of cases.

[b] Minus scores signify decreases in self-ideal discrepancy.

statistically independent dimensions that discriminate among treatment conditions, enabling the investigator to delete the correlated change measures, and thus is a conservative method in the sense of not overestimating the number of significant differences. Its weakness is that it will tend to produce a maximal discrimination among groups which may not upon replication be justified. At this stage of the research on encounter groups it was a method of choice for determining change dimensions that warranted further exploration in our data.

The picture participants presented at the end of the encounter groups was generally that of a satisfied clientele: 61 per cent of students reported that the group had changed them in a positive direction; of these, three-quarters expected the change to be lasting. At termination, participants' self-ratings significantly differed from those of controls on a number of behaviors, clustering in the areas of increased understanding of inner feelings and increased sensitivity to others. These findings are not surprising; they mirror our everyday experience that encounter group members are generally enthusiastic rather than critical of the experience and usually perceive it as having effected significant personal changes in themselves. Such evaluations tell the investigator little, however, about what the respondents are reflecting in such reports. Of greater investigative significance, but no more surprising, may be the ephemeral nature of participants' judgments of the benefit of the experience. Whereas at termination the ratio of high to low evaluations was 4.7 to 1, the comparable ratio six months later was 2.3 to 1. Of sixteen participants judged by the research staff from a review of eleven major outcome measures as having received high impact immediately after the group, only nine retained their change fully. The picture is not wholly one of "backsliding," however: Of thirty-one participants judged as having changed a moderate amount just following the group, eighteen maintained this change, six lost it, and seven added to their change, deserving the label of late bloomers.

The findings on social network perceptions of the participants' change were less expected. These data were unfortunately spotty, but for 64 per cent of the experimental group

and for 58 per cent of the control group at least one friend
responded. The mean number reporting per subject was a bit
over two. Regardless of the measure (number of changes,
number of people changing, verified changes, and so forth),
experimental and control groups looked alike, as judged by
members of their social network, who rated 80 per cent of the
participants and 83 per cent of the controls as having made at
least one change in a positive direction. For negative changes
the proportion was reversed; 27 per cent of the experimentals
were described as having at least one negative change, while
only 14 per cent of the controls were so described. Participants
did show a slightly higher number of mean changes (1.45 to
1.24), so that for those perceived as changing by their relevant
social network, the amount of change may have been judged
greater for the experimentals than for the controls. The belief
in change appears to be endemic in a college population; at any
rate, the encounter experience, as manifest in perceptions of an
individual's behavior toward significant others, did not demonstrate a singular potency. While methodological insensitivity
and the apparently high base rate of perceived change for
college populations may account for some of the lack of discrimination between participants and controls, a dramatic contrast between the participants' evaluation of self-change and
the evaluations of significant others remains undeniable.

The most powerful change discriminators between experimentals and controls were found in the self-system area. At
the end of the experience, participants saw themselves as more
permissive and less honest, with a greater self-ideal congruence
in the interpersonal area and lowered congruence in the instrumental area. Their self-image, in other words, moved away
from an instrumental, agentive conception of self, a self-view
which was reflected in other indices of change. Participants
changed on the FIRO-B toward a greater willingness to accept
influence from others. On terminal as compared to initial questionnaires, participants' choices of life goals reflected more
growth-oriented values; they also placed higher value on the
expression of angry feelings in relationships and were more
ready to use understanding and humor in solving problems. An

important difference between participants and controls was the participants' increased level of self-esteem, a difference which persisted in the long-term follow-up.

Many change measures did not reveal major differences between participants and controls: Areas such as interpersonal constructs (participants did change in the direction of seeing significant others as less permissive) and coping strategies were not highly affected, nor was there any evidence of major change in how the person related to significant others outside the group.

There can be no question that the encounter experience was meaningful to those who participated, but the impact of the experience seems to have been internal and not readily apparent to those in the participants' social network. At this stage of analysis, the impact of the group experience seems best understood as influencing a shift in the participants' value-attitude system, a shift which is accompanied by efforts to redirect behavior in forms consonant with encounter group values. In follow-up interviews with highly visible learners (defined as those individuals who gave high postgroup testimony —evaluating the group as a constructive, turned-on, high-learning experience—and who were also considered high-learners by their leader and/or peers), it appeared that they were trying to establish relationships akin to those experienced in the encounter group culture. They tended to be encounter-mode converts and often were ardent proselytizers who attempted to guide others into encounter groups. The encounter experience led to a process of resolution-making. These highly visible learners valued a different form of human contact and tried to relate to others in new ways—to meet strangers, to become more intimate; they expressed more courage to do or to try. Participants said they found themselves recalling specific communications or episodes from the groups which they used to orient their behavior. They also reported attempts to fortify themselves via positive images of the leader.

NEGATIVE OUTCOMES

The most disturbing finding, thus far, has been that four to eight months after the group experience 9.4 per cent of the participants who completed the experience (7.5% of total sample of participants, including those who dropped out) showed evidence of negative outcome (Yalom and Lieberman, 1971). We defined a negative outcome or encounter group casualty as an individual who, as a result of his encounter group experience, suffered some enduring psychological harm which was evident six to eight months after the end of the group. We did not include subjects who, in the follow-up period, underwent some psychological decompensation which in our opinion was unrelated to their participation in the group, nor did we include individuals who had a stormy, dysphoric, but evanescent episode following the group experience. We feel that our figures are conservative; we had a high degree of certainty about the identified casualties and were unable to contact for follow-up study some who seemed to be particularly high-risk subjects. The level of disturbance ranged from severe to moderate; one participant had a psychotic episode during the group, another suffered a severe depression with a forty-pound weight loss. Others suffered decrements in self-esteem, felt less trust in others, exhibited increased withdrawal from others. Still other members expressed increased fear of harm from others or a heightened sense of hopelessness or despair over whether they could break through some of the problems they had brought to the encounter group.

A detailed description of the methodology of identifying casualties is presented elsewhere (Yalom and Lieberman, 1971). In brief, our method was to identify a pool of high-risk suspects who were then interviewed briefly on the phone. If this interview suggested a negative outcome, we conducted a lengthy interview with the subject. To identify the potential casualty pool we developed a number of indicators: request for emergency psychiatric help, peer evaluation (at the end of the group all members were asked who, if anyone, got hurt in their group), dropping out of the group, steep decline in self-esteem (the Rosenberg self-esteem measure), subject testimony (self-rating of the group as destructive and unpleasant), leaders' negative ratings of change, and seeking psychotherapy.

The most accurate predictor of actual casualty status was

the peer judgment ("Who got hurt in your group?"). One of the least accurate predictors was the leader rating. In reflecting on these findings on negative outcome it should be stressed that the assessment of casualty was not limited to the period of the group's tenure. Such a procedure would have led to a gross underestimation of the degree of psychological risk; most of those eventually identified as psychologically harmed by the experience could not have been identified easily during the life of the group.

Thirteen per cent of the participants entered into psychotherapy during or after the group, compared to 3 per cent of controls. Interviews with these participants indicated that only a third of them could be considered casualties; for some, entrance into psychotherapy focused on problems that antedated their participation in the encounter group and perhaps the group only served as a further stimulus for this step. Others discovered aspects of themselves in the group which they wanted to work on further, so that for them entering therapy can best be seen as a continuation of growth.

Our interviews, and the quantitative data, showed rather clearly that pre-existing personality dispositions interacted with certain leadership styles and group climates. In particular, individuals who were psychologically vulnerable (had lower self-esteem, less self-perceived mental health, more sense of psychological distance from others) *and* who had very high hopes for the potential growth-giving properties of encounter groups were rather likely to experience negative outcomes when they attended groups with leaders who (in effect) believed that they could deliver the wished-for salvation (see description of Type A leaders in Chapter 8). Such leaders appeared to create group conditions in which strong attack or rejection occurred.

EFFECTS OF DIFFERENT GROUPS

The differing effects of the eighteen groups present a more striking picture than do the comparisons of experimental and control populations. Some groups had almost no impact; other affected nearly every participant. In one group, for example, 100 per cent of participants showed heightened self-esteem; in another group only 15 per cent showed a similar rise.

As with the experimental-control comparisons, linear discriminate analysis was used to determine what set of change discriminated among groups. Statistically significant differences in behavior were found in the use of avoidance or denial coping strategies, content of participants' self-perceptions, participants' personal construct system, and evaluations of significant others. Finally, various groups were associated with differences in casualty and dropout rates, as well as stability of changes.

Despite the preliminary nature of these illustrative findings, they may serve to emphasize an emergent direction—namely, that the experience of a participant in an encounter group is not a uniform event; particular kinds of encounter groups differ not only in how much change takes place but also in the patterning of changes and the areas of functioning affected. (See Chapter 8 for a discussion of leader style and outcome.)

Clearly, encounter groups have an impact on their participants. In large measure, what is carried away from the experience depends on particular characteristics of the group. The question of whether such experiences generally are productive or counterproductive—whether the positive changes noted are broad and deep enough to warrant the risks—raises a series of other complex, and to some extent unresearchable, questions leading, thus far, toward a metaphysical quagmire. Eventually, we hope to confront this question, for it is part of what has motivated the research. Much of the data upon which such judgment must be based, however, are as yet unanalyzed; more important, time has yet been too short for the available bits of information to be subjected to the fermenting processes that hopefully may clarify how they may be integrated into a meaningful whole.

8

Behavior and Impact
of Leaders

Morton A. Lieberman

How do encounter leaders go about the business of changing people?[1] A commitment to the production of personal growth through the group medium could well be all they hold in common. Small wonder that such a broadly defined charge has been broadly interpreted relative to the meaning as well as the means. Of the sixteen encounter leaders studied (for a description of the overall design, the approaches leaders used, and the various indices of outcome, see Chapter 7) some were primarily analytic (interpretative), some saw the management of group forces as their distinctive function, and still others offered

[1] This chapter is derived from the Group Experience Project—a study supported by the Ford Foundation Special Education Fund at Stanford University; The Mary Reynolds Babcock Foundation, Inc.; the National Institute of Mental Health #MH 19212; General Research Funds, Stanford University Medical School; General Research Fund, Division of Biological Sciences, University of Chicago; Social Science Research Committee, University of Chicago; W. Clement and Jessie V. Stone Foundation; Carnegie Corporation of New York; Foundation's Fund for Research in Psychiatry.

instructional, often non-verbal exercises almost exclusively. Some leaders believed passionately in love, others just as passionately in hate. For one leader the basic stuff of change stemmed from the experience of primary rage; for another, the idea that humans were dependent was anathema. Some leaders depended solely on talk-therapy; others used music, lights, the clench of human bodies.

The leaders were deliberately chosen, of course, to enhance such differences in style, methodology, and philosophy. Part of the reason for ensuring a divergence in point of view among the leaders was to discover whether the conventional labels they represented, such as Gestalt, sensory awareness, T-group, and so on, had any real meaning in differentiating what they actually did as encounter leaders. The more challenging goal behind the design, however, was that of generating the sort of data about leadership differences which would allow the development of an empirical taxonomy of leadership methodologies—a typology which might ultimately be related to different types or degrees of personal learning or change.

The intention to elaborate a typology of encounter leadership placed rigorous demands on the experimental design. As the major experimental variable, leader behavior had to be classified in a way that would make it truly capable of being associated with varying outcomes. The diverse orientations represented among the leaders added the requirement that observation methods be sensitive to the discrete characteristics of each orientation, yet sufficiently abstract to work for several cases and allow comparison. The relatively large number of leaders and their methodological differences suggested that studying the apparent function of their behavior held more promise for understanding its effect on outcome than would the analysis of their personality characteristics—a variable less likely to be associated with school of thought or ideological orientation.[2]

[2] For all the analyses presented in this chapter, the two Synanon leaders are treated as a single unit. The Synanon format involved changing the composition of the group at each session. Thus, the participants met varyingly with one or another of the two leaders.

To address such problems jointly, several observational schedules were developed which employed differing magnitudes in the units of observation. At the more microscopic end, observers rated how frequently leaders displayed each of twenty-eight discrete behaviors. At the more global extreme, observers recorded their overall impressions of "how the leader came across" to them at the end of each meeting, in terms of rather broad categories of leadership style. Three other assessments, made by observers or participants or both, struck at the midpoint of the continuum, tapping the focus of the leader's attention (whether group, interpersonal, or intrapsychic), his interpersonal attractiveness, and his symbolic meaning to the participants.

WHAT LEADERS DO

The first assessment of leaders determined how often they did such things as challenge, interpret, or stop an interaction among members. These discrete behaviors were grouped into five areas in terms of the function they seemed intended to perform; *evocative behavior* (behavior seemingly designed to get members to respond); *coherence-making* (behavior apparently aimed at altering cognitive perspectives); *support,* as evidenced in positive affective gestures; *managing behavior* (interventions concerning how people worked with one another or how the group was functioning as a whole); and *use of self* (behavior involving demonstration or modeling by the leader). Evocative behaviors were most frequently used (29 per cent), and next most common were those involving use of self (22 per cent). Supportive behaviors were used the least (12 per cent). Coherence-making (19 per cent) and management (17 per cent) were midway in per cent of use.

While leaders differed in their use of the five types of behavior, much that is similar can also be noted, particularly in their use of evocative behavior. This finding is not surprising, for despite their differences in philosophy and personal style, the functions the leaders served through these behaviors are generally necessary for any group of people to develop conditions useful for growth. All leaders must pay some attention to how their group is working, all leaders perceive the necessity of generating responsiveness in the members, and so on.

Behavior differences become more evident when a specific behavior within one of the functional groups is examined—when one looks at what kind of evocative behavior the leader used, what forms of coherence-making or managing behavior, and so on. The best sense of leader preferences for one type of behavior over another may be gained from looking at the number of sessions in which each leader employed a particular sort of behavior. Here, for most of the five types of behavior, leaders range from expressing no, or only occasional, examples of the behavior during a meeting to consistent use at every meeting.

Though this type of analysis goes slightly beyond what can be known through unaided observation, the five types of leadership behavior which it assigns are not intended to have any necessary theoretical meaning, nor are they considered equivalent or in the same metric. They represent a purely pragmatic ordering, based solely on the apparent function of what leaders commonly do in therapeutic groups. To provide a more systematic grouping, scores on the twenty-eight observable behaviors were factor analyzed. This operation produced seven clusters of behavior which were assigned brief descriptive labels. Table 11 presents the seven factored dimensions of leadership behavior and the items in order of factor loadings on each dimension.

Three of the seven factored dimensions of leadership behavior appear designed to elicit participants' response. *Intrusive modeling* represents behavior which gets response through direct, energetic demands via challenges, confrontation, and exhortation, as well as behavior which involves the intense participation of the leader as a self-revealing member of the group. (The clustering of behaviors grouped under use of self and evocative behavior, which had appeared distinct, suggests that high self-disclosure by the leader may have an effect similar to that of confrontation by the leader, insofar as it places an intense demand on members to reciprocate.)

Command stimulation groups behavior which directly

Table 11

Items from Factor Analyses of Leader Behavior

Factor I   Intrusive Modeling

Item #

25. Reveals Feelings (.80)
5. Challenging (.65)
6. Confrontation (.66)
26. Reveals His Personal Values, Attitudes, Beliefs (.62)
28. Participates as a Member in the Group (.58)
7. Exhortation (.54)
27. Draws Attention to Himself (.51)

Factor II   Cognitizing
13. Providing Concepts for How to Understand (.75)
8. Explaining, Clarifying, Interpreting (.59)
12. Providing Framework for How to Change (.54)

Factor III   Command Stimulation
1. Inviting, Eliciting (−.66)
2. Questioning (−.64)
18. Suggesting Prodecure for the Group or a Person (−.61)
23. Decision Task (−.52)

Factor IV   Managing or Limit-setting
21. Suggesting or Setting Rules, Limits, Norms (−.76)
22. Setting Goals or Directions of Movement (−.67)
19. Managing Time, Sequence, Pacing, Starting and
    Stopping (−.46)
17. Stopping, Blocking, Interceding (−.41)

Factor V   Stimulating by Drawing Attention To
9. Comparing, Contrasting, Finding Similarities (−.66)
20. Focusing (−.57)
4. Calling On (−.54)

Factor VI   Mirroring
10. Summarization (.69)
24. Decision-Making (.47)
3. Reflecting (.44)

Factor VII   Affective Support
14. Protecting (−.69)
16. Offering Friendship, Love, Affection (−.61)
11. Inviting Members to Seek Feedback (−.50)
15. Support, Praise, Encouragement (−.43)

Note: Number in parenthesis is factor loading.

requests members to respond, right now, and often in a particular form. It is probably associated with leaders who are termed "directive" in psychotherapeutic parlance. *Attention-focusing* clusters behavior which solicits response more indirectly than do the first two types; it permits greater latitude to respond or not or to choose from several types of responses.

The observation that so much of leader behavior is focused on getting members to respond is of more than passing interest. Although common to all forms of encounter groups, stimulation as a prime function of leaders is perhaps the most unexamined characteristic of this movement; yet, historically, emotional contagion was the first group phenomenon to interest investigators. Le Bon, MacDougall, and Freud were all intrigued with the powerful primitive affects that could be released in groups. Until the recent advent of encounter groups, however, most work with individuals in a group context emphasized the examination and management of such affects rather than the stimulus potential of the leader. This emphasis on stimulation perhaps most truly differentiates the activity of the encounter leader from other forms of help-giving through groups. This radical departure in conception of the leader's role undoubtedly explains some of the controversy and concern which the movement has aroused in many professional and lay circles.

Of the four other dimensions, *cognitizing* consists of teaching or instructional behaviors and includes the more traditional interpretative behavior. The fact that several behaviors pragmatically considered to be coherence-making (comparing, summarizing, inviting feedback) did not appear under cognitizing suggests that they may play a smaller role in the realm of cognitive behavior than had been assumed. *Managing* or *limit-setting* represents behavior relating to the conditions of the group as a social system. Again, some behaviors initially thought to be managing are not included in this dimension; it would seem that procedures and attention-focusing were associated more with stimulation than with management of group process. *Support*, the sixth factor, clusters positive affect behaviors—protection, friendship, love, affection, support, praise, en-

Table 12
Measures on Leaders

	Variables	#3 Gestalt	#4 Gestalt	#6 Psycho-drama	#13 Synanon	#1 T-group	#18 Trans. Anal.	#12 Eclectic
BEHAVIOR FACTORS	1. Intrusive Modeling	134	125	160	182	118	50	81
	2. Cognitizing	92	98	125	107	111	170	119
	3. Command Stimulation	150	121	91	65	101	77	122
	4. Limit-setting	109	106	95	133	101	78	72
	5. Attention-focusing	59	85	153	140	99	127	57
	6. Support	174	142	128	79	147	135	59
	7. Mirroring	68	63	86	66	105	142	62
STYLE	8. Interpreter of Reality	2.0	1.8	3.7	3.8	4.2	4.4	4.5
	9. Releaser of Emotion by Suggestion	3.4	3.6	4.3	2.8	4.0	2.2	2.3
	10. Releaser of Emotion by Demonstration	3.0	4.0	5.0	4.0	1.2	1.0	2.0
	11. Personal	2.6	3.1	2.5	0.0	2.2	4.6	2.3
	12. Social Engineer	0.8	1.1	0.0	0.5	1.4	0.6	0.8
	13. Charismist	2.2	3.8	5.0	1.5	0.0	2.6	0.5
	14. Teacher	2.6	2.2	0.2	1.3	3.0	3.6	3.8
	15. Resource	1.2	0.2	0.2	0.0	1.8	1.8	1.3
	16. Challenger	2.6	3.3	5.2	4.3	1.6	1.2	2.3
	17. Model	2.7	3.6	3.3	3.7	2.8	2.8	2.9
FOCUS	18. Group	10.0	17.3	11.7	3.8	16.0	1.2	11.4
	19. Interpersonal	42.5	42.2	23.3	36.3	48.0	23.8	18.6
	20. Intrapersonal	40.0	35.6	61.7	55.0	30.0	71.3	61.3
	21. Evaluation, Observer	6.3	5.3	6.3	5.3	4.8	6.6	6.0
	22. Evaluation, Participant	5.5	4.2	5.7	4.3	4.8	4.3	5.9
	23. Nonverbal Exercises	1.55	2.00	1.90	0.00	1.30	0.00	0.37
SYMBOL	24. Charismatic	2.0	3.2	8.1	6.0	1.5	2.4	2.1
	25. Love	3.9	3.2	2.4	2.7	3.6	3.8	3.8
	26. Peer	5.7	1.6	0.5	1.6	3.2	2.6	2.6
	27. Technical	1.6	3.5	2.6	4.2	2.4	2.6	3.5

Leaders

Table 12 (Continued)
Measures on Leaders

	Variables	#2 T-group	#5 Psycho-drama	11# Rogerian	#14 Verbal Enc.	15# T-group	#7 Psycho-anal.	#9 Trans. Anal.	#10 Esalen
BEHAVIOR FACTORS	1. Intrusive Modeling	37	72	56	101	92	52	77	59
	2. Cognitizing	53	44	49	76	54	109	94	153
	3. Command Stimulation	136	70	122	87	64	55	75	178
	4. Limit Setting	137	91	78	85	84	74	91	151
	5. Attention Focusing	114	110	40	128	97	98	64	74
	6. Support	102	72	90	80	57	50	94	83
	7. Mirroring	108	120	113	107	135	138	94	104
	8. Interpreter of Reality	2.9	3.4	2.3	3.0	3.2	4.0	4.0	2.6
	9. Releaser of Emotion by Suggestion	3.6	3.0	2.0	2.4	2.6	3.1	0.0	5.2
	10. Releaser of Emotion by Demonstration	0.4	1.6	1.8	1.2	1.8	0.0	0.0	1.0
STYLE	11. Personal	1.6	2.0	1.0	1.0	0.4	1.3	1.3	1.4
	12. Social Engineer	3.1	2.8	1.0	1.2	2.0	0.2	1.0	1.8
	13. Charismist	0.4	0.4	0.0	0.4	2.6	0.4	0.0	1.4
	14. Teacher	3.1	2.0	0.5	1.0	1.0	2.9	2.5	5.2
	15. Resource	2.4	1.4	2.5	1.0	0.4	2.2	2.5	0.0
	16. Challenger	0.9	0.8	0.5	1.8	2.4	0.4	0.5	0.6
	17. Model	2.0	3.3	2.9	1.7	2.4	2.3	2.1	2.5
FOCUS	18. Group	30.0	51.7	17.5	11.0	36.3	16.0	22.5	20.0
	19. Interpersonal	52.5	17.5	47.5	27.7	17.5	6.0	32.5	27.7
	20. Intrapersonal	17.5	25.8	35.0	48.0	23.7	77.6	35.0	50.0
	21. Evaluation, Observer	4.9	3.1	5.2	5.1	6.2	4.0	3.5	5.3
	22. Evaluation, Participant	4.8	3.4	4.3	4.1	4.2	3.1	3.2	3.1
	23. Nonverbal Exercises	1.37	0.00	1.25	0.71	0.11	0.00	0.28	2.70
SYMBOL	24. Charismatic	1.0	4.5	1.6	4.0	4.0	0.4	0.7	4.0
	25. Love	4.0	3.6	3.7	1.3	0.8	2.2	0.8	3.8
	26. Peer	4.0	6.4	7.0	1.3	3.2	2.2	5.6	1.6
	27. Technical	3.0	2.4	2.2	3.8	4.8	3.8	3.4	4.2

Leaders

couragement. Inviting members to seek feedback, which had originally been classified as coherence-making, appears on this dimension as a supportive behavior. *Mirroring*, the most puzzling dimension, combines summarizing, decision-making, and reflective behavior—all behaviors originally grouped under different functions. Conceivably, this dimension represents a cluster of leader behaviors that were reactive rather than proactive.

The differences among the leaders in their tendency to use one or another of the seven dimensions are depicted in Table 12, variables 1–7. On the three response-oriented factors, leaders who stemmed from the older, more traditional forms of sensitivity training and group therapy were distinguished by their scores from leaders associated with schools that have come into prominence in the last decade. Intense stimulation through intrusive modeling or command stimulation was more characteristic of the latter group, whereas those in the older traditions are better described by attention-focusing, since they seldom exhibited intrusive modeling and made only moderate use of command stimulation. This conclusion was tested by summing each of the leaders' scores on these three stimulation dimensions, an operation which yielded the following rank order from high to low: #6 (Psychodrama), #13 (Synanon), #3 and #4 (Gestalt), #14 (Verbal Encounter), #10 (Sensory Awareness), #2 (T-group), #1 (T-group), #7 (Psychoanalytic), #9 (Transactional Analysis), #11 (Rogerian Marathon), #5 (Psychodrama), #8 (Transactional Analysis), #12 (Eclectic Marathon), #15 (T-group). Again, these findings are not surprising. Traditional T-groups conceived of change as requiring group self-analysis and non-directive leadership, considering it crucial that participants establish their own goals and learning rates (see Argyris, 1967, for a detailed theoretical discussion of this point of view). The more traditional forms of group therapy generally have maintained a historically ingrained perspective of the group as a stimulating, "regression-inducing" environment, in which the primary role of the therapist was to help individuals understand and cope with these affective states as they arose in the interpersonal interplay of the group, rather than to induce or stimulate them.

On the cognitive factor the distinction collapses between representatives of older and newer forms; some cognitive structuring is characteristic of most of the leaders, although the particular behaviors differ. The two leaders who cognitized most did so in different ways—the leader representing Transactional Analysis stressed the teaching of concepts, whereas the other high scorer, the sensory-awareness leader, emphasized instructional exercises. The Rogerian leader, one of the psychodrama leaders, and two of the T-group leaders made least use of the cognitive dimension. On the whole, the more traditionally oriented group psychotherapists were less likely to display managing behavior than were the T-group leaders and those representing the newer forms.

The managing and cognitive dimensions are probably complementary; both emphasize structured behaviors of a highly specific and often unemotional character. Some leaders who were low in cognitizing appeared relatively high in managing behavior. One of the T-group leaders provided structure through managing rather than cognitive functions, whereas one of the Transactional leaders provided structure in his group through cognitive but not managing functions. High scores on both cognitive and managing dimensions, as with the sensory awareness leader, indicate a leader who "runs a tight ship," employing highly structured sequences of behavior. Leaders who were low on both of these dimensions, such as the Rogerian leader, exemplified a leader style of low control.

Levels of supportive behavior for each leader were unrelated in any way to differences in theoretical orientation; differences in frequency of supportive expression probably reflect personality more than theoretical positions.

A broader and more personal perspective on the leaders was afforded by the observers' impressions of the leaders' overall style for each meeting. As was to be expected, leaders showed greater uniformity in their characteristic overall style than in their employment of the more discrete categories of behavior; yet the observers' ratings of leadership style in great part paral-

leled and complemented the findings on the behavioral items.
(Table 12, variables 8–17, presents leader scores on the nine
style categories averaged over all meetings.)

Differences were considerable among the leaders in how
much time they focused their attention on total group, interpersonal, or intrapersonal issues. One leader almost never
focused on the group as a whole; another did so more than half
the time (Table 12, variables 18–20)—on the average, leaders
focused on the group just under a third of their time. The
intrapersonal factor yielded a smaller range. On the average
leaders gave such issues close to half their time, but one leader
focused on an individual well under a fourth of his time, while
another did so more than three-fourths of his time.

The overall interpersonal attractiveness of the leaders
was assessed through the reactions of both observers and participants—observers for each meeting, participants for the total
series. Both groups were asked to rate the leader on seven-point
scales in respect to his competence, whether they would like to
be in a group with him, whether they admired him or were
repelled by him as a person, whether they approved of his
techniques, how much they felt he understood the group, and
whether they considered him effective or ineffective. Table 12,
variables 21–22, shows the mean rating of each leader on interpersonal attractiveness; as can be seen, participants leaned
toward the positive view more than did observers.

In change-oriented groups, leaders may create surplus
meaning or possess symbolic value for those within their purview. Although entire systems of psychotherapy are based on
the symbolic meaning a therapist has for the patient relative to
transference phenomena, the present research has largely
ignored this view of leadership. A strict transference perspective would quickly require a consideration of the led (participants), in which phenomena were explained not in terms of
properties of the leader but of the members. Rather, the symbolic value of the leader is looked at here for its relevance to
charismatic attributes of the leader.

Some distinctions between positive transference in psychotherapy and the influence of charisma are worth considering.

Positive transference implies properties or characteristics primarily of the patient and not of the therapist. In contrast, in the relationship of encounter group members to charismatic leaders, the locus of analysis is the characteristics of the leader and not of the member. The second critical difference is that an operational definition of charisma rests upon the assumption of unanimity of perception in the led. To define the qualities of a charismatic leader one needs to define a set of perceptions that members share. A positive transference model permits variations in perception which do not fit the concept of charisma.

To assess symbolic value, a forty-item charisma questionnaire was devised which required participants to select the word which best described the leader from ten sets of four words. Each set contained a word associated with charisma, with a love orientation, a peer orientation, and a technical orientation.

Interest in charisma has waxed and waned in modern-day psychology; it has generally been introduced into the psychological literature as conceived by Weber regarding political ideology, and it has been used from time to time by political scientists interested in the psychological relationships of charismatic political leaders to the governed. The central properties of charisma in this view are a belief in the magical qualities of the leader—a sense that he is uniquely endowed; a sense of having a special or a unique relationship to him; and a willingness to be influenced by him. Characteristic phrases refer to his inspirational sense of a personal mission, his vision, bouyant confidence, sanctity, devotion, exemplary character, exceptional or divine power, or supernatural or superhuman ability. He does not communicate internal conflict but presents an appearance of an unruffled belief in himself and what he is doing. As portrayed in the literature of political science, charismatic leaders can sustain a shift from traditional norms or maintain adherents from a position somewhat outside the normative system of the society. The charismatic leader gives meaning to others' behavior; he validates the disciple's action and sanctions otherwise unsanctionable acts. The charismatic leader's person and ideology are intertwined and inseparable.

Following such themes in the social science literature, a charismatic encounter leader, on this assessment, was presented as one who was inspiring and imposing, really believed in what he did, was stimulating, had a vision or sense of mission, and so on. A love-oriented leader symbolized giving, understanding, genuineness, caring, sympathy, warmth, openness, kindness, and was a person with whom members wanted to be. The peer-oriented leader was defined as one who created little social distance—a "nice guy," related, relaxed, easy-going, one of us, a friend, easy to get close to. The technically-oriented leader was defined as one who expressed expertise, intelligence, solidity, decisiveness, competence, knowledge, skill. Table 12 (variables 24-27) presents each leader's score on these four qualities.

BASIC FUNCTIONS

These assessments of leader behavior by differing levels and kinds imply some redundance in what they tapped, although till now they have been discussed as separate approaches to describing leader behavior. In order to establish higher-order abstractions from the plethora of information yielded by these assessments, the twenty-seven variables describing leader behavior were intercorrelated. The number of high positive and negative correlations suggested that fewer variables were needed to describe leader behavior. When the twenty-seven variables were factor analyzed, four clusters emerged which accounted for 75 per cent of the variance. Table 13 shows the four rotated factors and the loadings on each of the twenty-seven variables.

Much of what the leaders do, as both participants and observers see them, can be subsumed under four basic functions: emotional stimulation, caring, meaning attribution, and executive behavior. These four dimensions may constitute an empirically derived taxonomy for examining leadership in all forms of groups aimed at personal change, be they therapy or personal growth groups. Table 14, which shows the scores of each of the leaders on the four basic dimensions, suggests that these dimensions can produce discriminations among leaders of highly varied orientation.

Table 13

Rotated Factors of Leader Variables

	Variable	1(30%)[a]	2(20%)	3(14%)	4(10%)
Leader Behavior Factors	1. Int. Model	0.91	0.16	−0.11	−0.00
	2. Cog. Inp.	0.03	−0.23	−0.87	−0.27
	3. Command Response	−0.12	−0.35	0.02	−0.71
	4. Set Limits	0.10	0.00	0.13	−0.86
	5. Draw Atten.	0.31	0.03	−0.05	0.02
	6. Mirror	−0.58	0.09	0.17	0.21
	7. Support	0.20	−0.69	−0.04	−0.10
Leader Style	8. Interpret Reality	−0.20	0.04	−0.50	0.38
	9. Releaser of Emot. Sug.	0.32	−0.37	0.13	−0.76
	10. Releaser Emot. Demo.	0.96	−0.18	−0.02	−0.05
	11. Personal Leader	−0.02	−0.82	−0.32	0.08
	12. Social Engineer	−0.36	−0.08	0.77	−0.37
	13. Charismist	0.71	−0.19	−0.13	−0.12
	14. Teacher	−0.44	−0.29	−0.47	−0.59
	15. Resource	−0.77	−0.20	0.09	0.51
	16. Challenger	0.90	−0.01	−0.15	−0.03
	17. Model	0.76	−0.41	−0.07	0.04
Leader Focus	18. Group	−0.15	0.08	0.79	−0.03
	19. Interpersonal	−0.04	−0.36	0.33	−0.24
	20. Intrapersonal	0.10	0.06	−0.89	0.15
Intp. Attract.	21. Obs Liking	0.34	−0.43	−0.13	0.10
	22. Member Liking	0.32	−0.21	−0.31	−0.12
	23. Games	0.44	−0.03	0.04	−0.89
Member Perception	24. Charisma	0.78	0.04	−0.03	−0.25
	25. Love	−0.22	−0.86	−0.08	−0.26
	26. Peer	−0.40	−0.18	0.44	0.37
	27. Expert	−0.18	0.88	−0.22	0.15

[a] Percentage of variance extracted by factor.

Intrusive modeling is the critical leader behavior on the *dimension of emotional* stimulation. Style characteristics related to emotional stimulation are the releaser of emotion by demonstration, the challenger, and the model. Observer and member ratings of high charisma are loaded heavily on emotional stimulation, whereas mirroring, teaching and resource function, and participant perceptions of peer-orientation are negatively associated. Emotional stimulation appears to be a dimension centered in the person of the leader; the very presence of the leader is a salient feature of the group experience. This dimension organized behavior which sends psychological signals adding up to "be like me," "see me," "I am here—omnipresent." Emotional stimulation is a high-input dimension, characterized by manifold uses of self.

Caring clusters support items and the stylistic rating of the personal leader as seen by observers and love-oriented as perceived by participants; a technical orientation is negatively associated. Caring is clearly a warm/cold, love/not-love dimension. (This dimension should not be confused with interpersonal attractiveness, for members' feelings about leaders are not associated with it. Liking leaders is more related to emotional stimulation than to caring.)

Meaning-attribution represents cognitive behaviors which offer the participants ideas, concepts, or values about change through the encounter group. This dimension clusters high scores on cognitive items (how to understand, explaining, clarifying, interpreting, how to change), a style rating of interpreter of reality and an intrapsychic focus. High scores on social-engineering style, group focus, and peer-orientation represent the bipolar aspect of this dimension. Meaning-attribution represents the naming function of leader behavior, wherein the leader gives meaning to experiences that members undergo. It refers to the translation of feelings and behavior into ideas. The perception of members that leaders who do not assume this function are more like peers suggests that qualities of parent, priest, or pedagogue may be associated with this dimension. Meaning-attribution, however, does not have the emotional valence of charisma.

Executive function clusters two categories of leader behavior—limit-setting (setting rules, limits, norms; setting goals; managing time; stopping) and command response (inviting,

Table 14

Leader Scores on Four Basic Dimensions

	Dimension 1 Emotional Stimulation			Dimension 2 Caring	
Score	Group Type	Leader No.	Score	Group Type	Leader No.
25			15		
	Psychodrama	# 6			
				Gestalt	# 3
20					
			12		
	Synanon	#13		Trans. Anal.	# 8
	Gestalt	# 4			
				T-group	# 1
				Gestalt	# 4
15					
	Gestalt	# 3	9		
10					
	T-group	#15		T-group	# 2
	Eclec. Mara.	#12		Psychodrama	# 6
	Sens. Aware.	#10		Eclec. Mara.	#12
	Verbal Enc.	#14		Sens. Aware.	#10
				Rogerian	#11
	Trans. Anal.	#18			
5	T-group	# 1	6		
	Psychodrama	# 5			
				Psychodrama	# 5
	Rogerian	#11			
	T-group	# 2		Synanon	#13
	Psychoanal.	# 7	3		
0	Trans. Anal.	# 9			
				Verbal Enc.	#14
				Trans. Anal.	# 9
				Psychoanal.	# 7
			0	T-group	#15

Table 14 (Continued)

Leader Scores on Four Basic Dimensions

Dimension 3 Meaning Attribution			Dimension 4 Executive Function		
Score	Group Type	Leader No.	Score	Group Type	Leader No.
15			18		
	Trans. Anal.	# 8		Sens. Aware.	#10
12	Psychodrama	# 6	15		
	Eclec. Mara.	#12			
	Psychoanal.	# 7	12		
	Synanon	#13		Gestalt	# 4
9				Gestalt	# 3
	Sens. Aware.	#10		T-group	# 2
	Gestalt	#14	9		
	Gestalt	# 3		T-group	# 1
	T-group	# 1		Psychodrama	# 6
	Verbal Enc.	#14	6	Synanon	#13
6				Eclec. Mara.	#12
	Trans. Anal.	# 9		Psychodrama	# 5
	T-group	#15		Trans. Anal.	# 8
3				Verbal Enc.	#14
	Rogerian	#11	3	T-group	#15
	T-group	# 2		Rogerian	#11
0	Psychodrama	# 5		Trans. Anal.	# 9
			0	Psychoanal.	# 7

eliciting, questioning, suggesting procedures). It is associated with observer style-ratings of releasing emotion by suggestion and member perceptions of a teacher-orientation, as well as with the use of structured exercises or games. The observer style-rating of resource leader is negatively associated. Executive function represents behavior primarily directed toward management of the group as a social system and behavior which also makes heavy use of structured material as a mechanism for goal-achievement.

These four dimensions are basic in the sense that all leaders exhibited some of the behavior they encompass. One further dimension accounted for a smaller percentage of variance—the leader's interpersonal attractiveness. It does not have the same properties as these basic dimensions, insofar as it is a derivative dimension, representing evaluation of leader behavior rather than the behavior itself.

Leader attractiveness to members was less related to other leader behavior variables than was attractiveness to observers, who were more specific in both their positive and negative evaluations. Participants liked leaders who produced high amounts of cognitive behavior and who were perceived as charismatic. They did not like resource or social engineering styles or those which were peer-oriented or group-focused. Observers liked intrusive modeling behavior, charismatic style, and leaders whom members perceived as love-oriented. They did not like mirroring behavior, group focus, or leaders who were perceived by members as technicians. Observers and participants both liked leaders who showed supportive behavior, who encouraged release of emotion by demonstration, and who were challenging. Caution, however, should be exercised regarding these relationships. Only charismatic style and challenging style, group focus, mirroring behavior, and release of emotions by demonstration reach .05 level of significance (.50 correlations). There may be some association between liking and particular behaviors, but it is not as high as one might expect.

BEHAVIOR AND OUTCOME

At the end of the experience, each participant was classified as having been a high-learner, a moderate-changer,

having been relatively untouched by the experience, as showing patterns of predominately negative changes, as having
dropped out of the group prior to termination for psychological
reasons, or as having become a psychiatric casualty. These
classifications were given numerical weights: plus three for a
high-learner, plus two for *moderate-changer,* 0 for *unchanged,*
minus one for a *dropout,* minus two for a *negative-changer,* and
minus three for a *casualty.* The details of classification procedure are beyond the scope of this chapter. Each case was
reviewed using test scores from a variety of instruments and
perspectives. Included were attitude measures, value measures,
self-rating of change, self-esteem and self-ideal discrepancy,
conceptions of others, measures of the person's propensity to
use adequate or inadequate coping strategies, interpersonal
behaviors, testimony, leader evaluation, judgments made by the
participants' social network, and the congruence between self-
ratings and peer perception, as well as interviews and other
collateral data when they were available (for approximately 50
per cent of the cases).

Table 15 shows how leader behavior is associated with
outcome. The most effective leadership style would combine
moderate stimulation, high caring, use of meaning-attribution,

Table 15

Relationship Between Leader Behavior and Outcome

	Levels of Leader Variables		
	Low	Medium	High
Stimulation	−04[b]	33	20
Caring	−12	23	55
Executive Function	−09	61	05

	None	Group Focus	Individual Focus
Meaning-Attribution [a]	−16	17	65

[a] Note that meaning attribution is a bi-polar factor. High scores
on the positive end indicate high meaning attribution directed toward individuals; high scores on the negative end indicate meaning attribution
behavior directed toward the group; and low scores indicate leaders who
did not engage in either of these two forms of meaning attribution.

[b] Scores in the body of this table show mean levels of outcome.

and moderate expression of executive functions. Conversely, the less effective leaders are either very low or very high on stimulation, are low in caring, do very little meaning-attribution, and display too little or too much executive behavior.

Another way to clarify these findings was to examine the relationship between four basic leader dimensions and outcome using correlations. The results of both the analysis of high, medium, and low and the correlations showed that stimulation is associated with outcome in a curvilinear fashion. Leaders who have too much or too little of it are unsuccessful. Similarly, leaders who exhibit too much or too little executive function tend to be unsuccessful. The caring dimension showed a linear relationship—overall success is associated with high caring. Meaning-attribution, again, is a linear relationship in the sense that meaning-attribution of either kind is associated with success while low levels are related to failure.

As these four dimensions are used to create leader typologies, some patterns of effective and ineffective leader style become more apparent. Thus, for example, high stimulation combined with high caring behavior takes on a different meaning when the leader also displays high levels of executive function rather than moderate ones. Or perhaps a better illustration would be that high caring behavior in the absence of meaning-attribution generates relatively low levels of success as compared with high caring behavior within a cognitive framework. Thus, for example, leader #1 and leader #8 are both moderate (see Table 14) on stimulation; they are both high in caring, and both engage in a moderate amount of executive function; they differ in that leader #8 provides a high level of meaning-attribution while this activity is absent in the behavior of leader #1. Thus, caring is a critical function of leaders, but it alone is apparently not sufficient to ensure high success. Another illustration is provided by examining the scores of leader #12 and leader #8. These leaders mirror one another on level of stimulation, meaning-attribution, and executive function. They differ in that leader #12 shows moderate caring, compared to the high level of leader #8. Their outcome scores are both positive, but leader #8 is the most successful leader in our study, while leader #12 is fourth in positive outcome. The two central functions, without which leaders rarely were successful, therefore appear to be caring and meaning-attribution. In other words, a combination of high levels of affectional behavior and high levels of cognitive input is critical.

BEHAVIOR AND SCHOOL OF ORIENTATION

As has been mentioned earlier, one question of interest was to assess whether conventional labels, such as Gestalt, T-group, sensory awareness, and so on, were meaningful descriptions of methodological differences among encounter leaders. The findings generated by the factor analysis which has just been described made it possible to find out. Using scores on the basic behavioral dimensions, a statistical clustering procedure yielded these groupings: a verbal-encounter leader and one T-group leader; the eclectic-marathon leader, a Transactional Analysis leader, and one T-group leader; the Rogerian marathon leader, one psychodrama leader, and one T-group leader; the psychoanalytic leader and one Transactional Analysis leader; one psychodrama leader and the two Synanon leaders; and the two Gestalt leaders. The Esalen eclectic leader did not resemble any of the other leaders.

Clearly, clusters do not support a view that leaders labeled similarly behave similarly in encounter groups. A less stringent method used to evaluate actual likenesses was to look at the degree of the similarity among leaders who might be expected to be similar. The three T-group leaders, for example, were examined to determine their similarity to each other as compared with their similarity to other leaders. This procedure produced two ranks per pair; for example, T-group leader #1 and T-group leader #2 had a rank of 9—eight other leaders were closer to leader #1 than was leader #2; leader #2, however, was ranked 3 with leader #15, so that only two other leaders were closer to leader #2 than was leader #15. The mean rank for these three T-group leaders was 5.3. The second pairing expected would be the two Gestalt leaders, who were paired by the clustering method. The rank for them was 1. The two psychodrama leaders—leader #6 and leader #5—had a

mean rank of 12. The two Transactional Analysis leaders had a
mean rank of 8. The two marathon leaders (leader #11 and
leader #12) had a mean rank of 7. Overall, except for the two
Gestalt leaders, the similarities based upon orientation were
indeed weak, if existent at all. Whatever the labels of the
diverse encounter leaders, the findings are indisputable that
conventional categories of leader orientation are poor predictors of leader behavior.

While the finding that encounter leaders' behavior is
highly varied diverges from reports in the literature on individual psychotherapy showing that experienced psychotherapists tend to do pretty much the same thing (as opposed to
novitiates), it is no surprise that in a new field characterized by
heavy borrowing, on the one hand, and the affirmation of doing
one's own thing, on the other, orthodoxy has little influence.
Marked similarities existed in how leaders approached the task
of running an encounter group, but these similarities were not
associated with school of thought.

LEADER TYPES

To develop an empirical typology of leaders derived
from the twenty-seven behavioral variables, leaders who shared
similar profiles were grouped. Scores for each leader on emotional stimulation, caring, meaning-attribution and executive
function were plotted on a series of graphs to provide a visual
image of the ways in which leaders were similar one to another. Leaders #3, #4, #6, and #13, for example, could be
grouped as high in emotional stimulation and meaning-attribution (Table 14). A more exact statistical procedure for developing a typology produced the same groups of leader types as the
inspection method. Six clusters or leader types were identified
from the two clustering methods. Type A—leaders #3 and #4
(Gestalt), leader #6 (Psychodrama), and #13 (Synanon);
Type B—leader #12 (Eclectic Marathon), leader #8 (Transactional Analysis), and leader #1 (T-group); Type C—leader #2
(T-group), leader #5 (Psychodrama) and leader #11 (Rogerian Marathon); Type D—leader #7 (Psychoanalytic) and
leader #9 (Transactional Analysis); Type E—leader #14 (Ver-

bal Encounter) and leader #15 (T-group); leader #10 (Esalen Eclectic) did not resemble any other leader, but represented a single type—Type F.

Type A—Energizers. The definitive characteristic of these leaders is intense emotional stimulation. They all gave moderate-to-high attention to executive functions and, with the exception of the two Synanon leaders, were similarly high on caring. They were perceived as the most charismatic. Among those studied, only these leaders were strongly attached to an articulated belief-system, as well as emotionally tied to the founder of their school of thought. Subsequent to leading the research group, the leader of group #6 was reportedly persuaded by the head of a Far Eastern religious sect to give up leading encounter groups because it elicited behaviors which the head of the sect felt to be "narcissistic" and not in keeping with the belief-system. Synanon exhibited characteristics of a revitalization movement and is more strongly influenced by the charismatic qualities of its founder than are any of the other types of encounter groups studied. Despite examples of other influences in the Synanon format, Synanon leaders perceive the founder of the movement as the originator of all innovations for changing individuals. Synanon rituals include a formal prayer, suggestive of the heavy religious overtones of the movement. The Gestalt school, founded by Fritz Perls, also has a sectlike flavor. Witness the published posters of Perls' sayings which have taken on the character of a Gestalt prayer.

The parallels among these five men as encounter leaders and as followers of "religiostic" movements are striking; all five communicated a faith in what they did that went beyond that which characterizes members of the healing professions as a whole. This is not to imply that other leaders possessed no similar qualities, nor that the zealousness of the charismatic type was not mixed with some of the more characteristic qualities of the traditional mental health professional. The religious quality of the behavior was dominant, however, in the charismatic type, allowing them to feel assured in taking over for participants and asserting firm control. They felt ready, willing, and able to guide participants forward, to "turn them on" to the road to salvation—they may even have seen this form of help as their most signal contribution.

As might be expected, the level of proselytizing behavior was highest for members of groups led by charismatic leaders, which again supports the grouping of these leaders under the banner of charisma.

Type B—Providers. Leaders of this type specialize in caring and meaning-attribution (two of these leaders were high on individually oriented meaning-attribution; one was moderate). They evidence moderate use of emotional stimulation and executive function. These were individually focused leaders who gave love as well as information and ideas about how to change. They exuded a quality of enlightened paternalism; they were good daddies; they subscribed to some systematic theory about how individuals learn which they used in the group, but which they did not press.

Type C—Social Engineers. The definitive characteristic of these leaders was their use of group-oriented meaning-attribution. These leaders were group-focused and were seen by observers as concerned with how people related to the social system. These leaders were not personal in style, in the sense that loving leaders were, but did exhibit a moderate amount of caring, indicating relatively high levels of support and affection. Type C leaders were uniformly low on emotional stimulation. Their exercise of executive function ranged from little to frequent, however. These leaders mainly offered the communication of support and steered the work of the group as a whole, rather than offering aid on individual or interpersonal issues. Their group members saw these leaders as low in charisma and high in peer-orientation.

Type D—Impersonals. These leaders were distant, aggressive stimulators; they were moderately high on emotional stimulation and low on caring and executive function. In a word, they were impersonal. Neither Type D leader was particularly high on meaning-attribution, although the differences in their scores on this dimension indicate that one was more group oriented and one more individually oriented.

Type E—Laissez-Faire. These leaders obtained the lowest scores on three of the four basic dimensions—emotional stimulation, caring (their behavior was characteristically impersonal), and executive function—and had moderate to high scores only on meaning-attribution. These leaders ape the classical descriptions of laissez-faire leaders because as a group they lack a cluster of any of the behaviors assessed in the study. They were generally low on input; they neither stimulated emotions nor controlled group conditions, nor did they offer support. They were generalists insofar as their behavior revealed no consistent pattern of the dimensions employed in the study. The symbolic meaning of the Type E leaders to their group members was as technicians. They had some views about how people learn in the encounter situation and communicated some ideas to group members, as shown by their relatively high scores on meaning-attribution. This communication, however, was not reinforced through behavior tapped by the other three dimensions.

Type F—Manager. This leader was uniquely characterized by his extreme score on the executive dimension. Unusual degrees of control were exercised on how, about what, and for how long members interacted with one another. The use of frequent structured exercises (an average of eight per group session) was the major, but not only, form of control used. The observers informally labeled him "top sergeant," which perhaps better than any other data characterize the sense of this leader.

CONSEQUENCES OF LEADER TYPES

This section considers, by using outcome data as well as participants' reactions during the group, the following questions: (1) How successful were the types in producing change? How many learners, how many unchanged people, and what proportion of negative outcomes occurred in groups led by these various types of leaders? (2) To what extent do particular leader types generate enthusiasm, and to what extent is such enthusiasm converted into postgroup proselytizing? (3) What are the perceptions of the participants about the time they were in the groups? What did they emphasize as unique to the experience?

As mentioned earlier, at the end of the experience participants were classified in six categories of effect. Table 16 shows these outcomes for the six leader types and the tape groups. Clearly, Type B leaders (Providers) were by far the most effective in producing positive changes while minimizing the number of participants who had negative outcomes—negative-changers, dropouts and casualties. Next to Type B leaders, the tape groups showed the highest *relative* gain score—a score that reflects the tape groups' extremely low number of negative outcomes combined with only a moderate number of high-learners and moderate-changers. Type C leaders (Social Engineers) displayed a relatively balanced picture of few dropouts and some casualties who were balanced by a large number of high-learners. Type A leaders (Energizers) produced some high-learners and many moderate-changers, but also a high number of casualties and dropouts. On balance, then, B, C, and A leaders as well as the tape groups produced a relative gain; Types D (Impersonals), E (Laissez-Faire), and F (Manager) all produced a relative loss—that is, a higher percentage of negative than positive or neutral outcomes. Type D and Type F leaders produced no high-learners at all; Type E had a few high-learners who were balanced by an equal number of casualties and a large number of dropouts. The poorest leader style is clearly Type F; not one participant showed positive change—there were no high-learners or moderate-changers, most participants were untouched, a few showed negative outcomes.

A not infrequent statement in the encounter group field is that what the best encounter leaders (the most successful) do involves high-risk procedures; these high-risk procedures are also seen as being the most productive for major learning or change. In short, there has been an association between high risk and high yield. When one looks at the percentage of high-learners or casualties produced by each of the six leader types, however, (see Table 16) it becomes clear that the Type B and Type C leaders, who are not especially associated with risk, produced the most high learning (one-fifth of all participants in their groups were high-learners at the end of the experience). The highest risk leaders, Type A, produced many fewer high-

Table 16

Leader Type and Outcome

Leader Type	N	High-learner a	Moderate-changer b	Unchanged c	Negative Change d	Dropout e	Casualty f	Weighted Impact Average g
A Energizers	60	8–13%	12–20%	19–32%	4–07%	10–17%	7–12%	+.15
B Provides	36	8–22%	13–36%	8–22%	3–08%	3–08%	1–03%	+1.06
C Social Engineers	34	7–21%	2–06%	15–44%	5–15%	2–06%	3–09%	+.12
D Impersonals	19	0– 0%	7–64%	3–16%	2–11%	5–26%	2–11%	–.05
E Laissez-Faire	27	2–07%	1–04%	13–48%	0– 0%	9–33%	2–07%	–.26
F Manager	10	0– 0%	0– 0%	7–70%	1–10%	1–10%	1–10%	–.60
G Tape Groups	27	3–11%	5–19%	13–48%	2–07%	4–15%	0– 0%	+.41

learners. A rank-order correlation between percentages of high-learners and percentages of casualties indicates that they were correlated —.33, clearly indicating that the data lend little credence to the notion that high risk is necessary in order to achieve a high level of growth.

As is also indicated by Table 16 the high-risk Type A leaders also produced the highest number of casualties. A case examination of individual casualties suggested overstimulation by the group leader as a primary pathway toward casualty status. Situations in which the leader inadequately protected someone under attack by other members of the group were also contributed to casualty status.

Both Type A leaders and Type D leaders conducted groups with high casualty rates; both types were characterized by aggressive stimulation and relatively high charisma. (The relatively high number of casualties in groups led by the laissez-faire Type E leaders was probably the consequence of omission rather than a direct result of leader behavior itself.) Aside from the tape groups, Type B leaders produced the smallest number of casualties; it is useful to recall that their behavior combined high support and moderate structuring with lower levels of stimulation. The tape groups, which produced no casualties, may provide a key to understanding the relationship of leader behavior to casualty status. An analysis of leader "behavior" in the tape groups indicates that the prototypical interventions are meaning-attribution and executive behavior. Thus, on one hand, the tape groups differ markedly from Type A leaders in that they provide low levels of stimulation; on the other hand, they do not resemble the laissez-faire leaders in that the tapes provide a highly structured environment with clear guidelines for behavior. Observer reports for the tape groups indicated that they tended to avoid intense conflict; the absence of high leader-induced stimulation and perhaps the high degree of structure made the tape groups safe.

Enthusiasm, being "turned on," is a psychological state which for many is synonymous with being a participant in an encounter group. Back (1972) describes such an affect state in terms of religiosity. Reflections on encounter groups that have appeared in the mass media clearly mirror high enthusiasm (as, for example, the movie *Bob and Carol and Ted and Alice*). That most participants in this study were enthusiastic at the end of the groups reflects the same theme. (Sixty-five per cent of those who completed the groups found the group pleasant, 57 per cent had been turned on to the group, 78 per cent said it had been a constructive experience, and 61 per cent stated that a person learned a great deal.) Turning to the implication of such psychological states in relation to personal change, Chapter 7 reports no correlation between enthusiasm and judgments of change by peers or by the leader. It is elsewhere noted (Lieberman and others, 1972) that enthusiasm was asymetrically related to change as measured by other tests, so that, while positive changes in many of the test indices were associated with enthusiasm about the experience, many enthusiastic participants did not show change despite their enthusiasm.

What of the relationship between being turned on and leader style? When the groups ended, all participants were asked to indicate the degree to which they saw the experience as pleasant, turned on, constructive, and beneficial to their learning. Mean scores (on a 7-point scale with 7 as high) were: Type A, 4.9; Type B, 5.0; Type C, 4.2; Type D, 4.2; Type E, 3.2; and Type F, 3.1. Overall, participants expressed moderate enthusiasm, with Type A and Type B leaders producing the highest degree of enthusiasm among their participants. Upon readministration of the same questionnaire six months later, there was some decline in the degree of enthusiasm, with large drops in the level of enthusiasm expressed by those with Type A leaders and in the tape groups and moderate drops for those with Type C and Type D leaders. Evaluations of those with Type B and Type F leaders remained stable.

These positive evaluations, of course, are not necessarily equivalent to the behavior and psychological meaning intended by Back in attributing a characteristic of religiosity, nor do they necessarily reflect the feelings mirrored in popular descriptions of encounter groups. To pursue this issue further, six to eight months after the encounter groups terminated, a questionnaire was administered to all participants which attempted to assess proselytizing behavior. The interest here was to understand the type of psychological response to encounter groups that is expressed in becoming a convert, wanting to spread the word. Participants were asked: "Since your group experience, have you encouraged others to participate in encounter groups?" Responses could range from "No, I've actively discouraged people," to "I frequently find myself encouraging people to get an experience in an encounter group." Proselytizing behavior was defined as frequently encouraging people. Of the 15 per cent who indicated that they had proselytized, 24 per cent represented Type A leaders; 20 per cent Type B; 7 per cent Type C; 10 per cent Type D; 0 per cent Type E; 17 per cent Type F; and 10 per cent tape groups. Clearly, these responses were not randomly distributed among leader types.

These observations on proselytizing behavior are not surprising. The description of Type A leaders as charismatic would lead one to expect their participants to behave as disciples. The enthusiasm generated in Type B groups and the high number of learners in those groups make understandable the positive aura and tendency to proselytize of participants in such groups. Less obvious is the reaction of 17 per cent of members in the Type F group who engaged in proselytizing, despite the absence of any learners in that group.

Clearly there are several alternative pathways to proselytizing behavior and conversion, not all of which necessarily depend on positive outcome for the participant. The high level of proselytizing demonstrated, particularly by members of Types A, B, and F leader groups, suggests that charismatic leaders, the experience of significant positive change, and highly structured activities ("games") (Drury, 1971) all have some role in leading to what has been described frequently as conversion behavior. No wonder then that the encounter group movement has created a rapidly expanding "cultlike" group. The prototype of the Type A leader is characteristic of a large number of encounter leaders; this was the most common style of leadership employed by the study leaders. When, prior to launching the study groups, each leader was asked to indicate on the leader questionnaire how he was usually seen by the groups he led, more leaders saw themselves as charismatic than as characterized by any other emotional symbol; often leaders saw themselves as more charismatic than they were seen to be by participants or observers.

A bit of reflection on the development of the encounter group movement and on the statements of its dominant leaders suggests that with few exceptions encounter groups involve activities and expectations heavily influenced by charismatic founders and that the movement appears to attract leaders who share or desire to emulate qualities of the founders. Although the total amount of enthusiasm observed cannot be associated specifically with leaders (for some comes from a specific type of activity), clearly leaders, particularly if they are charismatic, play an important role in creating a self-perpetuating movement by producing converts who wish to induce others to undergo the experience. Even some participants who suffered intense psychological harm from being in an encounter group were still quite willing to endorse encounter groups and saw them as useful for others.

Another perspective on the effects of the diverse leader styles is offered by the members' perceptions of the group during the life of the group. What kinds of psychological opportunities did the various leader styles offer to members of their groups? Significant differences among leader types were revealed in participants' evaluations of the degree to which groups provided opportunities for feedback, for knowing others deeply, for open and honest encounters with their peers, for being able to share with their peers, for novel experiences, and for opportunities to express trust or anger or being direct. Participants in Type A (Energizer) groups emphasized the increased opportunities for novel experiences and for the expression of anger, while those in Type B (Provider) groups emphasized the increased opportunities to share with their peers. Type C (Social Engineer) participants stressed the increased opportunity for obtaining feedback about their behavior. Members of Type D (Impersonal) groups evidenced no distinct reaction and reflect the average scores for the total participant population. Those in Type E (Laissez-Faire) groups were the most highly distinguished and rated the experience as decreasing the opportunity for feedback, knowing others deeply, sharing with peers, having novel experiences, and getting out their anger. Participants in the Type F (Manager) group stressed the lowered opportunity to share with peers and express anger. Those in the tape groups reported increased opportunity to know others deeply and share with peers.

These differing perceptions of the groups by the participants are consonant with the underlying behavior patterns of the leaders. Thus, for example, it is not surprising that the behavior of Type A leaders, which has been described in terms of intense stimulation and charisma, would lead participants to view their groups as providing increased opportunity for novel experiences and for the expression of angry feelings, an issue frequently associated with intensely stimulating behavior. The stress on increased sharing with peers by participants in Type B groups mirrors the characterization of Type B as displaying high caring behavior and high meaning-attribution with moderate levels of stimulation—to wit an emphasis on moderated conflict and on closeness or warmth. Similarly the emphasis of Type C leaders on group conditions articulates with members' perception of increased feedback. Participants in groups with Type E, Laissez-Faire leadership reflect disappointment in the experience in their uniformly low ratings of opportunities, perhaps because the character of the experience in no large way met their expectations of the special qualities they associated with encounter groups. The Type F leader, who was characterized by highly controlling behavior, restricted getting at other issues—relationships with peers and the expression of anger. Members of the tape groups, those without an actual leader, mirrored an obvious peer emphasis in their opportunity ratings of knowing one another deeply and sharing with their peers.

Another perspective of participants' perceptions may be gained by examining critical incident reports. At the end of each meeting, participants were asked to indicate what event in the group they felt most important for them personally and in what ways it was important. These critical incidents were

Table 17
The Effects of Leader Style on Participants' Perception of Their Group Experience

| | Leader Type | | | | | | | |
	A	B	C	D	E	F	G (Tapes)	Overall Means
Event								
1. Expression of feeling, unspecified	12%	16%	13%	20%	19%	24%	21%	16%
2. Expression of positive feeling	09%	08%	04%	05%	03%	01%	04%	06%
3. Expression of negative feeling [a]	21%	13%	10%	18%	17%	05%	12%	15%
4. Experience of positive feeling [a]	08%	04%	10%	03%	05%	03%	09%	07%
5. Experience of negative feeling [a]	05%	02%	04%	00%	01%	04%	10%	04%
6. Feedback [a]	10%	08%	18%	14%	11%	18%	19%	13%
7. Insight	06%	08%	04%	05%	02%	06%	05%	05%
8. Self-Disclosure [a]	16%	23%	22%	11%	18%	33%	11%	19%
9. Abstract Discussion [a]	13%	18%	15%	23%	24%	05%	10%	15%
Target								
10. Active self	28%	27%	28%	24%	35%	38%	33%	29%
11. Passive self	14%	08%	13%	13%	10%	14%	11%	12%
12. Not self [a]	36%	39%	33%	50%	26%	31%	19%	34%
13. Group [a]	21%	26%	26%	13%	30%	19%	36%	25%
Personal Meaning								
14. Love [a]	20%	20%	18%	04%	14%	12%	19%	17%
15. I'm like others	04%	04%	02%	00%	06%	07%	05%	04%
16. Altruism	02%	04%	04%	00%	01%	03%	00%	02%
17. Personal mastery [a]	10%	05%	08%	04%	07%	15%	09%	08%
18. Group mastery [a]	06%	06%	12%	14%	16%	08%	14%	10%
19. Empathy	06%	04%	04%	07%	02%	05%	01%	04%
20. All negative feeling	18%	19%	17%	25%	26%	20%	25%	20%
21. Insight	18%	20%	14%	21%	10%	15%	13%	16%
22. Information	14%	18%	22%	26%	19%	15%	13%	18%

[a] Significant at p = .05, one-way analysis of variance.

Note: Percentages add to 100 per cent in each classification: Event, Target, Personal Meaning.

categorized in terms of the event referred to, the target of the event, and the meaning participants attributed to it. The nine event categories, the four target categories, and the nine categories used to classify meaning are presented in Table 17. This table shows the percentage of total responses for each of the leader types as well as the tape groups. The last column shows the overall mean for the total group of participants (approximately fifteen hundred critical events were scored).

Participants in groups conducted by Type A leaders (Energizers) emphasized the expression of negative feelings and experiencing as prototypical events. Feelings of love and personal mastery were the prototypical meanings of the events cited as critical.

Participants in groups led by Type B leaders (Providers) did not emphasize the experiencing aspects of events and were not likely to see feedback as crucial—the events they most emphasized related to self-disclosure. Participants in Type B groups also emphasized love as a meaningful response and did not see personal mastery as crucial in their experience. Participants in Type C (Social Engineer) groups selected events of feedback and self-disclosure as crucial and did not see the expression of feelings, particularly positive ones, as central. Like participants in Type A and Type B groups, they emphasized love. They stress, however, group mastery in contrast to Type A's emphasis on personal mastery.

Participants in Type D (Impersonal) groups reported discussions as the prototypical event and emphasized the expression of negative feelings. Frequently participants in such groups chose events that happened to other individuals as most critical for themselves; unlike many participants in other types of groups, they did not emphasize group-level events. The meaning they attached to critical events differed in several important respects from that of all other participants. The response of love was almost totally absent. The emphasis was on group mastery as a meaningful aspect of their experience. Then, too, participants in groups led by Type D leaders did not emphasize self-disclosure or experiencing as salient events.

Participants in groups led by Type E leaders (Laissez-

Faire) emphasized events characterized by discussions and the expression of negative feelings, but not the experience of affects. They were more likely than most to emphasize as critical those events which involved the whole group; their most salient distinguishing response was group mastery.

Participants in groups led by Type F leaders (Managers) emphasized self-disclosure and feedback and gave little importance to the expression of feelings, particularly negative ones, the experience of positive feelings, or discussion. For these participants, the distinguishing prototypical response—that is, the meaning events had to them—was an emphasis on personal mastery. They were less likely to emphasize the feeling of love as a salient meaning of the event and they were less likely to emphasize group mastery. Members of the two tape groups emphasized the experiencing aspects of events and feedback and tended not to see self-disclosure as central in their experience. More often than participants under other leadership conditions, they emphasized group events. The meaning evoked tended to be love, personal mastery, and group mastery.

Table 17 points to a considerable communality among participants regarding the meaning of events, as well as the target and, to some extent, the events themselves. But there were important differences in what the groups felt like to participants under different leader types. There were uniform experiences associated with being a participant in a group led by a particular style of leader. A clear conclusion is that the type of leader one had did have some impact on the experience as seen through the eyes of participants.

SUMMARY

Despite the diversity of theoretical positions among leaders, the findings presented in this chapter suggest that a limited set of dimensions can successfully be used to describe leader behavior and, more important, that such behavior has consequences for the type of experience members have in encounter groups and what they take away from such groups. Lest these findings lead to an erroneous oversimplification, it should be noted that other aspects of the group examined in the overall project, such as norms, were found to be equally if not more influential on member outcome. Further, there was not a simple, point-for-point correspondence between leader behaviors and the norms groups developed.

In this sense, although the taxonomy of leader behavior described in this chapter does help organize and simplify the complexity of encounter groups, the abstractions presented are still in themselves complex. It should also be emphasized that some findings necessary for a fuller understanding were deliberately deleted for purposes of presentation. Specifically, we have omitted a discussion of leader behavior and specific outcome effects—for example, whether some leaders are more influential in altering values, while others affect the self-image. We have also omitted a discussion of long-term outcome (six to eight months after the encounter groups ended).

9

Marathon Groups: Toward a Conceptual Model

Frederick H. Stoller

A simple manipulation of an important dimension of the group procedure, the condensation of time, has had as a profound consequence the development of the marathon group.[1] As Phillips and Wiener (1966) indicate, time is one of the basic variables in psychotherapy against which other variables are revealed. The role of time, particularly time limitation, has been studied more extensively in individual than in group therapy,

---

[1] Frederick H. Stoller died on June 26, 1970, shortly after submitting this chapter on the marathon group. The editors are extremely grateful to his close friend and colleague, H. L. Myerhoff, for carefully reviewing the editing of this chapter and making the necessary revisions in a way that we all believe would have met with Stoller's approval. (The Editors.)

as Goldstein, Heller, and Sechrest (1966) suggest. *Monday crust* was the term Freud (1913) applied to the retreat that took place in his patients when they had one day off following six days of analysis. Such extreme arrangements help us to recognize the losses accruing to disruption in the therapy process, and this recognition has led us to attempt to diminish these inefficiencies.

Much of what happens in the usual group session becomes highlighted and vivid in the marathon. There can be spontaneous encounter or stereotyped manipulation, stalemate or accelerated movement, the use of delimiting cliches or open creativity. Whatever takes place is likely to have an unmistakable impact because of the intensity generated through the concentrated session.

As much as intensification has its own value, the marathon experience should not be mistaken for an extended session, an example of the American penchant for "more is better" or "efficiency over quality." While sharing much with the conventional group arrangement, such as the therapeutic mechanisms outlined by Corsini (1957), the marathon has characteristics which are unique; it leads to learnings which are likely to occur concisely only within this particular format. In order to understand just how this learning may take place and, in particular, the role of time in such a session, it is necessary to construct a model of what occurs within a marathon. However, before this construction can be attempted, it is desirable to specify what a marathon is and to describe what occurs within it. (The original writings on the marathon are Bach (1966) and Stoller (1968b). My presentation is an amalgamation of these views; many of the details can be found in these writings.)

Marathon arrangements can occur as a variation within an ongoing group, an alternative experience within an individual's growth program, or an experience which stands by itself. Even in the last instance, the individual marathon session is not expected to be the sole growth experience of the person involved; the marathon experience is simply not a programed part of his movement toward change. Whichever arrangement happens to be the case, a common goal should be that the marathon be ordered and conducted as if it were the only opportunity for the participant to engage in growth and movement. Fulfilling such a requirement has implications for the arrangement of the marathon and for the general style and atmosphere which prevail.

Initially, one may well ask why pretend a session will be a participant's only opportunity for growth and movement when it can be one of many opportunities if he so chooses. The answer lies in the goal of the marathon: to achieve a unique situation in which some aspect of the group member's particular life style becomes manifest, both to himself and to others, within an emotional matrix powerful enough to permit movement; important segments of the individual's feelings, behavior, or perceptions or all three will be appreciably different following the experience. The expectation brought to the session, then, by both the group leader and the group members is that the marathon will not merely be another session but rather a situation in which something of significance will happen, very likely a turning point in the individual's growth process. The importance of such expectations can scarcely be minimized in terms of defining the marathon experience, and a number of decisions concerning organization and procedure are determined by it. I now discuss four of these decisions—scheduling, accommodations, group composition, and approach.

If it is anticipated that significant movement will occur for a majority of the participants, sufficient time must be allotted for it. If an inadequate amount of time is scheduled, many things are stirred up by the experience, but there is little opportunity for movement. Experience with groups that have undergone twelve-hour sessions, for example, reveals a cranky dissatisfaction; something happens but there is neither resolution nor definition of what occurs.

Experience indicates that the minimum time for a marathon is eighteen hours. Extended sessions of shorter duration may have their own value, but they are not likely to exhibit the most important feature of the marathon: significant movement. It is not so easy to determine the maximum time, but a diminishing return likely sets in around forty-eight hours; people can deal with only a limited amount of input at a given time in terms of their personal growth.

In practice most marathons occur on weekends (Stoller, 1967), when people can find an adequate amount of free time, and the dimensions of the weekend have proven to be quite satisfactory. However, a number of arrangements have been used within this time span. Bach pioneered the twenty-four–hour nonstop session which foregoes sleep. Such a schedule is particularly useful when the problem of sleeping arrangements threatens to become a difficult one. With the twenty-four–hour group, continuity and the wearing away of defenses through fatigue are paramount. I have found particularly effective an arrangement which calls for a twenty-four–hour session starting Friday evening, allows the group a night's sleep Saturday evening (often following a party at the close of the first session), with another shorter session Sunday until lunch. In my experience the Sunday morning session can be extraordinarily fruitful, out of proportion to the number of hours encompassed. From my standpoint, the most preferable schedule starts Friday evening, allowing a few hours sleep each night and ending at a prearranged time Sunday afternoon. Continuity is not disturbed by such sleep breaks; much continues within the lapse for sleep, and the whole experience remains a unitary one rather than a series of connected experiences.

Marathons have been and can be held in a large variety of settings from the group leader's home (Stoller, 1968a) to an abandoned prison dormitory (Kruschke and Stoller, 1967). Successful groups can be held anywhere, but, all other things being equal, the least desirable setting is one which has an institutional or professional association. Most preferable are home or vacation settings, in which participants' roles are likely to be less fixed, allowing for flexible development. However, a determined group will overcome any limitations a setting may impose.

Food requires special consideration. Ideally group members should not have to undertake any responsibility for feeding themselves, and there should be a plentiful supply of coffee as well as fruit and other snacks. Meals can be as elaborate or as simple as people want. During the group simple meals are best, whereas there may be a desire for an elaborate meal at the close or when a party atmosphere prevails. Where it is not feasible to have the food catered, the whole group should take responsibility for preparation and serving, weaving such an endeavor into the marathon interaction. When a few members take on this responsibility, they find legitimate excuses for removing themselves from the group, diminishing the effect both for themselves and for the group.

The marathon can deal with a larger group membership than can the ongoing group, fifteen being the maximum size from my viewpoint. Since the marathon group accomplishes its purpose best when it approximates a microworld, too small a group can provide too fragmentary an arena in which to operate, diminishing the power of the experience to some degree. In an average-size group, there is some competition for time, a circumstance not dissimilar to that in the world outside the group. Thus, much of what the participant gains from the experience is a function of what he demands of himself and the group (although there are limitations to the usefulness of such competition).

Unless special goals are being pursued, a random selection of group members provides the most meaningful analog of the world. In line with this requirement, no special filtering system should be used to select group members. Also group members should be able to move through the group as free of prelabeling and prejudgment from the other participants as is possible; the group leader's prejudgments can have a particularly powerful impact. In order to preserve this freshness no attempt should be made to obtain case history material or other background information.

Surprisingly few problems have arisen as a consequence of this policy, suggesting the possibility that practioners tend to develop their own sets of unexamined security operations. An occasional group which has a poor composition can be anticipated, but the most careful method of selection (if such selection were indeed possible) still may return the same results. Possibly the most difficult misgrouping involves one or more subgroups who have had experiences together which excluded the remainder of the group. Unless dealt with relatively early in the session such a combination can seriously hamper adequate group development. Without a screening process, disorganized people also may enter the group. They do not necessarily represent a threat either to the group or to other group members, and their presence can result in an extremely powerful experience for everyone concerned; much depends upon the experience and training of the group leader. Members from the helping professions are the greatest threat to group development. Many of them come to peek at technique or to act upon rather than with people. A group heavily loaded with professionals can become a matter of the voyeurs watching the voyeurs: a result that is deadly but not fatal.

Style is a highly individual matter, and employment of style on the part of the group leader is mandatory rather than limited as Bennis (1964) suggests. Certain aspects of an individual's approach vary somewhat depending upon the circumstances. Expectations that significant movement will take place lend a high sense of urgency to the marathon session, and impatience gets translated into the prevailing style that the group develops. The emphasis is upon action and behavioral change rather than upon acceptance, understanding, support, or postponements for the future ("I will have to work on that"). The reactions that particular behavioral patterns of a participant elicit in others in a marathon mount in intensity as the hours pass. Participant behavior becomes stereotyped with increasingly intense feelings. The impact is therefore much more powerful than it may be in an ongoing series of sessions, where people often learn to accommodate to one another and to discount an individual's customary style rather than to urge change upon him. The marathon group insists upon inaction—a stopping of the customary behavior—rather than demanding specific acts on the part of the individual. Implicit in the group's demand is the concept that once a person ceases emitting responses high in his hierarchy, other response patterns are readily available to him (Stoller, 1969).

The group leader is likely to set the pace for the urgent

style, hopefully introducing helpful leads which facilitate the change. The group leader tends to be much more active in a marathon than in an ongoing session, partially because restraint rather than action results in fatigue, one of the major lessons of the marathon group. The urgency tends to mount as the group progresses and may reach a very high level during the final phase, enabling people to move in ways that may be inconceivable under other circumstances. (Sohl, 1968, presents a fictional version of one leadership style in a marathon.)

Quite often participants in a marathon find themselves in extremely painful positions, either having to face a disturbing truth about themselves or having to negotiate an anguished impasse with the group. Both group members and professionals find it very difficult to leave such an individual "bleeding," and they tend to engage in many maneuvers which amount to psychological first aid—succorance which fulfills the needs of the onlookers rather than of the sufferer. In a continuing group it may very well be impossible to allow an individual to go home too full of pain. However, since the marathon does not involve separation, it is often quite helpful to leave him alone with his turmoil. Generally such a person moves by himself and calls attention to himself at a later point in the session, ready to deal with the matters at hand from a new perspective. In this sense, the marathon allows group members to reach deeper levels of confrontation more quickly.

Now that I have discussed organization and procedures, it may be useful to attempt a definition of the marathon. I think of it as a continuous, prolonged group session, set aside from the usual routine, in which significant movement in terms of perception and behavior on the part of group members is anticipated and which is designed to stand as an experience by itself regardless of the arrangements various group members have for additional growth programs.

Let us turn now to how a marathon develops as an experience in growth. Exactly what is going to take place in a marathon session can scarcely be anticipated; after leading numerous marathons, I still find myself nervous before each session. However, the predictability of the development of a marathon has been sustained quite consistently over many sessions. Basically the marathon session can be divided into three major segments; as with most developmental phases they do not represent clean-cut divisions but phase out and phase in with much overlap.

The opening hours of a marathon invariably involve stiffness, discomfort, and stylized encounter on the part of the group members. People may attempt to tell their stories (spell out their predicament with the emphasis on external circumstances) or may focus overly much on a hapless victim, determined not to leave him alone until they have exhausted both themselves and him. Even prior group experience rarely allows people to aviod the stiffness of their encounter. The group members have a growing sense that what they are doing is heavy and clumsy and seemingly is providing little of the momentum they anticipated.

Such awkwardness is understandable because people are very much in the process of developing relationships, establishing trust, and building a sense of cohesiveness. Attempts have been made to cut through this initial impasse with microlab exercises, but the effect is generally very temporary. Bach and I have both noted this initial phase and have estimated that it takes about eight hours to work through it. Annoying as it may seem, it is extremely necessary, and it is shortsighted to bypass it entirely. Indeed, movement which occurs during this phase is often premature and frequently has to be repeated at a later phase. Too profound a sharing by one member may find the remainder of the group unprepared to deal with the heightened emotion. But participants are bringing into the group important aspects of their own dealings with the world, especially how they approach strangers—tentatively, suspiciously, guarded, with considerable maneuvering, attempting to deal with one another at arms' length. An important contribution can be made by helping people move through this aspect of their dealings with the world rather than by bypassing it through an overuse of technique. Also people are learning about one another and are beginning to accumulate responses and feelings which ultimately have an extremely important payoff.

Another trend, which may be unique to this continuous group, begins here and continues through much of the marathon. As when they enter any interpersonal situation, members have expectations as to how they will be received and treated. Within the marathon, as in most group encounter situations, their expectations are not likely to be fulfilled—quite the opposite, aspects of their conduct are reacted to in ways that they find has a negative impact upon themselves. Being received and dealt with in a negative way by others constitutes a crisis, the initial and ubiquitous response to which is a distancing from the others involved so that less pain is incurred in the future. It is precisely at this point that the marathon provides a unique situation: the individual is obliged to stay with rather than remove himself from the offending persons. He is in less of a position to seek out manipulative, avoiding ways of dealing with these people, and he also may have a part in developing their crises; at the least he is a participant-observer to their similar distress. The overall effect is for the individual to ultimately draw closer rather than to retreat, as he might in other noncontinuous encounters.

Eventually the group members begin to weary of the relatively narrow behavior repertoires to which they so rigidly adhere. They are reaching a stage in which they are ready to approach a flexible way of being with others—a readiness aided by growing familiarity and group cohesiveness. Although there are individual differences, trust is becoming possible for the group. These trends work upon the participants at different rates so that the new phase begins with one or two individuals and then many of the others follow.

Basically the second phase can be ascertained when group members shift from telling their stories to sharing themselves. There is a perceptible change from factual accounting to emotional sharing with a decreasing reluctance to show vulnerability. The crises do not necessarily fade away during this phase but, on the contrary, may mount in intensity. Although considerable warmth and appreciation of one another may develop, there is also a heightened aggressiveness in the negative feedback that is given—sharp, to the point, based on mounting feelings on the part of the people involved. People are rubbing up against one another, creating not only warmth but also heat. Thus, intense and very powerful crises may take place during the second phase side by side with breakthroughs on the part of some of the participants. And while there is movement, there is also frustration and seemingly insoluble stalemates. Meanwhile the world has almost become the group, hardly anything else existing for the time being.

The group members themselves would like to be able to establish a shift in their frame of reference and the kinds of behavioral patterns they are emitting. However, they are at a loss and feel the frustration, particularly in that they are looking for external solutions to what are basically internal problems. An almost undying hope is that someone will provide the answer—the group leader, another group member, the group itself. But in the long run the individual still must find within himself the answers to his frustrations, with others acting merely as catalysts rather than as primary agents of change. Accompanying the sense of frustration is a general feeling of depression which Bach has called "the slough of despond."

The third phase emerges as the group approaches the end of the marathon session. Movement now can be very swift as the urgency intensifies. Interaction during this phase is characterized primarily by an almost total absence of defensiveness; people are able to express themselves with the utmost spontaneity, forgetting to watch themselves or to gauge what they emit. They are also free to take in what is given them. As a consequence, crises tend to become resolved rather quickly. There is an elated feeling of intimacy, and many are able to express very succinctly what they have learned from the experience as a whole: the investment in withholding and the greater cost it entails than does "going with"; the possibilities in intimacy; the feasibility of creating one's world rather than being a mere reactor; and the importance of using one's talents and assets as fully as possible.

Here begins the extremely important work of integrating the experience, a complex and not completely understood process. So much has taken place, so much has to be abstracted that it is difficult to see how people can truly develop new organizations out of this mass of data. And yet this integration takes place, often several weeks following the experience. In the process of integrating the complex experience for themselves many participants have the opportunity to gain insights which they may acquire only in such a situation. In order to speculate how and why this learning takes place and to specify the conditions under which it is most likely to occur, it is necessary to attempt to construct a model of what takes place within the marathon session.

One important aspect of learning about oneself is to be in a position to say, "when I do such and such, this tends to happen," or "when so and so takes place, I tend to do such and such." In other words, a person learns to connect or associate features of the environment and his own reactions and behavior in ways that did not occur to him before, and this connection enables him to alter the automatic conduct that characterized him previously. The group setting offers a particularly rich culture for such associations to take place because of the wealth of interactions it offers among its members.

If we look at the events that occur in a single hour of a group, we can organize them as they are in Table 18.[2] The bottom line, *observable events,* represents events which could be recorded on sound film or videotape. The letters symbolize all the statements, actions, movements, facial expressions that occurred. This representation is a great simplification since the events being symbolized include not only overt behavior on the part of various group members but nonresponse signs of disinterest and distractions. The *subscript* "1" refers to the fact that this is hour 1 in a series. Since events are not perceived without some organization, the next line refers to *incidents* and indicates the way an observer would tend to order the events into groups.

Obviously this is an extraordinarily complex series of

[2] When Stoller died the model described here was in an early stage of formulation. We include it as he presented it, rather than second-guessing him to artificially refine it, for the heuristic value it might have. (The Editors.)

Table 18

Observable Events at Various Levels of Organization

Career	$(B_1C_1D_1E_1)$	$(G_1H_1I_1J_1)$	$(M_1N_1O_1P_1)$	$(R_1S_1T_1U_1)$	$(X_1Y_1Z_1)$
Account	(C_1D_1)	(H_1I_1)	(N_1O_1)	(S_1T_1)	(X_1Y_1)
Incidents	$(A_1B_1C_1D_1E_1)$	$(G_1H_1I_1J_1)$	$(M_1N_1O_1P_1)$	$(R_1S_1T_1U_1)$	$(X_1Y_1Z_1)$

Observable events	A_1-B_1-C_1-D_1-E_1-F_1-G_1-H_1-I_1-J_1-K_1-L_1-M_1-N_1-O_1-P_1-Q_1-R_1-S_1-T_1-U_1-V_1-W_1-X_1-Y_1-Z_1

phenomena, and a participant must simplify what he recalls; such simplification is a function of his selective inattention. The next line, *account,* indicates how a participant may recall what occurred in that hour from his own point of view. Other participants, however, in attempting to organize what occurred to this group member would give a somewhat different version, including details which he had left out but which give a different color to what occurred. Their accounts can be found in the line *career.* A career description of what happened to an individual is much richer than and presents a different perspec-

Table 19

Unobservable Events

Observable events	A_1-B_1-C_1-D_1-E_1-F_1-G_1-H_1-I_1-J_1-K_1-L_1-M_1-N_1-O_1-P_1-Q_1-R_1-S_1-T_1-U_1-V_1-W_1-X_1-Y_1-Z_1
Unobservable (self)	a_1-c_1-e_1-g_1-i_1-k_1-m_1-o_1-q_1-s_1-u_1-w_1-y_1
Unobservable (others)	a_1'-b_1'-c_1'-d_1'-e_1'-f_1'-g_1'-h_1'-i_1'-j_1'-k_1'-l_1'-m_1'-n_1'-o_1'-p_1'-q_1'-r_1'-s_1'-t_1'-u_1'-v_1'-w_1'-x_1'-y_1'-z_1'
Retrievable (self)	a_1-g_1-k_1'-o_1-s_1-u_1'
Retrievable (others)	a_1'-d_1'-g_1'-j_1'-k_1'-l_1'-o_1'-n_1'-r_1'-s_1'-u_1'-v_1'-x_1'
Irretrievable	b_1'-c_1-e_1'-f_1'-i_1-m_1-p_1'-q_1-t_1'-w_1-x_1'-z_1'

tive from the person's own account. Getting the person to appreciate the difference between these two versions and to attend to the specifics of this career line is one of the goals of the group.

However, the task is, in reality, a much more complex one than this. A whole order of events takes place which cannot be recorded and filmed, and these covert events occur on a subliminal level, which is symbolized in Table 19. The unobservable events include inner responses, emotions, associations, perceptions, and bodily sensations; these occur both in the individual who is concerned with giving an account of himself and in the others who are participating in the session. Some of these unobservable events are accessible, that is, retrievable (there should be several levels of retrievability—certain feelings and responses are much more accessible than others, but these other levels are not diagramed for simplicity's sake); others are, for all practical purposes, irretrievable.

For an individual to make some sense or to get any meaning out of the discrepancy between his account and his career, linkages with some of the unobservable events should be made. Increased perception of the organization of what occurred results when he realizes that a set of feelings preceded certain of his behaviors, and these behaviors elicited feelings in others which precipitated their behaviors in turn. Similarly, it is helpful for him to realize the degree to which his perceptions are shared by others or are idiosyncratic. In this manner his organization of what occurred comes closer to the career attributed to him than does the account he has of himself; associating the unobservable events makes this a meaningful trend rather than an arbitrary one. This process can be symbolized as in Table 20.

Table 20

Integration of Career With Unobservable Events

Summation $\quad a_1 a_1'(B_1 C_1 D_1 E_1)d_1' \qquad g_1 g_1'(G_1 H_1 I_1 J_1)h_1'$

$$k_1 k_1' j_1'(M_1 N_1 O_1 P_1)o_1 o_1' l_1' \qquad s_1 s_1'(R_1 S_1 T_1 U_1)n_1' r_1'$$

$$u_1 u_1'(X_1 Y_1 Z_1)v_1' x_1'$$

Table 20 suggests that an individual can summarize his career in a meaningful manner through association of his own feelings and reactions as well as those of others with what occurs to him; his ways of acting and reacting are now somewhat comprehensible.

Technically it may be feasible to accomplish a level of understanding of what occurred within a group hour by careful examination of a videotape with recall by the participants. Aside from the fact that the group members are not likely to have deep feelings for one another and are not likely to share too much if relationships have not yet been built, it is questionable whether the individual would see much relationship between the summation and the remainder of his life patterns. What is required is a trend, a repetitive cycle which indicates that what has developed is typical.

The opportunity for such repetition occurs as other group hours accumulate. Therefore, the figures can be repeated with A2-B2-C2 . . . A3-B3-C3 . . . A4-B4-C4 . . . An-Bn-Cn, for as many hours as the group runs or the individual participates in it. Patterning, a more or less typical trend of behavior, can be diagramed as in Table 21.

Table 21

Patterning and Complex Patterning Across Many Group Hours

Patterning $\quad$ $g_1\, g_1'\, (G_1\, H_1\, I_1\, J_1)h_1'$ $\qquad$ $g_5\, g_5'\, (G_5H_5I_5J_5)h_5'$

$\qquad\qquad\qquad$ $d_{12}\, g_{12}\, g_{12}'(G_{12}\, H_{12}\, I_{12}\, J_{12})h_{12}'$

Complex
patterning $\quad$ $a_1\, a_1'(B_1\, C_1\, D_1\, E_1)d_1'$ $\qquad$ $k_6\, k_6'\, j_6'(M_6\, N_6\, O_6\, P_6)o_6\, i_6'$

$\qquad\qquad\qquad$ $s_9\, s_9'(R_9\, S_9\, T_9\, U_9)n_9'\, r_9'$ $\qquad$ $u_{14}'(X_{14}\, Y_{14}\, Z_{14})v_{14}'\, x_{14}$

Patterning develops when repetitive behavior occurs and is recognized by the individual, particularly when he is able to catch himself entering into it. The repetition adds strength to the pattern observed, and the applicability of the pattern to behavior outside the group becomes increasingly manifest.

In addition to patterning, Table 21 shows complex patterning, which is learning of a difficult and subtle nature; connections are made between incidents that take place within different hours. Complex patterning occurs when unobservable events, such as feelings, do not occur when their eliciting external events occur but do occur at some later time removed from the eliciting event and in association with other unobservable events. In this learning, apparent inconsistencies on the part of the person are seen by him as being related; the relationship between expectations and subsequent events is clarified, and, above all, elaborate maneuvers of the individual to foist particular stances upon others are recognized. Bringing together discrete events spread out over time in this way is difficult for anyone and doubly so for the individual himself. Complex patterning is of particular importance in that it connects those aspects of our behavior which are least visible and which are least likely to be specified by others except in a therapeutic situation. It has special relevance in the group in that the individual is least likely to report the kinds of events which get linked in complex patterning, being able to specify merely the consequences; the group is then the arena in which the antecedent behavior is enacted and connected to its consequences.

Up to this point, the model is applicable to therapeutic groups in general. When considering the marathon as a special case, however, an important dimension is significantly changed: the temporal distances between A1-B1-C1 . . . A2-B2-C2 . . . A3-B3-C3 . . . An-Bn-Cn. The process of establishing patterns and, in particular, complex patterns is accelerated by the group remaining in contact throughout its development. Patterns can be established rapidly so that their impact upon others is clear and readily determined. In similar fashion, complex patterns are much more perceptible and emerge much more quickly than they do in the more ongoing group arrangement. Even more specific to the marathon is the possibility that incidents of disparate hours can become linked together in complex patterns, which, because of the many weeks involved, may take an exceptionally long time to emerge or may never emerge in an ongoing group.

Finally, complex patterns become linked in new combinations referred to as the group career: the specification of how incidents, emotions, patterns, and complex patterns merge in a coherent fashion to lend credence to what occurs to the individual within a marathon experience. When the individual internalizes his group career, he has undergone a partial reorganization of how he sees and feels himself moving through the world.

With this model I can attempt to answer the question raised previously as to how the marathon influences the kinds of learning under discussion. Internalization and reorganization of self-perceptions occur when there is a vivid emotional milieu: when something happens to the person rather than being studied by him in academic fashion. The emotional climate of the marathon mounts in intensity in a relatively continuous fashion. In their study of individual therapy Lennard and Bernstein (1960) identify a fading away of emotional intensity before the session ends, as if in preparation for its closing. The likelihood is that the emotional development of an ongoing group session parallels this finding. It is almost inconceivable that it can ever have the sharp, steady rise in emotion found in the marathon arrangement. Therefore, at the time that participants are likely to undergo the integration of their group career, they are also attaining an intensity of emotion which is quite marked. Thus, the kind of reorganization and integration they are likely to undergo has a particularly vivid quality about it and accelerates the self-learning process enormously.

If we examine once again the phases of the marathon in the light of this model, we can see that the initial period involves not only preparation for what occurs later but also recognition of patterns. In many ways these patterns are ones the individual finds most recognizable and which he is most likely to have heard about before. While such information is useful, it neither is very exciting nor presents new vistas in terms of possible alternative behavioral patterns.

Within the context of the present model, in the second phase of the marathon, complex patterns begin to emerge and to be recognized by the individual. Very often a particular complex pattern is perceived and internalized yielding closure and completion and leading to changes in behavior which can be recognized as breakthroughs. However, while these changes are taking place other complex patterns which do not lead to this satisfaction develop with varying degrees of recognition. They yield puzzlement and discomfort—a sense of unfinished business. Thus the second phase of the marathon brings discoveries and breakthroughs and also a sense of the complexity of the drama which has unfolded.

Within the final phase of the marathon the various strands of complex patterns can be integrated into the group career. Thus the overall pattern of the marathon experience begins to have a consistency and meaning which lend a sense of completion and enormous satisfaction. The process of integration may merely begin within the marathon experience and may well take a number of weeks to be completed. What is important is that a broad spectrum of abstraction takes place rather than a narrow and pinpointed one, and this broadened integration has a marked impact on aspects of the person's life outside the group situation. He is now in a position to make bridges between his group experience and his life, which can be particularly meaningful if one parallels the group career with the life career. Premature attempts to build bridges or to provide solutions to presented problems can cut off such important learnings. A tremendous sense of excitement and exhilaration can accompany such a process, in which large and important elements suddenly fall into place.

10

Promoting Growth with Nonverbal Exercises

William C. Schutz and Charles Seashore

One job of the professional group leader is to help people move from what are essentially pathological cycles to some kind of growth cycle. Assuming that this is a generally understandable and agreed-on job, we have a variety of further assumptions about how to accomplish this goal and a variety of ways to go about it. Some of us like to intervene in the cycle at only one point—a dominant point of entry; and some of us like to use multiple entries—that is, to help the person change not just one thing in his life but many things at the same time, so that he can switch cycles.

Some professional workers concentrate on the inter-personal system as a point of entry. They seek to break the pathological cycle by intervening where people interact—in the family, work group, or other interpersonal systems. "Change behavior in these systems, and then you can move toward

188

growth." Another approach might be to help the individual ask, "What cooks inside me? What are my attitudes, feelings, aware-nesses, sensitivities, energy levels?" This entry can be accom-plished by treating the person in a counseling or therapeutic relationship.

The pathological cycle we commonly find is one of help-lessness, an attitudinal response of withdrawal—a closing up —a stance toward other people and the world that leads to a cognitive attitude of "I have very few options available; I'm not aware of many. I'm almost stimulus-deprived, so that when I try to make decisions they end up in the control of other people."

The individual finds himself buffeted around by people he does not care about in the sense that one cares about family or friends. Impersonal "theys" or structures such as the estab-lishment are in control. This sense of manipulation leads to further hopelessness, to deeper convictions that events are uncontrollable. "I really don't know how you change the red tape," the victim seems to be saying. And his hopelessness bears with it feelings of impotence and incompetence which reinforce his attitude that the only way out is withdrawal.

This closed system within the individual keeps com-pounding itself—a closed system of hopelessness. It may get worse, or at least reinforce itself, so that the person never builds a greater awareness of what he can do. Moving him toward growth involves starting a cycle of competence which leads to his ability to initiate personal action. The person discovers where to get needed information and becomes aware of alterna-tives that are not controlled by others. He begins to feel that he can make decisions by himself, without needing the cooperation of a large bureaucracy, a small office, or even of very many people outside his immediate world.

Although we have chosen to talk about a pathology cycle and what movement out of it would involve, some people see the problem as one of immaturity. Instead of saying, "This person is sick; he has learned to do things in the wrong way," these people say, "That isn't true; he's only in an immature state; very much like that of a child starting school. He can't read the first day in first grade, not because he's sick, but because he just hasn't reached that level of maturity." According to the proponents of the immaturity concept, the person needs only such things as information—information that can be picked up just by being exposed to it—or money, the wherewithall to get started. In other words, he is ready to move; he's just immature.

But those who believe the problem is one of pathology see a kind of game going on which has to be broken up before the individual can function in a healthy manner. In an analogous situation, if a person were to go to China and begin learning the language, he would have a "pathology"—he speaks English and would have to do a certain amount of unlearning. However, the child coming into the world has no pathology; he is just immature and can pick up the language on the basis of pure exposure. The child requires information; the other person needs to be brought into contact with resources of which he is usually unaware and which he does not use. This process we call *coupling*. In facilitating the pathology-to-growth phenomenon, coupling provides still another method for making entry for the professional worker, one that requires strong initiative.

We can begin by saying, "What can we do to break into the part of the cycle that has to do with low awareness?" We can help the individual get the new information he needs to understand and control his environment. By looking at the person's internal systems, we can try to help him answer the question, "What can I do to take an initiating stance instead of a withdrawing stance toward my environment?" Hopefully, these approaches are mutually supportive and break the self-reinforcing cycle, freeing the person to begin new growth.

We have found that nonverbal methods are frequently more successful than traditional verbal therapy in changing old patterns of thought and feeling. In our nonverbal, group-oriented attempts to break into the cycle, we choose two points of entry—the internal and the interpersonal systems. Many techniques are available for nonverbal exercises in group situations. Usually a combination of several is used, because no one method works well for everyone. By having a variety of approaches from which to choose each person can find one or more techniques he can use profitably. Also, each person is at a different point in his psychological development. For one person, one technique might be just what he needs to enter a new, better phase of life. For another, it might just start a series of events which needs to be followed up by more similar experience. (See Schutz, 1967, for a fuller discussion of these exercises.)

Our interest is to put these techniques together into one integrated approach, and one way to start is with a Brief Encounter Microlab. The microlab is designed to condense a regular one- or two-week laboratory into an hour and a half. A five-minute meeting replaces a two-hour meeting; and instead of having a one-hour general session, we have a one-minute general session, and so on. A typical brief encounter microlab might be made up of the following sequence of exercises and meetings as explained by the instructions that follow:

INSTRUCTIONS

Meeting 1 (Encounter group). You are to meet in a regular encounter group for five minutes. The rules of this meeting are: Talk about your feelings; talk about the here and now; be open and honest. I will tell you when the meeting is over. Go ahead.

Meeting 2 (General session). Please stop. Now we'll have a general session. How did it go? (Discussion for one minute.)

Meeting 3 (Encounter group). Begin another five-minute encounter group.

Meeting 4 (General session). Please stop. How did it go this time? (One-minute discussion.)

Meeting 5 (First impressions). This time I would like you to have another encounter group but with a special task. I would like one person in each group to stand, walk over in front of another group member and look that member in the eye, touch him however you feel like touching him, and tell him as honestly and openly as you can your first impression of him. Then proceed around the group until you have given your first impression of each group member in this fashion. When the first member has completed the cycle, I want a second group member to get up and give his first impressions of all other group members. Repeat this process until all group members have given their eye-to-eye, touch, first impressions of each other member. (This usually lasts about ten minutes. It is stopped after all groups are through, or almost.)

Meeting 6 (Encounter group). Please stop. Now have another regular encounter group meeting. (Five minutes.)

Meeting 7 (Dyad encounter). Please stop. Now will each group select the two members who feel least close to each other. (Allow two minutes.) Would the pair from this group please stand up? One of you please go down to that end of the room and the other stay at this end. Now I'd like you to look each other in the eye and maintain eye contact throughout. When I give the signal start walking straight toward each other very slowly and when you get close enough do whatever you feel like doing without words. Try not to plan anything ahead of time but do what you feel impelled from within to do.

Meeting 8 (Encounter group). Now go back to a regular encounter group meeting (Five minutes.)

Meeting 9 (Nonverbal). This time I'd like you to have another regular encounter group meeting except without using words. Communicate to each other nonverbally. (Five minutes.)

Meeting 10 (Encounter group). Begin another five-minute encounter group.

Meeting 11 (Fantasy). This time when I give the signal would you please close your eyes and have a fantasy. Imagine the other members of your group advancing toward you. Just begin with that fantasy and let your imagination go in whatever way it wants to. I will give you the signal to open your eyes in about three minutes. Go ahead.

Meeting 12 (General session). Would someone like to tell us what went on in his head? (Five minutes.)

Meeting 13 (Encounter group). Now let's go back to a regular encounter group. (Five minutes.)

Meeting 14 (Roll and Rock). I'd like you to select one person—or I will choose him if you like—who seems still to be somewhat reluctant to let himself go in the group. (Give groups time.) Now everyone stand up and each group make a circle facing in with the selected person in the center. He is to shut his eyes and try to relax entirely and the group will pass him around from person to person. After he has been passed around for a while, lift him up into the air, rock him back and forth, and let him down to the ground gently. Go ahead.

Meeting 16 (Farewell). Now please stand and walk slowly toward each other and say goodbye in whatever way you wish.

The main idea of the brief encounter microlab is to introduce a number of techniques in a certain sequence that will get the group moving as quickly as we know how to get it moving. A one-and-one-half-hour session is equivalent to about thirty hours of regular group meetings. In this length of time, groups can get very close due to a combination of methods, including talking, but more importantly through the nonverbal and fantasy methods.

We usually find that the fifth meeting (First Impressions) is crucial. When it is not included, the group takes much longer to reach the point of expressing groupness—true feelings, honesty, candidness, and so on—than when it is used. The eleventh meeting (Fantasy) is a good way to get deeper when groups are going well and have almost exhausted the kind of interpersonal contact usual in such groups. Meeting seven (Dyad encounter) is a simple but very effective procedure in which all kinds of things happen—combat, play, and impasse, to name three. People pass each other, turn their backs, or do any number of things. The exercise probes beneath the conscious defenses, for when a person is standing in front of someone, he feels the experience with his whole body. And that sensation is more important than is merely talking. It is often a little frightening to anticipate being in such an encounter, and this fear is one indication that the experience is getting at something important. Meeting fourteen (Roll and Rock) has several purposes. It involves trust, for the selected person really has to give himself up to the group, and the group receives a feeling of unanimity. The fact that all the group members work together to give pleasure to somebody, or to support him, usually makes the group feel better about itself. The ninth meeting (Nonverbal) can always be used when the group has gone pretty far. If the members have not attained much groupness, the exercise usually falls flat; they will do stereotyped things that do not have much meaning. At the beginning, this procedure is almost always uncomfortable, as most of these exercises are, but if the people let it "go," it can evolve into something meaningful.

It is important to tailor what one does to what is happening in the group. A number of other exercises may be used, such as forming dyads for five-minute meetings if the group is not going well, giving and receiving affection nonverbally if the group is very advanced, the press, the push, arm wrestling, group fantasy, and many others. They are all described, both as to method and use, in the book *Joy.*

Many of our methods come from . . . psychotherapy (making sick people well), training (making well people better), from the arts, especially dance and drama, and from eastern philosophy and religion, especially meditation. . . .

A cornerstone of our approach is honesty and openness. These qualities are seemingly simple to express but they are not. Training people to be direct and not devious, to express their feelings honestly, is difficult, often fraught with risk, but enormously rewarding. It deepens and enriches relationships and opens up feelings of warmth and closeness that are rare in most of our experiences.

This approach is in many ways countercultural. We have many words for hypocrisy, such as tact, diplomacy, discretion. And these concepts are very dominant in public life, usually unchallenged. Sometimes they lead to spectacular failure, as in the current credibility gap that is eroding an administration, or in the situation that has led to youth's demand that we tell it like it is. Much more candor will, we believe, lead to much more joy for all (Schutz, 1967).

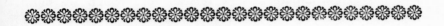

11

Use of Physical Contact

Bertram R. Forer

It is firmly established that physical contact early in life is an essential determinant of adult capacity to relate interpersonally with members of one's own species (Harlow, 1958). This finding is true of mammals, including dogs (Freedman and Roe, 1958; Igel and Calvin, 1960); and it is more significant in primates (Harlow and Zimmerman, 1959) and human beings (Spitz, 1946), who must, in order to survive, internalize complex interpersonal patterns and schemata of their worlds.

Homo sapiens has the most complex potential for a vast array of behaviors and for internalizing self-contradicting events. He is the most intelligent of animals and most capable of transcending his animal nature. He also must endure the most persistent and involved process of physical, emotional, and cognitive contact with other human beings to evolve an idiosyncratic personality that also achieves some kind of congruence with a variety of other human beings. He must develop an internal system that has continuity—that builds upon past events—yet is capable of adapting to changing circumstances that may be radically unpredictable. To single out any one factor as the determinant of the developmental process is to oversimplify the complexity of becoming and remaining human and the process of psychological growth during the autonomous adult years. But physical contact between human beings seems to be essential to the socialization process and to the main-tenance of adult psychological growth.

Psychotherapy can be viewed as a variety of somewhat systematic approaches designed to help the individual resume an interrupted process of humanization and loosen the rigid psychological structures that limit flexibility or adaptability of feeling, cognition, or behavior. Early interpersonal relationships have much to do with the kind of human being one becomes, and their outcomes ordinarily limit considerably the individual's freedom to participate in new relationships which are more than just frustrating repetitions of the self-limitations of earlier ones (Forer, 1969b). Early relationships both shape and limit the range of perception of self and others, affective expressions, the use of body parts, interpersonal roles, and the kinds of persons with whom one chooses to relate and how one trains them to respond. Psychotherapy has the dual function of help-ing the person to recognize and experience the invariant, repeti-tive, nonempirical (hence nonadaptive) aspects of himself and to experiment with suppressed or dissociated parts of himself that have been locked into rigid adaptations to significant per-sons earlier in his life. Thus, psychotherapy stimulates a resump-tion of the growth process.

Traditional psychotherapies have attempted to effect resumption of growth almost exclusively by verbal communica-tion by the therapist and almost exclusively about the client. The therapist (psychoanalytic) intended to expose *the* trans-ference neurosis by maintaining an emotional and perceptual neutrality that would prevent contamination of the client's self-exposure by the therapist's personal self.

Many therapists, some of them psychoanalytic in orienta-tion (Forer, 1961a,b), have come to believe that exposure of transference neurosis does not in itself effect sufficient change; new introjections of attitudes from new people are necessary to expand the self, because each early structural fixation limits the variety of experiencing and action that could be incorporated into the self. Furthermore, new openness without experimenting with new coping methods too often reinstitutes old maladaptive patterns.

Physical contact is one aspect of emotional responsiveness between the client and other persons that can lead to a broadened experience of self and others, enhance trust which is the open door to new introjections (Fromm-Reichman, 1959, pp. 69–70; Forer, 1965, 1969a), and free the individual to participate more boldly in the world. Only recently physical contact between therapist and client, among clients, and in the public at large has erupted from a long period of repression instigated by the isolation-intellectualization of our Puritan, engineering culture. As is so common among breakthroughs of tabooed behavior, initial expressions may be impulsive, defiant, and self-destructive. I have been experimenting for about fifteen years, admittedly in tentative, even gingerly fashion, with physical contact with clients because they forced me to recognize my own reluctance to participate beyond the verbal level. Now I am alarmed that this potent force may be getting out of hand; it may at the least lose its power and at worst become injurious to the therapeutic growth process. I therefore provide a framework for describing the role of touching in psychological development and formulate some preliminary guidelines for its constructive use in psychotherapy.

Skin-contact is a primordial anxiety-reducer, the source of soothing, calming sensations. Even skittish horses and other domesticated animals are calmed by gentling. Household pets become partly human because of their responsiveness to and dependence upon physical contact with human beings. Children not only recover from anxiety states when stroked and held (Freud, 1949, p. 101; Ferenczi, 1955, p. 316), but become attached or even addicted to the sources of skin nourishment. This kind of interpersonal contact is not only a lever for socialization but, in seriously disturbed persons, a source of added turmoil (Forer, 1969a). At this primitive level lifelong interpersonal stances can be fixed by absence of skin contact or a mixture of contact and pain, so that being touched is experienced as either alien or as a threat. Absence of soothing contact can produce psuedoadults who are unable to make emotional contact and who become and remain alienated from their bodies. A cultural example is that of child-rearing practices in New England which limit physical contact (Whiting, 1963, p. 947). Schizophrenia which derives in part from an early interruption of humanization sometimes has a source in sensory overloading and a confusion of comforting and pain. And it is often manifested in adulthood by literal terror of being touched lest ego boundaries be lost. Being touched soothingly or cuddled foster the comfortable establishment of ego boundaries and the development of an integrated body image (Federn, 1952, p. 43; Mahler, 1952) which are necessary for the development of skills in reality-testing.

Because one of the earliest fears is that of abandonment, the result of inconsistent soothing contact, or contact contingent upon self-renunciation, or warm contact confused with more sensuous experience may be an anxious need for (Balint, 1958) or distrust of the persons who are needed for reassurance that one is a safely separate person and not alone. Reasonably consistent gentling seems necessary for the development of a stable self with separateness, boundaries, autonomy, and the capacity to seek social nourishment from other persons. Without frequent reinforcement throughout life the maintenance of humanness is difficult under the best of circumstances. When skin hunger has been spoiled by defective parenting, the individual resists the one antidote to his early infection. The interpersonal nourishment that he thus rejects is more important psychologically than food: it is nourishment of the psychological structure itself.

Sensual skin contact has different psychological repercussions. Though Freud wrote that skin is passive, others (Reich, 1949, p. 227) emphasize its motor characteristics, especially vasomotor. Some skin contact stimulates the vascular system and autonomic responses. Excitement is generated, and genital arousal may occur as part of a general arousal pattern. This is the point at which skin sensuality may be perceived as a threat of loss of parental affection; this perception may lead to splitting or dissociation of skin motivation. In adults the split can persist as isolation between affection and sensuality or between sensuality or affection and sexuality. Adult sexual behavior is frequently confused by encouraging one form of contact when the personal need is for another form. Many people indulge in sexual intercourse when the need for cuddling is suppressed out of fear or anxiety or shame. Others settle for passive touch or non-sexual sensuality out of inhibition of sexual excitement.

Hence the most complex of body contacts is sexuality, which encompasses images and attitudes toward parts of the body, interpersonal attitudes and expectations, and the entire history of infantile sexuality—essentially the discovery and exploration of one's own body and others'. As tactile experience moves from soothing contact through sensuality to sexuality, a variety of conflicts can develop from the internalization of others' attitudes, real or fantasied.

Different psychological effects derive from active touching of one's own and others' bodies. Early auto-erotic self-discovery, an essential component of laying claim to oneself and to the development of a body ego, is often an instigator of parental taboo. Touching and exploring parents' bodies is crucial to a realistic sense of orientation in space and the establishment of clear body boundaries so often lacking among schizophrenics (Federn, 1952). It is the exploration of the environment with one's own body that makes the world real. Those whose early contact experiences were curtailed tend to have a verbal, visual, or otherwise abstract concept of the world that can differ radically from their bodily image of it. Passive touch is particularly liable to stimulate fear of annihilation, disintegration, pain, penetration, and loss of autonomy. Active touch is subject to inhibition, internalized social taboos that are experienced with feelings of shame, and embarrassment and guilt that are the internalization of public opinion rather than the personal affects of drive-expression. Such feelings can persist throughout life as an interpersonal barrier constructed of the attitudes of internalized authorities behind which the individual hides himself and his contact needs.

The client seeks therapy and may join a group. He enters with a complex pattern of adaptations to his early human

relationships, limited ranges of behavior and feeling, and powerful though possibly covert expectations based on childhood
experiences. He carries out dialogues with fantasies of people.
He seems to be living in the present, but much of his self, his
feeling, his motivation is directed toward and governed by his
internalized childhood public. His outer self makes superficial
contact with people; his inner selves are largely dissociated or
free-wheeling (Forer, 1969b) and may reveal themselves only
inferentially through the defenses erected against them. He is
virtually immune to modification by present persons. He may
have lived in an environment that provided few challenges to
old adaptations or he may have selected or trained a mate or
friends who, by recognizing him as he presents himself, reinforce his old ways and treat him in the manner to which he is
accustomed and committed.

Some aspects of the process of inaugurating and effect-
ing change can be summarized as follows. The individual who
seeks therapy has in most cases lost his adaptation or become
aware through anxiety of its ineffectiveness. Either external
circumstances have changed and no longer support his rigid
roles or his internal integration has somehow been loosened.
Anxiety arises when hitherto dissociated parts of himself call
for expression. The pain and unpredictability of himself or his
life are uncomfortable. Therefore, he is open to some palliative
input; usually he seeks a change in circumstance or removal of
the pain rather than a reorganization of his own self (Forer,
1963).

His continual need of and search for social nourishment
of some kind or approval or love provide the kind of dependence
that gives the therapist and the group power to affect him. If
his internalized parents or authorities (introjects) do not approve or like him, he must seek approval or affection from
persons in the present.

Consequently, his dependence on the group for soothing
and for validation of his childhood capitulations and his fear of
aloneness motivate a reliving of his earlier dependence on
parents and provide leverage which the group can eventually
use to restructure old adaptations in terms of adult here-and-

now criteria. Group members as well as the therapist begin to compete with the undependable introjects for power to guide. They become gradually allied with those parts of the self which were renounced or dissociated as they begin to emerge.

The group's power and its members' needs for intimacy and support confront the individual with his ritualistic behavior, which is oriented to the requirements of childhood introjects rather than to his peers. They force him to recognize that he is truly living in a world in his own mind, that he is dealing with fantasies of people (transference) rather than with the real people around him.

Loosening the rigid adaptations to introjects encourages an emotional breakthrough of feeling and the recollection of critical turning points in his history. As a reaction becomes more intense, its repetitive reliving quality becomes more apparent. The intellectualized defenses against earlier pain and emotional recollection wane.

As in hypnotic age-regression, the client experiences a split: One part of the self is in contact with the group while the childhood level struggles with responses derived from his childhood introjects. The client is now reliving his past with the options of changing his history in its structural properties or of succumbing to it once more. He is in the past and the present simultaneously. The group sees that the client is on the borderline of introjecting, or rather reintrojecting, the traumatic experience (which he may be projecting onto the group) or extrojecting it and no longer keeping it as part of himself. The therapeutic goal is to help him loosen the attachment to the punishing or frustrating person and return to the state of being that existed prior to the relived experience, thus to eliminate that particular contamination of his self and let the group neutralize or replace the voice or behavior of the introject with its own benevolent, supporting attitudes. It is the regressed self that requires and can be reaffirmed by supportive contact rather than the post-traumatized self, which represents a fusion with the early authority. The "bad" child needs love and reinforcement, not the role-playing psuedoadult.

When in the throes of regressive reliving, the client

exposes those parts of himself that became dissociated in response to real or fantasied authority. When the client is urged to identify with that part of himself rather than with the internalized disapproval, he is likely to experience anxiety, shame, embarrassment, and guilt because he expects the same kind of negative response from the group as he experienced with the original person. Most crucial for lasting personal change is how the individual experiences and utilizes the recrudescences of parts of himself.

An essential condition for change is revalidation of the formerly opposed parts of the self through social reinforcement, that is, the genuine approval or affection of the group for the newly emerged facet of the self and contradiction of the voice of the introject. This process is literally a battle to the death between past and present, between childhood ties and real people in the present.

The client does not, however, easily accept the new social response as nourishing. At first he is likely to perceive it as phony or as a threat to old securities with parents or as another trap with the same self-destructive outcome. He and the group have the intensely emotional challenge of dealing with the discrepancy between internal standards and transference expectations on the one hand and the group's real reaction to him on the other. The client is testing in social reality the fearful fantasied risks that had historically turned him against his self. At this point the therapist's active emotional participation and pressure to perceive are extremely important.

If the reemergence of self is successfully worked through, it brings about extrojection of the authority figure (sometimes with actual vomiting) and the introjection of the positive attitudes of the group toward the revealed self. The introjection of positive feeling is crucial for changing the "bad" self into a newly accepted lovable self.

The double-faceted nature of this process of relearning who one is involves replacement of antiself attitudes with proself feelings and reinclusion of the dissociated parts of the self as *me*. Excessively authoritarian or charismatic approaches or the imposition of approval on the wrong parts of the self or after insufficient struggle with the introject can add other layers of internalized demands upon the client, producing lessened rather than increased freedom.

One such experience, and it is clearly not the same as insight, can be immediately therapeutic because it generally culminates a long period of preparation, development, and experimentation. And it involves a dynamic restructuring of forces already operating within the person. But more often many similar episodes are necessary to free large areas of the self and to increase the amount of self that can be brought to bear upon any one issue. Each experience of this kind brings about ego expansion.

The therapist who uses physical contact to maximize his impact should keep in mind the following considerations. Which clients should he touch or encourage to touch? A suspicious paranoid, a person in homosexual panic, or one suffering from contact phobia might be excessively threatened and find his anxiety and impenetrability increased rather than improved. Verbal expression of contact wishes can sometimes be a useful beginning because it is less likely than actual touch to be threatening and can foster expression of fantasy concerns.

At which points in therapy is some form of contact likely to be both personally meaningful and corrective? Casual contact as training or as impulsive behavior on the part of the therapist can operate as another meaningless ritual or encourage isolation and intellectualization.

Which form of contact is appropriate? Sensuous contact or exploration during periods of fantasied abandonment or oversexualization of body curiosity may confuse communication and increase defensive hiding. Touching with a toe rather than a hand may communicate ambivalence. In either case the client will rightly feel misunderstood again.

Who is the important person with whom the client might make contact? At times the therapist's leadership can break through a group's inhibition about touching, particularly when the group talks of wishes for contact and discomfort about initiating it or asking for it. If there is excessive transference discomfort about contact with one member of the group or with the therapist, a more neutral person may prove to be a successful temporary substitute, possibly a person of a different sex or age in the case of homosexual or heterosexual fear, shame, or guilt.

What kind of therapeutic effect is being sought? The issue with which the client is struggling will ordinarily reveal what ought to be worked out. Whether he needs reassurance that he is acceptable, safe from abandonment, whether his sensual or sexual needs will get out of control, whether he is testing gingerly to discover how far he can go in exposing or expressing himself, whether he is testing the reality of his expectations or discovering how bodies are made—all require different responses from the therapist. If the client is experimenting, which part of him is to be affirmed—his introject, his capitulation to it, his pain, his struggle, or his final expression of self?

Let us now turn from the theoretical to the concrete.

A female client in individual therapy has had little tender contact from her father or from any other man. She is bright and sensitive, but her sensual and sexual needs are subordinated to the belief that she is untouchable and unlovable. Her sexual expression, which has occasionally occurred under alcoholic freedom and sometimes erupts during dissociated states, is ordinarily hidden behind paralyzing shame. During one session she was tearful with no awareness of the content. I offered to hold her hand from across my desk. She was incredulous and hesitant. After a time she permitted contact, talking vaguely of fears of what this might lead to; what if she wished to hold my hand again? She was able to communicate surprise that I would hold her hand knowing that she had used it in masturbating. My impression was that this was a turning point in therapy in that my reassurance broke through the barrier of shame and accepted the person behind it. At the same time it was possible to separate longing for nourishing contact from sexuality which had contaminated it. Subsequently the client showed many signs of reintegration: spontaneous affect with a broad range, open communication, and a more clear-cut sense of identity.

A male homosexual is sobbing with feelings of loneliness and isolation. I tell of my impulse to hold him. He becomes agitated and forbids contact. He relates contact even with a man to surrender of himself and fusion with another person. Later he was able to desexualize contact and to discover that sexuality as faceless promiscuity was a way of avoiding his terror at becoming addicted to another person who offered warmth like his mother, who was undependable.

A seriously regressed schizophrenic woman is outraged that I have not offered to hold her, although she gave no outward indication of wishing it. She had recurrent dreams of holding someone's hand and running away, of contaminated food. She imagined my hand as so hot as to burn her skin. After many months of my holding my hand out to her, she dared to touch it. Gradually she could experience my hand as having normal temperature. Her icy-cold hands gradually became warmer. She continued to test the reality of her concrete ideas and her bizarre body image by touching my head, face, arms, and chest and gradually accepted that I had no breasts like her mother. She built gradually an image of my body as three-dimensional, carrying blood. She was extremely attentive to cuts in my skin which she attributed to her destructive fantasies. She more frequently asked me to hold her or lie on the floor with her; at times she placed her ear on my chest so that she could hear and feel my reassuring heartbeat. She said, "Contact with you pulls together the fragments and makes me feel like one person." The painful headaches and shoulder muscle tension subsided. She said, "My feelings in my body have changed. Before, I was a little girl, stiff and rigid. Now I feel flexible. It feels like a woman's body." She was able slowly to differentiate between me and her mother and sister. She had never known her father. She later lived through a symbiotic tie with me in which she experienced physical separation as a plucking away of her flesh. She phoned frequently to discover whether I really existed and whether she could begin to visualize me. She was enraged at my vacations as punishment for her "badness." She learned to accept and experience body boundaries and separateness, to discriminate between fantasies of persons and their reality. She was becoming empirical rather than living in a world projected from her chaotic early years. Working with someone at this level, with a person whose humanization was interrupted so early, provides much evidence about the bodily basis of ego and self-development. It is also a painfully challenging task.

A married woman, dominated by a sense of duty, limitedly aware of her own needs, becomes anxious and trembles during a group session. Her mind is blank. She says she needs something from the therapist, but does not know what it is. I offer to hold her to allay her anxiety. In an almost hypnotic state she places my hand on her breast. The group is uncomfortable and so am I. I discuss my discomfort with the group but intend to follow through with whatever is happening. The client becomes calm and recollects earlier dreams about fear of exposure, her breasts being visible, and her shame. The group approves her act rather than condemning it as she had expected. Months later in connection with her symptom of perspiring hands she talks of her relative comfort in being touched and her panic about actively touching others. Through successive phases she describes and lives out her anxiety and embarrassment in touching a male client's genital area. She is amazed at how different this experience is from similar behavior with her husband when they both intended to have sex together. She relives age five with her father and both speaks and feels from this period. While perspiring profusely and admitting to excitement, which is childlike curiosity rather than sexuality, she dares to touch the breasts of a lesbian woman. The male members are particularly apprehensive until I point out that the client is not being erotically seductive. I suggest that she is recapturing her wish for exploratory contact with her mother and sisters and that this inescapable need is more difficult for women to meet. The group admired this client's courage in exposing and expressing her little-girl wishes. Her heterosexual life became more rewarding as she no longer sought from men what she needed from a woman. All these activities grew out of her partially repressed fantasies and were accompanied by anxiety, shame, expectation of criticism, and temporary regression in this competent, functioning woman. Subsequently, women in other groups have enacted the same kind of recovery of old longings that had been disavowed.

A homosexual woman had established relationships in which she touched women both warmly and sexually in order to maintain control over them. She, herself, was afraid of being touched. She enacted simultaneous roles of mother and child in her relationships but could not tolerate the cuddling she knew she needed. After a time in group she was able to ask women to sit by her and gradually invited them to touch various parts of her body. Whenever her anxiety became pronounced, she stopped the contact. During these episodes she abreacted and extrojected childhood experiences of being misused sexually by father-surrogates and of being slapped by her mother. She gradually lost all anxiety about being touched in group and began to enjoy the sensuality without fear of being taken over. She began to experiment with touching a male homosexual in the group who himself had been terrified of contact with a woman. Later she permitted him to touch her. Her wishes for childlike mutual body exploration with this man emerged along with feelings of trust. They planned to spend an evening together and had occasional dinners to share their fears and to set limits on themselves. Both feared intercourse, and the therapist cautioned them that intercourse was not the appropriate goal at this time, that the underpinnings of sexuality such as trust and reassuring body experience were the crucial issues. I pointed out that many adults force themselves to have intercourse as the adult thing to do when their real needs were to cuddle or to have literally child's play: fun and exploration. The adult standards which they and the heterosexual members of the group pursued were sidetracking the childhood needs which had never been expressed.

A middle-aged man feels rejected by the women in the group because they omit him in their fantasies of affection and contact. He has devoted much of his life to fantasies of his ideal image of the stalwart, tough male. He cannot understand why the women prefer other men whose emotions cover a wider range and who reveal their weaknesses. He clings to the belief

that they would like him if he were more "manly." While recounting his mother's death, he tried to stifle his tears. The
group brushed aside the adult veneer and encouraged his tears
and sadness despite his shame. When he sobbed openly the
group supported him, the women held him, approved of his
openness, and contradicted his feeling of shame. Both therapist
and group convinced him that his child-sadness was more admirable and lovable than his pseudoadult pose. He became
able to discard the masculine image, to identify with his feelings, and to experience genuine affection from both men and
women. He became open and tender and perceptive, rather
than stiff, complaining, and oblique. He was startled to learn
that women felt more sexual toward him when he felt soft and
weak than they did when he was supermasculine. He became,
in fact, more tough and realistic in his business dealings than
he had been.

In most of these cases the pressure of the therapist or
group encouraged renunciation of the role playing that hid the
vital child feelings and motivations behind the mask of pseudoadult, and stimulated the revelation of repressed aspects of self;
the individual could expect and receive the always needed love
only for showing those parts of self that had been relinquished
for early adult approval. To reward and reinforce self-renunciation in any of its aspects is to settle for approval for one's best
behavior while surrendering hopes for love of oneself. So long
as the precious emotional-motivational self is unshared, social
disapproval cannot change one's self-concept. There is always
the doubt: "If you really knew me you wouldn't like me. Touching my outer surface does not touch me." To comfort or re-
assure prematurely precludes contact with the important aspects
of the person that require reexpression and revalidation.

A young woman, formerly a model, overweight, seductive, masking her childlike dependence, announced to the group
that she felt depressed. It was suggested that she share the full
feeling of her depression with the group and let us into that
part of her. She refused to do so but asked me to comfort her
by putting my hand on her knee. I refused and she became
angry, accusing me of having a problem with girls because I

had hugged men in her presence. I commented that her request was a trick because she was asking for sensual recognition or admiration rather than letting me into her depression, where I might be able to get under her skin. I would have felt seduced as other men had been by the somewhat sexual adult pose and she would have escaped the risk and reward of exposing the sad little girl.

A woman who had long hidden her sadness and self-loathing behind obesity and jollity has been confronted and begins to cry. Another woman, who uses maternalistic giving to avoid fears associated with receiving, rushes to hold her. I suggest that holding her is not being helpful. She continues. I insist that she stop holding the crying woman, who later admits that the holding stifled her feelings before she could fully experience what was upsetting her.

A homosexual male engineer, generally rational but prone to tears when others reveal their anguish, dares after having experienced contact with women in the group to ask a woman to hold him. He could remember only one incident of affection from his mother, a time when he had been injured. This particular woman said she could not feel affectionate toward a computer and that is how he appeared at the moment. It was difficult for him to understand why he would be less acceptable when rational, responsible, and productive than when he showed weakness, childishness, sorrow, and self. The experience of rejection sent him into an episode of lonely sobbing. At this point the woman began to hold him and talk to him tenderly. He clung to her and said in amazement that he seemed to be getting approval for the wrong reasons, for being a child rather than for being a hard-working, self-denying adult. Everything seemed topsy-turvy.

The therapist, too, is a person who uses his body as well as his mind, even though he may avoid direct contact. His untouchability is as much a communication as his touching or openness to being touched. His own adaptations to his and others' bodies, to physical dependence, sensuality, and sexuality, will have much influence on what he does. If he is willing to make contact, he has the problem of assessing his clients and predicting his impact on them. He will sometimes find it difficult to discern whose needs are being met, his clients' or his own. The contact may be most effective if both persons' needs are being met in some constructive way. He will not always be able to discriminate between his personal and his career self; the borderline is often fuzzy and shifting. He may use contact to express his need for power, or he may deceive himself that he is warmer and more capable of intimacy than he really is. He may touch in moments of desperation when his professional arsenal is bankrupt. He may touch routinely or allow himself to be touched too casually and thus encourage intellectualization and avoidance of clinical issues. He or his client may experience a momentary thrill whose impact quickly fades. Or he may foster the development of a counterphobic layer that hides a lack of real change. He may fear his clients' fantasy life or his own excitement. He may encourage action without self-exposure and induce further self-destructive anxiety or guilt in his clients or himself.

He is likely more than once to misread his clients out of his own unrecognized needs and his own incomplete humanization. The underpinnings of his own contact needs, sensuality, sexuality, and interpersonal patterns are under constant stimulation and challenge from both within and without (Forer, 1965). If he is reasonably honest, open with himself, tolerant of anxiety and uncertainty, and well-trained in his work, he may grow almost as fast as his clients.

12

Audio-Tape Programs for Self-Directed Groups

Betty Berzon, Lawrence N. Solomon,
Jerome Reisel

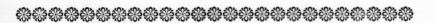

"I'm Dr. Jerry Reisel, one of the people who designed this program, and it's my voice you'll be hearing on these tapes, suggesting in each session ways in which you might get the most out of this group." So begins one of the two audio-tape programs for personal growth learning through encounter groups which we developed at the Western Behavioral Sciences Institute in La Jolla, California.[1]

The encounter group is an excellent medium for personal growth learning. The group process enables participants to look closely at their own feelings about themselves, to see how

[1] This investigation was supported, in part, by Research Grant No. 1748-P from the Vocational Rehabilitation Administration, now part of the Social and Rehabilitation Service, Department of Health, Education, and Welfare, Washington, D.C. 20201.

those feelings affect their behavior, and to see how their behavior makes other people feel toward them. On the basis of what they learn, group members can test personally fulfilling ways of relating. They can extend their repertoire of behaviors and strengthen their emotional resources so they are better able to accomplish what they want to happen between them and other people.

Since these goals are very much in line with those of any counseling or rehabilitation activity, the encounter group can be an important resource in such programs. However, its application is limited by the same problem that limits the usefulness of much we have learned through behavioral science research and through less organized means of inquiry into human affairs. Who will implement the ideas? Where can we find the professional manpower to put into practice the knowledge we have gained?

Long, drawn-out graduate training programs in the helping professions are not going to provide manpower in sufficient numbers to meet the current need. An obvious alternative is to help people do for each other what they previously asked the professional to do for them. One such means is the self-directed encounter group, where individuals meet together without a professional leader present and, through the immediate shared experience of the group, help each other learn and grow.

To implement this approach we at WBSI began, twelve years ago, to study self-directed groups. First, we tried to learn what, if anything, was lacking in the absence of a professional leader. After five years of observation, data collection, and comparison with professionally directed groups meeting under similar conditions, we felt we understood some of the missing ingredients. The basic finding was that participants would not, over an extended period of time, assume responsibility for what happened in the group (Berzon, Pious, and Farson, 1962; Berzon and Solomon, 1964). We had to find ways to promote interpersonal responsibility, to orient the participants to facilitative interaction, to provide opportunities for them to confront each other, and to structure these experiences so as to maximize learning.

PILOT PROGRAM

In 1965 we began a three-year, federally supported project to develop structuring materials for self-directed groups. Our first program consisted of eighteen booklets, one for each of eighteen sessions. Each group member had a booklet; the contents were read aloud, a paragraph at a time, by the group members taking turns reading. The program was tested in eight small groups of vocational rehabilitation clients who met twice weekly for nine weeks. Four groups were professionally directed and did not use the structuring materials. The other four groups were self-directed and did use the materials. Evaluation was made using a battery of research measures. The self-directed groups compared favorably with the professionally directed groups in that both enabled participants to become more self-disclosing and to develop more positive self-concepts. However, direct observation of the self-directed groups made it apparent that the program material should be much less cognitive, less structured, and more experiential (details regarding experimental design, data analysis, and results are presented in Solomon, Berzon, and Weedman, 1968).

VOCATIONAL IMPROVEMENT PROGRAM (VIP)

In 1966, an entirely new eighteen-session Vocational Improvement Program was developed to enhance an individual's ability to make fuller use of his social and vocational potential through better understanding and a broadened experiencing of himself in relation to other people.

The program was presented on audio-tape, rather than in booklet form—a major change from the previous year. The audio-tape recordings provided a way to intervene with additional instructions during sessions and to present dramatized examples of points made in the instructions, making the program more vital and involving than it had been. Group members were told, during a brief orientation period at the beginning of each group, that they would find a different tape on the machine at the beginning of each session and that they need only turn on the recorder to begin the session. Instructions for each session's exercise usually took about ten minutes. A participant's notebook included forms needed for certain exercises, as well as some of the material presented on the tapes for the participants' later reference.

In addition to changes in format, the content of the program was completely revised, based on learnings from the first year. Twenty-four vocational rehabilitation clients participated in a Self-Improvement Workshop, using the VIP tapes. They met in groups of approximately eight persons for two two-hour sessions a day, over nine consecutive days.

Since we felt that results of the professionally directed and the structured self-directed groups in the previous year had been sufficiently alike, the professionally directed condition was eliminated in this study. One experimental condition and one control condition were compared. The experimental condition consisted of self-directed, structured groups in which the subjects met without a professionally trained leader and used the program materials to guide their interaction. There were three groups of approximately eight persons each in this condition. The control subjects were vocational rehabilitation clients who were given no group experience. Pretests and posttests were administered to control subjects concurrent with data collection on the experimental subjects.

Quantitative assessment was made using a battery of seven research instruments. They included pretests and posttests to measure self-concept change, self-disclosure, motivation to work, and self-understanding: (a day-by-day self-and peer-rating instrument); and session-by-session process ratings made from tape recordings, attendance and attrition records, and the subject's ratings of his own self-disclosure.

A series of assumptions regarding personal growth guided the interpretation of results. Personal growth was judged to occur if the participant: 1) experienced self-concept change in a positive direction, as measured by a semantic differential rating form; 2) experienced change in a positive direction in his motivation to work and his self-understanding, as measured in interviews rated by experts; 3) became more open with others, in his own perception, as measured by the Who Knows You

Inventory; 4) came to perceive greater congruence between his subjective feelings and his overt behavior in the group, as measured by a Self-Disclosure Index; 5) became more genuine, personal, risk-taking, and sensitive to others in the groups, as rated by other group members on the Group Experience Rating Form; 6) came to see himself as others saw him, as measured by a decreasing discrepancy between self- and peer-ratings on the Group Experience Rating Form.

Results of the study support seven of these ten specific assumptions: These self-directed groups, using program materials, did promote positive changes in the participants' ability to be more open, sensitive to others, self-disclosing, self-accepting, and self-motivating. Control subjects (no group experience) showed no such changes. A more detailed description of the evaluation procedures and results is presented in Solomon, Berzon, and Davis, 1970).

VOCATIONAL IMPROVEMENT PROGRAM (REVISED)

On the basis of research results and direct observation of the groups, the program was revised. The number of sessions was reduced from eighteen to twelve. A brief description of each follows.

Session 1: Orientation. The main purpose of this session is to establish group norms along the lines of trust-building and facilitative behavior. Members are presented with a set of group ground rules and a list of ten characteristics which employers look for in a "good employee," the latter heavily weighted with interpersonal factors. The exercise is to rank-order the ten characteristics in terms of their relative importance. This is a group task, and the rank-ordering must be consensual.

Session 2: Listening lab. In this session, rules of good listening are presented and a checklist using these rules is provided in the participant's notebook. The exercise is to form triads, or three-person groups, in which one person takes the role of the talker, one the listener, and one an observer who uses the checklist to rate the listener on his listening behavior. The talker's task is to talk for ten minutes about why he came to this group. The roles are then rotated so that each person has a chance to take each role.

Session 3: Paraphrasing. This exercise is built on the previous session's material. Each person tells the group what his talker told him about why he came to the group. This task serves the dual purpose of underlining the importance of listening to understand others and of making information about each participant available to the entire group.

Session 4: Self-appraisal. In a go-around, each group member selects and talks about one of the ten characteristics of a good employee that he thinks he needs to work on to make himself more sought after as an employee.

Session 5: Feedback. The tape-recorded narration presents information regarding the importance of giving and receiving feedback in the group. Definitions and examples of facilitative and nonfacilitative feedback are given on the tape. Group members then practice giving and receiving facilitative feedback in a go-around exercise.

Session 6: Unfortunate circumstances. Each group member tells the most unfortunate circumstance in his life and discusses his feelings about it.

Session 7: Descriptions of others. Each group member describes each other group member metaphorically, thus initiating here-and-now interpersonal feedback in an indirect way.

Session 8: Descriptions of self. In another go-around each individual describes himself metaphorically, giving the group an opportunity to know more about him.

Session 9: Feeling pooling. In this session, each individual anonymously writes on a slip of paper a strong feeling he has about another group member. The slips are placed in a pile, drawn out one at a time, and read aloud by others, who comment on why they think someone would feel that way about the person named. The group members are encouraged to elaborate, drawing on their own feelings toward the person.

Session 10: Secret pooling.[2] Each group member is asked to write down a personal secret anonymously on a slip of paper.

---

[2] The authors are grateful to Dr. Gerald Goodman for this exercise.

The papers are folded, scrambled, and each person then takes one. He then reads aloud the secret he selected from the pool and tells how he thinks it would feel to have a secret like that. (Paper and pencils of uniform nature are provided to insure anonymity.)

Session 11: Strength bombardment.[3] Each group member takes a turn in which he spends 1) three minutes telling the rest of the group about his strengths and 2) five minutes listening to the other group members tell him what they see about him that is good and strong.

Session 12: Self-reappraisal. Each participant is asked to look again at the list of ten characteristics of a good employee and to select the one he thinks he needs to work on most or to talk about any other way in which he thinks he needs to make an effort to change.

PLANNED EXPERIENCES FOR EFFECTIVE RELATING (PEER PROGRAM)

In 1967, a third program was developed, titled Planned Experiences for Effective Relating. In line with the broadening definition of vocational disability, we decided to use a less goal-oriented approach in the content of PEER. We wanted to provide a higher payoff in learning experiences for participants whose vocational problems have a broad social and/or emotional base and to give the program wider applicability in the counseling and rehabilitation fields.

The goal was redefined as follows: to help learn to relate more fully and effectively to the world around them. To accomplish this purpose, PEER provides a series of structured opportunities for each participant to 1) express more easily his genuine feelings and receive the genuine feelings of others; 2) inquire more actively into his own experience; and 3) try new behaviors in the group. The individual increases his awareness of choices available to him, understands better how he functions in groups, and gains more control over what happens between him and other people. The PEER goals are based on those defined by Bennis (1962).

[3] The authors are grateful to Dr. Herbert Otto for this exercise.

In comparison with the revised VIP, the PEER program had two fewer sessions and stressed experiential learning even more. The approach is illustrated by the following brief review of the PEER sessions.[4]

Session 1: First encounter microlab. This session uses the concept of the compressed-time microlab (see Chapter 10), in which a series of short, timed meetings and a variety of activities bring the participants into confrontation with one another. Activities include the following: *Impressions*—Group members stand in a circle and one at a time go around the circle, stopping in front of each person. They are to touch the person to make contact, look directly at him, and tell him their impression of him. *Break-In*—Group members stand in a circle, and one at a time each individual steps outside the circle, then tries to break in, to become part of the in-group. The other group members are instructed to keep the person from breaking in. *Rolling*—Group members stand in a circle; one at a time each individual goes to the center of the circle, relaxes as completely as he can, and allows himself to be passed around by the other group members—literally putting himself in the group's hands. At the beginning of each activity, the recorded narration relates the activity to a personal growth issue, such as honesty, affiliation, or trust. After each exercise, a timed discussion period is provided in which participants are encouraged to discuss their feelings about what they just did.

Session 2: Ground rule. The narrator presents a ground rule which emphasizes the importance of expressing feelings and of learning from the immediate, shared, here-and-now experience of the group. The rule is 1) to tune into what is happening inside yourself and in the group, and 2) to talk about it. Examples of tuned-in and tuned-out groups are presented

---

[4] The exercises in the PEER Program are based upon experimental work done over the last decade by a number of people associated with personal growth learning in small groups. William C. Schutz contributed actual exercises (Impressions and Giving and Receiving), synthesis of previously developed techniques (Break-In, Rolling, Break-Out), and ideas for program format and organization. The work of Joyce and John Weir and Hannah Weiner, with nonverbal techniques in small groups, influenced the design of several exercises in PEER.

on the tape. Group members then pair off to practice this kind of tuned-in interaction and later reassemble as a total group to discuss what has happened.

Session 3: Feedback. Same as VIP Session 5.

Session 4: Progress report. Concepts presented in the first three sessions are reviewed on the tape, and group members are asked to report to themselves on how they are doing relative to the ground rule, giving and using feedback, and so on.

Session 5: Secret pooling. Same as VIP Session 10.

Session 6: Break-out. Group members stand in a ring, and one at a time each individual goes into the center of the circle. He is asked to deal with the circle of people as a problem that stands between him and his freedom. The instruction to the person in the center is to break out of the circle. The instruction to the other group members is to do everything they can to keep the person in the circle. Following the exercise, group members discuss what has happened and how they felt about it.

Session 7: Descriptions. Participants are asked to go around, one at a time, and describe each member metaphorically—such as an animal, a piece of furniture, a car—telling everything they can about what they are describing, including how they feel about it. Examples of this kind of metaphorical description are given on the tape.

Session 8: Strength bombardment. Same as VIP Session 11.

Session 9: Giving and receiving. Participants are asked to select three people who have had the most trouble letting the other group members get close to them. Then, one at a time, these three people step into the center of the circle. Also one at a time, the other group members go to the person in the center and nonverbally express the positive feelings they have toward him. The person in the center is instructed to receive this expression without returning it—to have an undiluted experience of receiving without giving back. After the three people, and anyone else who wishes to, have taken their turns, the group members discuss what has happened and how they feel about it.

Session 10: Last encounter microlab. This session again involves a series of timed meetings, with varied activities. As in Session 1, the group members do Impressions and Rolling, each of which is followed by a discussion of what happened and how people felt about it. Opportunity is provided for participants to focus on how group members have changed in the PEER group. It is then suggested that they use the rest of the session to take care of unfinished business and to say goodbye to each other.

Evaluation of this study shifted away from examining the self-directed programed approach as such, since it was thought that the feasibility of the approach had been adequately demonstrated by previous studies. Emphasis in this third and final year of the project was on refinement of the program content, format, and presentation. Research instrumentation, therefore, was drastically reduced from that of the first and second years of this project.

Eight experimental groups of approximately eight persons each met in two different settings oriented toward personal growth: a county honor camp with a strong treatment focus and a university YMCA. Three groups were composed of honor camp inmates (n=28) and five of university students (n=47). The control condition was no group experience. Control subjects were comparable individuals from the same two subject populations described above. Pretests and posttests were administered to them concurrent with data collection on the experimental subjects. There were forty-four control subjects in all, twenty-five honor-camp inmates and nineteen university students. All groups met for two two-hour sessions each day for five consecutive days. In each setting, all groups met during the same five-day period.

There was no provision in either of the experimental settings for observing groups, and we felt that it was important for further program development to have feedback on group members' responses to the exercises. Therefore, in each of the eight groups, one member was asked to be a participant-observer. This person kept a log and met with us after the program was completed to report, in some detail, on the sessions. Prior to the first session, the group was informed about the participant-observer. This person was identified for each group, and his duties were described. It was also explained that he was not a leader, had no special training, had never heard the tapes, and was going to participate as just another member of the group.

Attendance and drop-out records were kept for both experimental populations in order to compare results with the 1965 and 1966 studies in this project. Two instruments were used to evaluate pre-post changes in participants: a self-concept scale and a scale to assess the individual's sense of personal efficacy. Both quantitative data provided by the research instruments and qualitative data provided by reports of participants and participant-observers were used to assess the effectiveness of the PEER Program.

The quantitative data yield outcome information about format and content. Results indicate that 1) subjects who went through PEER groups experienced positive change in their self-concept, while (no group) control subjects did not; 2) those subjects who went through PEER groups did not experience change in their feelings of personal efficacy, nor did (no group) control subjects; and 3) attendance and attrition rates in the self-directed groups tended to be more favorable than were those rates in the 1965 and 1966 studies. As in the previous studies, the self-concept does appear to be positively affected by this approach to personal growth.

Qualitative data were obtained from participant-observer reports and group interviews held with participants after completion of the program. Participants found the program to be an effective unifying and focusing instrument in the groups. Presentation and format were favorably received. It appeared from subjects' reports that an unusual degree of group cohesion was attained very early in the sessions; this occurrence was probably due to the physical contact involved in Session 1, which would tend to decrease the psychological distance among participants sooner than might happen without such activity.

Apparently, participants were given adequate personal freedom, since they were able in many instances to modify the instructions to fit their needs of the moment or to ignore them altogether. As one student member put it, "We discovered that we could turn off the tape-recorder, that 'The Voice' was not inviolable. Once we did that, we felt we could do it anytime and we were freer to hear what 'The Voice' had to say."

As would be predicted, the physical contact was much more acceptable in the coeducational student groups than it was in the all-male inmate groups. However, the inmates reported that their discomfort with the physical contact evoked much discussion about men living in close and continuous proximity. They felt such discussion was helpful and believed it never would have occurred if they had not been confronted with the PEER exercises.

In particular, activities that participants liked best involved use of feedback in any form. This finding is in line with results of the two previous years in which those sessions featuring feedback were most highly valued both in self-reports and in process ratings. See Solomon and Berzon (1970) for further details of this study.

CONCLUSIONS

The three studies described here lead us to conclude that self-directed groups, using carefully planned program materials, can effectively facilitate personal growth for the individuals who participate in them. Program materials provide minimally structured opportunities for people to give constructive feedback to each other, to experience themselves in new ways, and to extend their repertoire of behaviors. The materials seem to make their most valuable contribution in these aspects of personal growth learning in small groups.

The authors see PEER and VIP being used for a variety of purposes: to increase personal effectiveness for the individual group member; to train people to use their membership in groups more effectively; to help potential group leaders learn through experience about group processes; to provide both an experiential and a conceptual basis for a long-term self-directed group that will continue beyond the ten sessions; and to identify indigenous leadership in community health, education, welfare, and social action programs.

The Vocational Improvement Program will be most appropriate for clients whose problems are primarily vocational. In either an agency or a residential setting, the VIP might be part of the intake process, or it might be used with clients or job trainees who are not making adequate use of the training they are receiving or have received. Because of PEER's more general focus, it will undoubtedly have applicability for counselor education, staff development training, and clients whose problems are not only vocational but have a broader social and/or emotional base.

For the future, custom programs offer particular promise. For instance, a program might be written especially for children, or for families, or for parties to a negotiation—labor, foreign power, or civil rights. Programs could be developed for any group of people who have a special problem or concern in common. With sufficient interfacing of such programs, social systems might begin to evolve that would enhance rather than inhibit the creative growth of individuals. That goal seems worthy of a very special continuing effort.

13

Self-Directed Groups
and Community
Mental Health

Richard E. Farson

Human relationships in modern American life are appallingly
superficial. Urbanization has increased our physical proximity to
each other but at the same time, somehow, has widened the
emotional distance between us. Even the physical intimacy of
family life is rarely matched by emotional intimacy. Many of us
go through life without knowing the security of a single deep
or significant relationship upon which we can depend for support and understanding, for sharing problems and feelings, and
in which we can be truly and simply ourselves, without fear or
facade.

Indeed, the mental health problem of mid-twentieth-
century America is primarily a matter of dealing with the
pervasive feelings of loneliness, alienation, frustration, general-

ized anxiety—the supposedly normal feelings which beset us all. How few of us feel that we are really important to others; how few of us have any opportunity to care about others or to be cared for, to share our concerns and hopes, to share ourselves as we really are, openly and honestly—in short, to become fully human. And how much more exaggerated these feelings must be in the socially deprived, the jobless, the dispossessed. How we prize those rare, authentic moments of humanness, moments when we can make contact with another human being. We all need such moments because they give us back ourselves. To the professional interested in community mental health, the basic challenge is to find a way to provide such experiences for great numbers of people—for everyone.

The professionally directed unstructured group, by whatever name it is called, affords just such moments of deep human encounter and is being used in a great variety of settings, from mental hospitals to rehabilitation projects to management development programs. For several years, at the Western Behavioral Sciences Institute, we studied the feasibility of the self-directed group as a means of providing this very rewarding experience for large numbers of people who might not otherwise have access to it. We had found in our early research on professionally led groups that they are effective in large part because they make use of the simple fact that people help each other. Of course—people always have! Our work on the possibilities of self-directed groups was based on the premise, therefore, that people are resources for each other. Probably whatever advances we make in community mental health programs in the near future will be grounded on this neglected phenomenon.

Our first research on self-directed groups was carried out in the institute's group laboratories where we could screen the participants and observe, rate, tape-record, and otherwise monitor the interactions. Comparisons with concurrent professionally directed control groups made it overwhelmingly clear that self-directed groups are almost indistinguishable from professionally directed groups in very important ways, and they entail no greater risks of negative effects. The leaderless group seems to be not only practical and economical but a thoroughly satisfactory format for enabling people to discover themselves and each other (Solomon and Berzon, 1970).

We began to wonder how such a promising mental health resource might be made available to much greater numbers of people. Could self-directed groups be set up throughout the community? But how could they be directed away from the familiar discussion-group format and moved toward interpersonal exploration and involvement? Suppose such groups were to watch a professionally directed group in action. Why not try television? Would the televised, unrehearsed sessions of a basic encounter group, edited to fit time limitations and with suitable commentary, serve to stimulate and guide totally naive groups? These questions prompted our research efforts.[1]

The public affairs director of the San Diego NBC station, KOGO-TV, was enthusiastic; so was the director of the University of California's Extension Division. Our first step was to send a letter and application form to approximately five hundred people on our institute mailing list, people who had attended our lectures, been volunteer research subjects, or expressed interest in our work. We invited them to participate, as members of a community group or a studio group, in a combined educational-and-research project on interpersonal relations in small groups.

We received 155 applications, about half of which indicated willingness to be in the studio group. We selected forty-four for personal interviews. From these we composed a group of seven persons, six of whom had no previous group experience or acquaintance with each other or with the leader, who were typical of the community with respect to background and age range, and who could meet one morning a week for thirteen weeks. The four women, ranging in age from twenty-six to fifty-five, included a wage-and-salary administrator for an electronics

[1] I am deeply grateful to all those individuals who contributed their time and talent to this project, including Hope Warren Shaw, C. A. Lewis, Melinda Sprague, Toni Volcani, W. H. McGraw, Jr., Dorothy Edwards, Lorraine Gibb, Elizabeth Allison, Helen Rogers, Kathy Ritter, Mavis Holley, Carol Sprague, Harriet Washburn, and Ann Dreyfuss.

firm, the manager of a telephone answering service, a volunteer worker for the Democratic party, and a housewife. In addition to the leader, the men were: a twenty-two-year-old college student majoring in business administration, a civil servant in the county administration office, and a physicist employed with an industrial research organization.

The group met once a week for an hour-long session in the television studio. Each session was videotaped; important incidents from the session, plus brief commentary by the leader, were shown a week later as a half-hour episode in a thirteen-week TV series entitled Human Encounter. (Incidentally, the studio group members generally forgot about the cameras, just as we have found that in the group laboratories people soon ignore the tape recorders and the observers behind the one-way vision windows.)

The project had two overlapping objectives: first, to explore the potential of television for showing people being genuinely themselves. We felt that the medium's great intimacy and immediacy might make it an important mental health resource —for example, as a sanction for the expression of genuine emotions or as reassurance that we all share similar perplexities, fears, and aspirations and are a part of the human condition. I think we confirmed this view; all the episodes fairly well demonstrate that TV can be used to show people developing caring relationships, deepening their understanding of themselves, and helping one another in a variety of ways. And we found, too, that the public quite readily accepts so unexpected a program, sandwiched between commercials on a network station. One viewer wrote:

My viewing friends and I often talk about what has happened each week and find ourselves feeling quite involved in the experience. The people in the group are certainly real to us and help us to see ourselves in old—and new—ways. I feel it is true to say that each of us has been affected, in some way, by the program; each has had his own unique relationship and experience with the show. It is marvelous to think about the possibilities inherent in this sort of show.

Here is another in its entirety. "Please continue Human Encounter; it is helping me to communicate more effectively with my wife. Sunday 12 noon is most ideal. Thank You."

Our second objective was to explore the feasibility of the self-directed group itself, as a community mental health resource. So, let me describe how these groups were organized, how we monitored them, and how they worked out.

For the convenience of the 120 participants, the community groups were composed on a geographical basis. Except for an effort to distribute the sexes as evenly as possible throughout the groups, the assignments were random. We did no screening, nor did we try to establish any criteria of psychological adjustment as we had in our previous research on self-directed groups.

In setting up our groups, we tried to devise a format that could be used on a much larger scale. Thus, after sorting the applications geographically according to home addresses, we arrived at twelve groups, each containing eight to twelve persons. In each group we included one person whose application had indicated willingness to be a convener—to provide a meeting place. We talked to the conveners by phone, making clear that their function was only that of host and in no way that of leader. With few exceptions, this was the extent of our personal communication with any of the participants until the project ended.

Each participant received a list containing the names and phone numbers of the other members of his group; the name, address, and phone number of the convener; and a request that he contact the convener. The accompanying letter outlined the research aspects of the program in greater detail and asked each participant to keep a research diary describing his experience in each session and incidents, if any, that had affected him negatively or positively. Diaries were to be mailed to the institute within forty-eight hours after each session. The community groups met each Sunday to watch the TV program and then proceeded with their own self-directed session.

The diaries were read by volunteer research assistants,

women with extensive group experience. Each volunteer, or *diary mother* as they came to call themselves, was assigned to monitor the diaries of a single group for the duration of the project. At weekly conferences, each diary mother abstracted the material from her group and presented the development of the group as she saw it.

As might be expected, after the first few weeks the research diaries became sparse, both in quantity and quality. Much of what had at first gone into the diaries was being expressed in the group meetings. And as those who at first viewed their participation as a contribution to research began to be more deeply involved in the human-encounter aspect of their experience, their attitude tended to be "to hell with the research." As the "my group" feeling developed, participants seemed to resist such formalistic intrusions as reporting drop-outs (surprisingly few) or new members—some of whom we did not know about until their research diaries appeared or even until the project was over.

Perhaps we all have to face the fact that carrying out community studies by mail or telephone will be frustrating for those of us who are accustomed to working with more pliable and accessible laboratory subjects. Nevertheless, we were able to monitor the groups satisfactorily, assure ourselves that no seriously negative incidents were taking place, and get some feeling of what their experiences meant to the participants.

One man wrote: "A few more sessions like this and I could be changed into a more sensitive person. There are vague stirrings of an inner nature that are disquieting and hopeful." An older woman wrote: "I have definitely let down some of the barriers I kept up for so many years. I've learned to give a little, maybe initiate friendly overtures. I don't know just when it happened. Maybe it's just that I've become conscious of doing it now."

A forty-year-old man said:

I found myself in a position of being able to help someone, just by talking with them. Someone asked me for help. . . . *I don't think I have ever been so concerned over anyone, except my family, as I am over her. I have often questioned myself, "Does anyone in this world really need me?"*

A young married woman:

My experience in this session was the most exhilarating and exciting thing I have ever gone through. I feel like the new and real me finally came to the surface. I felt such a warmth in the group and such a freedom never before experienced. Our group broke up about five, and even then I hated to leave. It was a very enriching experience and I'm looking forward so much to next week.

This from a young woman:

I approached this meeting with some feelings of dread. I wanted to go, but I didn't want to go. Last time, I had expressed myself rather emotionally at one point and I think I was really feeling a little embarrassed about it. I decided this time I would just keep quiet. I was surprised, however, when they praised me and seemed to feel that I had been the only one to really express some strong feelings, but even if they hadn't, I don't think I could have kept quiet. I really want to talk.

Shortly after the Human Encounter series ended, each community group came to the institute for an unstructured follow-up group interview conducted by professional staff members; we tried to determine the quality of the relationships that had developed and to discover if any participants had had significantly negative experiences. The interviewers uniformly felt that the participants had by and large benefited significantly and that the groups had developed a great deal of cohesion.

In general, we found (1) the plan was feasible. The use of the television program as a stimulus for the community groups, in this instance only twelve, could just as easily have involved 1,200 or 12,000 groups. (2) Most people did watch and make use of the television program. (Interestingly, the television program gave rise to spontaneous groups about which we heard only indirectly—groups formed in churches or bars which met regularly throughout the series, evidently with outcomes similar to those of the research groups. There was no mention of the community groups on the broadcasts.) (3) Of seventy-two respondents to a questionnaire, sixty-nine regarded the experience as helpful. (Interviews with the three people who regarded the experience as not helpful led the interviewers to feel that these people had been stirred out of habitual attitudes and were in fact as deeply involved in the group experience and as committed to it as the rest.) (4) The overwhelming majority of the group members felt that their group was considerably better than the televised group on the basis of freedom to expose true feelings, the ability to talk honestly and directly to others, cooperative efforts to understand and help each other, and the development of an atmosphere which made it easy for people to explore and show feelings. Most people did find the experiences valuable and important. (5) The groups developed such cohesiveness and importance that nine months later seven of the twelve groups were still meeting, and all but two of the twelve groups met for a longer period than they had expected. (6) Diary material showed that one member in each of three groups was disturbed enough to cause professional concern. However, it is not clear that these people could have been screened out in any circumstances, and in each case the diary monitoring showed that other members responded constructively to a remarkable degree and that the groups had not been disrupted.

CONCLUSIONS

The phrase *community mental health* conjures up an image of clinics. We must broaden our view to include programs that will pervade the basic institutions of society—family, schools, churches, industry. In such programs, and in many other ways, too, television can be an important resource. Vicarious experience, identification with participants in a televised group, may in itself be beneficial; in our previous research we found that vicarious experience is an important factor in growth and change. Seeing people as they really are, rather than playing roles as actors or as public images . . . the reality of the relationship between the person in front of his television set and the person on the screen—we know almost nothing about the great variety of ways in which television makes an impact. We know it is an enormously potent medium. We need to explore, understand, and use its great potential for helping us solve the ever-increasing problems of living together in a computerized society. In the future, I can see community mental health, education, entertainment and so on as being so close to the same thing that they truly become one.

This concept of mental health is so much bigger than what we think of today; in group activities alone it would demand professional help far beyond our ability to train enough people. We must therefore go to mass methods. And television can be one of the best, because of its possibilities for intimacy. It can get right inside. If part of the problem of clients of mental health agencies has anything to do with how they see themselves as human beings, and I think it does, then that is a problem area which is vulnerable to change from the outside, and television is one of the best agents for assisting that change. I see televised group activity as having two points of impact: The first is the use of the medium as stimulus material for groups that could meet in the community. The other is the ability of this type of programing to simply show what it's like to be a human being. In the latter sense, the televised group program becomes a vicarious experience for the viewer, legitimizing the type of behavior that group activity demonstrates.

Our study of the results of the program confirms previous studies. The self-directed group is indeed an important new resource for community mental health—for bridging the emotional distance between people; for freeing people from the constrictions and superficialities of so much of our social interchange; for helping people experience the humanness of others and, through that experiencing, accept their own fundamental humanness. We can enable people to use what we know to be true—that people really do help each other, that we are surrounded by others longing to reach out—to make contact, to be able to say, "I'm not alone."

14

Use of Videotape Feedback

Frederick H. Stoller

All psychotherapy and counseling can be seen in terms of providing a client with an objective view of his behavior, goals, and attitudes and how all these tend to mesh with each other. One of the major technical problems in the field is the difficulty of presenting such feedback in a way that facilitates its acceptance by the individual as well as maximizes its potential usefulness to him. As anyone who has attempted to help people change in significant ways knows all too well, learning about one's self in a precise and concrete way is one of the most difficult tasks there is.

The opportunity for one to see one's self as he is seen by others is one of the most important functions that an intimate, freely interacting group can provide. Such groups are particularly valuable in that they encourage people to interact in a context that mirrors the effect the individual has on others, and that provides a picture of how he moves through the world and what he tends to elicit from those he rubs up against. Perhaps, most significantly of all, the group may help a member determine the discrepancy between that which he wishes to receive from the world and that which he makes the world give him—the difference between the interpersonal message he would like to give and the one he actually gives. In a well-conducted group, where direct interaction is encouraged, a person gets a reflection of his behavior with others rather than discussions about his interactions. However, it is easier to gather this data in the arena of the group than it is to have it processed by the recipient; it is difficult to get a person to be truly aware of his own conduct. Even when motivation is high (and it is generally ambivalent) the information given by others is integrated and used only with very arduous effort.

Many group leaders use mechanical aids to stimulate feedback, such as audio-tape recorders, though there is no evidence that this device has been developed or explored in any systematic manner. Photographs and movies also are used, as in the attempt of Cornelison and Arsenian (1960) to present photographic images to psychotic patients. They report a wide range of reactions resulting in some changes in the psychopathological state of the subjects.

Videotape, a new tool for enhancing the presentation of feedback, has a number of advantages: It involves the audio-visual channels of information; playback can be either immediate or delayed; selectivity is readily accomplished; repetition of viewing as well as stopping the action is very easy; and the tapes can be stored for as long as is required or can be used over again. Closed-circuit television cameras function quietly, modern equipment needs only ordinary room lighting for an excellent picture, and small cameras can be placed unobstrusively in a group setting. Television has the ability to be intimate—to bring a person on screen closer to the viewer than is generally considered comfortable in Western society, as Hall (1959) has indicated. The closeness is sometimes the equivalent of standing nose to nose. When Kogan, Krathvohl, and Miller (1963) experimented with TV in individual psychotherapy, they termed it a breakthrough in methodology. Moor, Chervell, and West

(1965) presented hospital patients with self-viewing on video-tape and reported more improvement for them during their hospital stay than for those who had not had the opportunity.

The primary disadvantage of videotape is its high cost relative to conventional audio-tape recorders. However, the technical aspects of videotape are developing so rapidly that prices are diminishing. In the next several years, the videotape recorder is likely to be within the reach of most moderate-size settings. It is already being used for training in psychotherapy at a number of neuropsychiatric institutes as indicated by Schiff and Reivich (1964).

Experience with this instrument has suggested certain technical arrangements which are most useful. While a particular approach and technique will be described, work with videotape is still developing; experimentation and innovation as well as experience are absolute necessities for this instrument. Above all, fresh ways of looking at interaction, at behavior, and at behavioral and attitudinal change are required in this framework that differs from the usual dynamic-speculative approach to groups as advocated by such innovators as Slavson (1947).

Contrary to what might be expected, it is entirely possible to conduct a group session in front of television cameras without forfeiting the spontaneity and naturalness of group interaction. Both Farson (see Chapter 13) and Stoller (1965) have amply demonstrated that group interaction quickly absorbs the attention of members and they can ignore the presence of the cameras, as well as crews, to a surprising extent. Probably the most important factor is the comfort of the group leader in operating in an open setting, under the surveillance of cameras and videotape. Groups conducted with outside people present, as well as considerable distraction, can still experience only minimal interference with group development.

However, technical considerations should not overwhelm group participation. Large cameras, extremely hot lights, and extensive manipulation of equipment can hinder group development. Considerable acquaintance with the electronic gear is necessary in order to foster smooth group development.

Under ideal circumstances, a group should be seated in a

circle, as is customary in group practice. Approximately three closed-circuit television cameras (or however many are required to cover all group members) around the periphery of the group should be mounted so as to shoot over the participants' shoulders. The cameras should be equipped with zoom lenses (for closeups) and remote controls (for panning and raising or lowering the camera angle). Ordinary room lighting is satisfactory for these cameras, although some attention will have to be given to their placement so as to avoid distracting shadows. In the adjoining control room, each camera should be hooked to a monitor under the control of a director, who can manipulate the cameras by means of the remote controls. Ultimately, the director decides what will be recorded on the videotape, and thus he must be attuned to what is significant in the group interaction at the moment. Not only must the director have some acquaintance with television equipment and programing, he must have considerable feeling for and knowledge of group processes.

It has been found useful to equip the group leader with a signal to indicate a portion of the group interaction to which he wishes to return in the feedback session. For example, pressing a button turns on a light which signals the director to take note of the number on the recorder counter; this notation makes it quite easy to return to a specific portion of the tape when the group wishes to view themselves.

A monitor for viewing should be present in the group room, turned away from the members when they are in their interaction session. Remote controls for the video recorder should be available to the group leader so that he can start and stop, go back or go forward with minimum interruption of the group's forward movement. There should be as little manipulation of equipment as possible in order to avoid interfering with the intimate nature of small group interaction.

In order to be most effective, the group leader should have a clear idea of what would be useful to look at on the videotape. He must pay some attention to what is being captured. The most significant aspect of the process is that the actual behavior of individuals in interaction with others is recorded. Thus, video feedback provides the unique opportunity to see oneself dealing with people: explaining oneself away, painting a particular picture of oneself, listening, being superior, pleading, being angry, or being annoyed. Only under these circumstances can one actually see oneself as seen by others. The person literally confronts himself.

By placing himself in the role of his audience, an individual can objectify the role-taking part of his behavior (Coutu, 1951). He can do consciously and deliberately, and therefore with the possibility of change, what he does unconsciously and as a matter of course. Shibutani (1961, p. 48) sums it up as follows:

Thus role-taking is an important part of role-playing. The two concepts are not to be confused. Role-playing refers to the organization of conduct in accordance with group norms; role-taking refers to imagining how one looks from another person's standpoint. It involves making inferences about the other person's inner experiences—pretending temporarily to be someone else and perhaps even sympathizing with him.

Personality may usefully be examined from an interaction point of view. Mead (1934) generated a concept which has considerable power and utility for emphasizing group confrontation. An important element of his thinking concerns the capacity of man to objectify his view of himself, to approach himself as he thinks others would view him. To quote Shibutani again:

Mead argued that human beings are able to control themselves because of their capacity to act toward themselves in much the same manner as they act toward other people and as others act toward them. . . . Thus, a man becomes conscious of himself as a distinct unit, through role-taking; he responds to his own activity as if he were someone else. He responds covertly to his own behavior in the same way in which he expects others to respond overtly [p. 91].

An individual's imagined reception governs, to a considerable extent, the course of his conduct. The *generalized other* becomes a part of an individual's repertory as he grows and becomes a socialized human; it is formulated out of the early reactions and expectations that are made toward him. Once formed, particularly in adulthood, the anticipation of others' reactions becomes relatively fixed; the anticipated responses are our version of what the culture expects of us.

A person's approach to himself constitutes his self-concept. Once established, his behavior toward himself tends to become autonomous, so that an individual's self-concept does not actually conform to reality in terms of how others actually react to him. Much of what enters into a person's reception by others is determined by his expressive style: how he communicates rather than what he says. In order to make more accurate predictions about a person's behavior, one who has investment in another because of some joint involvement tends to pay close attention to the fine nuances that can be seen in the other's face. What is being seen and interpreted in deliberate fashion are the expressive movements which are largely involuntary, that is, outside the awareness of the person producing them. As such, they do not contribute to the goals directly and consciously embraced by an individual and, under ordinary circumstances, cannot be evaluated by him. Thus, discrepancies develop between what he believes he is generating and what the world is actually receiving and acting upon.

These anticipations of others' behavior toward us soon become closed systems, and our image of how others react tends to remain fixed. This picture of others' perceptions generally remains narrower than is necessary because we do not feel we may ask others what their impressions are. Even when we do ask others, as in group therapy, we are often too busy defending ourselves and altering what they say to us in order to fit our preconceptions to listen very carefully. So, while our needs may change, our ability to change the way we anticipate others does not necessarily match the change; in fact, the picture may remain relatively fixed. Goffman (1959) discusses the various social staging techniques that enable people to preserve their self-concepts.

At most, then, successful people keep their behavior

within a narrower frame than they need to. Those who encounter considerable difficulty generally have grossly distorted
versions of the reactions of others; the picture of society which
they have constructed often emphasizes one aspect to the detri-
ment of others, so that their image of the audience is markedly
at variance with what is actually the case. Their behavior as
well as their concerns (that is, their attitudes) become increasingly out of step with the actual reactions of those with whom
they come in contact. Under these circumstances, they really do
not believe what others tell them about themselves, even when
they are told in a direct and straightforward fashion.

The videotape of group interaction is an objective picture of how people appear to others. When they have the
opportunity to view this in very close contiguity with the
actual interaction (one of the major values of the videotape is
its immediate availability), people can react to themselves.
Particularly where this viewing is done in a special social milieu
where objectifying the image of how others react to one is the
major value adopted by the group, objectivity about oneself
becomes possible.

The significant questions to ask the individual who is
watching himself on screen are: "How would you react to that
person? What would your behavior be if you had to deal with
him?" The videotape feeback does not substitute for what the
group itself attempts to do, since these questions are, to a
considerable extent, part of the major endeavor of most encounter groups. The videotape is merely an instrument to enhance and amplify their major task; under no circumstances
should this form of feedback supplant the wider effort.

An encounter group differs from social groups in that it
works toward a goal, and it has to work hard to achieve that
goal. Its major purpose is direct confrontation rooted in what
takes place within the room. The group may go off on tangents,
discussing comfortable topics, or it may enter into speculative
side roads purporting to explain why someone has to be the way
he is. These are, however, attempts either to escape the discomfort and risk of direct confrontation or to gain relief from
this frequently uncomfortable style. In this respect, the video-

tape feedback can be seen as a kind of magnifying glass which forces the group into confrontative encounter. This feedback not only aids the group in its major work but alters the group process itself.

Focused feedback has been developed to be used with an encounter group within the framework just outlined. This technique presupposes that certain aspects of group interaction are more valuable for self-viewing than others. Experience has suggested that passive viewing is not the most effective way to use feedback. Geertsma and Reivich (1965), using videotape feedback with an individual psychotherapy patient, discovered that "it was frequently necessary to maneuver the subject to examine her taped performance. . . . In general, the therapist served the function of directing attention to cues he deemed important in the playback tapes."

Immediately following the group session proper, the group views the tape. The monitor is turned to the group, and the group leader takes control of the video recorder. He turns to those portions of the tape he considers worth reviewing, as noted during the session by his signals to the director. (The director should tape members who are not necessarily in direct interaction because the group may want to focus on a participant's manner of listening as much as any other behavior.) For the most part, the leader emphasizes those scenes in which participants engaged in typical interactions showing a lack of congruence between what they anticipate from others and what they actually receive.

A variation of this method was used in a two-day group session. Interaction was continuous so that there was no break between sessions during which the tape could be viewed. Instead, at appropriate places during the two days the group watched the videotape, generally what had just happened. This feedback was particularly valuable when a marked struggle over confrontation and resistance to confrontation was taking place. We originally feared that stopping for videotape viewing would slow down the interaction. Instead, the viewing intensified the work of confrontation and often helped the group move on to new levels.

During the playback, the group leader may point out aspects of what is being seen. After a significant portion of the tape has been shown, the monitor is turned off and the participant may be asked to react to himself. Sometimes he is asked a direct question: "What would you think or feel if you were dealing with him?" Or he may be requested to give his general reactions to viewing himself. Participation of the other group members is encouraged, and interaction may continue extensively.

The tape often will have to be replayed to let the participant look at himself again in view of the discussion that just ensued. Not infrequently, people miss important aspects of themselves that others have noted and consider important. Because reducing the number of channels of information being given to a viewer tends to amplify concentration on what is being presented, the sound may be turned off sometimes so that the individual can appreciate the nonverbal cues he is sending out.

These variations should be used judiciously. Automatic application of these techniques kills an important part of the group process: its spontaneity. Again, mechanical gadgetry must not be allowed to overwhelm the much more important aspects of the group. Creativity and flexibility are needed in the group leader to avoid mechanical use and denigration of a powerful tool. The leader should have a clear idea of what he is trying to accomplish so that the power of self-confrontation is not confused and dissipated.

Even more important during the videotape feedback session is the ability of the group leader, as well as other group members, to provide alternative behavior for the self-viewer. When they do help him, the maximum usefulness of the technique can be demonstrated. When they fail to provide choices, the individual may become merely self-conscious. Self-awareness is often a necessary step in learning to stop what one is currently doing, particularly when the behavior is relatively automatic. However, the person must be helped to develop an alternative way of behaving. The focusing technique furthers this goal by fixing attention on discrete behavior which can be altered relatively quickly and for which very concrete alternatives can be provided. Under these circumstances, learning and change can take place much more quickly than one might imagine. In order to accomplish this result, the leader must be aware of and tuned to the kinds of behavior with which he can help a participant.

Where large discrepancies exist between a person's image of himself and what is actually being received by the world, a marked reaction often occurs when he sees himself on screen. In one experiment, a patient who had been hospitalized for seven years remarked: "My God! I do look like a patient." He then promptly got himself discharged from the hospital before the week was up, almost ruining the experiment. However, discrepancies are usually small and subtle and require considerable judgment on the part of the leader. As a technique, focused feedback places great responsibility on the group leader's skill and sensitivity rather than bypassing them.

Videotape feedback can also be used in special situations, such as vocational rehabilitation, Johnson (1960) showed TV teachers videotapes of their presentations. In this case he found a decrease in the effectiveness of a subsequent presentation. Providing feedback without also helping the individual with alternatives will probably result in the person's becoming more self-conscious about his performance. Since self-viewing brings about a slowdown in semi-automatic behavior, such results are not too surprising. Slowing someone down provides a chance to introduce new learning; unless advantage is taken of this opportunity, the potential of the situation may be lost.

Keeping in mind that the optimal moment for introducing new learning is directly after the tape feedback, programs for performance evaluation have been devised based on the experience of Griver, Robinson, and Franklin (1965) with a parallel technique called *augmented feedback*. Purchasing agents were given audio tapes of their own telephone orders so they could experience taking orders from themselves; then suggestions were given for improving their method of order-giving. The results showed a remarkable drop in delivery errors. Videotape programs have been prepared for employees whose work situations are largely interpersonal in nature: executives, sales persons, and bank tellers. In some cases, role playing is introduced, and in others a group situation is used. These programs are still too new to be evaluated effectively, but they do suggest that performance enhancement is feasible through videotape feedback if more than feedback is offered.

Many work situations call for considerable use of the self; the way the worker approaches others is as much a part of what goes into transactions as his knowledge and skill. Therapists and counselors are prime examples of people who must combine knowledge and interpersonal skill; focused feedback has been used in their training to help them function effectively within the therapeutic situation. In addition, focus upon their ways of relating to others in general situations has been provided. Any vocation which calls upon someone to influence others in particular directions could conceivably benefit from focused feedback. As anyone in this position is well aware, self-presentation is an important ingredient in the influencing. Many of these professions already are using encounter groups, such as motivation laboratories and sensitivity training, to achieve this end. Videotape could enhance these programs.

Even where use of the self is not so important, as in crafts and other skilled and semiskilled fields, those having difficulty obtaining or maintaining jobs could benefit from focused feedback adapted to their needs. Such workers are generally unaware of the impact they make on others; they evidence little appreciation of what they are really telling people through their behavior. Very often, these individuals are simply unlearned in the personal skills required to obtain and hold a job. Because videotape is graphic, rather than merely verbal, it can provide feedback much more effectively than can conventional means.

Focused feedback is based on the assumption that there is value in attending to the style of communication presented to the world. Videotape is a method for using such feedback to enhance small group confrontation. Since much behavior depends on one's anticipated reception by others, providing an opportunity to objectify this constant component of personal behavior has particular value. In order to provide alternatives to that behavior which seems to be inconsistent with the conscious goals of the individual, specific and concrete units of behavior receive focused attention in the feedback session. Videotape feedback can strengthen and heighten some of the most important phases of an encounter group.

15

Gestalt Therapy

Abraham Levitsky and James S. Simkin

Although Gestalt therapy is a relatively recent innovation (Perls, Hefferline, and Goodman, 1951), it is already a highly elaborated system, as evidenced by the long array of concepts on which it makes its characteristic statements (Simkin, 1971). However, a strong unifying thread ties together the various rules, games, and techniques. The importance of this framework is symbolized in the name which has been chosen for this approach.

In 1966 Simkin tape-recorded a biographical interview with Fritz Perls, during which Perls dealt with his search for a label for the therapeutic approach he was developing. Out of several possibilities, he fixed on the name Gestalt therapy. He had been profoundly influenced by the German school of gestalt psychology with its emphasis on total functioning, on problems of structure, configuration, wholeness, the interrelationship between parts, and, above all, on the phenomenon of moment to moment shifts in the definition of foreground and background.

The gestaltist's concern with the question of completeness—the nature of complete functioning and completed experience—suggests an underlying question which the therapist asks both himself and the patient: "What is the nature of complete living?" The answer, of course, may be recognized as open-ended and eternally expanding and emerging.

This underlying concern with totality of functioning— the gestalt of one's life, the gestalt of one's being at this moment —constitutes the ground from which stem all other detailed considerations of method and technique in this therapeutic approach. Techniques are seen as merely techniques, and a broad range of stylistic differences are therefore represented within this school of therapists. As Levitsky and Perls point out (1970, p. 140), "Any particular set of techniques such as our presently used rules and games will be regarded merely as convenient means-whereby, useful tools for our purposes but having no sacrosanct qualities."

We now turn to some of the formal aspects of group formation. Typically, the small group in Gestalt therapy practice consists of a therapist and from five to eight patients and is conducted on a regular (usually weekly), ongoing basis. Most groups of this size meet for approximately an hour and a half, but the length may range from one to three hours. Some groups have co-leaders and vary in size from eight to as many as fourteen people. Usually, the larger the group, the longer the time period spent in group.

Many therapists follow Perls' lead in the use of the "hot seat" technique and will explain this to the group at the outset. According to this method, an individual expresses to the therapist his interest in dealing with a particular problem. The focus is then on the extended interaction between patient and group leader (I and Thou). The patient sits in a chair directly facing the leader during this exchange.

Inevitably it sometimes happens that no one comes forward to "work." Depending on how he views the dynamics of this situation, the therapist may elect to wait it out or to try any one of a number of techniques or games which serve as warm-up (Levitsky and Perls, 1970). Among these is the basic method of "making rounds." Here each person is asked, either in turn or randomly, where he is at this moment. The question "What are you in touch with?" in the Gestalt framework is laden with practical and theoretical implications. There is a world of difference between "What are you in touch with?" and the more usual "How are you?" or "What are you feeling?" In the "What are you in touch with" formulation we imply the individual's active choice of a particular mood, feeling, body sensation, or image to be in the foreground of his attention at a given moment. This way of asking also seems to allow far wider latitude of response than does the more conventional opening gambit.

Making rounds may lead to one person's discovering that he wishes to work through some unfinished material, in which case rounds are suspended and the focus is switched to the individual and therapist working together. As they work, occasions arise in which the patient is asked to carry out some particular exercise, such as "Could you repeat what you just said, but this time with your legs uncrossed?" or "Could you look directly at me as you say this?" The attitude with which these exercises are carried out is an important element. The patient is gradually educated and encouraged to undertake them in the spirit of experiment. One cannot really know the outcome beforehand even though a specific hunch is being tested. The spirit of experiment is taken seriously and the question raised, "What did you discover?" Discovery is the most potent form of learning. It is far more one's own possession than is any information fed in from the outside. The open and flowing personality expresses a natural and spontaneous curiosity. When we are skillful enough to elicit this drive in unhampered fashion the patient will make discoveries that reflect his unique interests, his unique needs, his stylistic trademark. At that moment he stands on his own two feet; at that moment he is self-actualizing and is doing quite nicely without the benevolent wisdom of therapist-guru.

To some observers, the practice of Gestalt therapy in a small group appears to be essentially individual therapy which takes place in the presence of a group. To a large extent this is true, and Perls (1967, p. 309) outlined the value of this approach as follows:

To the whole group it is obvious that the person in distress does not see the obvious, does not see the way out of the impasse, does not see (for instance) that his whole misery is a purely imagined one. In the face of this collective conviction he cannot use his usual phobic way of disowning the therapist when he cannot manipulate him. . . .

Behind the impasse . . . is the catastrophic expectation. . . . In the safe emergency of the therapeutic situation, he [the patient] discovers that the world does not fall to pieces if he gets angry, sexy, joyous, or mournful. The group supports his self-esteem; the appreciation of his achievements toward authenticity and greater liveliness also is not to be underestimated.

Gestalt therapists also use the group for doing collective experiments—such as talking jibberish together or doing withdrawal experiments in learning to understand the importance of the atmosphere. . . . The observation by the group members of the manipulative games of playing helpless, stupid, wailing, seductive or other roles, by which the neurotic helps himself in the infantile state of controlling, facilitates their own recognition.

By its very nature Gestalt therapy places considerable stress on extensive and intensive interaction between the therapist and whomever is working at a given moment. A number of therapists specifically ask other participants not to join in during the thirty- or forty-five minute period of working with one individual.

The reason for this restriction is germane to the Gestalt approach: The therapist wishes to participate in and enhance the flow of feeling from the patient in the here and now. He aims to seek out and liberate those feelings which at the moment are in the foreground of the patient's awareness. The methods he uses are both intriguing and unique and have unusual efficacy. The best illustrations are in the transcripts of taped interviews between Perls and members of his workshops (Perls, 1969b), as well as in the Simkin training film.

Having a background of both gestalt psychology and Reichian psychiatry, the Gestalt therapist assumes that the individual is a totally communicating unit. As is now widely accepted, important and unwitting messages are constantly being sent through body language. Much of the skill of the Gestalt therapist lies in his facility in reading body language. A characteristic move of the shoulder, a clearing of the throat, an irregularity in breathing—these may profitably become the focus of concern in the therapeutic session.

There is another way of saying this: One of the basic modes of Gestalt therapy is to look for significant microscopic bits of behavior. Enright (1970, p. 269) offers a beautiful example:

Many times, the movements or tensions that substitute for, and therefore block, awareness are far more inaccessible, often being "miniaturized" into tiny movements that are almost invisible and yet sum up and sustain a whole point of view and set of expectations about life. For example, one medical student in a group punctuated almost every remark (made in a very intense voice) with a flick of his head to the right. I had another student stand behind him and hold his head fairly tightly. After a minute or two, the head movement disappeared and the man began to flick his right wrist slightly at the end of each comment. Another student held his wrist. Soon a fairly noticeable shrug of the right shoulder appeared to replace that. At this point, I had him then exaggerate the shrug extensively, turning it into an entire body movement; within a minute or two, he was able to put this gesture into the words "Who cares?" This was the miniaturized organismic counterpoint to his overtly expressed close interest in what I was saying.

Although the practice of focusing on small movement is common this particular emphasis has not yet been clearly articulated. Apparently all Gestalt therapists have absorbed this theoretical and practical point so heartily that they have not bothered to describe it. The rationale is that these microscopic units of behavior often convey attitudes and bind emotions. Attending to these elements of gesture and style can be particularly dramatic when the patient has little or no awareness of their existence. It is commonplace that even after this feedback is given to the patient he needs to make special efforts to gain this awareness himself. What is obvious to the observer may be thoroughly hidden from the self.

Another aspect of the therapist's activity deals with the role of sensation both in communication and in combating intellectualization. A major criticism leveled by Gestalt therapy against psychoanalysis and other traditional therapies is that they resulted too often in dry and unproductive verbal insights. They had meager success in uniting thought with feeling. In frequently invoking one of his favorite dicta—"Lose your mind and come to your senses"—Perls was focusing on just this danger. This dictum applies, naturally, to therapist as well as patient, and much of the training in Gestalt therapy is a highly refined sort of sensory awareness training in which the therapist learns to sharpen his eyes and ears and to be aware of his own body sensations as clues to his total emotional reaction to the patient (Enright, 1970).

Many therapists have acquired the freedom to tell the group about a particular body sensation or image which they are experiencing. At the moment of sharing this private experience, the therapist may have no inkling of its significance and be quite in the dark about where this disclosure will take the current interaction between patient and therapist.

The freedom to use these intuitive processes on the part of the therapist is developed only through painstaking practice. It must be evident also that the therapist accepts his job as a high-risk undertaking. By this acceptance, he makes a powerful statement to the group on the role of risk in authentic living.

Unfortunately the exhaustive concern with seeming minutia of gesture and feeling easily lends itself to misinterpretation by those who have only a cursory appreciation of Gestalt methods. We often hear the accusation that the Gestalt therapist is controlling or authoritarian. Gestalt techniques do indeed require an almost fiercely active and leader-centered approach. But this approach is to be sharply distinguished from authoritarian control. Within the session the Gestalt therapist is quite active in making suggestions for exercises and experiments. These are designed to heighten and broaden the patient's capacity for experiencing himself and others. The suggestion-giving is obviously quite different from telling the patient how to conduct his life. If anything, many therapists in the Gestalt movement feel that autonomy has perhaps been emphasized too much at the cost of underplaying human interdependency. Here there is much room for debate.

As already suggested, the methods and techniques of Gestalt therapy flow from a number of general principles. Gestalt therapy is a broad and very ambitious approach not only to the problems of psychotherapy but to the problem of existence. Inasmuch as Gestalt therapy contains a philosophy of growth, of healthy human functioning, it is essentially a philosophy of being.

As such, Gestalt therapy stands firmly among the existential therapies. As Laura Perls has pointed out with great clarity (1970, p. 128), "I am deeply convinced that the basic problem not only of therapy but of life is how to make life livable for a being whose dominant characteristic is his awareness of himself as a unique individual on the one hand and of his mortality on the other." The phenomenon of self-awareness and the recognition of one's finiteness lead to the experience of existential anxiety, an unavoidable part of existence. The Gestalt therapist, therefore, is not concerned with curing the patient of anxiety. The aim is rather to help him accept anxiety as part of the very nature of things. Our emphasis on such matters as risk, confrontation, the importance of chewing over and assimilating emotional experiences (Perls, 1969a)—all these reflect the strong existential component in Gestalt therapy.

If we were to choose one key idea to stand as a symbol for the Gestalt approach, it might well be the concept of authenticity, the quest for authenticity. The concepts of existential anxiety and authenticity are more closely allied than may be apparent. In seeking authenticity we must break many bonds and face many challenges. It is the courageous and repeated struggling with these bonds—of society, family, one's own nature—that confers authenticity. Authenticity is a state of individuation, of truly being one's self. It is the most impressive human accomplishment. It *is* the state of grace.

The methods of a truly existential therapy are more readily delineated if we keep clearly before us the idea of authenticity. Let us rely momentarily on the metaphor of the therapist as teacher. Obviously he is not teaching a specialized skill such as mathematics or dancing. What, then, is he teaching? He is teaching living; he deals in the art of truly being.

If we regard therapy and the therapist in the pitiless light of authenticity, it becomes apparent that the therapist cannot teach what he does not know. If he tries to cover up the thinness of his understanding through facile reliance on skills, techniques, and gimmicks, then he is simply imparting to his patients that particular neurosis or bit of phoniness: The patient is subtly learning to pretend a knowledge that he does not have.

A therapist with some experience really knows within himself that he is communicating to his patient his (the therapist's) own fears as well as his courage, his defensiveness as well as his openness, his confusion as well as his clarity. The therapist's awareness, acceptance, and sharing of these truths can be a highly persuasive demonstration of his own authenticity. Obviously such a position is not acquired overnight. It is to be learned and relearned ever more deeply not only throughout one's career but throughout one's entire life.

There is good reason to believe that Perls was quite right in his feeling that the innovations of the Gestalt method are decisive contributions to psychotherapy. This thought gave him much personal satisfaction, a satisfaction which seems warranted by present developments in the practice of psychotherapy.

An exciting feature of Gestalt work, unique to this school, offers a special sort of fascination to therapist and patient. We refer to the dramatic and utterly unpredictable unfolding and development of the patient's interior space which occurs in the therapist-patient interaction. Elements of artistry and surprise occur with such regularity that surpirse is no longer surprising.

What is especially intriguing is that the patient need not start with a question or problem or conflict or program. He need only be there. The simple question "What do you experience now?" accompanied by the reliance on present-moment awarenesses is enough—in the hands of a skillful Gestalt therapist—to start the unfolding of a fascinating exploration.

At the same time, these self-appreciative remarks need not blind us to the limitations of Gestalt method in groups. The main limitation stems from the very feature of leader-centeredness which we discussed. The emphasis on extensive interaction between therapist and patient is particularly stressed by Simkin, who makes clear to the group that his individual work with group members takes precedence over all other group activity.

This type of structure has important consequences for the kind of group experience which then develops. Group initiative is considerably underplayed. The complex group dynamics which develop through efforts at decision making—for example, about admitting new members, planning vacations, arranging meeting times, about ambiguities with regard to fee payments—do not get prominent attention in Gestalt-oriented groups. In addition, the patterns of interrelationship among individuals, with their frequent parallels in family structure, are also usually underplayed.

It would be an exaggeration, however, to say that the group plays no role. In fact, we believe there are several advantages to individual work within the group setting. Frequently, while one person is working in the hot seat, some or most of the others present are on a similar trip and doing important work for themselves subvocally. The work being focused on will frequently trigger recall of unfinished business in other group members who are thus motivated to work through freshly stirred conflicts. The group can be very supportive and permit some people to get into material they may have been unwilling to deal with in an individual therapy session. Finally, group reaction to an individual's work as well as to that of the therapist can be an excellent criterion of the authenticity discussed earlier.

A number of workers in the field are combining Gestalt

methods with other therapeutic approaches, both individual and group. Thus, workshops are being offered with such titles as Gestalt and Encounter, Gestalt and Hypnosis, Gestalt and Massage. More specifically, some therapists are seeking to develop techniques which deliberately maximize the creative participation of group members and thus achieve integration of Gestalt techniques with the rich potential of group dynamic processes.

16

Psychodrama and Role Training

Lewis Yablonsky

Role playing has been used for more than twenty-five years to explore the skills and emotional background individuals bring to particular life situations. In a proper role-playing session, the group can provide a sounding board for evaluating the individual's abilities and thus give the subject of a session the benefit of its viewpoint. Group members can also observe themselves through the subject's acting out.

This analysis examines role playing in the context of the overall use of psychodrama. Basically, psychodrama encompasses simple role-playing, as well as a variety of action therapy techniques. Psychodrama was originated in 1911 in Vienna by J. L. Moreno, who found that allowing children to act out their problems spontaneously produced therapeutic results. Since that time, largely due to Moreno's efforts, psychodrama has developed as an action theory and a method for understanding and resolving interpersonal problems in many settings, including mental hospitals, correctional institutions, industry, vocational rehabilitation, schools, and private practice.

Psychodrama's broad acceptance is due primarily to its adaptability and flexibility. All that is required for a session are the problem, the group of individuals, and a psychodramatist (although psychodrama is practiced more formally in most cases). The office, the couch, a chair, the stage, or other formal elements may be used but are not necessary for psychodrama; the problem, the group, and the subject are at the center of the session, and all artifacts are on hand to help structure problem situations with the aid of the director and his aides or auxiliary egos. Freedom for the client to act out his problem is represented in the freedom of space—the stage or any open space— as a vehicle for production.

The theoretical system which defines the practice of psychodrama is found in the hundreds of books, monographs, and articles on the subject (most notably Moreno, 1953). Psychodrama's scientific roots are buried deep in Moreno's philosophies of spontaneity, creativity, the moment, and his theories of role and interaction. The sociometric system for understanding human networks and acting on individual and group structure is a foundation of psychodramatic procedure. The web of theory which Moreno and others have spun in sixty years of psychodramatic progress is unified and strong but requires further academic interpretation. The major theoretic considerations will be presented after a preliminary discussion of psychodrama practices. Such aspects of the psychodramatic school as sociodrama, societry, role research, and the concepts of spontaneity, creativity, and cultural conserve will be touched on.

PSYCHODRAMA PRACTICES

The psychodramatic procedure, as suggested above, has five essential components: the group, the subject or protagonist, the psychodramatist or director, his aides or auxiliary egos, and a system of methods and techniques adaptable to the requirements of the situation.

In a group warm-up the following may take place. About fifteen people enter the room and become seated. The director opens up a discussion on feelings about working, for example;

One person may say, "My main hang-up with work is that my mother wanted me to become a doctor and anything else I do is considered inferior. Somehow I agree with her and anything I do seems second-best." Another may say, "All bosses bug me. I just can't take orders from anyone."

After the discussion widens, the director may, for example, take the individual with the authority problem as a protagonist. An obvious scene would be to have the individual act out a situation with his father in which he was subjected to some orders and discipline. Then the entire group might discuss the relationship between work in the family setting and work in an outside job.

Once the group selects the area of concern and chooses the subject—that is, the person in whose personality the problem area is most clearly shown—action begins. Essentially, we have established channels of communication through which the action on stage and the feelings of the group can merge into beneficial processes of catharsis, the development of insight, and relearning. Vicariously, the entire group benefits from the action process through catharsis and the expansion of perceptual fields.

As the subject warms up to the roles he is playing in relationship to the people who are causing difficulty in his current or past life, other group members are selected to portray people in his environment, or social atom. These auxiliary egos are people for whom the experience of taking these particular roles will be useful.

Psychodrama is primarily a group process, although it may shift from the group to an individual's problem at varying points in a session. The director constantly tries to mobilize the group to work together on their problems. Even though one participant may serve as the session's focus, he functions as a focal point for communication within the entire group. Therefore, production on the stage is an intensified and a controlled extension of the problem of the total group. While action goes on, each person participates through identification with individuals and emotional themes, extending these experiences in his own fantasy and often moving into the action.

When a member becomes destructive by becoming

spokesman for those who represent the opposite polarity of the central theme, the group may deal with this through discussion and further psychodrama to bring about modified behavior and attitudes on the part of both extremes. Through this dynamism the group begins to evolve behavioral standards and insights. Response of people not on stage to actions being dramatized is often greater than that of people on stage. The intensity of response to a psychodrama session does not necessarily relate to frequency of participation in the stage action.

Growth in psychodrama takes place through effective channeling of the group's dynamics for the benefit of its members. In a spontaneous group which is free to express its underlying sociometric dynamics, progress occurs immediately. A client, for example, who acts out his problem through hostility (for example, toward an employer or a parent) is confronted with the consequences of his expression on the spot, where the expression can be dealt with by the entire group. In psychodrama, the individual can work out his conflicting emotions as they occur, in direct relationship to a host of other personalities who are not passive but who react; all dimensions of the problem are explored and dealt with in terms of the entire group structure.

The protagonist in a production represents the group through his actions. Before relevant action takes place, the protagonist must warm up to himself as he functions within the group setting. This warm-up allows him to bring forth pertinent concerns and to exclude those unrelated to the concomitant group process. Some defenses and blocks become so obviously superficial in this setting that the protagonist moves spontaneously into deeper levels of his problem and achieves a greater realization of himself.

The protagonist, with the aid of auxiliary egos and methods such as role reversal and the double, objectifies his problem in a situation. His perception of the situation—his here-and-now construction of it—is what counts. What happened "in fact" is not the immediate concern of the group or director at the time of psychodramatic action. The group and star are accepted on their levels of function, and an attempt is made to create a climate in which these levels of functions may be improved. For example, if an individual is grossly distorting a portrait of a person known to the group, he has license to do this because the session is involved with his personal perception of the situation.

The role of the director fluctuates continually. His function is dictated by what is happening at any given time. He may be passive, aggressive, directive, and so on. At times he may become an authoritarian father or a demanding mother. There is no limit to the range of roles demanded of him, and the roles he may take are limited only by his own anxieties and the requirements of the moment. He must constantly diagnose the situation within the group—including the action—and create new opportunities for self-defeating patterns to be broken. It is essential that he thinks on his feet and observe nonverbal as well as verbal communication cues while carrying on his primary function of directing the session so that learning is achieved.

Auxiliary egos are used as extensions of the director in the role-training situation. They facilitate production and intensify the meaning of interpersonal situations, acting on their own or at the direction of the director. Auxiliaries may enlarge their roles in order to help the subject examine new dimensions of his problem. The group setting in general, plus the use of auxiliaries, allows a diffusion of transference phenomena. The range of personalities available for interaction, as supplied by the auxiliaries, helps the subject move quickly toward total involvement in the therapeutic setting, especially when auxiliaries take the part of significant figures in the life of the subject or when the behavior of certain group members reflects prototypes of familial figures. This spread of transference phenomena affords greater mobility, and perhaps greater objectivity, to the director than seems likely in individual therapy settings.

Auxiliary egos sometimes are trained professional personnel. In some situations, such as working with an extremely deteriorated and regressed group, this type of auxiliary is necessary. However, in a group which embodies a range of problems, members usually function quite well as auxiliaries, and there is a certain pride and advantage in the autonomy thus gained. Usually, the auxiliary functions on a spontaneous level, responding to the demands of the situation within the group. The auxiliary role may be highly defined. For instance, if the director wishes to test a hypothesis concerning a particular subject's ability to function when confronted with a specific problem pertinent to his living, he instructs the auxiliary in how to play his role. Auxiliaries taken from the group are often given assignments; for example, a person having a problem with his wife may develop understanding of his own marital interaction by portraying other people's problems.

All behavior of group members is subject to group analysis, and the director is in no way excluded. In a psychodrama therapy atmosphere, he is not able to blame his difficulties with the group on transference or other defenses; he is forced to recognize that a subject who accuses him of being overly hostile, for example, is quite right and that this accusation may bear little, some, or no relationship to another authoritarian figure. The director must always be willing, in his relationship with his group, to allow this criticism and to deal with it on a person-to-person level when it develops. The psychodramatist is seldom a catalyst. He participates as a member of the group, as well as its leader.

Numerous production techniques are used to aid the protagonist and group in achieving a state of spontaneity and in structuring relevant problem situations. These clinical techniques, designed to bring about maximum creativity, productivity, and growth, have evolved from the experiences of many years. They are applied in the course of the production when they seem indicated and usually are not planned in advance. The director must be sensitive to the group production so that his use of these techniques has real impact.

Role reversal is the procedure in which A becomes B and B becomes A; for example, a protagonist playing his role as husband may reverse roles with his wife. Role reversal may be used for any of the following purposes: First, the protagonist playing the role of the relevant other often begins to feel and understand that person's position and reactions in the situation, thus possibly adding effective telic sensitivity (two-way empathy). Second, role reversal may be used to help the protagonist see himself as in a mirror. The employee playing the role of his boss will see himself through his boss's perception. This instrument elicits better understanding in the protagonist as he sees himself through the eyes of another. Third, role reversal is often effective in augmenting the spontaneity of the protagonist through shifting him out of defenses. In general, however, role reversal helps the protagonist understand others in the situation by being them. Fourth, role reversal can help an auxiliary ego to better understand how a role was played in a particular situation. The auxiliary, although he was not present in the actual scene, attempts to fulfill the requirements as projected by the subject. The subject, who is usually the only person who has experienced the situation, takes the role of the other, through role reversal, so that the auxiliary may learn how to fulfill the necessary role. This process helps the protagonist and auxiliary move more effectively into the problem situation.

In *the double* technique, the double attempts to warm up to and become the subject. If the protagonist is A, the double is A. (The double usually stands behind him, like a shadow, during the scene.) Unlike an empathetic situation, the double experience produces loss of separate identities for the two people in the action. The result is a single production of two people. The double can give the protagonist necessary support. At other times the double will express feelings of fear, hostility, or love which the protagonist, when alone, is unable to act out. The double may take a chance and express certain hypotheses which appear in the situation. For example, a double in the case cited earlier might say to his boss, "I hate you because you're just like my father." The subject may confirm or deny the double's statement; he may or may not agree with many thoughts which the double expresses. In this respect, the double helps the protagonist produce new cues for further understanding. The double produces an added dimension which the subject, for various reasons, cannot present himself.

The *soliloquy* is a familiar technique in theatrical history. Like Hamlet, the protagonist thinks aloud in the middle of the action, expressing his hidden thoughts and action tendencies. As the protagonist voices his inner concerns, he may clarify and structure insights and perceptions and prepare himself for future situations. The double technique may be combined with the soliloquy, in which case the double soliloquizes for the protagonist throughout a production or at crucial moments, stepping in and out of the situation.

The *mirror* effect is produced by having auxiliary egos portray the protagonist in his presence so he sees for himself how he acts. The mirror is used whenever it is indicated that seeing himself in action, as if in a psychological mirror, would be productive. This technique helps withdrawn subjects warm up to self-presentation. The protagonist is always encouraged to comment on, or react to, the auxiliary playing the role. At times the protagonist will participate, come forward, and take over his own role from the auxiliary when he is sufficiently warmed up.

As stated, methods and techniques are only aids for helping to produce therapeutic production and interaction in psychodrama. They are never ends in themselves. Used with sensitivity, they benefit the protagonist and the group.

ELEMENTS OF PSYCHODRAMA THEORY

In psychodrama, both the group and the individual are the focus of the therapeutic process. Their inextricable relationship is considered at all points in practice. Although one or the other may be the focal point at a particular time, the psychodramatic director is aware of his responsibility to both.

The psychodramatist's guiding principle is that problems cannot be resolved without focusing on the network of relationships as well as the individual's personality dynamics, which are hinged to his social atom. Awareness of the group's dynamics and of the behavior manifestations of underlying social and personal difficulties is an intrinsic part of sociometry. We must understand the individual's social structure in order to understand his particular problems. Psychodrama therapy tries to help the individual understand his own unique social atom—his structure of primary interpersonal relationships.

When working with specific problems of one group member, the director recognizes varying involvements among other participants and he uses these to further the processes of the whole group. He may assign particular auxiliary ego roles. When a subject acting out his problems appears to dominate the situation, the skilled psychodramatist assesses the group's sociometric structure to be sure that all members are receiving what they need. Psychodrama has a built-in diagnostic method: The director continuously examines the group's structure through sociometric analysis to determine which moves will produce maximum benefit.

Technique and method are adapted as the group dictates; they do not dictate to the group. The axiom is to do what helps the subject and the group most. The psychodramatic principle is that what helps most are those techniques which facilitate spontaneous action and promote testing of alternate solutions to future situations. In the course of this testing, insight into the dynamics of group structure is sharpened and broadened. The psychodramatist is frequently challenged to produce, on the spot, new methods and techniques to meet the needs of the group. His imagination is guided in such critical moments by his knowledge of the dynamic forces propelling the behavior of the group. He tries to infuse the group with an understanding of the creativity necessary for living effectively in society. The protagonist is encouraged to face the situation and act—not talk about it.

Psychodrama approximates the problem-producing setting more closely than does any other form of therapy. Immediate problems, born of the group's interaction, are dealt with in situ. By reenacting problem situations which exist with significant people outside the group, corrective emotional experiences can occur. Defeatist, repetitive patterns can be seen and treated. Perhaps more important, distorted perceptions of interpersonal relationships are recognized, and the group immediately attempts to bring about more realistic views. Critical thought is stimulated. Group members express insights and interpretations and form new relationships with each other which can be useful to rehabilitate goals.

The subject and group discover they can handle a problem after they find they have done it. Psychodrama probably comes closer to the lifeline of human experiences than does any other therapeutic format because participants live their problems more intensively and extensively than they could under the stresses of living outside. The psychodramatic world has characteristics of surplus reality. Intensive psychodrama encourages each person to develop a realization of himself and all his facades, in a setting in which errors of judgment and behavior are not so traumatic as they would be elsewhere. The individual works toward an expanded and integrated self-perception, with its concomitant attributes of interest in others and concern, not with the existence of problems, but with the ability to deal with them—in other words, he moves toward being a freer and more spontaneous person. Acting in the theatrical sense has no place in psychodrama, as the goals are to aid in self-realization rather than to promote the development of facades.

The spontaneous subject pulls the group with him into the light of sociometric experience and understanding. New light is thrown on symbolic behavior on the psychodramatic level of action because it surpasses and encompasses life. In action, nonverbal communication patterns become apparent, and maximal use may be made of them. Gestures, facial expressions, pauses, and body attitudes often indicate fundamental feeling tone. Conflicting feelings are revealed when nonverbal communication consistently is at variance with verbal communication.

Time is significant in psychodrama. Although a production may focus on past, present, or future, psychodrama is always the here and now. The subject is giving his current conception of a situation. The problem, objectified with the aid of the group and auxiliary egos, is what troubles the subject at this time. It may refer to similar conflicts in the past and to potential ones in the future. If the conflict gets clarified and understood, the subject and group can experience their handling it effectively. If they cannot handle the problem to their satisfaction, the action may be repeated until anxiety and conflict are reduced or resolved. This reality testing and evaluation is taking place within the session itself. The subjects learn to live and to communicate directly. Experience indicates that when a subject has not resolved an issue or conflict satisfactorily, the difficulty will reappear in the psychodramatic session. However, when he does work out the problem, it is apparent in the group session; proof is already visible in the psychodrama. Later, reality testing in the actual situation will validate the individual's progress in the practice setting of the role-playing group.

17

Encounter Groups in a Small College

Morton H. Shaevitz and Donald J. Barr

Since 1960 there has been a remarkable increase in both the number and variety of intensive small groups on college campuses. Self-analytic groups in the classroom have become almost a tradition at Harvard. Similar classes, where groups are used to help students understand the dynamics of groups and the complex nature of interpersonal relations, take place at the University of Michigan, the University of California at San Diego, and numerous other institutions.

Other types of groups, for counseling or therapeutic purposes, are offered within the programs of counseling services and mental health clinics. At times the naive observer has difficulty distinguishing between goals, means, and techniques, lumping all meetings of a continuing nature as "another damn group." With further experience, however, the observer becomes aware that the classroom group for didactic purposes looks quite different from encounter groups for personal growth.

While students flock in increasing numbers to group experiences, considerably less enthusiasm, occasionally bordering on overt hostility, has been shown by two other populations of the academic community—faculty and staff. It is the rare academician who does not have a strong position regarding encounter groups, sensitivity training, or groups for classroom learning. Most often the strength of the opinion is negatively correlated with the amount of his direct or indirect experience with the small group movement.

Participation in a small group is anticipated by the adolescent and young adult, viewed with cautious puzzlement by those in their generative years, and avoided whenever possible by those in their fifties and sixties. There are numerous exceptions. Many adults have had intensive small group experiences at professional conventions, in their churches, or in one of many training programs conducted by a variety of well-known organizations.[1] We venture to say, however, that while student groups have become common, the geriatric group is still a rarity.

Most participants have come to groups for individual reasons, including a desire for greater awareness, resolution of long-standing personal problems, or better understanding of the relation between group pressure and conformity. But group or organizational reasons are now in the foreground. During the 1950s and early 1960s, sensitivity training, the most widely used term for the intensive group experience, was a method of promoting both individual change and work effectiveness. In recent years organizational development programs, planned systematic attempts to promote change in an organization by the use of social sciences processes, have become frequent. Often, the sensitivity encounter group is an integral part of such programs. An early attempt to apply the concept of organizational development to schools was the work of Miles (1963). Most efforts using an organizational development approach in school systems have focused on elementary and secondary schools (Schmuck and Miles, 1971). Almost nothing systematic

[1] National Training Laboratories Institute for Applied Behavioral Sciences; Center for Studies of the Person; Esalen Institute; Institute for Social Research, University of Michigan.

has been done at the college level. A major factor in this discrepancy is that elementary and secondary education has been concerned with effectiveness, and federal funds have often been available to support educational programs.

What would happen if an entire college became involved in a series of encounter groups? Who would participate? How would they react? What would be the differences among students, administration, and faculty? How would people change? How would the college change? How could one document the findings if participation were voluntary? These were the questions confronting us in the summer of 1967 when we were asked to become an outside evaluation team for an educational change project relying on the use of encounter groups.

In 1967, Carl Rogers described a program to create a climate for self-directed, self-perpetuating change in schools. He invited those interested in participating in that type of experimental program to contact him. The sisters of Immaculate Heart, then an established community of nuns (now a lay community) in southern California, had participated heavily in primary, secondary, and collegiate education. They were actively involved in teaching at the elementary and secondary levels and were seen within the Catholic education community as an active, questioning, liberal group. Immaculate Heart College was and continues to be a respected liberal arts college best known, perhaps, for its work in art and drama but generally seen as providing quality undergraduate education. A subgroup within the college quickly convinced the administration that participation in a change program would be highly beneficial. Initially, Rogers was not too enthusiastic about installing his program in a parochial school system but finally agreed after a group of very persuasive nuns convinced him that the system offered unique opportunities.

Two organizations came together in the educational change project. One was the college, located in the middle of Hollywood, with a total enrollment in 1967 of approximately twelve hundred female students (four hundred full-time). Students tended to be from middle- to upper-middle-class backgrounds. The faculty of 102 was primarily female, two-thirds were lay people, and most held the doctorate. Although Immaculate Heart College (IHC) might be seen as similar to any one of a dozen small, Catholic, primarily female colleges in the country, in some important ways it was unique. The institution and its members were heavily involved in reassessment, looking at how the college should function and at the college's relation to other parts of the educational community. Key personnel were highly creative, dynamic people, actively seeking new methods, techniques, and structures. It was clear to us, from the beginning, that this was no ordinary Catholic girl's college, but a melange of contradictions.

The other organizational participant was the Western Behavioral Sciences Institute, located in La Jolla, California. The institute was a relatively new organization of applied behavioral scientists started in 1959. During the summer of 1968, Rogers and most of the educational change project staff left WBSI to form a new organization called Center for Studies of the Person (CSP). The central staff that stayed with the project over the two-year period were all men, three held Ph.D.s, and three of the four had been working together for two years prior to the project. Women were involved in the project but not in leadership roles. A major cornerstone of the CSP philosophy was that potential effectiveness should not be dependent on formal training but that individuals should be judged in terms of competence.

Many types of programs took place from August 1967 to June 1969, but all were in some way related to the process of the small group, in accord with the basic philosophy behind the project: "The major purpose was to utilize the encounter group, intensive group experience to bring about self-directed change in an educational system. The aim was to use a series of intensive workshops with administrators, students, faculty, parents, and others to improve communication and to bring about more openness to educational innovation and organizational innovation" (Rogers, 1967).

Three types of workshops were held (the word *workshop* is synonymous with encounter group program). First, two preplanned workshops for faculty and administration were held in the fall and winter of 1967. Each took place over a weekend (the first in a residential setting) and all faculty and administration were invited to participate. Second, a series of brief workshops, lasting from two hours to a full day, were held in response to specific requests. Natural groups, such as individual classes, student government, and the newspaper staff, were the usual requestors. Most involved both students and faculty.

The third type was intercollegiate workshops. Male students at a nearby college (California Institute of Technology) invited Immaculate Heart students to join them for three weekend workshops. NonCSP consultants conducted task-oriented meetings with some faculty and administration, but this chapter does not include an evaluation of the effect of these task-oriented groups.

These workshops had some distinct characteristics. The following description is based on our discussions with facilitators, participants, and staff and on attendance at a weekend workshop conducted by staff members from the Center for Studies of the Person. Participants were randomly assigned to groups of ten to fifteen persons. For the preplanned workshops, an attempt was made to equalize the sex distribution within each group, but no other demographic variables were considered. Each group had two facilitators; whenever possible mixed-sex pairs were used. Often the leader team was composed of a senior and a junior member; seniority was based on amount of group experience but not necessarily on formal education. For those workshops in which there was more than one group, relatively little time was spent in community sessions—whole-group gatherings for a specific activity or major presentation.

The format was usually an unstructured group. No previous topic had been identified, and participants were encouraged to express immediate reactions on an affective level to other group members. Topic-oriented discussions were discouraged, while interpersonal confrontations and the sharing of personal and interpersonal problems were sanctioned. Staff facilitators participated actively and shared their own experiences, expressing both positive and negative feelings toward others in the group. They placed little emphasis on group issues or general developmental themes.

Evaluation of the project was conducted by two colleagues at the University of Michigan with backgrounds in clinical and counseling psychology and with extensive experience in conducting sensitivity-encounter group sessions. Both had completed internships at the National Training Laboratories Institute for Applied Behavioral Sciences and had special interest in research on encounter groups in educational systems. Both had worked on such projects in past years.

The research team had definite ideas about appropriate evaluation techniques. They felt that questionnaires which asked individuals to rate themselves or colleagues on either attitudinal or behavioral dimensions were prolific but had limited validity. While questionnaires offer the advantage of statistical comparisons, the research team believed they would not be useful for purposes of research. Instead, the evaluators used a case study design, with heavy emphasis on observation and interviewing, as their primary data-gathering method.

From the fall of 1967 to the middle of spring 1969, the evaluation team made five visits to the college and spent a total of twenty days on campus. They sampled heavily among participants in encounter groups but also spoke to people who had not been actively involved, as they were interested in changes both at an individual and organizational level (only the former will be reported in this chapter). Interviews were either taped and transcribed or the evaluators dictated a summary at the end of the interview. Some people were seen individually, some in groups, others in classrooms, some while walking around campus, and still others at social events. An interview schedule was used; some items remained constant, while new questions were added when the project began to be less active.[2]

Our findings showed that a number of the major responses to the encounter group experience took place within a few months of participation. The long-range behavioral and attitudinal changes began to assert themselves some time after the actual experience.

[2] Readers interested in more explicit descriptions of both research methodology and technique may write for an expanded version of this area to Morton H. Shaevitz, University of California at San Diego, La Jolla, California.

During visits to the IHC campus the first year, we focused on the degrees of change in the functioning of various members of the IHC community. Our initial questions centered on significant events which had led to changes either in personal life or in professional role function (administrator, teacher, or student). After a series of general questions, we concentrated more specifically on what experience the interviewees had with the WBSI/CSP program, their evaluation of that experience, and the possible relationship of the experience and personal or professional change. We asked them whether they could identify other individuals they felt had changed in some significant ways, either interpersonally or professionally, and to specify precisely what these behavioral changes were. We attempted to go beyond the initial affective response (I feel better; It was a marvelous experience; I'm more comfortable now; It was terribly disruptive; There were bad consequences; and so on) by asking them to be as specific, detailed, and situationally oriented as they could be.

Obviously, we were unable to talk with everyone. The WBSI/CSP staff and the IHC coordinator were helpful in identifying individuals they felt had had varying personal experiences at the WBSI/CSP workshops. Because our third visit was made during the first summer session 1968, some personnel whom we had wished to reinterview and others who were identified as being relevant data sources were not available. But we were able to interview a large majority of college administrative personnel, a representative sample of teaching faculty, and, during the first year, a smaller and possibly less representative sample of the students. Similar interviews had been conducted during the September 1967 and November 1967 visits, and at times we were able to compare the participants' initial responses to a workshop with their views after some time had elapsed.

We were troubled by the question of how to present our findings most meaningfully. A numerical summary of individuals who had changed or not changed seemed inadequate, and we did not have sufficient representational data to make this type of statistical assessment meaningful. People who had been interviewed were candid and specific in their responses and accepted the implicit assumption that we would be handling this information in a way that would insure a relative degree of confidentiality. Our decision was to present composite pictures of different categories of individuals, who were grouped according to their degree of exposure and their reactions.

There were responses to the WBSI/CSP program even by those who had not attended any workshops. It was decided to present findings for these individuals as well as for those who had attended. The groups that emerged are represented in Table 22.

Table 22

		Attended		Did Not Attend	
		WORK/ROLE BEHAVIORS			
		Positive	Neutral	Positive	Negative
P E R S O N A L	Positive	1	2	5	6
	Negative/ Neutral	4	3		

Evaluation of faculty and administrative responses to workshops was reported in terms of the following groups of individuals: (1) those who had a positive personal experience and reported positive change in their work/role behavior; (2) those who had a positive personal experience and reported no changes in work/role behavior; (3) those who had a bad or neutral personal experience but reported no effect on work/role behavior; (4) those who had a negative or neutral personal experience but reported positive behavioral work/role changes; (5) nonattenders with strong positive evaluations; and (6) nonattenders with strong negative evaluations.

People (Group 1) who felt they had both a good personal experience and had changed in how they functioned included full-time administrators, those who both taught and had administrative functions, and some who only taught. The age range of the participants was from late twenties to middle fifties, and all those who gave positive ratings attended both of the preplanned workshops and had a number of contacts with the training staff, either in short workshops or on their own. They were not universally positive in their view of the staff, and some were critical of how the facilitator functioned during the encounter group. Most participants in this category had attended encounter groups previously or had heard about encounter groups and were prepared for the emotional nature of the experience. The reported changes in professional function had to do with being able to listen more acutely, using a variety of group techniques in the classroom, and changing their interpersonal relations with students—for example, by encouraging the use of first names. They felt more able to argue, to confront when appropriate, and were quite enthusiastic and specific about behavioral changes.

Demographically, Group 2 is quite similar to Group 1 in terms of role and age. In addition, these individuals also had attended both the preplanned workshops; although they did not have as much experience with the staff, they did participate in some other other workshops. In contrast to the first group, there was a greater range of personal evaluations. Some participants were laudatory and had had very positive personal experiences; others, while reporting the encounter group as having been pleasant, said it was not highly meaningful. In general, this group used fewer affective terms to describe their experiences and seemed somewhat more sanguine about the whole idea. Most members of this group had manifested new behavior patterns that were quite similar to those in the first group. They felt they had been changing, but they related change not to the encounter group experience but merely to a continuing evolution in their own attempts to become better teachers, administrators, and people.

Most people in Group 3 were older, had administrative responsibility, and had expected the encounter group to be task oriented rather than personally oriented. They were loud, certain, and strident in their dislikes of how the encounter groups were organized, what went on in them, and, in most cases, the behavior manifested by the group facilitators. Many felt that the basic contract of individual responsibility for participation was violated by pressures for self-revelation. Many, but not all, appeared uncomfortable in the world of affect; they stated that they rarely talked about how they felt and experienced discomfort when others became personal. Their needs were not met by the structure of the encounter group, and they looked back on the experience with responses ranging from anger to a shudder. When asked about how the encounter group might have affected functioning in their jobs, most expressed astonishment that there was supposed to be a relationship. The major theme was that work must be talked about if work behavior is going to change; talking about personal things is not relevant to how one functions as a teacher or as an administrator. Their general feelings can be summed up by the comment, "I don't see how the workshop experience has any connection with my role as a teacher."

Group 4 was established as a category because the research team thought a participant might leave the encounter group believing nothing had happened yet later realize that the experience was affecting him in indirect but positive ways. Such a result is possible, but the evaluators found no evidence to support this view, and no participants fell into this category.

Group 5 was composed of a small group of faculty and administrators who strongly supported the notion of encounter groups despite their lack of personal experience with it. Their support came mainly from two sources: talk with participants who had positive experiences and who articulated these quite well, and a general sympathy with the ideas behind both encounter groups and the educational change project. In spite of their strong emotional commitment to encounter groups, none of these people observed specific role-related behavior changes in their group-experienced colleagues. Rather, on a personal level, they felt their colleagues were more energetic, easier to relate to, and more exciting to be with. They did express some caution regarding the methods and goals of the facilitators. All

Group 5 people evidenced a strong desire to participate in a workshop.

People in Group 6 (no experience, negative evaluation) generally confined their complaints to two major areas: one, the lack of relationship between an encounter group and the solving of educational problems ("How can people becoming emotional with one another do any good?"); two, concern with how participation in encounter groups might negatively affect students in terms of their being able to pursue academic goals. These nonparticipants recounted stories they had heard in which individuals had had cathartic experiences or revealed personal issues. There was little concern with "people going crazy," but a typical question was "Why aren't they talking about education instead of themselves?" Many of these people admitted great discomfort in talking about feelings and in this way were quite similar to those in Group 3. They gave few examples of students having negative experiences. They just felt "things were not right." When we asked for greater specificity they referred to third-hand reports generally related to heightened expressivity but of a rumored nature.

The findings after a year of the change project show clearly that individual faculty and administrative personnel varied widely in their responses to the encounter group experience. Generally, those who were most positive in their response and seemed to have made maximum use of the experience were prepared for the encounter group. They were younger, had some previous experience with, or knowledge about, intensive groups, and were ready to become involved. One might consider them close to the descriptive adjectives of open, flexible, and involved. In contrast, those who were most negative about the encounter group were somewhat more defensive and stolid. It must be said, however, that among this negative group there were some very creative and productive individuals. While they seemed to be ready to move and grow, the encounter group experience with its emphasis on personal revelations and interpersonal confrontations "was not their cup of tea."

More than half the faculty and administrative staff participating in encounter groups had both their personal and professionally related needs met; the other 40 per cent did not.

In addition, one organizational consequence, which markedly influenced the second year of the project, was intense polarization between supporters and nonsupporters of encounter groups.

Although the same six-group approach was designed to describe the student response, we found it inadequate. Students were unaware that involvement in an encounter group was supposed to have a bearing on their functioning as students. For the most part they saw groups as opportunities to deal with personal and interpersonal relations. Also, the vast majority of those attending had positive reactions, while the bulk of negative student responses came from nonparticipants. We therefore grouped student response in only two categories—positive and negative.

The greatest proportion of positive responses was obtained from those students who had attended heterosexual groups with students from another college. Most were highly enthusiastic and talked about the continuing relationship between them and fellow students after the workshops ended. While there was some reference to one-to-one pairing, the great stress seemed to be on interchangeability and availability to one another: "A fellow could just come over to the dorm because he needed to talk to someone and any one of us who had been there would try to help him." Those students participating most actively and reporting most favorably were freshmen, sophomores, and transfer students. This selective factor seemed to parallel life at the college, where during the junior and senior years there is much less involvement in programs and greater moving into the community.

Overall, those who were most positive about the encounter group were new to the campus, attended workshops with male students, and probably participated in a brief classroom encounter group. They found the experience personally meaningful and informative, but were unable, except in rare cases, to see the experiences related to their student role and felt this was not an expected outcome. They were favorable toward faculty and administrative participation, and they observed significant positive changes in some specific teachers and administrators.

The most vociferous negative responses were from students who had had the least personal experience with and knowledge of encounter groups. These students were upper-classmen who had not attended the weekend encounter groups with the men's college; however, some were involved in class-room encounter groups. In all of our conversations with college people, these students were the most reluctant to talk with us, the least responsive, and at times were overtly hostile.

They seemed to have little knowledge about encounter groups, were uncertain as to who was participating and what it was all about, but seemed fairly definite that whatever was going on was not good. They believed that encounter group experiences were personally disruptive and should be avoided. They were concerned about the emotional outpourings that were reported to have taken place and had fears that people could be permanently damaged. Some expressed intense anger toward those students who had participated in groups in such terms as "they think they are so hot"; yet they were somewhat curious about what these other people had found so exciting. The ideological split was along liberal/conservative lines, with the nonparticipants identifying participants as being different, less responsible, and uncontrolled. Finally, there was general disapproval of the notion of encounter groups and some nega-tive reactions to specific staff members with whom they had had contact.

A clear and consistent picture emerged of students. Pre-disposition to participate was a primary factor determining student responsiveness. Those who were fearful and uncertain about what to expect found evidence to support their views. The negative students were angry about encounter groups and openly hostile to those who were participating. The negative students felt alienated from the things they observed happen-ing. Neither positive nor negative students expected that par-ticipation in encounter groups would lead to any meaningful change in terms of classroom or classroom-related behavior. However, student supporters of groups were enthusiastic about their experiences.

During the second year of the project, *no encounter group sessions took place*. This phenomenon was rather remarkable since it had been expected that the number and variety of such meetings would proliferate. Apparently, the lack of encounter was due to the enormous ideological split that developed on the campus about the groups. Talk continued about getting different types of encounter groups going, in dormitories or classrooms, but absolutely none occurred. There were a series of task-oriented meetings led by nonCSP consultants and a series of attempts to do problem-solving in the college community. We continued our evaluation despite the lack of activity.

Faculty and administration retrospective responses at the end of the second year are discussed in relation to the six original categories. Those who had originally reported their experiences as being positive and as having specific role relevance (Group 1) reported making greater use of their earlier training. A small cluster participated in a program developed to teach them to be facilitators during the summer of 1968, but because of the campus atmosphere, they never had an opportunity to use their skills at Immaculate Heart College. A second cluster, while continuing to maintain that their experience had been highly positive, had gained more cognitive mastery of the notion of planned change, and with this knowledge they became somewhat more critical retrospectively about the method used. They did continue their own development and in some instances made remarkable changes at a personal and work level.

Those in Group 2 maintained their view of the experience and in a somewhat passionless way continued to support the idea of encounter groups, its objectives, and their own experiences. At the conclusion of this second year, most members still did not relate any personal positive experiences of the workshop to changes in professional role function. One might summarize their responses as: "It was nice, I like it, I may even want to do it again—but I am not sure that it made any real difference."

Though Group 3 people continued to negatively evaluate the encounter group experience, as well as criticize techniques, goals, and personnel involved in conducting groups, two unique subgroups emerged. Most intriguing to the evaluators were those individuals who strongly maintained their criticism of encounter groups yet formed positive working relationships with some members of Group 1 who were trying hard to change their functioning as teachers or administrators. This subgroup was willing to experiment with different behavioral models and attempted new ways of dealing with traditional problems. They tried out new methods of teaching and relating to students or shared decision making with subordinates. They began to act like those in Group 1 but still felt very differently about the experience.

The second subgroup is the clearest example of professional dysfunction which could be related to the encounter group experience. Some of these people held major administrative responsibility and exercised power primarily by the use of sanctions. As other members of the faculty and administration became somewhat more sophisticated about certain areas of decision making and interpersonal relations, the actions of the blocking group became obvious and they were responded to negatively at both a personal and organizational level.

Those who had not participated in the program (groups 5 and 6) maintained their opinions throughout the second year. Their reactions, however, were less intense. We predict that given future opportunities to participate in an encounter group those who were supportive would become quickly involved and those who felt strongly opposed would avoid the situation.

Student retrospective responses at the end of the second year remained essentially positive. During the summer following the first year of the project, four of the several students trained as facilitators during the year had been deeply involved in encounter group experiences away from school. They were highly productive, exceedingly bright students who had become strongly committed to increasing the number of encounter groups made available to students and also increasing the number of students involved. On their return to campus, however, their plans to initiate a number of encounter groups were not supported by the students. By the end of the second year they felt somewhat disappointed and alienated.

Other students who were positive about encounter groups seemed willing to talk about their perceptions of temporary negative aftereffects of group participation. Three students were multiply identified as constantly questing for confirmation, asking for feedback, and directing almost all conversations into a personal area. For them, it seemed that no content was independent of the affective dimension, and they began to be seen by their fellow students as tiresome and boring. They had also became dysfunctional with regard to more traditional student roles, both on the basis of observations and self-reports. At least these three were clearly identified as having decreased attendance at classes, taking incompletes, and being less willing to participate in classes.

Positive students felt they were more able to communicate with teachers and that a different level of dialogue was taking place. A number of these students became active participants in student government and other leadership roles. It is difficult to pinpoint causal relations; those who most often participated in encounter groups tended to be students who were already involved in campus politics, organizations, committees, and so on. It did appear, however, that their effectiveness was increasing, due to both increased skill and reciprocal receptivity of the faculty and administration.

It was difficult to find students who were very concerned about encounter groups during the second year. Several factors probably account for this occurrence. First, encounter group activities had ceased. Second, a number of those who were most vehemently opposed the previous year had graduated. Third, the student body was not as polarized as it had been the first year. Those who supported the basic encounter group and the general outlines of the educational change project seemed to be less monolithic in their views of the outcome. Their attitude change seemed to reduce the concern of the negative students.

Before summarizing the overall results of the project, we will make some general statements about encounter groups for students in an educational system. First, the intensity of the responses, positive and negative, was much greater for students than for faculty and administration. Students had more difficulty gaining distance from their experience, and they tended to transfer actual behaviors rather than principles of behavior to a new setting. While adult members might learn that the expression of anger can be useful, they often modulated this learned behavior in a work situation and the way they expressed feelings was significantly different from their method in the group. Students, however, tended to transfer behavior directly, so that the same degree of intensity was exhibited outside the encounter group. Thus, the behavior change sometimes wound up being inappropriate and at times frightening to their peers.

Those who experienced the workshop in a highly emotional fashion often went through a period of nonfunction following the group. We are not aware of instances where this happened for faculty and administration. Such dysfunction seems more likely among a population whose emotional structure was considerably more labile than that of the adults. In most instances, these periods were brief, later integrated, and were not debilitating. For some, as we have already mentioned, involvement in the group experience became a prominent part of their lives, and this result may be viewed as having a long-range negative effect. The students themselves did not see it this way, and therefore this may be seen as an issue of values. We believe that one outcome of intense involvement in encounter group experiences was the dissociation with more traditional student role behaviors. In contrast to the more careful work of Lieberman, Yalom, and Miles (see Chapters 7 and 8), we did not find any casualties.

The decision to work with students in a basic encounter group carries with it the possibility of rapid and intense change along with the risk of temporary dysfunction. Two critical steps should be taken if one is going to work with this population. First, sufficient time should be spent on the issue of transfer—what the experience means in terms of other relationships and how the learnings can be translated into new, adaptive behaviors. Second, follow-up counseling should be available to those students who are unable to adequately reintegrate in a productive fashion. Participants should understand that this possible consequence is not necessarily negative but should lead to help from professional sources.

The responses of students, faculty, and administration to encounter groups were more varied than we expected. Some major conclusions were: (1) The most positive responses to the encounter experiences came from those who knew what to expect or were able to adapt to the situation most easily. (2) The number of people able to integrate a limited intensive group experience in a way that significantly affected their interpersonal behavior was relatively small. For these individuals, however, the degree of change was highly significant. (3) The intensive group experience was rarely responded to neutrally. For all those who participated, it was a significant event. (4) The level of response and later integration of the intensive group experience by college students was qualitatively different from that of faculty and administrators. (5) Though there were cases of transitional nonfunction, we were not able to document a single case of severe long-term disability as a function of participation in the intensive group experience.

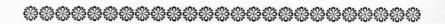

18

Organization Development Groups in Industry

O. S. Farry, S. M. Herman

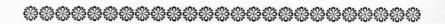

A great deal has been written and said about the use of sensitivity training or encounter groups in industry.[1] Much of this output has been highly controversial and characterized by partisan statements ranging from: "They represent the real hope for building authentic personal relations and thereby for rehumanizing organizations" to "They are the same as communist brainwashing and tend to destroy individuality and

[1] Person-to-person encounter is central to sensitivity training. In this sense sensitivity training and encounter groups are synonymous. However, because encounter groups have so diversified in meaning in recent years we use the term sensitivity training to clarify the base from which the experiences described generated.

initiative and foster divisiveness and permanent antagonisms."
Based on our personal experience with sensitivity training over
the past ten years at TRW Systems [2] and elsewhere, and reports
from other companies where it has been used, we find both
positions extreme and extravagant.

Controversy, of course, is exhilarating. However, our
purpose is not to elaborate, attack, or defend sensitivity training
as such. Rather, our primary intent is to highlight and discuss
organization development, a relatively new methodology for
the application of sensitivity training theory in task-oriented
settings.

Before proceeding to these specialized applications, however, some aspects of sensitivity training and its use in an industrial environment are worth noting. Well-run sensitivity
training groups support the development of a person's individuality. They can help people both to express themselves
more adequately and to understand and accept the expression
of others' individuality. In our view, a sensitivity training group
conducted for employees in industry, as well as for people outside organizations, has the following objectives. It should be a
personal growth experience which emphasizes personal awareness, taking responsibility for one's self, experiencing behavioral
options, their personal meaning and consequences; and it should
support heightened awareness of the processes of interaction
among individuals in a group setting.

Many possible discoveries and values derived from sensitivity groups contribute to improved functioning in organizations. People learn to appreciate the similarities and differences
among people—especially those in varied occupational specialties. They begin to recognize the reality and effect of
feelings as well as opinions and observations. They gain a sense
of optimism, or at least a broader perspective on the possible.
In a spirit of inquiry and experimentation, they find out what
is real and try things out.

Participants discover a vital approach to change which

[2] TRW Systems is an operating unit of TRW Inc. With headquarters at Redondo Beach, California.

helps them move to the future from a base of better understanding of the present, its potentials and pitfalls, rather than leap to a fantasy future to avoid present realities. They gain a sense of people and organizations in movement—not static and unchangeable—as dynamically flowing between processes of differentiation and integration. Group members also learn to appreciate trust as a keystone to effective communication among people and trust in oneself as essential to productivity and creativity. They begin to see how focusing organic processes is critical to the evolution of organizations. They also learn to appreciate conflict as an expression of vitality, not catastrophe, and gain a sense of individual responsibility—for necessary risk-taking, for appropriate openness and direct communication, and for person to person confrontation.

Critics of the sensitivity training process raise some concerns. They argue that since it is a group endeavor, it must represent an attempt to substitute the irresponsibility of group anomie for individual responsibility. They state that this training overtly tries to correct people (who do not conform or who do no function well) through methods of subtle seduction or overt coercion by the group and that it represents a move to eliminate operating structure—to substitute randomness for organization and to encourage everyone to do his own thing regardless of consequences. While these possibilities may be real dangers in some organizations, in our experience they have not occurred. In fact they are antithetical to our primary principles of reality focus and individual responsibility.

Two other frequently expressed concerns relate to the risk of psychological disturbance and the possibility of generating unresolved personal antagonism among organization members. There are, admittedly, some risks of psychological disturbance in a sensivity training group, and even a likelihood that most members will experience tension and temporary discomfort as they begin to explore and open their behavior and feelings in areas that have been relatively closed in the past. However, based on our experience, as well as information collected from other organizations that have had extensive experience in the use of sensitivity training, the dangers of serious psychological disturbance are hardly greater for participants in the sensitivity training setting than they are for the general population in the day to day work environment. There are even indications that some emotionally troubled individuals may actually find the freer, more authentic environment of a sensitivity group to be strengthening rather than harmful.

While cases of unresolved personal antagonisms among coworkers have arisen in groups, these are really quite rare. More often, a well-functioning group encourages people to express their differences, to discover the bases for them, and to work these differences through to the point of achieving more functional and satisfying relationships. In those few cases where strong personal animosity becomes apparent in a training session attended by members of the same organization, the antagonisms probably existed prior to the session but at a more covert level. They may even have been more dysfunctional and harmful in this hidden state.

To make the experience as useful for individual participants as possible and to minimize chances of negative consequences, care should be taken to ensure that any sensitivity training group efforts have the following characteristics: clear objectives, voluntary participation, prescreening, training goals, and sound leadership.

The learning objectives for the training laboratory should be clearly stated and understood by prospective participants before they attend. These objectives should not be confused with any attempts at evaluation, certification, standardized indoctrination, and so on. At TRW Systems, we typically conduct orientation sessions and distribute written statements of lab objectives, as well as conduct individual interviews to ensure this point. Further, the lab has a limited goal: to introduce interpersonal process that can later help personnel perceive and deal with complex organizational problems in a different setting and with professional consulting help.

Individuals should not be sent to a sensitivity training session. Special efforts should be made to assure that an individual has full freedom to attend or not according to his own desires. Further, the more subtle pressures to attend sensitivity training (because it is fashionable or an organization status symbol) should be minimized. At TRW Systems, a personnel administrator interviews each candidate for group sessions. The administrator determines whether the individual is feeling any pressure to attend or whether his interest is merely in getting in on a popular thing.

Prescreening of participants also occurs during these interviews. The administrator asks the individual whether his experience includes any history of psychological upset and whether he is presently experiencing any particular difficulties either in his job or personal life that might be placing an inordinate amount of stress on him. If the candidate is feeling significant problems, it is recommended that he postpone, at least temporarily, his participation in the group or explore other learning formats more appropriate to his current situation.

We make clear to all managers and others responsible for organizing group sessions that sensitivity training is not intended to be a therapy group but a training group, and therefore it is not a place for the manager to send problem cases.

All sessions are conducted by adequately trained group leaders. We also assure adequate time for the program, sound planning of the process, and availability of professional psychiatric help should the infrequent need for such help arise.

When these preconditions are met, sensitivity training usually provides a personal growth experience for those who participate. Many individuals who attended sensitivity training sessions at TRW Systems report that they achieved significant personal insight; others developed or reinforced a more optimistic orientation toward people and groups. (They became more comfortable and confident being with people or experienced a heightened appreciation of the differences among people and a sense of the processes which occur in a group when these differences interact.) Some have reconsidered their stereotypes, simply discovering that they could talk with other people in the organization of whom they previously were only vaguely aware. They were surprised to find, for instance, that a contracts manager, or a nuclear physicist, or a systems engineer could understand their problems and even be willing to help. For some, not much happened, and for a few the experience was sour.

For many who participated in the lab, the concluding attitude involved the question: How can I sustain this style of interaction back on the job and use what I have learned in my own organization? This question brings up a critical point relative to the use of sensitivity training in industry: Sensitivity training is not enough. Unless an organization's culture can modify itself to provide a supportive on-the-job environment consistent with the values learned in the group, the effects of sensitivity training on individuals after their return to the organization setting will almost invariably be short-lived indeed.

Most of us who have worked in, or are familiar with, organizations whose approach to change is limited solely to "sending managers away" to one- or two-week sensitivity training laboratories have encountered some of the sad results after their return. Few people become more frustrated or more disillusioned than the manager who goes away to a lab, learns the value and satisfaction of personal openness, direct confrontation, and freer expression of feelings, then returns to his own work setting only to find that these new-found modes are considered inappropriate and unfit for a business world. Thus, participation in encounter groups needs to be incorporated in some broader effort of organization development oriented toward culture change as an overriding objective.

This necessity is supported by a National Industrial Conference Board survey (1969):

The companies expressing the most satisfaction with their behavioral science programs are those that do not view them as programs at all. Instead they see them as a completely different way of improving and managing the enterprise. These firms are trying to impact the total organization by applying behavioral science principles at all levels. Their behavioral science applications extend beyond trying to develop managers. Instead, they encompass every facet of the company's operations in terms of meeting such objectives as long-range planning, career development, productivity, and profitability.

At TRW Systems sensitivity training laboratories played a large part in our initial activities several years ago and still play some part; however, they currently account for only a small fraction of the total activity in organization development. For instance, we have found that rather than try to recapture the laboratory experience (which is, of course, gone) the most satisfying and productive follow-up to sensitivity training tends to have the following characteristics. First, the participant gets together with a member of the industrial relations staff (often the IR staff man takes the initiative). Next, they begin to identify the operating problems or specific things they would like to change in the organization unit in which they are involved. Third, they develop a specific action plan to involve others in a process of change. Virtually all the lasting payoff for individuals or for organizational groups develops directly from some effort other than the sensitivity training event as such— although impetus for change is often sparked there.

How to induce positive change in the organization culture is the subject of the remainder of this chapter. In this context, our organization development efforts include: an approach to the management of organizations that recognizes interpersonal (interactional) process as well as formal structure and content as important and legitimate subject matter to be examined; a set of methods (behavioral science technology); an organization ethic that seriously and purposefully attends to the humanness of the people who work within; and a long-term, committed effort by the organization and its management to improve its total capability and effectiveness.

Let us begin by examining what we mean by an organization culture. Clearly, a complete definition of the organization culture must include everything that goes on, is used by, is generated by, and influences the organization. For our purpose, however, we can focus on those facets having to do with the prevailing assumptions, values, and norms which characterize the management and personal interactive processes that occur in the day to day operation of the organization. These are the areas where much of organization development is most relevant. Some examples of such assumptions, values, and norms are given in the following questions.

Are people seen as inherently lazy and selfish, requiring motivation by carrot and stick approaches, or is the assumption that people would naturally rather work than be idle, that they are concerned about others as well as themselves, and that they are normally responsible and conscientious? Is it assumed that supervisors must maintain personal distance from subordinates to be effective, or that close personal relationships can exist between supervisors and subordinates and that these relationships may actually enhance satisfaction and effectiveness? Are people judged according to their rank and status, or according to their ability and personal effectiveness? Is it assumed that power is the only way to get things done, or are participation and consensus considered legitimate processes?

Is profitability the sole criterion for decision making in the organization, or do management decision makers really take into account relationships between profits and people? Are line people considered first-class citizens and staff people second-class, or are equivalent status and recognition available to all specialists depending upon their abilities? Do communication and action occur only through the chain of command, or does the system allow functional interaction as required by the situation? Is competition the only means through which an individual can achieve success and recognition, or are there also rewards for collaborative efforts? Is an individual required to stay within the limits of his formal job definition, or do the scopes of jobs have permeable boundaries? Is the rule "don't contradict the boss," or is it legitimate to raise questions and issues at all levels?

Are only organization needs considered legitimate, or are individuals' personal desires also taken into account? When something goes wrong, is there an emphasis on blame-placing or an emphasis on problem-solving? Are there tight boundary constraints on organizatioanl subunits, are charters so clearly drawn that no one has any business in another area, *or* is there adequate allowance for some overlap and necessary ambiguity? Is all the reward for making no mistakes, or is reasonable risk-taking to achieve higher stakes encouraged? Are mistakes viewed as events from which to learn?

Even this brief set of examples makes clear that prevail-

ing assumptions, values, and norms provide an extremely powerful framework within which any individual member must
operate. It would be a rare manager, indeed, who could carry
home the learnings of a sensitivity group and successfully apply
them in a hostile culture—a culture, in other words, characterized by the first alternative in each of these questions.

In addressing the processes of diagnosis and change in
an organization culture, it is important to recognize that an
organization consists of more than its formal structure and
mechanisms and that organizational dynamics include more
than the formally prescribed channels of interaction. Organization development can help individuals appreciate this fact. In
addition, its methods can help generate ideas and mechanisms
for dealing effectively with the complex processes of these organization dynamics. A model we have found useful for char-
acterizing organizations is the Organizational Iceberg shown in
Figure 2.

The upper portion of the iceberg represents the formal
statement of the organization. Such items as organization struc-

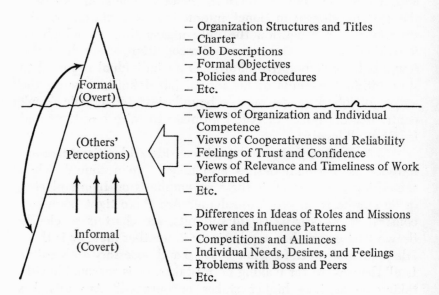

FIGURE 2. The organization iceberg.

ture and titles, charter, policies, and job descriptions are typical. Traditionally, in most organizations, when a serious operating problem is encountered, managers, organization consultants, and others interested in improving functioning tend to concentrate their attention in this area. Thus, characteristic proposed solutions to operating problems often call for changing the structure of the organization or the responsibilities of individual units, adding a level of management or deleting one, moving a subunit from one reporting relationship to another, and so on.

In some instances, such proposals are relevant and useful. At other times, though, all they accomplish is the shifting of the same problem from one location in the total organization to another. Even when appropriate structural solutions are imposed from above by directive, those affected may become very resistant (often in subtle, indirect ways) and exert a great deal of energy to making sure the solution will not work. In the practice of organization development, therefore, we believe attention must be given to other dynamics—those below the "waterline"—in addition to (not instead of) those represented by the formal organization statement.

In the lowest third of the diagram, the informal or covert area, are the intrapersonal and interpersonal dynamics of those who staff the organization. Different concepts of roles and missions are important elements at this level. For example, does the personnel manager view himself and his staff as controllers and monitors of personnel policies and requirements, or does he see his function as one of facilitating and helping operating managers and employees to achieve their aims in the context of the organization setting. What about his "customers," the operating managers and other personnel he services? How do they perceive what his role ought to be? When the personnel man sees his role one way and those he services see it another, and these issues are never explicitly confronted, the result can be continual conflict and resentment. In some companies, these long-standing and unresolved differences, typically between line and staff functions (though they can also exist between any organizations that interface with each other), can become so bad that the servicing group is seen more as an obstacle than a help.

Power and influence patterns are also important and frequently do not coincide with the hierarchical lines on an organization chart. Confusion, resentment, and frustration are often a concomitant of the lack of clarity and explicitness in power and influence modes. Again, illustrations are abundant. The covert resentments and political games played between managers as they compete for power or the boss's favor are commonplace. Unless these issues can be addressed and dealt with frankly, there is little chance to improve the situation.

There are probably few organizations, whether industrial, educational, social, or governmental, in which certain subgroupings of people have not formed into temporary or sometimes even permanent blocks for the purpose of mutually supportive alliance or to compete against other subgroups. In typical staff meetings any proposal made by members of one group is opposed by another group, no matter what the nature of the proposal. Dysfunctional behavior stemming from these interpersonal patterns frequently obscures and hinders the work of the organization. Often the basis and form of these alliances and antagonisms are disguised, resulting in what are commonly called hidden agendas.

The business itself demands that decisions be made regarding a wide range of variables relating to the products or services being offered. The decision-making process is much more complex in some industries than it is in others. A by-product of these decisions is their substantial effect on the interests and careers of people in the organization. Usually an individual has a lot invested in some piece of the action—in the short term (for example, getting the product out today) or in the long term (for instance, planning for the future). Others have heavy investments in the technological state-of-the-art, finance, marketing, and so on. How these people get involved in setting priorities for the organization and in the process of decision making can make a major difference, not only to the company's success but to the development and careers of individuals as well.

The hidden agenda phenomenon is also common when the personal needs, desires, and feelings of individuals are considered illegitimate in the organization setting. A prevailing organizational myth, especially in industrial companies, implies that employees are paid to devote their entire concentration to the needs of the organization. They are supposed to leave their personal needs and concerns at home so that they can operate objectively in determining and implementing what is best for the organization. But individual needs and feelings do not go away merely because they are considered bad form. Rather more frequently they are expressed in disguise and therefore in less accessible ways.

In one recent case a high-level executive was developing a plan which called for a series of major activities of one organization to be redistributed among several others. The executive decided to get the opinions of the affected managers before finalizing his plan. All agreed that it made sense except the manager from whose organization the functions were being removed. This man, a highly competent and respected member of the executive's team, raised one objection after another over a period of weeks. As each point he made was answered he found another in its place. Soon it was apparent that his points were becoming less and less relevant.

Only after a lengthy private conversation between the executive and the manager, arranged with the aid of a third-party consultant, did the manager's objections finally emerge as desperate efforts to prevent a change because he was personally worried about the effects of such a change on his own career (job interest, status, opportunities for promotion) and the careers of his affected subordinates. After these concerns were dealt with successfully by the executive, the manager was asked why he had not raised them earlier. He replied that he had not believed that personal worries were appropriate in a business situation or that his boss would be willing to consider them.

Other problems of fear, insecurity, and anxiety stemming from superior-subordinate relationships hardly need further illustration. Numerous cases of suspicion and unproductive self-protective adaptations made by people and groups when there is a lack of trust between them could also be discussed at length. The time and energy used in some organizations to maintain "Pearl Harbor files" or to place the blame on someone else sometimes seems greater than the time and energy used for getting the work done.

The middle portion of the Organization Iceberg represents perceptions of the organization by others outside it. To the extent that they influence outcomes of the organizational enterprise they are part of the culture. The arrows drawn through the broken line from the lower to the middle third of the Iceberg indicate that what happens at the covert level is often recognizable and has its effect on those with whom the organization interacts. These may include clients, customers, or other organizations.

Those who interact with an organization cannot help but have views and feelings about the competence, reliability, and effectiveness of the organization and its members. Is this a group of able, up-to-date people or a collection of over the hill, uninterested incompetents? Do personnel try to help you with your problems, are they willing to work out give-and-take solutions, or are they rigid and uncompromising? Are they tuned in to what is happening or are they ivory-tower dreamers out of touch with the real world? Will they produce what they say they will produce and deliver on time?

More important than general answers to such questions is specific information about specific functions and the way they are handled. Knowledge of how others react to these problems could be of great value to any organization. Yet few outside people feel free to comment openly and honestly about their perceptions and impressions directly to members of the organization. Even less frequently would the management or members of most organizations possess the knowledge and skills required to actively solicit these impressions, even if they were so inclined.

Organization development provides the basic philosophy, theories, and methods for enabling open, constructive communication of relevant personal concerns in addition to operational information. It also encourages identification of specific corrective action required.[3] The philosophy and techniques have evolved from experimenting with both the formal and informal aspects of organizations in a variety of formats. The common theme of all this effort has been the need to create, maintain, and change a large organization and its subunits in order to achieve a dynamic whole that meets the requirements of rapidly changing markets and technology. Out of this effort have come (frequently tried) methods and an orientation toward continued experimentation.

The most fundamental of these methods, team building, bears a close relationship to sensitivity training, though it is different in significant respects (Davis, 1970). *Team* in this instance refers to a group of people (usually fewer than twenty) who have a common manager or who have some common task or tasks to perform. Thus, rather than being strangers or casual acquaintances as in the typical sensitivity training group, the participants have a continuing relationship focused by work requirements or organizational arrangements. The second difference is that the team-building meeting is not a self-contained event; it is but one event in the ongoing stream of the whole organizational process. The third difference is that the agenda for the team-building meeting usually focuses on "how can we work together more effectively" as opposed to the focus on personal growth and awareness of sensitivity training groups.

As part of team building, an outside consultant or a member of the personnel department skilled in organization development who acts as internal consultant interviews each member of the team prior to the meeting and says, "We are going to spend a block of time looking at how we can improve our effectiveness. If we are going to do that, what are some

[3] Organizations involved in organization development include American Airlines, several Bell System companies, Pillsbury, Syntex, Union Carbide, Texas Instruments, and the Hotel Corporation of America. Each has approached its situation differently because of such factors as the nature of the business, how the effort was initiated, the state of the culture at the outset and its readiness to change, and the personal proclivities of those most active in the process.

things you think should be looked at and that need to be dealt with?"

The team leader starts the meeting by explaining the purpose of the group. A typical explanation: "I think we need to improve what we are doing. I believe we can do so if we make the process of improvement a deliberate and joint effort. Let's ask ourselves what we can do better. I have a few ideas and I'm sure you do, too." The consultant then continues the meeting by feeding back the interview data he received and highlights the problems the interviews have uncovered. These problems are delivered as nearly verbatim as possible. The rest of the meeting is spent dealing with that data.

Usually, but not always, the feedback process starts with issues relating to the top man on the team. There are inevitably things he is doing (or at least perceptions of him) that need discussing—and if he is not going to be open to the team-building process, the rest of the team probably will not be either. The third-party consultant interviewed him in the preparatory stage, listened for issues involving him, and now uses his willingness to learn how his subordinates feel about his leadership as a lever to get the discussion going more broadly. For this reason the leader must genuinely want to do team building and have good rapport with the consultant from the beginning.

Other aspects of team meetings are predictable in a general sense. Typically, the members will first deal with accumulated misperceptions, exaggerated perceptions, and resentments in the interpersonal systems of their particular subculture—that is, things that have gone on over the years that are still bothering them but which have not yet been identified, talked about, dealt with, or worked through. The range of expression here can be very wide; it can be very personal. In one group, for example, a member was told he was very competent but extremely cold in dealing with other people. They misperceived his coldness, personally experiencing it as arrogance and rejection. While he did not warm up toward his co-workers as a result of this confrontation, there was less misperception and more understanding of his manner and attitudes. Some of these perceptions and resentments get worked through by discussing them, or merely by talking. Matters of trust are raised. Somehow, just the act of being able to say, eye to eye, that trust levels between two people are low begins to help the problem. The work in this phase of team building is extremely important; if it is well done it can clear the way for other important business.

Usually the next general phase is an attempt to introduce some specific recommendations for improvement. Matters of an organizational nature often come up: "We need to have more staff meetings. The meetings should be shorter. We ought to take time in the staff meetings to actually solve problems and to give a critique of what we are doing"; "Joe needs to be involved in the X43 project"; "We need to set a high priority on increasing our capability in marketing."

In a later phase the team begins to examine how it relates to other groups. Again, as in the first phase, misperception and resentment have accumulated. Often they wish the president of the company would do something to straighten out those purchasing people, or tell the electrical engineers, or say something to personnel. They feel someone else with more authority should take some constructive action and straighten out the people who are really the problem. After a while the group tires of this approach and begins to question: "Are we part of the problem?" This insight is very important, because they usually are part of it: The problem is in the relationships. "Can we do something about our troublesome relationships with others and not wait for the president to issue the magic memo, which probably wouldn't work anyway?"

Team-building sessions are designed to bring to light problems that interfere with task accomplishment. Each meeting produces an action list of specific items to be worked on after the meeting when everybody is back on the job. These on-the-job applications may range from the airing of differences between individuals to the resolution of a difficult interface between divisions or even between the company and a customer.

Team building has led to the use of other methods which focus on individuals, departments, and even larger organization segments. Some of these that have broad application are briefly outlined. *Intergroup building* is a step beyond team building in which interfacing and interdependent work groups meet to identify and resolve problems between them. The *organization mirror* is a method whereby any organization unit actively seeks out its "internal customers" (other units using or affected by their services) to receive their critique and feedback on the quality of their services. In *the confrontation goal-setting meeting* all individuals from a large organizational unit (as many as 100 people) and including two levels of management meet for a day to identify goals for change and subsequent action steps.

Diagnostic techniques are part of the ongoing process of evaluating the health and climate of the organization and facilitating communication. Prominent among these techniques is a procedure called sensing. Rather than have an outsider come in to measure attitudes or collect information, appropriate individuals are brought together face to face so that an individual or group may get a reading on a particular problem area or segment of the organization. For example, rather than depend on memos or a consultant's report on a particular program, the president might listen while persons (usually several levels below him) directly involved in carrying out the program discuss among themselves its problems and progress. The president does not participate, except to ask questions or request clarification.

Joint exploration *workshops* are conducted or developed to respond to specific subject interests, such as personal effectiveness on the job or organization development methods for managers. A *behavioral science consulting team,* composed of prominent behavioral scientists, works with various segments of the organization, both offsite and onsite. Typically these consultants team up with a member of the industrial relations staff and an operating manager to provide organizational development consulting services to an organization unit.

Organization units wishing to explore change use *third-party consultation.* Someone outside the unit, either someone on the industrial relations staff or another line manager, assists them in focusing on changes they wish to make and facilitating their process. For instance, a member of the industrial relations staff skilled in these methods works with each major organization unit. He has responsibility for the total range of personnel functions, including acting as a third party and consulting on organization development.

Several common themes in all these approaches can be identified. They tend to support or enhance personal and open communication, making data necessary to deal with a problem situation available to those who need it—those who, in a direct sense, have the problem. They provide a method for collecting data and setting priorities to focus on issues that potentially have highest leverage and greatest payout for the people involved. These methods provide a framework for diagnosing a situation with the people involved so that its critical elements can be dealt with by them. They also provide a structure or format for dealing with problems which is generally consistent with the nature of the problem to be addressed and permit it to be dealt with in a whole way—they do not arbitrarily select pieces for attention.

These techniques clarify objectives or outcome expectations and demand a resolution satisfactory to those involved. Assessment criteria and method are implicit as part of these objectives. They build in an external frame of reference (often someone outside the group concerned with the problem) to assist in establishing perspective and guideposts for accomplishment. They legitimize dealing with uniquely personal matters— feelings, attitudes, perceptions, assumptions—when they are part of the problem. They focus both choice of action and responsibility for action on those people who are most involved with the problem. They recognize critical external influences and the need to develop a format to deal with them.

As we see them, these methods are tools to be used in a connected and planned change effort which involves all aspects of an organization culture. They are not isolated activities. The progressive use of these methods generally moves from basic education (such as the sensitivity training experience) to small group work (team building) and on to broader organizational formats (intergroup building or organizational mirror). All approaches involve the interested people and include, in some form, the fundamental action research steps of data collection, diagnosis, action planning, implementation, and assessment. (For more detail on these methods, see Fordyce and Weil, 1971.)

To conclude, these and other methods applied in a concerted and planned way can contribute significantly to the growth of an organization and its culture. Especially important is the way the organization manages its processes of change and the consequences of this change for its members. Our eight years' experience with organization development reveals that organizations which used this approach successfully had several characteristics in common. The general spirit of the organization was one of expansion and optimism; the need for managing complex patterns of interaction was critical and urgent. A lot of people got involved in all parts of the organization. The efforts were not considered as just a luxury but were seen as essential to effective functioning in a complex business—the focus was on concrete job-related issues. The key people in the organization were relatively young, were not hindered by long-standing traditions, and were willing to experiment. They agreed to invest in a long-term continuing effort rather than a quick fix. Work toward change was championed by a few people inside the organization who were willing to risk initially negative reactions from others and to persist.

Perhaps most important, in support of the effort and the methods developed, the top management generally shared a set of values consistent with those values and discoveries from sensitivity training outlined at the outset of this chapter. Thus, organization development efforts have served to focus and accentuate these values in people-terms and have helped to integrate them into the operating processes of the organization.

Encounter Groups for Married Couples

Richard Pilder

The marital dyad in our day is burdened with unprecedented strains. It has, in a unique way, become the victim of the compartmentalized depersonalization of Western technological society. Having been isolated from the traditional family, which offered an extended range of interpersonal contacts, today's marriage is expected to absorb the intensified emotional needs produced by contracted contact (Keniston, 1965). The temporary nature of modern systems also impinges on the married couple. The unstabling effects of rapid change and high mobility produce increased demands for the alleviation of heightened insecurity and meaninglessness (Bennis and Slater, 1968; Toffler, 1970).

In light of the burdens which the social situation imposes on today's married couples, and in view of the fact that an alarming number of these couples experience the marital relationship as dissatisfying, there has evolved much speculation about the adequacy of traditional conceptions such as permanence and sexual exclusivity (Leonard, 1968). This discourse, though important, is perhaps premature. Possibly, it is a manifestation of the lack of nobility which Camus (1955) says characterizes our age: abandoning the world before having exhausted it, lack of fidelity to our limits and lucid love of our condition. The fact that the behavioral sciences have only minimally communicated their learnings and skills to the married couple leads me to agree with Camus. Let us first exhaust our knowledge on improving the condition of today's marital relationships before resorting to redefinitions.

One application of behavioral science knowledge to the possible improvement of marriages is the encounter laboratory for couples. As an educational innovation specifically designed to increase interpersonal competence, the laboratory method (Bradford, Gibb, and Benne, 1964) seems ideal for aiding the marital relationship. Controlled empirical study on the applicability of this method to married couples is sorely lacking. To date, growing numbers of couples are being exposed to this experience and yet the literature reporting the outcomes of these groups is still sparse (Golembiewski and Blumberg, 1970).

Despite the absence of empirical study, it is possible to extrapolate possible applications to the marital dyad. The following remarks discuss the desirability of a laboratory (or encounter) approach for married couples, some specific goal-objectives of couples groups, the unique contributions which couples bring to the laboratory setting, design requirements for couples groups, and finally a model design which has proven effective experientially.

Research has shown that change in the direction of growth occurs as a result of laboratory training in a number of areas: improved self-acceptance (Valiquet, 1964), a greater openness to and acceptance of others as other (Bunker, 1965), and increased sensitivity to personal needs as well as the needs of others (Miles, 1965). Such outcomes are directly related to interpersonal functioning. If we accept that self-love is the basis of love for others (Fromm, 1956) and that interpersonal sensitivity and acceptance are prerequisites for all growth-producing dyadic relationships (Carkhuff and Berensen, 1967), then these outcomes would strongly suggest the creative possibilities of the laboratory environment for married couples.

Research findings on the relationship between interpersonal competence and successful marriages also lend support for the laboratory approach (Katz, 1965; Navran, 1967; Dymond, 1954; Stimson, 1966). Further support is found in the fact that many marriage counselors and therapists make improved communication (a known outcome of laboratory training) their major objective (Kadis, 1964; Ellis, 1958; Satir, 1964).

Apart from the supportive findings of related research, the very nature of the laboratory environment provides couples a unique opportunity to increase the breadth and depth of their relationships. A common problem in marriage is that roles tend to become rigid and interaction becomes fixed, stable, predictable. If such rigid roles are prolonged, boredom is inevitable. The laboratory environment provides a unique culture whose aim is to unfreeze and thus decrease routine behavior (Bennis and Schein, 1965). Couples can alter the stereotyped patterns of their relationships and consequently avoid the stagnation which produces boredom.

To speak of the positive possibilities of the laboratory method is not to overlook its limitations: It was not designed to replace therapy. Similarly, laboratory training for couples should not be seen as a substitute for marital counseling. It is definitely no panacea for marital problems. In fact, like that of other laboratory experience, its creative potential would seem most beneficial for the basically healthy. A couple using the laboratory as a last-ditch effort to salvage a seriously degenerated relationship will probably not benefit greatly from the experience. Such couples also detract from the experience of others due to the excessive amount of time they consume (Clark and Clark, 1968).

Accepting the desirability of marital laboratories, what specific goal-objectives may be identified for such groups? Four possible objectives are: to develop (1) greater congruence in the relationship, (2) a clearer understanding of the relationship patterns, (3) an increased openness to and acceptance of the full range of feelings within the relationship, and (4) greater realism regarding the relationship.

Rogers (1961) has said that the therapist possesses congruence when within the relationship he "is exactly what he is—not a facade, or a role, or a pretense." The same idea may be applied to marriage: Relational congruence occurs when both partners not only are what they are but are perceived and accepted by the other as they are, specifically within the relationship. The relationship is thus seen and accepted by both parties for what it is. A frequent difficulty in interpersonal relations is that the relationship itself is approached and thus experienced differently. In common parlance we speak of being on different wavelengths. The laboratory experience offers couples an occasion to realign frequencies in the direction of greater congruence.

Achieving greater relational congruence does not necessarily result in perpetuating the marital relationship. An honest goal of couples laboratories cannot be to perpetuate or strengthen the marriage, as some would suggest (Golembiewski and Blumberg, 1970). With actualizing individuals, greater congruence could well lead to a decision to end the relationship. Any a priori conceptions of specific outcomes would contradict the basic values of the laboratory environment.

Clark and Clark (1968) speak to the point of congruence as a goal-objective when they say that couples are helped to "establish a new norm about how open they are with each other." This statement can be expanded by adding "or how open they want to be." Though many would consider total honesty in the marital relationship an idea, it is surely not an absolute. Some couples prefer not sharing certain things. The point of congruence is that whatever the final norm, both members are aware of it and accept it.

A second goal of couples laboratories is to help the participants come to a clearer understanding of their relational patterns. Shostrom and Kavanaugh (1971) hypothesize that all male-female relationships or even all manifestations of male-female interpersonal interaction fit into six categories. Mother/Son, Daddy/Doll, Bitch/Nice Guy, Master/Servant, Hawks, and Doves are descriptions of truncated and thus manipulative male-female interactions. Due to an inability to express all feelings spontaneously, many individuals become fixed at one end of the feeling continuums of love-anger and strength-weakness. Such fixations create individual styles. In relationships these individual styles combine in a complementary or symmetrical way to create relationship styles. In light of this sixfold categorization, the laboratory setting can be an ideal place for couples to experience and observe these patterns in themselves and in other couples. Such an experience is nonthreatening and enables observing couples to understand more objectively the nature of these patterns. With this clearer understanding couples can more easily detect and admit their own personal patterns and thereby end a great deal of manipulation. The laboratory environment, with its open and supportive character, helps couples to honestly experience their manipulative patterns and, hopefully, change them.

A third goal of couples groups is to help the participants experience and accept the full range of feelings within the relationship. One important countercultural norm characteristic of the laboratory environment is that all feelings are legitimate. Within the nonevaluative climate of the laboratory, both positive and negative affect are sanctioned. Acquiring this value alone would enhance most marital relationships. It is known of actualizing relationships that the full range of feeling expression is characteristic (Shostrom and Kavanaugh, 1971). In the laboratory environment couples learn not only the acceptance of all feelings but also acquire the skills to express them creatively.

A fourth goal-objective of married groups is to provide space wherein realism about the marital relationship may be attained. Today's marital dyad is frequently isolated from opportunities to share intimate problems. Often common problems are seen as uniquely personal, and perspective has been lost. Much energy is spent in conjuring up idealized mates, and the problems are merely intensified. In the laboratory environment such problems may be openly aired. Airing often results in a renewal of realistic perspective. When idealized imaginings cease to distort existing problems, solutions are often easier to attain.

The benefits couples may derive from the laboratory experience are heightened by their contributions to the group. The classical stranger laboratory suffers the anxiety of the initial vacuum experience until sufficient data and direction are generated to arrive at interpersonal interaction. Although the values of this initial floundering period have been described (Bradford, Gibb, and Benne, 1964), one disadvantage is the time expended before trust and openness emerge. Such an environment also allows a great deal of innocent, yet nonproductive game playing to occur. Married couples, on the other hand, come to the laboratory with established personal intimacy and much interpersonal data. If the focus of the laboratory is kept on the relationship, the intimacy and data act as levers to rapidly bring about group trust at an intimate level. Unreal gaming behavior is eliminated, for the most part, because of its familiarity to the marital partner and because of the difficulty of prolonging such games at an intimate level.

An interesting aspect of this focus on the relationship and thus on intense levels of interpersonal intimacy is that the laboratory environment has the support of the larger culture. The distancing behavior which characterizes strangers' groups is sanctioned by the larger culture, while the same culture sanctions intimacy within the marital relationship (Clark and Clark, 1968).

Couples also bring established behavior patterns to the laboratory. In an established relationship, patterns are more readily discernible, in comparison to the hit and miss interaction among strangers. When the focus is kept on the patterns of the relationship, there appears to be a more rapid and direct emergence of each partner's "true" self. Such exposure affords group members real feedback and thus provides opportunity for personal growth. My impression is that much feedback in strangers' groups is counterproductive because the "true" self has not emerged. Often such feedback merely reinforces uncreative behavior.

Couples also contribute a natural ongoing unit (the dyad) which offers great promise for the long-term effectiveness of the training. Behavior patterns are not altered in a weekend, and thus follow-up is an important factor in sustaining change. A husband and wife, as an ongoing unit, can facilitate each other's continued growth process. Couples groups avoid the pitfall of the classical laboratory, which has been plagued by a lack of transfer and a waning effect of the training experience. The lack of follow-up support has been a primary cause of poor carry-over and transfer of learning.

All these advantageous contributions which couples bring to the laboratory can also be seen as disadvantages. The creative value of temporary and anonymous relationships has been described in the sensitivity training literature (Bennis and Schein, 1965; Golembiewski and Blumberg, 1970; Mill, 1965). Yet the value of anonymity and temporariness may have been overstressed. Effective transfer of laboratory learning, which couples groups are more likely to achieve, is essential if encounter experiences are not to degenerate into weekend catharsis —idyllic interludes in the midst of depersonalized routine.

Couples groups should be designed to capitalize on these special contributions. A primary concern is to concentrate attention on the marital relationship. With such a focus, the individual is not overlooked but is revealed more rapidly and honestly. This emphasis also capitalizes on the already established interpersonal intensity and thereby may facilitate rapid development of group trust and openness. Designs which separate men and women into different groups or create cross-couple dyads tend to have dissipating effects. The advantages of structures which do not focus on the relationship would be those already enumerated: anonymity and temporariness. Under certain conditions they may be effectively employed, as, for example, in role playing marital relationship difficulties in cross-couple dyads.

A second design consideration is the necessity for acquiring clearly conceptualized behavioral skills. The behavioral emphasis in couples groups may vary, yet it is essential that participants retain some specific tools to aid them in continuing the process begun in the laboratory. Such skills would be ideal for all laboratories; yet with couples, this goal assumes added importance because they leave the laboratory as a continuing unit.

One such tool is a concrete model of communication

which facilitates listening with understanding, direct reporting
of feelings, and nonevaluative feedback. The model should be
as simple as possible and should be consistent with what has
been experientially emphasized in the laboratory. Whatever the
laboratory design, the skills emphasized should be directly
related to interpersonal processes. The ability to diagnose
groups is of little direct value to the marital relationship.

Designs may also incorporate observing activities for
members. Couples may practice skills of listening, empathizing,
and detecting relational patterns while observing the interaction
of other couples. The aim of such training is to enhance couples'
skills as competent facilitative agents for interpersonal processes
and at the same time to promote group cohesiveness by providing an opportunity for supportive cross-couple help. In the same
process, the observing couples often obtain insights regarding
aspects of their own relationships. Through observing, they may
attain a greater openness and objectivity, since personal interests and emotional involvement are lessened.

Where a total residential experience is not possible, some
compensating arrangements should be made to alleviate the
distractions of returning to family situations. Adequate time is
also an important design factor. Twenty to twenty-five hours of
group work seems to be the minimum essential for groups of
five couples. Sufficient time must be provided to avoid possible
lack of closure.

Designs should also provide space for couples to be
alone. Privacy is important, especially in sleeping arrangements.
This suggestion may seem obvious, yet there are couples groups
which do not make such provisions. If privacy is not available,
the design may tend to dissipate the experience.

The following model presents what theoretically and
experientially seems to be a creative design for couples laboratories. The design presumes the presence of a professional
trainer and is presented here in the hope of stimulating more
thought about and experimentation with couples groups.

The laboratory is a total residential experience which
provides twenty to twenty-five hours of group exposure. The
laboratory is advertised specifically as a couples group with

focus and goal-objectives clearly explicated. Couples know exactly why they are coming, what it is they are buying, and the type of contract they are forming (Egan, 1970). This clarity not only alleviates confusion but facilitates a more rapid development of the group process. Everyone knows and agrees beforehand why they are coming together.

Upon arriving, each couple is privately videotaped for ten minutes. The directions for this taping are: "Talk about what you are interested in talking about; be as honest as possible." After each couple has been taped, the group begins. There is a brief introduction by the trainer specifying that we are here to help one another grow as persons and that the effectiveness of the workshop depends on everyone taking responsibility for what happens in the group. He explains that the focus of the workshop is on the marital relationship but that other interaction is not excluded. The use of the video is then described as a means of getting to know one another, as well as an opportunity for each couple to obtain feedback from other group members.

After clarifications and informal introductions, the tape of the first couple is played. Feedback, as well as here and now interaction, follows. Before proceeding to the next couple's tape, sufficient time is given for any interaction generated by the tape or subsequent conversation. The time required for each tape is usually between one and two hours.

In using videotape in this manner, the interaction can become very analytic and clinical. Trainer modeling of non-evaluative feedback and direct interventions by him when necessary are thus important during this phase of the group's life. Such modeling behavior and interventions expose participants to the interpersonal skills which are emphasized throughout the laboratory—listening with understanding, empathizing (Rogers, 1961), and direct reporting of feelings. This video phase of the workshop usually lasts about eight hours.

The second phase of the lab begins with a brief review of the skills emphasized earlier. These skills are summarized in a simplified model of communication, consisting of listening with understanding, communicating acceptance, and reporting one's own position. Such simplicity is important if conceptual tools are to facilitate transfer behavior in nonlaboratory situations.

After this brief input, it is suggested that each couple get in touch with the central conflict in their relationship and, using the model, attempt to work it through within the group. By this time, the trust level is such that couples volunteer. This phase of the laboratory lasts about ten hours. During this phase couples get a chance to observe and facilitate other couples' growth. The advantages of such activities have already been described.

During the third and final phase of the group, each couple is asked to go off by themselves and, using the communication model, come to an agreement on the important norms regarding their relationship which they feel need attention. Such norms may deal with how honest they are or want to be with each other, with marital or extramarital sexual behavior, and so on. Couples are given several hours for this interaction. Help from the trainer is available for those who request it. Following this, the group reconvenes and couples share what happened in their dyadic interaction. Finally, clarifications of theory are made by the trainer, and the group tries to bring final closure to the whole process.

Though the focus of this design is the marital relationship, other group processes should also be handled. Such interaction usually occurs spontaneously, yet it appears helpful to provide space at specific intervals during the workshop to facilitate this process.

I have discussed the desirability of the laboratory method for married couples, the goal-objectives of such laboratories, the contributions which couples bring to the laboratory setting, and some design requirements of such groups. Hopefully, future empirical research in laboratory training will examine the applicability of this educational method to married couples. Until such time, current experimentation remains limited. If, in fact, laboratory training does benefit the marital relationship, lack of empirical evidence becomes a central obstacle to the possible rejuvenation of an ailing social institution. The possibilities are great. What remains is the process of scientific verification.

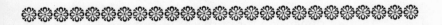

20

Groups, Families, and the Karass

James Sorrells

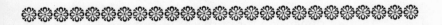

The group experience has enjoyed unprecedented acclaim and application in an amazingly brief period of growth. Only a few years ago, *group* meant psychoanalytically oriented group therapy, and NTL was an infant pioneer. Now, group experiences are widely used in education, industrial management, training for civil service jobs, and even churches; *encounter*, *sensitivity*, and *marathon* have become household words.

Our rapid growth has not lacked unfortunate consequences. We have only recently begun to tackle such knotty questions as: What kinds of training should the group leader have? Who profits from group experiences and who doesn't? Are some people harmed by group experience? What kinds of interpersonal systems benefit from encounter, and what kinds may be obstructed?

In order to solve these issues, we must first be able to differentiate the many varieties of group experience. One basis for differentiation is that of procedure, what takes place in the group. In a recent text (1971), Egan contrasts the T-Group, which focuses primarily on the group's dynamics or process, and the sensitivity group, which deals more with individual and intrapsychic material. Are both T-Groups and sensitivity groups simply different breeds of encounter? Is an academic class which utilizes experiential learning and self-disclosure an encounter group?

At best, these distinctions are poorly grasped by the layman and even those who lead groups. Many people now hold a deep distrust for anything labeled encounter ("You just sit around and tell each other off") or sensitivity ("those touchie-feelies") yet eagerly participate in other groups which strive for authenticity and emotional openness. Students applaud an experiential course yet would avoid the same course if it were labeled as encounter. Some professionals skirt the problem, or hope to, by speaking instead of growth groups or awareness experiences.

Another dimension for purposes of comparison is that of constituency—who is in the group. In this book, there are chapters on interracial groups, industrial groups, couples groups, groups for young children, and so on. This chapter, which relates family treatment to encounter experience, belongs to the dimension of constituency. The assumption is thus implicit that what goes on in a conjoint family therapy session bears enough resemblance to an encounter group that it is worth our while to consider them together.

A more basic assumption here is that, in understanding better the procedures and techniques of different styles of groups and the implications of varied group constituency, we will be able to provide a better match between the two factors. The expertise of the seasoned facilitator probably lies in his sensitivity to the idiosyncratic needs and tensions of each group and in his capacity to respond, not in role nor with standard gimmicks, but with flexibility and authenticity.

What implications may we derive for the people-helper when the group consists of a family? Again our labels obscure our purpose, because family, like group, is an ambiguous word. Most of us share a general denotative meaning of the word, pointing to a traditional pattern of marital/legal and biological relationships among three or more people. Fewer and fewer families fit the mold, however. As divorce becomes increasingly acceptable in society, we find more and more families with one parent or in which the children are "his, hers, and ours." An increasing number of homosexual couples, especially female couples, are rearing children. In some ethnic and economic groups, the grandparents may live with the nuclear family and exercise a more important influence on the children than do the parents.

Furthermore, many of us feel a sense of familyness with others in relationships which are neither marital, legal, nor biological. Communes are the most obvious and prevalent example. Many young people feel few roots with their biological families of origin, and much more with their peers. To an increasing degree, they shun the traditional pattern of marrying one person of the opposite sex and instead enter into deep relationships of commitment with several persons of both sexes.

In spite of these difficulties in designating what is meant exactly by family and group, I want first to compare and contrast some aspects of conjoint family therapy and the encounter group. To that end, I will assume a traditional notion of the family constellation. I will also think in terms of a hypothetical encounter group made up of individuals who have no important relations with each other outside the group, coming together for a fixed period of time. (Even the open-ended group shares the expectation not to go on forever.)

Because I am unhappy with this arbitrary mode of posing the contrast, I will turn finally to a model of interpersonal interaction which I will call the *karass*. The terms family and group have surplus meaning which diverts our attention from important dimensions of interaction. In using the neutral and novel term *karass*, I hope to reestablish the importance of some of those dimensions.

GROUP AND FAMILY SIMILARITIES

The encounter process and conjoint family treatment share the fundamental premise that personal growth occurs in

relation to others. Both procedures assume that growth can be
facilitated with greater ease, validity, and completeness when
the therapeutic process focuses on the individual in the process
of relating rather than after the fact. I want to stress that the
attention of a truly interactional approach is on those ties that
bind person A and person B; in group therapy, each person has
a turn at being the center of focus, while the other group members serve more or less as assistant therapist.

The focus on relationships has at least two historical
roots. First, psychoanalysis eventually concluded that resolution
of the transference neurosis was the essence of the analytic
process. That is, the patient must reach a stage of relating to the
analyst where he recapitulates a significant parent-child (usually) relationship. It was also observed that peer relationships,
especially marital ones, may be distorted by feelings or
memories about either parent. The analytic context and contract provided the possibility of resolving these distorted perceptions and response patterns, thereby terminating the analysis
and theoretically improving the analysand's peer relations.

From sociology and social psychology comes a second
line of evidence that our salient feelings about ourselves are
almost always in relation to other people. Clinical and experimental findings bear out the notion that we form images and
attitudes about self in substantial accord with how significant
others have perceived and evaluated us. We learn low self-
esteem from scorn, ridicule, embarrassment, failure, and misunderstanding. We learn positive self-esteem through empathic
understanding, support and reassurance, and achievement. If
significant others expect us to fail, failure is, indeed, more likely.
If they expect us to succeed, we strive all the harder to validate
their expectations. We also evaluate ourselves against the scale
of how well we expect others to perform: "I will do as well as,
better than, or less well than X."

In individual treatment, these reflexive self-images ("this
is how I see them seeing me") must be dealt with vicariously,
as when the therapist or patient enacts roles of others, or in the
transference neurosis. In the encounter group, self-other relationships are available for examination. In an atmosphere of

trust and authenticity, an individual may receive genuine feedback about how others perceive him. He may also risk responding to others in honest and direct ways, expressing feelings which have customarily been stifled.

While new behaviors are encouraged in the context of an encounter group, these explorations probably become real learning only after an individual's customary repertoire of interpersonal behaviors has been thwarted or exhausted. And unless one assumes that encounter group behavior mirrors an individual's interpersonal behavior outside the group, in some basic sense, the group experience could not be seen as very meaningful or relevant. In fact, one issue confronting group leaders is the problem of how to transfer new behaviors and attitudes from the group into the day to day world. In an informal discussion, Richard Farson once commented that encounter experience is probably closer to attending a symphony concert than going to a physician. One visits the doctor to be cured, definitely not with the goal of repeating or prolonging the curative treatment. A symphony concert, on the other hand, would hopefully inspire the listener to want to attend more concerts, start a record library, and so on. The goal we strive for is that of encouraging the group participant to grow in the direction of greater authenticity in each of his important relationships outside the group. Those of us who have experienced weekend encounters know too well the reentry problems of returning to the same old job, family, and the expectations others have maintained while we have been away.

It was precisely this reentry problem which was a major impetus to the growth of family therapy. Workers with schizophrenic patients were dismayed to observe that fully remissed patients, when returned to their families without any therapeutic intervention, would soon reappear at the hospital, fully or partially relapsed. This recurring phenomenon prompted the formulation of an interactional conceptualization of schizophrenia (Bateson, Jackson, Haley, and Weakland, 1956) and gave new blood to interpersonal theories of personality, which had, in fact, been with us since Sullivan (Carson, 1969).

Bear in mind that these theories said neither that the

parents drove the schizophrenic crazy nor that the so-called identified patient drove his parents crazy (although we did pass through a period of blaming first the "schizophrenogenic" mother, then the father, and finally both of them). What the theories did postulate, however, is that deviant behavior, schizophrenic or otherwise, may indeed be adaptive when one views the interactional pattern of the whole family (Laing, 1967; Halleck, 1971). Jackson further hypothesized that all families behave with such interpersonal regularity that it makes sense to speak of the family's "rules" and even "homeostatic mechanisms" which serve to reestablish violated rules (1965a and 1965b).

This is a more complex notion than is the simple relationship between an individual's self-esteem and the support or criticism he received as a child. It is even more complex than Freud's description of Oedipal conflict, which I appreciate most as a pioneering effort to understand the interaction of more than two people at a time. A fully interactional view of the family as the basis of personality is Gestaltlike: Each person has a role, if you will, within the family, and all the roles must mutually fit. The whole is greater than the sum of its parts, and the entire family pattern necessarily changes with changes in the dramatis personnae, such as the birth of new siblings, the departure or death of a family member, and so on. In addition to these roles, which may remain central in one's personality throughout life, one also learns some extremely basic, often out-of-awareness assumptions and expectations about males and females and male-female interaction, adult-child interaction, and peer conflict resolution.

Is it any wonder, then, that so many groups which focus on personal, intrapsychic material (as opposed to pure group process) find themselves reenacting a group member's familial relationships? Especially in psychodramatically oriented groups, the roots of a person's interactional problems with his peers are usually sought and found in the family. Whether one examines Janov's primal therapy, the bioenergetic therapy of Lowen and others, or the garden-variety encounter marathon, he is likely to find group members attempting to resolve unmet needs for affection from parents, risking the forbidden expression of anger or frustration or defiance toward them, or pleading for acceptance in spite of a failure to measure up to parental expectations.

Conjoint family therapy affords the opportunity to work with these processes directly. I have often had the eerie feeling, while witnessing the evolution of a new relationship between parent and child, that the child before me could be projected ten, twenty years forward in time and be seen attempting as an adult in an encounter group to resolve the issue with which we are dealing at that moment. My friend and mentor, Fred Ford, once said, "Resolve your feelings toward your parents now, while they are still alive. It's a lot tougher once they're dead."

Because intrafamily problems are of such a perennial nature, and because all mothers were once daughters, and so on, the family therapist frequently catches a glimpse of the grandparents, even though only two generations are present. In one family I treated, the mother and sixteen-year-old daughter were constantly at odds. Using a Gestalt technique, I moved an empty chair in front of the mother and asked her to speak to her "self", at age sixteen, in the chair. Complying, the mother began to weep as she recognized her own mother's expectations and admonitions to herself and how these had resisted her own life experience. As Jung stated it so well:

I feel very strongly that I am under the influence of things or questions which were left incomplete and unanswered by my parents and grandparents and more distant ancestors. It often seems as if there were an impersonal karma within a family, which is passed on from parents to children. It has always seemed to me that I had to answer questions which fate had posed to my forefathers, and which had not yet been answered, or as if I had to complete, or perhaps continue, things which previous ages had left unfinished. It is difficult to determine whether these questions are more of a personal or more of a general (collective) nature. It seems to me that the latter is the case. A collective problem, if not recognized as such, always

*appears as a personal problem, and in individual cases may give
the impression that something is out of order in the personal
psyche. The personal sphere is indeed disturbed, but such disturbances need not be primary; they may well be secondary,
the consequence of an insupportable change in the social atmosphere. The cause of disturbance is, therefore, not to be
sought in the personal surroundings, but rather in the collective
situation. Psychotherapy has hitherto taken this matter far too
little into account [1963, p. 233ff].*

Having established kinship between the goals of the encounter group experience and the conjoint family session, I
turn now to a brief discussion of the tools I have found useful
in both contexts. In contrast to the therapist whose work is with
individuals, the group leader and family therapist must focus
upon interaction. I will therefore organize the discussion around
aspects of interaction which are of prime importance in family
therapy.

Family members must talk to each other. Families seeking help usually see the therapist as either the doctor who will
cure them or as the judge who will arbitrate conflicts and
decide who is right. In either case, most remarks will initially
be addressed to the therapist with very little interchange among
family members. Mrs. X will tell the therapist how awful Mr. X
is, and vice versa, or both of them may tell the therapist how
awful little Mary is while Mary sits in the same room like a piece
of furniture. This is a familiar phenomenon in groups as well as
families, and the therapist must encourage the participants to
talk to, not about, each other. A family which has taken full
responsibility for its own growth will use the therapist as an
observer/facilitator, often ignoring him as they talk together.

Families must learn to communicate accurately. Dysfunctional families are often characterized by vague, ambiguous
verbal communication, sometimes so subtle that the therapist
may think that everything said made perfect sense until he
listens to a tape recording of the session (Watzlawick, 1964). He
must teach the family to communicate clearly, directly, specifically, and congruently (Satir, 1964). It is absolutely essential

that the beginning family therapist study tapes of his own sessions, both to appreciate the complexity of the family's interactions and to ensure that his own verbal behavior is an exemplary model for the family.

Each family member is important and unique. Any event will be seen, heard, interpreted, and felt differently by each family member. When the therapist asks to hear from every member, he affirms the uniqueness and value of each person, and this part of the therapeutic process cannot be overestimated.

Some parents still feel that children should be seen and not heard. They will want the therapist to help them in obtaining obedience from their children, rather than mutual understanding, and they will regard the therapy as a failure if this end result is not obtained. (A popular set of phonograph records, texts, and games on family living entitles the section on childrearing "How to Bend a Twig.") When the therapist views children as unique individuals in their own right, he may be radically violating a norm held deeply by the parents. Halleck (1971) comments on some radical aspects of conjoint family therapy, but I believe he overlooks the very radical implications of fully recognizing children in the therapeutic process.

Family members may need help in contacting their own true feelings. I described earlier an example of the enduring influence of grandparents on the conflicts within a nuclear family. A parent's feelings toward one or more of the children may stem directly from that parent's experiences with his or her own father and mother. Later in this chapter, I will stress the importance of blame as an escape from individual feelings and responsibility. Another obstruction in family therapy is the family's desire to appear reasonable before the therapist, a motivation which may produce hours and hours of intellectualization to the obfuscation of underlying feelings.

There are no easy solutions to this difficult problem, in leading a group or in treating a family. Family therapists who are most successful, it seems to me, are those who can creatively and imaginatively abandon our traditional models for proper therapist behavior—reserved and detached. As a rule, these therapists have a healthy appreciation of drama and a generous capacity for role-enactment which are used to intensify and dramatize the family's relationships and dilemmas.

At one time or another in family treatment, I have used every therapeutic tool and technique with which I am comfortable. With highly intellectualizing families, I have made good use of nonverbal techniques to portray feelings rather than talking about them. I have used meditation to reduce the level of a family's anxiety and to aid in contacting feelings about self. I have found that some families may be able to reveal themselves through clay or painting to a far greater degree than is possible verbally.

Surely the most valuable techniques have been psychodrama and the tools developed by the Gestalt school. The therapeutic hour is most powerful when the focus is on the here and now, fully as much with a family as with a group. Both psychodrama and Gestalt allow family members to experience themselves during the hour, in contrast to a dull rehashing of the family's history since the last appointment. I find no conflict whatever between the premises of family therapy, psychodrama, and Gestalt and strongly encourage the family therapist to incorporate these tools in his work.

The family therapist needs a picture of the workings of the family system. Using traditional interviewing techniques, it may be weeks before the family system emerges for him. In essence, he needs to see the family in action, solving a problem or attempting to cooperate on a joint venture. I am speaking here, of course, about diagnosis, and any useful diagnosis depends on an appropriate instrument, applicable to many families, and a clinician who is sensitive to variations in response to the instrument. For example, one may ask families to draw together on one large sheet of paper. Having witnessed the response of a large number of families to this task, one is able to sense a great deal about the family and relationships between various members. It is possible also to ask two families to observe each other drawing together, a procedure which may yield valuable insights.

I personally favor the structured family interview developed by Virginia Satir and Paul Watzlawick (1966). This particular interview consists of seven tasks for the family, tasks which usually clarify patterns of coalition, scapegoating, self-concepts, and so on. Having administered the interview to many, many families, I now have a fairly broad frame of reference within which to assess a particular family. While the Satir/Watzlawick interview was carefully designed for purposes of family diagnosis, any such format which elicits family interaction could be useful in the hands of a skillful therapist.

To conclude, there are many, many styles of working with families (see Jay Haley's essay, "Whither Family Therapy" [1971], for a hilarious spoof on some eminent family therapists and their idiosyncratic approaches). There are just three ideas which should be borne in mind: First, no one ever became a competent family therapist from the starting point of being a lousy individual therapist. (I feel the same about group leaders.) Second, any therapist who adopts styles and techniques which do not flow from his own personality, feelings, and values is headed for disaster. Third, techniques should be used to intensify, or give handles to, what is already surfacing in the family or group. The therapist who utilizes a technique to make something happen is merely filling time and easing his own anxiety. Finally, all technique must originate from the conviction that "to understand himself man needs to be understood by another. To be understood by another he needs to understand the other" (Hora, 1959, p. 237).

GROUP AND FAMILY DIFFERENCES

Egan (1971) makes a case for describing the encounter process as "therapy for the normal." To the extent that this is true, we have an immediate point of contrast between the encounter group and conjoint family therapy: Whereas a great many individuals now seek out the group experience as a means of growth and expansion, families usually seek therapeutic help only when confronted with great emotional pain. Virginia Satir and others at the Mental Research Institute in Palo Alto, California, contemplated some years ago establishing a well-family service, but to my knowledge no such service has yet been developed. Frederick Stoller and Ann Dreyfuss have conducted weekend encounters for relatively healthy families, but by and large, families seek help when some family member is labeled by the family or community as "sick, bad, stupid, or crazy" (Satir's parlance).

Rare, too, is the family that seeks help as a family. More often, they hope and expect the therapist will cure the Identified Patient (IP). Especially if the IP has been hospitalized, the other family members may deeply resent and resist the therapist's attempts to involve them in therapy. They, of course, do not wish to be blamed for the IP's symptoms, much less to be regarded as somehow disturbed themselves. I have had most success when my approach (and my sincere attitude) to the family has been, "I need your help in providing the patient the most thorough treatment possible."

The question of blame and responsibility is significant for family therapy and another point of contrast between groups and family treatment. Families usually come for help with extreme feelings of guilt concerning the plight of the IP. Parents feel especially guilty when one of their children is faring badly; spouses may blame themselves for driving the other crazy; and even children may feel guilty for their parents' problems. Generally, this sense of guilt produces nothing worthwhile in terms of behavior change; for some strange reason, people often prefer to feel guilty and even to atone for the guilt rather than change what they are doing. Furthermore, the guilt that X feels on account of Y often seems to relieve Y of the responsibility of changing his own response to whatever X is doing.

Thus, in conjoint family treatment, the goal is to teach each member to be responsible to and for himself. I said earlier that families operate according to regular patterns of interaction, the family's rules, that the family behaves as a system. Each family member does not have to understand the overall workings of the system, at least in the same sense that the therapist may understand it. Instead, each member must begin to perceive his own behavior as a stimulus for the behavior of others (as opposed to "I just did this because he did that") and recognize the possibility of alternative responses in his own repertoire to the stimuli that other members provide. When individual responsibility is truly a realized feeling in a family, there is simply no room for any member to be blamed for the behavior of any other member.

Should this sound like an easy task, it must be remembered that families evolve their rules and mechanisms of blame over years and years of interaction. The families of origin of the parents are often the source of deeply held expectations which are seldom or never questioned in conscious awareness. The circumstances of birth of one of the children, or even the name given to the child, may have lasting and salient influence over how the child is perceived and related to. (We often speak of the family's ghosts to refer to kin whose influence on the family is historical yet abiding.)

The quality of the relationship between the parents at the time of a child's birth and during his formative years is of singular importance. Children are often brought into the world to save the marriage, and they learn appropriate roles of peacemaker or distractor quickly enough. Or when the parents are at odds, the child may be pressured to form coalitions with one parent against the other, at great cost to the child. Or the child may receive messages which are at once implicit, simultaneous, and discrepant (for example, when a parent verbalizes warmth and acceptance yet emits nonverbal cues of resentment and hostility). He may develop psychotic behaviors as an attempt to respond to all parts of the discrepant message at once. All of these roles, once formed, may then become somewhat autonomous and stimuli for the parents' response.

I do not believe that these phenomena have any parallel in the encounter group. Group participants may regret having held back (or not having held back) some response or feeling, but group members seldom carry enduring feelings of guilt for one another. Groups, to be sure, evolve their own rules (the group's process or shared level of trust), but these interactional regularities are much more amenable to swift change than are family regularities. And whereas the group's process may serve as an obstacle to the growth of each person while in the group, as when a group implicitly contracts to avoid painful issues or deeper levels of intimacy, the process does not, presumably, enter into each participant's life outside the group in the same manner as do family rules.

There are some obvious reasons for these differences between the family and the group, although I deem them worth listing. First, in a group, the cast changes as members leave, new members enter, and as the whole group adjourns or convenes. In the family, the cast remains fairly constant, thus providing ample time and millions of interactions to establish and reestablish patterns of interaction and, therefore, identity. Second, in the group there is an expectation of change and variety; a member may even be censured by the group if he continues to demand excessive attention from week to week. In the family, there is a particular resistance to change, a desire to maintain the status quo. The dysfunctional family rigidly adheres to the status quo, even in the face of demands for new rules: Changes in age, responsibility, or activities of a family member create tensions which may give rise to symptoms, the surest clues that something is wrong in the family's operation. One family member, the IP, may serve as the scapegoat for months and years with the full cooperation of the other members. Third, most group leaders would hope that individuals in the group grow in the direction of becoming more internally directed, freer of the expectations of others. In the family, young children have neither the means nor social sanction for violating parental expectations to any significant degree. In the functional family, the parents accord the children autonomy and responsibility in degrees that are appropriate to the child's capacity; but we have the paradoxical situation that a child must often demonstrate to his parents the capacity for more responsibility before the capacity is acknowledged. Even here, one party (the parents) grants the second party (the child) a privilege, a thoroughly one-up/one-down interaction: The child does not seize the privilege. Few people approve of parents being called by their first names by their children, a further manifestation of symmetry, reciprocity, and mutuality. In most families, the standard steadfastly remains, "As long as you are living in our house (meaning the parents'), you will do as we say."

Finally, it should be noted that few encounter groups, with the possible exception of Synanon, have any expectation of commitment beyond the stated duration of the group. Also, members are not expected to meet many of their continuing needs for affection, sexual expression, esteem, and others in the sole context of the encounter group. In contrast, the family is based, usually, on the expectation of commitment, for a lifetime in the case of the parents, and until maturity for the children. This expectation is often the most serious question for the family and the therapist. Should the parents remain married? Should the children remain in the home? In our society, divorce is still regarded as a sign of failure, especially on the wife's part, rather than as a possible sign of new growth and creative problem solving. It is also clear that for a home to be judged unfit for the children is a devastating blow to the parents and a sure mark of failure in the community. It is unspeakably tragic that families cannot re-form with social sanction, as in Aldous Huxley's *Island.* Many, many lives are ruined and wasted because of it.

THE KARASS

Having suggested some distinctions between encounter and conjoint family treatment, I want now to propose that individuals who have no legal or biological relation may come together in special ways which render the collective more like a family than a group. To label the collective, I have borrowed a term from Kurt Vonnegut's *Cat's Cradle* (1963): the karass. "We Bokononists believe that humanity is organized into teams, teams that do God's will without ever discovering what they are doing. Such a team is called a *karass.* . . . If you find your life tangled up with somebody's life for no very logical reasons, that person may be a member of your *karass.* Man created the checkerboard; God created the *karass* [which] ignores national, institutional, occupational, familial, and class boundaries" (p. 11ff).

Leaving God's will to the side, we nevertheless observe

that people's lives do indeed become entangled. The entanglement might be described in many different ways. Jourard tells us that "no man can come to know himself except as an outcome of disclosing himself to another person" (1964, p. 5). Jourard then developed research in order to discover who we disclosed ourselves to. Members of a karass disclose themselves to each other, verbally and nonverbally, and thus know themselves through each other's eyes.

Another way to express or describe the entanglement: "I am what I become in the process of responding to what you become in the process of responding to me" (Wilmoth, 1971). The feeling or experiencing that accompanies this reciprocity is that of *involvement*, the awareness that "we're in this together." Satir speaks of "shared outcomes" to call attention to the interdependency of lives.

A superb article by Auerswald (1968) described the karass of a twelve-year-old Puerto Rican girl which included her mother, the mother's boyfriend, her grandparents, the school, the neighborhood clinic, and the girl's peer group. If we realize that membership in a family system is important in determining an individual's self-image and behavior, we must also admit that each person belongs to several interpersonal systems, each of which contributes some piece to the individual's identity.

I am willing to introduce a novel term, and a fictional one at that, to call attention to certain qualities of interpersonal involvement. As facilitators, we find ourselves working with a rich variety of multiperson collectives. If we continue to carry fixed expectations of what a family is, or a management team, we may too easily overlook important interactional regularities which are thwarting the needs of the members. Or we may feel at a loss when working with collectives for which we have no traditional expectations, such as communes.

A pointed example: One may begin a simulated family interview with the help of two males and two females. Ask the males to negotiate who is to be the father and who the son and the females, to determine their mother-daughter roles. Then ask each person to select privately a name and an age. When the participants reveal their assumed ages, it sometimes happens that one of the children has chosen an age which is close to, or even greater than, the age of one of the parents. Most participants will want to revise their ages to match our usual expectations of family relationships. Yet, in my own practice, I treated a family in which the wife was twenty-one years of age and the eldest daughter was seventeen. Clearly, the relationships between age, role, and authority were a matter of great contention in the family.

Another example may be found in this currently popular riddle: There was a family automobile accident. The father was killed and the son seriously injured. The son was rushed to the hospital, and the attending surgeon said, "I can't operate on this patient. He is my son." How is this possible? The answer, of course, is that the surgeon was the boy's mother. Liberationists use this riddle to demonstrate the rigid connections we make between gender and professional roles. The facilitator may have to confront some of his own rigidity in the midst of a collective which violates some of his expectations.

I will now describe the general characteristics of a karass and some of the parameters which may be used to compare one karass with another. To be sure, I might have used the term *system* instead, but system refers to nonhuman entities more often in the literature than to human collectives. I also dislike speaking of people in mechanical terms, and I think we may often be misled in doing so. The reader may find it useful to recall various collectives he has experienced with respect to each of the dimensions to follow.

Readers who are unfamiliar with communication theory might wish to refer to Watzlawick and others (1967) or to Sorrells and Ford (1969). For our purposes here, these principles may be summarized as follows: (1) One cannot not communicate. Every element of behavior in the presence of another person, even silence, has message value for the other person. Since one cannot not behave, it is then literally true that in the presence of another one cannot not communicate. (2) The message sent is not always the message received. A great number of the grievances between people occur when one person wrongly interprets the feelings and motives underlying the behavior of another. (3) Communication is multileveled. The context, tone of voice, facial expression, and posture of the sender may reinforce, disqualify, or be irrelevant to the literal, verbal message. (4) Communication always includes a definition of relationship between sender and receiver. The sender is intrinsically saying, in addition to the content of the communication, "I perceive our relationship as one in which I may do or say the following in your presence." Seemingly pointless yet bitter and heated quarrels may take place over implicit definitions of relationship, such as who has the right or authority to tell who what to do, rather than over the content of the disagreement.

I have already proposed that our definitions of and feelings about ourselves are saliently rooted in interpersonal interactions. The characteristics of communication outlined above have their greatest impact when areas of critical definition of the self are involved. Those who have been arrested in peace demonstrations report that the greatest stress comes not from physical mistreatment but from being perceived as a criminal rather than someone acting from conscience.

I have stated that families behave in regular patterns of interaction, the so-called rules. I now mean to apply this concept to the karass, since these regularities certainly are found in nonfamily groups, yet not in all groups. These rules apply most significantly with respect to definitions of relationship, especially the relationships of symmetry (equality and mutuality) and complementarity (inequality and reciprocity). The status quo of the overall pattern of rules may be referred to as the homeostatic balance of the karass. When the rules are violated, other predictable behavior patterns, homeostatic mechanisms, will be enacted to restore the status quo.

Owing to the mutually interdependent nature of the self-concepts of individuals in a karass, it is impossible for one or more persons in the karass to be in continuing emotional distress while other members of the karass are content. If one hurts, all hurts.

The following dimensions apply to any karass. Although the dimensions are generally more qualitative than quantitative, the reader might imagine profile analyses of two or more karasses in his experience for comparative purposes. The therapist/facilitator might find these parameters useful in working with a karass experiencing internal strife which somehow lacks definition. The parameters are by no means independent.

Authority. Authority is best indicated by the decision-making processes of the karass. Coalitions and disproportionate leverage in resolving disagreements are signs of where the power lies. Members may silently resent having too little power or, paradoxically, being given more power than they desire.

In one community I have experienced, the founding members ultimately made all the major decisions, although verbalized policy had it that the community was egalitarian. In another community, similar in size and in distribution of seniority, each person could veto any major decision, including the continuing membership of any member of the karass. In biological karasses, older members, the parents, usually make most decisions because the authority dimension is bound up with the one to follow.

Dependence, Responsibility, and Structure. In the biological karass, some members must survive an initial period of multifaceted dependence. In other karasses, the dependence may be purely economic. Problems may arise in the karass when the dependence outlives or overextends its necessity or when dependence unduly contaminates the way authority and responsibility are handled by the karass. Each karass also evolves some degree of structure to accommodate questions of responsibility.

In one karass, the implicit assumption was that individuals would be irresponsible unless a very strict structure were developed; thus, each person was assigned specific duties and a minimum number of hours per day of work for the maintenance of the karass. In a very different karass, literally no responsibilities were assigned, with the assumption that needs would be recognized and filled as they arose by all members of the karass. Some parents feel they must strictly enforce the performance of duties by the children yet are puzzled when the children sense a minimum of responsibility and initiative toward those and other needs of the karass.

Purpose and Centrality of Need Gratification. Some

karasses are formed when people come together for a commonly shared purpose: economic, spiritual, political, and many others. Others are formed accidentally, as when an individual takes a job or is born into a biological family. People are likely to feel a higher degree of commitment to the karass when their membership is due to conscious, active choice and when the choice reflects highly central needs and motives.

Karasses differ in the degree to which members expect the karass to meet their various needs—sexual, emotional, esteem, and so on. In one karass, the members came together simply for the sake of more economical housing; many members were unwilling to attempt to meet their other needs through the karass, much to the consternation of the remaining members. In another karass, by virtue of geographic isolation, there was very little opportunity for interaction outside the karass, and members were forced to meet all their needs through each other.

Emotional Openness, Intimacy, and Feedback. Some karasses may share a high degree of commitment, yet a very low level of openness and intimacy. Still others may be quite intimate within the context of low commitment. One karass I have experienced had convened for the purpose of spiritual growth. Early attempts to encounter regularly had produced a feeling of disenchantment with the whole process and a consequent firm avoidance of self-disclosure and feedback of interpersonal feelings. Such activities were regarded by the karass as a waste of time. In another karass, which incidentally was also founded for purposes of spiritual growth, encounter and feedback are part of the daily agenda.

Trust. I use trust here with two meanings in mind. The first is the belief that one's feelings will be taken seriously and responded to authentically. The second meaning approximates Jackson's quid pro quo (1965b), a shared expectation that X's needs can be delayed and will eventually be met if Y's needs are temporarily the dominant focus. Trust is thus used in the second sense as a temporal dimension and depends on the shared belief that neither of the parties involved is being exploitive. The first meaning of trust, I would postulate, varies directly with the level of openness and intimacy, almost by definition. The second meaning, however, seems to be a different matter; some karasses feel selfish, while in others people seem willing to devote great energy and time to helping one member.

Privacy. I refer here to proprietorship of both property and direction. In one karass, there was no sense of private ownership of property, all clothing and other articles being considered available for anyone's use. There was, however, little interference with one's management of time or personal practices. In another karass, property was privately held, yet individuals were frequently called to task for idiosyncratic actions.

Differences. Within some karasses, diversity is valued; individuals are expected to contribute in accordance with their own unique talents and interests. In others, homogeneity is valued, and uniqueness may be regarded as a threat to the community's cohesiveness. One of the spiritual karasses I have mentioned stressed uniqueness. Whoever liked to cook, cooked, and so on. The result was a somewhat chaotic yet individually gratifying solution to the nutritional needs of the karass. In the other spiritual community, tasks were rotated each week, and people were discouraged from becoming overly attached to a particular role or service in the karass. It should also be mentioned that in dysfunctional families, individual uniqueness is threatening and discouraged while sameness and conformity are fostered.

The Value of the Status Quo. All karasses evolve homeostatic patterns and mechanisms. Changes in the membership of the karass, external pressures confronting the karass, or many other factors may necessitate an adaptation of the homeostasis, what Watzlawick and others (1967) label a "step function." Some karasses adapt to change only with extreme difficulty, especially when the homeostasis of the karass is postulated by the members to represent some species of enduring truth. Other karasses in their processes have built-in conditions and allowances for changes. A karass characterized by inflexibility may give the initial appearance of determination and perseverance yet may prove brittle in response to the changing needs of its members.

Biological families must evolve new relationships each

time a new child is born and each time a family member reaches a new stage of development (entering school, attaining puberty, and so on). The therapist most often is called in by the family when the family's rules do not change to accommodate new growth, capabilities, responsibilities, and needs. Points of stress and tension are thus the outgrowth of individual needs in conflict with archaic family patterns.

Conjoint family treatment and the encounter process share the basic conviction that behavior is grounded in interpersonal relationships and that growth, therefore, takes place in relationship. Special conditions, which I have discussed, make a family different from an encounter group. If we are truly to focus on relationships, we must look beyond our expectations of traditional collectives of people, seeing the quality of relationships therein. The wise facilitator is he who can respond to each karass in terms of its unique qualities and in terms of his own authentic response to the karass, with a minimum burden of expectation.

Encounter Groups
for Women Only

Betty Meador, Evelyn Solomon,
Maria Bowen

Anyone who is aware of the women's liberation movement will
have no trouble understanding the rationale behind encounter
groups for women. Women in our culture are taught certain
basic values which stand in the way of their full development as
persons. They are taught to be passive and accepting. They are
taught to look to authority outside themselves, namely to men.
They are taught that true fulfillment lies in one path, marriage
and motherhood. To the extent that a woman assimilates these
learnings and the complicated manners and morals which sustain them, to that extent she truncates her very private, individual, personal potential for growth and development.

Encounter groups for women in this time of cultural
change are a vehicle for personal liberation, a place where

women can look at the cultural expectations they have assimilated and begin to make intentional choices with an enlightened self-understanding. Personal liberation is a necessary part of the wider movement for social equality for women, and the encounter group offers women a chance to share the excitement of self-discovery.

We do not intend to explore here the dividing line between culturally imposed restrictions and personal human limitations to growth and actualization. If such a line exists, and many people, particularly in the women's movement, say it does not, it is unclear at best. We do intend to report what we see happening in women's groups, namely the eagerness with which women are chiseling away the walls of traditional expectations, responding to societal restrictions with anger and resentment, and thus making way for their own growth in directions formerly closed to them.

Before going further with this discussion, we would like to locate ourselves, as women, with regard to the women we are writing about. Our socioeconomic backgrounds are similar to those of the women we worked with. The majority of them were married and had children. We are all married and have children. Some of the women worked outside their homes. We are actively involved in professional careers. The three of us have been struggling with many of the issues brought to the groups—specifically, the issues of independence, conflicting role-expectations, and establishing self-identity. These issues have been, and continue to be, difficult ones for each of us. From our own needs, personal experience, and professional concern emerged the idea of encounter groups for women only.

We had had the idea of conducting groups for women for several years. Our original notion of the validity of a group for women, though somewhat vague, was based on the principle that as women psychologists we could bring to the groups not only our experience as facilitators but a primary understanding of being female. We had no clearcut conception of the problems of women, although we were aware of innumerable women whose development had been thwarted by the demands of the roles they were playing. We saw these women expending their energies being the good wife, mother, lover, or manhunter at the expense of their own feelings of self-worth.

We were correct in our anticipations as far as they went. Our being women did enhance our understanding in the groups, and most of the women who came discovered they were neglecting their self-development. However, we did not expect that the experience of an all-women encounter group would be so multifaceted. The impressions we recall as most important came to us as surprises.

The first and most outstanding surprise was the sheer pleasure of being with women, which confronted us with our own negative bias. Prior to our first weekend group, we anticipated the idea of spending three days in a room with twenty women with little enthusiasm. We could never have predicted the good fun we had together, the playfulness, the caring and understanding which we experienced. Most of us had not felt this way with women since preadolescence.

Second, we discovered that women in encounter groups without men very quickly discard much of the superficial role behavior they have learned. Contrary to our expectations, most women found that it is only a small step from playing the roles to seeing their absurdity. Our willingness to sabotage cultural expectations is apparently just beneath our willingness to conform. Much of the fun we had together was in laughing over the ridiculous games we had learned to play.

A final surprise was the extent to which women in the groups were involved in reexamining social values and mores. The age range of the women was from nineteen to sixty. Most were married and had children. They came from middle- to upper-middle-class backgrounds and saw themselves as responsible citizens, participants in the mainstream of culture. All had some college education, and many had advanced degrees. Those who worked held jobs ranging from dean of women at a university to a night club entertainer. The majority of them had not been in an encounter group prior to this experience. Many of the women referred to the group as their class or seminar. The Women's Liberation Movement was not a major concern of the group, and only one member was actively involved in any type of women's liberation group. Yet almost without exception, these women saw the necessity of beginning to carve out a life style which suited them individually, rather than blindly following traditions in which they were raised. This theme was so prevalent that we began to see the groups primarily as an occasion for women to discover within themselves their individual road maps. The group members met the painful self-explorations of individual women with nonjudgmental support, caring, and confronting feedback. There was no doubt that the groups were filling a deep need of women in this particular historical time, providing the space in which women can step back from traditional role expectations and share the common search for individual, intentional choices from a wider set of alternatives.

The three of us have been conducting encounter groups, for women only, for a year. Some groups met once a week for eight weeks, and others met for a weekend. This chapter draws together our impressions, learnings, and a few biased opinions on encounter groups as consciousness raising experiences for women.

The question men often ask when we mention encounter groups for women is, "How are women's groups different? What do women talk about with each other that they don't talk about with men?" The foregoing section gave an overview of what women talk about. In the remainder of the chapter we will be more explicit about the content of the women's groups and their differences from male-female groups.

What do women talk about? Women talk about themselves as persons, their doubts, fears, hopes, and fantasies. They explore ways to discover and actualize who they are. They talk about role expectations for women. And they talk about the pleasure of being with women, why it is so, and how to make it happen more often. In all three of these areas women together talk differently from the way they do in the presence of men. The cultural conditioning which most women have assimilated rises to the fore even if only one man is present. The women's groups provide a place for women to be together in deep, personal relationships where this influence is at least held in abeyance.

In contrast, a mixed group tends to be a microcosm of society with its sexist, paternalistic structures. Consequently, it tends to reinforce the traditional patterns and roles of relationships between men and women. Encounter groups are most often led by men. If the male leader succumbs to shamanistic tendencies, by misusing his personal charisma and expertise, he exaggerates even more the male-authority-figure pattern of the culture. In a group without men, women have more freedom to examine themselves in terms of their role expectations and their relationships to other women. In the next three sections we discuss each of these separately.

Women in the encounter groups are encouraged to look at themselves quite apart from their primary relationships outside the group. We as facilitators are repeatedly struck with how difficult this is for most women. For them, their development as persons, their needs, dreams, and potential are subordinate to those of husband, children, or lover. Thus thwarted, these women leak out their resentment in a series of complaints. In the groups we try to break this cycle of subordination and complaining by asking individuals to focus exclusively on themselves, their feelings, fantasies, needs, and dreams. Most of the group work centers around two primary problems: The first is that women attach large portions of their self-identity to their men and children, and second, women have difficulty feeling and expressing their own potency. Certainly some women come to the groups who have broken out of this cycle, but they are the minority.

The first step toward discovering her own unique identity is usually a woman's struggle to dispel the notion that she is primarily somebody's wife or lover. Many women have difficulty accepting that they have equal rights to fulfill themselves as persons. The manifestation of this tendency is somewhat different for single women than for married. A young single woman, a talented dancer, was so overwhelmed by her dependency on her lover that her dancing as well as her graduate study and other personal interests began to lose all meaning for her. She was in her late twenties and feeling pressured by her parents (and undoubtedly by herself) to get married. Her lover was treating her badly, and she felt basically unsuccessful as a woman because she did not have a "permanent" man.

Married women, on the other hand, feel quite guilty over the thought of spending more time just for themselves. "I should be happy, I have a wonderful husband and lovely children" is a common remark. The implication is that something must be wrong with me that I am not happy. Success as a woman is so traditionally tied to having a man that women, married and single, have trouble displacing that priority and looking to themselves for their own fulfillment.

As women become able to consider their own personal development, they begin to face squarely the traps into which they have gotten themselves. As one woman expressed it, "I feel like I've spent my life waiting, waiting to take a child someplace, waiting to fix supper, waiting for the baby to wake up. When does my time come?" This same woman started going to classes two nights a week. "I know he [her husband] doesn't like it. I can tell by his humor. We aren't allowed to get angry, so he lets me know his displeasure through his humor." After a pause, she added, "If he'd let me, I'm sure I'd go out every single night!" (A frequent phrase we heard was "If he'd let me." At the same time we became aware in social situations of husbands using the phrases "I let her" or "I don't let her.")

The process of allowing one's own feelings to emerge and to accept them as valid and rightful expressions of one's personhood is frequently a painful and risky step. We began to form new hypotheses about the emotionality of women, as woman after woman in the groups let go of feelings she had held back, sometimes for years. Invariably, the withheld feelings were for herself. That caused us to wonder if woman's proverbial easy tears in emotional situations did not represent an overflow from the package she is holding inside, namely her anger at not allowing her own honest feelings. One woman expressed with tears and anger her feelings about a year's separation from her husband early in their marriage. "I've never told anyone how *I* felt," she said. Another woman laughed and cried, "For the first time in my life I'm allowing myself to cry when I feel like it. And the tears are for me! My feelings are just as valid as my husband's or my children's." On the other hand, more than one woman said in one way or another, "I can't allow myself to feel about my situation. I can go only so far; then don't ask me to go any farther. I just can't afford to right now." "If I do I will have to make some decisions and some changes in my life and that's too scary." The insight which many women had in the groups involved the extent to which their identity depended on their man or children. The work toward actualization was in the area of feeling and expressing their own potency.

Liz walked into the group the first day, a strikingly beautiful woman of thirty-eight, hair, face, and body held very taut. In her stylized, accentuated manner of speaking, punctuated with a nervous laugh, she told of moving eleven times in her twelve years of marriage, of being up and down financially several times, and of never having a single close personal moment with her husband. In the process of the group she expressed a fear, close to terror, of leaving him and having to rely just on herself. This brought out the issue of the dependence trap in which so many married women find themselves—the trap of an easy life, with someone to take care of you. To be liberated from this a woman needs alternatives; she must feel capable of making it on her own. To be totally dependent on a man can be destructive, not only for the woman, but also for the relationship. Until coming to the group, Liz saw no alternatives, but by the end of the eight weeks there were visible changes in her. Her face and body seemed more relaxed and she had lost all traces of her tight, clipped speech. She said calmly and with confidence, "I think the two of us may make it now. But if we can't, I feel like I can make it alone." Liz had begun to feel her own potency.

For women who are able to express their strength, other problems may arise. Even in an all-women group, powerful, aggressive women will ask, "Am I coming on too strong?" We are so sensitive to the cultural epithets for the aggressive woman that it takes conscious effort for most women to allow themselves to express this part of their personalities. There is much cultural unlearning to do before a woman can feel free to fully express her strength.

The labels for the aggressive woman which are used in a mixed group all have negative connotations: castrating bitch, hard, ballbreaker. In the face of such pressure, aggressive women are likely to come away thinking they are deficient rather than questioning the values of the group. On the other hand, the soft, caring, mothering qualities of a woman are encouraged, reinforced, and labeled positively with such epithets as mother earth. Roles which are culturally acceptable for women have an exaggerated potency in a mixed group, while the assertive, straightforward, self-confident woman who is willing to contend with men as equals, instead of protecting and soothing them, is frequently "put in her place." Little wonder that in such an atmosphere women "do their shuffle." The consequence of such attitudes is that women who are already way overboard on the side of passivity, acceptance, and dependence do not even begin to get in touch with their sources of strength and assertiveness. We see women's groups as a place where women find permission to develop all parts of themselves.

These women are questioning what they have been taught they should be primarily in three areas: sexuality, motherhood, and childrearing. The hold of traditional roles on women is being loosened as we get in touch with our own personal needs.

To be sexual or, better, sexy is a role constantly reinforced in the woman's socialization process. Women are very aware, particularly in the presence of men, how others are successfully or unsuccessfully playing that part. They compare themselves with one another and develop a sense of competitiveness. Often in a mixed encounter group, so much energy is spent in comparison and competition that it is difficult for women to listen to each other and to be aware of each other as whole persons. In the absence of males, women are more available to be sensitive to each other as human beings, not only because they are not busy being seductive and pleasing to men, but also because they can look at the roles they play in heterosexual relationships without acting them out. Instead of competitiveness, a sense of cooperation, patience, and understanding develops, and women are free to share their sexual experiences, wishes, attitudes, and lack of knowledge.

In a mixed group if a woman talks about her sexual needs or her desires to be aggressive sexually, it may be interpreted as a come on. Women in our groups were much more eager than might be commonly assumed to confront the myth of the passive sleeping beauty as the desired position of the female. In the group they explored, freely, their sexual fantasies. A woman in her late forties candidly told of her multi-faceted love life. She was the initiator in a variety of sexual experiences, her latest being a twenty-six-year-old fellow student. A shy young woman came out of her corner and asked the question on most of the women's minds, "How do you do it?" Whereupon the older woman gave very explicit directions. Following this, a number of women "confessed" their successes at being sexually aggressive.

One must grow up female in order to understand fully the power of the taboo against women being the aggressor in a sexual encounter. Women do not forget such epithets as hard, common, cheap, or slut which have been ascribed to a woman going after a man for sexual pleasure. Being in a group where most of the women expressed such desires was like discovering a hoax which had somehow been played on all of us.

Women freely talked in the women's groups about their body images and their feelings of sexual inadequacy, two topics women seldom explore in the presence of men. An important moment for one of the groups occurred when a woman said she was separating from her husband after sixteen years of a rocky marriage. "Last night," she said, "for the first time since I got married, I looked at myself naked in the mirror. I saw a thirty-eight-year-old, overweight woman with varicose veins, and I'm really scared." The stereotyped female body image is taught to women to the point of overkill. Most women introject the 36-24-36 profile into their self-concepts and suffer real feelings of inadequacy as they fall short of this supposed ideal.

When the woman felt free enough to discuss sexuality, the issue of orgasm became a concern of the group. Many women admitted they had never had a vaginal orgasm. A few told of never having an orgasm at all but of pretending to in order to please their husbands. They felt completely responsible for pleasuring themselves as well as their mates and were experiencing feelings of inadequacy and guilt. One woman said her need to please her husband was so great that it was impossible for her to relax and enjoy sex.

Jill, one of the younger women, asked with great embarrassment, "Have any of you seen your clitoris?" Most of the women admitted they never had. The clitoris is, in essence, the seat of female sexuality, and yet few women are familiar with the appearance of this highly controversial part of their anatomy. The women's groups provide an atmosphere where women can explore their hidden feelings about their bodies and sexuality in a nonthreatening situation.

Women traditionally receive ample instruction on the characteristics of the good mother; they receive little or no instruction on how to cope with their negative feelings toward pregnancy and motherhood. The ideal of the beautiful pregnant woman and the warm, accepting, good mother is another myth women candidly look at in the groups.

It is a rare woman who does not experience some negative feelings toward pregnancy or caring for an infant. Women recall feeling trapped, odd for not experiencing the great surge of motherly warmth that is expected of them. One woman in our group expressed feeling queer and unnatural for not finding motherhood the supreme fulfillment of her life as a woman. Traditional upbringing does not prepare women to cope with these negative feelings. Rather, the simplistic teachings of the culture imply that these negative feelings are unfeminine, unnatural, and in some cases pathological.

One woman shared this experience in our group. When pregnant with her first child, she was scared, confused, and feeling "like a human incubator." She decided to try exploring some of these feelings in a mixed encounter group. As she entered the room, one of the women said to her, "Why could you possibly be here? You're young and in the bloom of motherhood. What problems could you have?" Needless to say, this beginning reinforced all her feelings of self-doubt, and she never had the courage to talk about her real attitudes. Upon sharing these feelings twelve years later with a group of women willing to challenge traditional expectations, she found understanding and support.

Another woman told of frantically thumbing through her copy of Dr. Spock, looking for the section which said mothers sometimes feel desperate. She had two babies at the time. All she found was a mild suggestion to get out of the house once in a while. There was no one she could go to who would simply listen to her feelings and accept them as valid. The women's groups provide a place where young mothers are allowed to have their own feelings, regardless of how contrary they are to cultural ideals. The despair and desperation mothers sometimes feel is seldom heard for what it is; rather it is glossed over with pink and blue superficiality.

Women feel most alone, find the guidelines of the culture most useless, in the area of childrearing. In a time of rapid social and technological change, children are influenced by external events, such as man traveling to the moon or living under the threat of total annihilation. When, as a result of growing up in a world very different from that of their parents, children have values and experiences their parents find difficult to understand, the children have to teach their parents what this new world, its values and experiences, is like. In the groups, these phenomena are expressed in the struggle women are going through with their children to understand their new values, to keep communication with their children open, and to find ways in which whatever wisdom the women feel they have can still have an impact on their children's lives. For one woman the struggle was to accept her son's long hair. For another it was the decision to have her seventeen-year-old daughter fitted with an IUD. Wherever the women are in their own personal acceptance of their children's mores, they are experiencing the difficulty of carving out new guidelines for child-rearing as a lonely and risky task.

Many women feel themselves caught in the middle of a transition in which their own values are changing, and they find having one foot in the past and one in the future a very confusing position. One woman said her fantasy of the ideal life for herself would be to "live like a hippie" alone in the mountains with only the bare necessities. On the other hand, this was the woman who forced her son to cut his hair.

In the groups the women can face squarely their own confusion and fears and find consolation in discovering other women in the same position. The sequence in the groups seemed to be that a woman had first to face her own value dilemmas before she could begin to see the variety of alternatives to her particular childrearing problems. If the women's groups did nothing else, they could justify themselves as a place where women can come together to work on the fearsome task of childrearing in the present world.

As we mentioned earlier, rediscovering the goodness and fullness of relationships with other women was one of the pleasures of the encounter group. Most women could recall the fun of being together as children but felt that at adolescence their relationships with men became the primary focus. Though they still had close women friends, their relationships with women took on a new competitive aspect. This change, plus the generally accepted idea in our society that men are better, kept them from seeking out female relationships with energy to equal that spent on relationships with men.

A professional woman put it this way: "Before the women's group, I really didn't like women. I much preferred to be with the men in my profession. I know I got status in my own mind from being liked and respected by them. I was trying to be like a man in my job. Now I've come to like myself as a woman. I can see now that the woman's way of doing my job is perhaps quite different from the way a man would do it. I am excited about discovering what the woman's way will be."

Another participant found she was behaving quite differently in social situations. "I used to measure my success at a party by the number of men I thought I was pleasing," she said. "I can almost make myself sick when I think of the games I was playing and how untrue I was being to myself. This all hit me last night at a party as another woman and I were getting to know each other in a very real and deep way. I felt the same sisterly bond with her that I feel with you, here. A few months ago, I wouldn't even have noticed her."

Women in the groups frequently developed close friendships as they came to trust each other with the most intimate parts of their lives. They found a richness in the quality of woman to woman understanding. They were easily able to be loving and openly expressive of affection.

Some women were considering the alternative of a life style without men, where the need for companionship could be met by another woman. Most of the others accepted and understood this alternative, whether or not it involved a sexual relationship. Some women freely discussed their lesbian experiences or fantasies, while others, though not interfering with the discussion, found this subject still taboo.

A real joy in the groups came when the women would break into a mood of playing together. "I've never laughed so hard in my life," said one woman, after a siege of joking with each other. The climate of the groups was frequently one of relaxed fun, with no one needing to impress anyone else, no one having to play games. We could simply be ourselves. It was this atmosphere more than any other which made us realize how much we have been missing by not creating occasions for women to be together.

We hear from all directions that this is a time of upheaval, culture change, and reexamination of values and institutions which have gone unquestioned for decades. The effect of this upheaval on women hits first the traditional role expectations which they were taught from early childhood and which have been rather rigidly held by the larger society. Women are questioning how many of these roles they are still willing to choose for themselves and are seriously searching for alternatives.

We see encounter groups for women as a vehicle through which women can begin to make their own transition from the rigid, well-defined roles they were expected to fit, to the unique alternatives they discover within themselves. For some women the step they make in the group may seem like a small one. For others it will seem like a leap of genuine personal liberation. No matter what the size of the step, the trusting, supportive atmosphere of the encounter group appears a significant approach to helping women see more clearly what their individual alternatives might be.

Human Development in the Elementary School Classroom

Harold Bessell

For most patients, therapy is a painful, expensive, and protracted experience that often comes too late. Encounter group
techniques, as helpful as they can be, invariably labor under
this shadow. The damage has been done; pain and guilt have
twisted a human life into their own grotesque image. And the
therapist must somehow piece this fragile, pain-filled human
thing back together. Little wonder that therapy is rarely wholly
successful. Our skills and knowledge abound in palliatives, but
lasting cures are still rare. Moreover, for every patient we treat,
it is an unhappy fact that there are hundreds, even thousands,
more who desperately need therapy but cannot afford it or,

even if they could, would not be able to find a qualified, let alone effective, therapist available to help them.[1]

These are disturbing truths that must perplex and trouble every therapist as he struggles with his responsibilities. They raise vital, nagging questions for all of us. It was in answer to these questions—and the frustration we all feel at the issues they imply—that the Human Development Program was born.

Simply described, the Human Development Program (HDP) is a curriculum designed for use in schools to foster the positive emotional development of children. Its basic structure consists of a daily encounter group, called the Magic Circle, whose purpose is to stimulate and support emotional development. Provocative cues that are significant but nonthreatening are used to open children to a discussion of their feelings and life in such a way as to leave them feeling self-confident and worthwhile—and not eviscerated as many adults feel after intensive sensitivity sessions. Curriculum materials, including a theory manual and curriculum guides which I developed with Uvaldo H. Palomares, spell out the teaching techniques and provide a set of tested and sequenced cues for daily use in preschool through grade three. Additional curriculum guides for the upper levels are currently in preparation. A set of developmental scales has also been developed to profile the individual affective progress of each student. To date, a series of teacher training institutes [2] has trained more than twenty-five thousand teachers in HDP techniques and methods, exposing some five hundred thousand children to the program. While evaluation studies are currently in progress, teachers nevertheless report highly gratifying results: reduced discipline problems; greater personal involvement; increased verbal expressiveness; higher motivation to learn; greater self-confidence and constructive

[1] Acknowledgment is given to *Psychology Today* for permission to use passages from an article by the author which appeared in the January 1968 issue, entitled *The Content is the Medium: The Confidence is the Message.*

[2] Teacher Training Institutes are conducted on a pre- and inservice basis by the Institute for Personal Effectiveness in Children (IPEC), organized by the author and Dr. Palomares.

behavior. Teachers also verify the effect of the program on their own teaching styles and attitudes: They find themselves more flexible and able to cope with teaching problems, more comfortable, and less hostile and distrustful toward children.

The basic premise of the program can be summed up in two words: emotional development. Or to put it another way, the program is designed to prevent emotional problems by developing in each person a set of positive, adaptive skills to cope with problem situations. Therapy certainly has a continuing, useful role to play in treating emotional disorders, as do encounter group techniques. But in the absence of a certain cure for emotional problems, the old canard about an "ounce of prevention" became a challenging imperative. A new strategy was needed, one that focused on the emotional development of children.

Such a program does not spring out of the head of Jove or drop from the heavens; the Human Development Program is no exception. It was the outgrowth of more than seventeen years' experience as a practicing psychotherapist. A selected collection of psychological theories formed its theoretical base, and extensive, continuing research with children in classroom settings gave the program its present form.

The personality-development theory of Karen Horney (1950) provided the major theoretical basis of the program. Horney, who related personal growth to social relationships, concentrates on the basic drives to achieve mastery and to gain approval. Her conviction is that the competent, approved child develops a healthy self-concept and the incentive to strive for further self-realization.

In addition, the phenomenon described by Harry Stack Sullivan (1947) as the "delusion of uniqueness," the notion individuals have that they are different from others and therefore somehow inferior, became a focus for the Magic Circle groups. In these groups, children see and hear that others feel unsure and have fears, and each child can perceive that others in the group are much more like him in their thoughts and feelings than they are different from him.

The basic psychological thrust of the program—its content and organization—grew out of an observation based on years of practical experience. Patients in therapy invariably are deficient in three things: awareness, self-confidence, and an understanding of interpersonal relationships. They are not really aware of the emotional motives that influence their behavior; they lack a real and steady confidence in themselves as whole persons; and they only dimly understand why and how other human beings react to them. Thus, these three main areas of human experience and feeling became the basic themes of the program: awareness (knowing what your thoughts, feelings, and actions are); mastery (knowing what your abilities are and how to use them); and social interaction (knowing other people and how your behavior affects them and influences their behavior toward you).

The theory of awareness is as old as Plato, who discussed feelings and thoughts as they motivate man's behavior. From Plato (Jowett, 1946, pp. 425–434) through Freud (1961) to Bernard Bloom (1956),[3] philosophers and psychologists have arrived at the same notions: Awareness is a major area of human functioning, and a long array of disorders can be associated with insufficient emotional awareness.

Freud and his followers have described extensively the nature of and treatment for problems caused by limited awareness. They say in essence that the neurotic person is suffering from gyrations of his alienated, unacceptable, unconscious impulses. Therapy consists of allowing the unconscious impulses to enter into conscious awareness where they can be dealt with in integrative and constructive ways.

Our problem, then, was to find a way to provide emotionally meaningful experiences which would help children keep the awareness—the emotional openness—they have as young children. To preserve their awareness, children would need special experiences and skills. And most of all, they would need a language—a vocabulary—about awareness with which to express themselves and listen meaningfully to others. Thus,

[3] Bloom's contribution was his division of the educational process into three domains: the cognitive (thinking), the affective (feelings), and performance (behavior).

we began to talk with them about their feelings, thoughts, and actions. When they readily dealt with these terms, we knew we were on solid ground. The prospects for keeping children aware of their feelings—and hence their motives—have turned out to be quite good.

Adler (1965), who identified the inferiority complex as a major cause of personal maladjustment, emphasized the fact that every child is born into a state of helplessness. The early experiences of childhood confirm this sense of helplessness. But the child resents the feeling of frustration caused by his helplessness and strives to become capable so he can satisfy his needs and desires. He struggles to obtain the feeling of power, of "I can." He wants to believe in his own capability. He wants and needs to perceive himself as a person who, when presented with a reasonable challenge, can overcome it, can succeed. This perception is the root of self-confidence.

Our task was to find a method that would build children's self-confidence. Psychological theory, as well as clinical experience, provided the basic developmental ingredients: involvement, achievement, and adult praise. First, the child had to be personally involved; the challenge had to mean something to him. Secondly, the task had to be easy enough for the child to succeed, yet difficult enough to provide a real challenge. Finally, the most powerful reinforcement a child can receive in building self-confidence is the praise of a respected, credible adult in authority, particularly if the praise occurs immediately after the child's achievement (Skinner and Ferster, 1957). So we began to develop tasks designed to build self-confidence. While we could guess what would interest children, only they could confirm what excited and challenged them. In this way, the children themselves selected the tasks for building self-confidence.

All philosophies and psychological theories recognize man as being socially equipotential: capable of kindness and cruelty; of emotionally rewarding or damaging behavior; of good and evil. Charles Darwin (1871) epitomized this dualism when he commented on the great contrast between the cooperative behavior within a tribe and the destructive behavior between tribes. Within the tribe he observed "sympathy, fidelity, obedience, courage, mutual aid, and self-sacrifice." But between tribes there was "deceit, plunder, destruction of property, and murder." Children exhibit the same dual potential for positive and negative social behavior.

Our deepest challenge has been to develop a truly meaningful set of experiences that would stimulate constructive social interactions. We began by setting up simple experiences in which children could learn to talk about how people do nice and mean things to one another. Our goal was to develop a vocabulary for dialogue about feelings and to help children learn to perceive the emotional dynamics of social interaction. The four- and five-year-olds learned the language very quickly and enjoyed the chance to express themselves and to listen to one another. At this juncture the modified encounter group technique we employed demonstrated special value. When the children sat around in a circle, they tended to show and express understanding, kindness, inclusiveness, and helpfulness to a markedly greater extent than they did when they were not seated in a circle arrangement. The children, recognizing this difference in themselves, named the circle sessions the Magic Circle.

To test our basic theories and assumptions, we enlisted the aid of Anna Lord at Twin Trees Nursery School (La Jolla, California). Here we set about to discover a number of vital things: Would children get involved with us, and could a simple vocabulary be devised to enable children to discuss awareness, confidence, and social interaction. The answers were affirmative. Several other practical considerations also became clear. To accomplish any growth, children must be exposed to emotionally maturing experiences every day. Teachers were willing to make this effort, but they needed a daily guide that would name the lesson and its objective, describe the procedure and its rationale, and provide some guidance on how to deal with problem situations. After a year's research testing various lessons, an organized set of lesson plans was devised and published as part of a basic theory manual (Bessell and Palomares, 1967).

The lesson guides were organized to expose children to a series of six-week units on each theme. On the awareness theme, the children devote one week to pleasant feelings, followed by one on pleasant thoughts and another on positive behavior. These same topics are then repeated for further development and reinforcement in the circle process.

On the theme of self-confidence, a six-week program progresses from mastery in naming things to mastery in numbers, motor coordination, performance skills, dress and hygiene, and social comprehension. As the children mature, these six categories are continued in the second semester at a more advanced level. We found that it was crucial to emphasize the fact that they were succeeding at their tasks and to give only secondary emphasis to the actual skill they were achieving. We were not as interested in what the child was learning as we were in the growth of his confidence in himself to cope effectively with any challenge.

On the social interaction theme, the six-week unit treated the following topics: one week each on what we do that people like and dislike; what other people do that we like and dislike; and how to ask for and offer kind behavior. While these six-week units make up a planned program, it is not rigid. Once the focal point of the session is identified by the teacher, the children can discuss it as freely as they wish.

One such early session that lasted seventy minutes instead of the usual twenty suggested a simple but important discovery about the attention span of children. While it was a fact that a four-year-old's attention span was quite short when he was made to listen to something that interested an adult, his attention span grew quite long when someone listened to him discuss his thoughts and feelings. From that point on, the adult posture in the program became one of listening rather than of talking.

Another thing we found was that every child will talk. At Twin Trees and later in other preschools, we found that shy children, who had never spoken before in the school setting, talked for the first time during a circle session. The fears that impeded their speaking were apparently removed by both the example of other children expressing themselves in a safe and comfortable atmosphere and the efforts of the other children to include and directly encourage the shyer ones.

Another issue dealt with during this period was measurement. How could we measure individual emotional development? To accomplish this, we adapted Horace Champney's version (1941) of the Fels Rating Scales for use with nursery-school children.[4] The scales combined qualitative and quantitative measurement of development in several traits: awareness of self; considerateness; eagerness; effectiveness; flexibility; interpersonal comprehension; self-confidence; sensitivity to others; spontaneity; stability; and tolerance.

On these scales, each trait is described, and accurate cue descriptions are agreed upon; ratings for each trait are located along the scale from high to low. To the extent that the program is successful, the scores should rise. Each child is profiled every six weeks, not as a test but to indicate progress and discover needed areas of development. A residual value is that the profile compels the teacher to assess children in a way that often reveals valuable psychological and behavioral assets not considered by the regular educational apparatus of cognitive tests and report cards.

The first phase of our research resulted in a program for four- and five-year-olds consisting of a theory, daily semistructured procedures, and a crude means of assessing results. Since then extensive research has modified and improved the program and additional levels have been added. Levels IV, V, and VI have been developed and are currently being researched in the field. Meanwhile, a bird's eye view of the program as currently organized and operating might prove helpful. Table 23 covers five levels ranging from preschool to grade three and describes meeting arrangements, strategies, and program objectives.

The Magic Circle with its discussion cues and personal interaction is the heart of the Human Development Program;

---

[4] Champney believed that by describing a trait articulately and making quantitatively and qualitatively accurate cue descriptions along a continuum, he would have a superior kind of rating scale.

Table 23

Human Development Program

Level	Grade	Age	Groupings	Strategies	Objectives
A	Preschool	4	Single circle; 8–14 children	Encourage to talk, listen, and succeed; positive aspects only.	Improve ability to sit still, listen, and express; develop self-confidence and understanding of interpersonal interaction; promote tolerance for individual differences.
B	Kinder-garten	5	Single circle; 8–14 children	Encourage to talk, listen, succeed. Deal with negative as well as positive aspects.	Develop self-control and confidence. Increase understanding of social interaction, individual differences, and tolerance. Increase verbal expression and listening skills.
I	First	6	First one circle, 8–14 children; then add self-controlled outer ring until whole class is in two rings.	Discuss ambivalence in feelings, thoughts, and behavior; effective and ineffective behavior; reality and fantasy. Discuss social variables of inclusion, exclusion, warmth and coldness, decising making. Begin leadership experiences.	Effective self-control, ability to comfortably experience ambivalence; improve reality testing, self-confidence, effective meeting of needs; increase responsibility, tolerance, and empathy; increase skill in making helpful suggestions. Sharing in decision making and recognition of leadership abilities.

Table 23 (Continued)

Human Development Program

Level	Grade	Age	Groupings	Strategies	Objectives
II	Second	7	Whole class in concentric circles. Teacher and child leaders alternate.	Teacher leads one-third of new sessions. Child leaders are guided by teachers in remainder. Continued presentation of awareness, coping, social interaction. Character development is hastened by challenge, commitments, and confrontation of peers.	Effective self-control, articulation of wide range of experience in positive and negative feelings, thoughts, behavior; strong realistic self-confidence, positive self-concepts, personal pride, esteem; ability to distinguish between reality and fantasy. Motivation to be responsible, productive, kind. Sharing in decision making. Leadership skills as service instead of exploitation. Ability to make helpful sugestions to guide leader to better functioning.
III	Third	8	Whole class in concentric circles. Teacher and child leaders alternate.	Further challenge to self-sufficiency, integration, honesty. Emphasize awareness, responsibility, keeping commitments. Challenge to overtly recognize differences between and interest across sexes.	Self-control as a matter of pride. Verbal facility; skillful and tolerant listening. Ability to tolerate ambivalent feelings in self and others with skill in detecting discrepancies between verbalization and behavior. Wise decision-making and responsible, constructive leadership. Courage in taking the initiative to build good social relationships.

it is the engine that makes it go. Its basic strategy is to develop affective communication skills in children in their early, formative years while their emotions are still open to positive adaptive development. These skills are learned through daily practice of the two basic ingredients of communication—perception and expression.

In essence, the Magic Circle functions as a highly efficient and sophisticated communications system. The circle configuration enables information, both cognitive and affective, to pass among children and the teacher quickly and in all directions. Each child in the circle sends and receives affective information; every day he becomes the focus of vast amounts of instant feedback. For the children this feedback is an impressive experience at receiving attention, praise, or acceptance. Thus, the Magic Circle becomes a vehicle for enlarging the child's emotional experience.

The teacher gently structures this deepening experience so that the child can learn important, adaptive lessons. Like a good facilitator, she generalizes explicitly about the experiences the children relate: "Johnny and Simpson and Fernando and I have all told about a bad dream we had, so you see everybody has them and they're scary, but there's nothing bad about you because everybody has them." In this way, the teacher gives children the support they need to learn important facts about themselves and their experiences.

Much of this information is conveyed verbally, and this in itself represents an important accomplishment. Most people do not really know how to talk about their emotional experience. They have never really learned to name what goes on inside them. The Magic Circle provides children with the opportunity and help to develop an affective vocabulary: "You're teasing me and I don't like it, but it probably means you like me and want to be my friend, so why not be friends."

But verbal communication is by no means the complete story. People express many of their emotions in nonverbal ways. We tap our feet, bite our nails, blink our eyes, or slump in our chairs. In the Magic Circle, children learn to notice and pay attention to such nonverbal signs and learn to read them so accurately that by the time they are eight years old they can spot and discuss the discrepancies between what a person says he feels and what his behavior implies he feels.

In the Magic Circle, there are no lessons which the children passively absorb. On the contrary, the children are the lessons: Their own experience is the subject matter; their words and feelings, the learning medium. What children learn is what they emotionally want and need to learn—how to be more effective, how to feel better, and how to get along with people. These lessons are learned because the relevant information gets expressed and is then shaped, corrected, and refined by continuous feedback, not only by the teacher but principally from the other children.

These lessons are also learned more deeply at an affective level; children quickly perceive and translate attitudes into their emotional meaning. For this reason, positive attitudes—gentleness, friendliness, politeness—are critical to the shaping process of the Magic Circle. The teacher's example is crucial; she sets the tone. She must always be courteous and polite. Children are spoken to by name, thanked by name, and always responded to in a polite manner. In this way, children experience themselves as being taken seriously as persons and can begin to interact accordingly. On the one hand, her courtesy confirms their sense of self-worth; and on the other, it becomes a way for them to operate within and without the circle.

Teachers, like children, need some assurance of success. Consequently, to make the Magic Circle viable as a classroom instrument, there were several practical considerations every teacher had to know: group size and seating arrangement, the length of the session, and criteria for selecting groups. The guiding principle was to make the circle process as easily manageable and effective as possible.

At the preschool and kindergarten levels, we found that ten to twelve children were ideal. This number provides enough children for meaningful interaction but does not create long delays between turns. However, some teachers are more effective with a few less; others do well with a few more, the optimum range being eight to thirteen. Once established, the membership of each circle group should remain constant. Children gain an increased sense of security when they deal with the same people day in and day out. They get to know one another better and are more able to observe one another's development.

The place and time of the session should also be consistent. The room and its facilities should be familiar to the children and subject to an absolute minimum of distraction from other people or activities. Preferably, sessions should be conducted at the same time each day, relatively early in the day. Children are then less tired and can adjust more quickly to what is expected of them.

Three criteria are used to select children for each group. First, it is best to have an approximately equal number of boys and girls. Second, the more highly developed children should be placed in one group, the less developed in another, and the least developed in yet another. Children will make fewer negative comparisons when they are all about equally advanced. And third, no more than two children with relatively severe personal problems should be in any one group. It must be emphasized that HDP is not a therapeutic program. If a child is highly disruptive or maladjusted, he should be referred for professional care.

The teacher should try for a seating arrangement as closely resembling a circle as possible. It is important for every child to be able to see all the others clearly—their gestures, facial expressions, and bodily movement. At the same time, nothing in the arrangement should signify a different status between children. Boys and girls are seated alternately around the circle.

A duration of twenty minutes for each circle session seems best. This should not be thought of as a rigid limit but rather as a mean. Some sessions last longer, others less. In no case, however, should a session exceed the logical point of closure.

Apart from these basic guidelines, there are only a few other necessary notes. With four- and five-year-olds, the children need a summary to learn the general significance of what they have been discussing. In the final few minutes of each session, the teacher reviews what each child said or did and relates this behavior to the broad implications of personal and social effectiveness.

Generally four- and five-year-olds present few disciplinary problems. When misbehavior is not due to confusion or inexperience an effort should be made to determine the frustrating element for the child. A slight adjustment or accommodation to the child's needs solves the problem.

In addition, the teacher should explicitly state the need for silence, whenever necessary, so everyone can hear the child speaking. This basic courtesy is essential to communication. For this reason, before each session the teacher follows a simple orientation procedure to acquaint the children with the basic ground rules of the Magic Circle. When the children are seated, she tells them there are three things they must do to enjoy the session. Rule 1: Everyone should sit quietly. Rule 2: Only one person should talk at a time. Each person must raise his hand to get permission to talk. Teacher wants everyone to have his say, but they must take turns. Rule 3: They must listen. To show that they are interested in what a person is saying, they have to be able to repeat what that person just said.

There is one persistent, sometimes difficult question that every teacher asks: "What shall I do with the other children when I'm working with a circle group?" In a preschool or kindergarten setting, teaching aides are an obvious if not always available solution. The other children should be engaged in activities in another room or the farthest section of the room to minimize distractions. Where there are no aides, arrangements might be made for another teacher to include the remaining children in her classroom. When the teacher completes her session with the first group, it is advisable to have an intervening period with a different activity for all the children. Later on, she can conduct a circle session with the next group.

Despite our preferences for smaller groups, we came to find that an entire class of first, second, or third graders could interact effectively in a single session. In this case, the circle configuration consists of two concentric circles: an inner circle containing one-third of the class and an outer circle containing the remain two-thirds. The most obvious reason for this arrangement is the convenience of the teacher. But the main reason is that the children can do it; they become involved even with as many as thirty-five children. Another reason is that it offers children an opportunity for leadership training. A four-stage process prepares the children and the teacher for this arrangement.

First graders must make a gradual transition to the concentric-ring arrangement, even when they have had Level B (kindergarten). This four-stage building sequence, shown in Figure 3, can be varied according to the readiness of the chil-

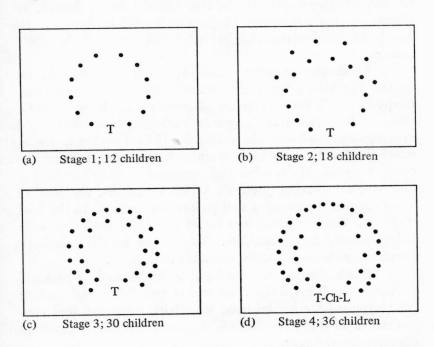

(a) Stage 1; 12 children

(b) Stage 2; 18 children

(c) Stage 3; 30 children

(d) Stage 4; 36 children

FIGURE 3. Development of concentric rings. (a) First six-week unit: Teacher works with one-third of class only; makes arrangements for remainder. Next day works with different third; some lessons condensed or omitted. (b) Second six-week unit: Teacher works with one-third of class; has some better-controlled children sit as observer-participants in outer ring. Repeat next day with more children; encourage participation. (c) Third six-week unit: Teacher works with one-third of class in central ring. Rest of class sits in outer ring, except the least controlled. These children participate as soon as they can in a controlled way. It is made clear they are wanted, if controlled. (d) Fourth six-week unit: Teacher works with one-third of class in central ring; all the rest in outer ring. Next day, different third are in center; following day the last third.

dren or the competence of the teacher. For the remainder of the year, the double concentric ring continues, but the teacher brings in children to serve in the role of leader-trainee. She invites the child to sit next to her and to perform some of the group leader functions.

By far the most surprising finding has been the discovery that almost all children have a desire and moderate aptitude for effective leadership. While this drive depends upon the readiness of each child, we found it to come much earlier than we expected—around age seven. Consequently, leadership training is built into the Magic Circle at late Level I. Its aim is to develop child-leaders who can facilitate the circle session.

Leadership training is best acquired in several stages. In the first stage, the child observes the teacher, acquiring leadership skills through simple observation and later by imitation. Second, the child acquires leadership capability—and demonstrates readiness—by taking the risk of serving as leader when the teacher asks for a volunteer. In the next stage, the child sits beside the teacher and performs the activities he has observed the teacher perform. When he falters, the teacher lends support, encourages, and guides as necessary. In the final stage, the teacher withdraws to let the child lead the circle independently and effectively. She remains on the periphery to reinforce the constructive elements that occur.

The leadership role is a highly valuable tool for personal development. It gives the child real responsibility and explicit peer approval for his fairness, sensitivity, patience, and consideration. In this way, the child-leader is exposed to powerful developmental forces.

Another important facet of the Magic Circle is to give the children a decision-making role. At an early stage, children are permitted to chose the game or topic of the day. Because they have a stake in this choice and its outcome, they have a natural opportunity to be responsible and committed. At the same time, they learn to participate in the democratic process through an experience that directly affects them.

The advanced levels of awareness, mastery, and social

interaction each introduce more complex issues for the children's consideration and development. In awareness training, children are exposed to and discuss unpleasant feelings, thoughts, and behavior. These experiences prepare them to describe and assimilate the negative experiences that inevitably arise in their everyday life. The concept of ambivalence in feelings, thoughts, and behavior is introduced in a very personal way through discussions of their own mixed feelings and reactions. Children are also encouraged to express their wishes, fears, and resentments as a means of defusing Sullivan's delusion of uniqueness. In addition, they are encouraged to distinguish between reality and fantasy. The basic aim here is to develop their capacity for reality testing. A person who can discriminate accurately between reality and make-believe—as well as the possible and impossible—is in a better position to deal effectively with life's challenges.

In mastery development, the emphasis is on responsible competence—ability to function with awareness of consequences. The development of this vital skill depends on personal involvement, a perceived, assured success, and approval. Utility is critical for personal involvement; the child must perceive that what he is to learn will be useful as he sees it. Adult approval is an equally important motivation for competence (A. Freud, 1935). Once children have a repertoire of skills, focus shifts to feelings of power. These game experiences are then extended from what "I can do" to what "I fantasize doing." These experiences test the temptations of fantasy and act as a cathartic. (Both Axline, 1947, and Rogers, 1942, discuss the benefits of cathartic release.) The theme of responsibility is further explored in terms of making and breaking commitments. The most important commitment, children learn, is the commitment we make to ourselves. The issue of congruent behavior—doing what we say we do or want—is dealt with in a series of experiences designed to build self-respect and integrated behavior.

In social interaction training, advanced themes and skill development include: power (the ability to exert influence on another's feelings and behavior); attention (positive strategies to get it); kindness (the ability to give it); social involvement (boy meets gang and girl); and frank discussions about the way children feel toward one another. The variables identified by William Schutz (1960) as the basis of every interpersonal relationship—*inclusion, control, and affection*—are especially emphasized. Such games as "I Let Somebody, Who Wanted to, Play with Me" and "Somebody Made Me Do Something I Did Not Want To Do" deal with issues of inclusion and control. Children learn the importance and need for balance in these elements in social relationships; they learn that social relations that endure are those in which there is a mutual sharing and meeting of needs. Frank discussions about how others feel toward them are fostered by such games as "Tell Me Something You Like or Dislike About Me." In a protected atmosphere, children can articulate their real concerns and learn from one another how to improve.

The Human Development Program was developed as a guide for leading discussions in which children are given the license to express what is on their minds and to provide each other with helpful suggestions. A teacher does not have to be a trained psychotherapist to do these simple but vital things. But she must care about children, have faith in them and their capacity for development, and be able to listen patiently to what they say. Most of all, she must make her own commitment to their development; she must be willing to work with her children day in and day out even in the face of no apparent results. She must allow them the freedom to develop without becoming permissive. In short, the Magic Circle becomes an opportunity for her own development as a teacher and as a person.

Many teachers fear this role and would avoid it under any pretext. Many protest, "Children don't have feelings; it is not the business of the schools to develop children's emotions; we are not qualified." But children do have feelings and teachers can be trained. And the day is coming when schools can no longer afford such consequence of affective neglect as racial strife, juvenile crime, drug addiction, and dropouts.

The true fact is that the teacher affects childrens' feel-

ings all day long, regardless of her willingness to admit responsibility for it. Unfortunately, in a vast majority of cases,
children come away in worse condition than they were. Nothing
the teacher or the system can do can avoid this interaction; it
is essential to human relationships. For the well-being of children this interaction must be dealt with positively. As long as
affect is neglected, children will remain essentially uneducated.

All children present one managerial problem or another.
But the way they confront the teacher with their developmental
problems reflects their perception of the teacher. If they perceive her as humane and willing to listen, they are ready to
behave supportively. If they perceive her as mean, fearful, or
irrelevant, they will behave accordingly. In this context, the
Magic Circle acts as a bridge between child and teacher. It
opens up the teacher to her children and enables her to discard
the fears that limit her effectiveness with them. In this way, she
can develop as a person and as a genuine educator.

In concept and purpose, the Human Development Program is a bold and ambitious undertaking. One of our major
tasks was to develop tools that would increase communication
between teacher and child; the Magic Circle represents that
tool. Its success in classrooms across the country has given us
real hope that by teaching adaptive skills to young children
we can develop a generation of children capable of becoming
truly effective persons and citizens—a generation that will be
aware of themselves and others, integrated and effective in their
functioning, and humane and constructive in their social relationships. Today that vision is largely a dream. But even as we
seek with our children to develop more sophisticated tools to
realize such a generation, we know that the first steps have been
taken.

Homosexual Encounter in All-Male Groups

Don Clark

Sex is a pale, undernourished part of self for most Americans. We live in a culture that is phobic in its fear and obsessive attention to sex. We have learned to feel most comfortable when the sexual aspects of self develop in darkened areas of our being where the light of awareness, understanding, and acceptance rarely penetrates. And of this neglected and distorted part of self called sex, whose facets that might be called homosexual are the most carefully hidden.

In working with all-male groups, it has become increasingly clear to me that men need more from one another than they believe they are permitted to have. Expression of positive affect, or affection, between men is seriously inhibited in our culture. Negative affect is acceptable. Men can argue, fight, and injure one another in public view but they cannot as easily hold hands, embrace, or kiss. When emotions in any area are blocked in expression they seek other outlets, in distorted form if necessary. Affection between males finds outlet with only mild distortion in such forms as competitive body-contact sports. Some war behavior is probably an outlet for extreme distortions of these feelings.

Encountering homosexuality in all-male groups can be helpful in recovering awareness, understanding, and acceptance of male-male affectional needs. The scarecrow of homosexuality can be appreciated for what it is in the accepting warmth of brotherhood. Uncontaminated homosexuality is nothing more than a sexual expression of affection. Taking other needs and the context of his current life style into consideration, a man can choose whether or not he wishes to express affection sexually. It is one of many possible means that can be used to express affection between men.

Work with real and presumed homosexuality in all-male groups is a constant reminder of the ancient wisdom that in order to be yourself, you must first know yourself. And knowing yourself involves friendly acceptance of all the basic ingredients of self no matter how unattractive they appear when first compared to current community manners and morals. Affection for other males is one basic ingredient of self. Homosexuality is one possible way to express that affection. Fear and misunderstanding have led us to view homosexuality as pathological and have made most expressions of masculine affection seem homosexual. The all-male group is a suitable place for a man to stop running in fear, to search for full awareness of affection for other males, and to consider all personally satisfying forms of expressing that affection.

I began conducting all-male groups in a college setting in 1968. These groups were for young men who were teaching in disadvantaged urban schools as an alternative to participation in the Vietnam War. They were fondly called "draft-dodger" groups, and when they began no one knew what would happen. I knew only that I would use encounter techniques in conducting the groups and hoped that these inexperienced teachers would get on better terms with their feelings about themselves and their pupils so they could give more energy to the job and not be too separated from their students by barriers of guilt, insecurity, and resentment.

What happened is not very surprising with the wisdom of hindsight. A room full of males paying attention to the here and now began to sort negative and positive feelings. As positive feelings were differentiated, someone mentioned the unmentionable with words like, "You're good looking. I mean, I guess what I'm saying about my feelings is that you're sexy looking to me, and I guess that means you kind of turn me on!" This kind of revelation in turn led to even finer distinctions, such as sometimes wanting to sit next to a particular man or wanting to touch hands, or hug, or put a weary head in his lap. Sometimes the feeling was relatively nonsexual; sometimes it was obviously sexual.

The group gained skill in differentiating various feelings that have to do with affection and that would ordinarily be lumped together as homosexual and therefore dealt with in hidden ways. In the early weeks a lot of attention was paid to sexual and other affectional feelings, then, gradually, attention went more often to other subjects. Male-male affection remained a matter of concern, however, and the group's acceptance of these feelings accomplished something special.

It seemed to me that the open exploration and acceptance of man to man affectional feelings acted as a catalyst. It was as if, having faced the unmentionable and having made friends with it, we were afraid of nothing. Anything could be brought up in the group, any feelings could be said aloud, anything could be tried. We viewed ourselves as close to emotionally fearless. I had seen some of these same ingredients at work in other encounter groups, but what seemed different in the all-male groups was the pace. We usually met only two hours a week but things sped along. Barriers to communication were unusually weak. Bonds of mutual support were unusually strong.

We spent a lot of time examining male roles. We were aware of cultural definitions for man, teacher, husband, brother, son, father, lover, and friend. Each of us had had those cultural definitions reinforced daily for years. Now we paid attention to self-satisfying definitions of those roles. I remember someone saying, "I don't want to be John Wayne. I want to be the man that is me, but I've been so busy trying to squeeze into the right categories that I don't even know my personal wants."

Like everyone else in those groups, I did a lot more thinking about homosexuality than I had before. Because I am book oriented, I started looking for books to read but had a hard time finding much beyond the patronizing bigotry of psychoanalytic attempts to cope with the fearsome monster. Some fiction helped to give understanding that had a truer ring when compared with my learning in the groups, but I had yet to grasp the universality of homosexual feelings and the pernicious quality of our society's prejudice against it. Like other professionals, I had read the Kinsey findings with blind eyes and learned to present an accepting but uninvolved facade when homosexuality was mentioned.

Part of summer 1969 had been set aside for delicious indolence with time to enjoy beach and family. There was time for catching up on leisure reading. I went on a spree of black authors and did some emotional catching up in that area. Phrases about white liberals began to come clear. And then a curious thing happened. Sometimes while reading, my mind's eye would pop *homosexual* in place of *Negro,* or *gay* in place of *black.*

At the end of the summer I went to the yearly meeting of the Association for Humanistic Psychology and participated in a leaderless encounter group. As the tension of the early hours mounted, a friendly young man with a charming smile said he would like some help from the group on "something specific." An attractive blond housewife sitting next to him said, "I think I know what your trouble is—boys."

"You mean I like boys better than girls?" he asked.

She nodded, and he agreed that was true when it came to sex but not in all areas of his life.

The group began to look more alert. As they spoke, my jaw dropped lower and lower. I heard phrases like, "Some of my best friends are queer"; "I think homosexuals make very loyal friends"; "I don't care if he's gay as long as he doesn't act like a screaming queen or try to put his hands on me"; "They'd be a lot better off if they weren't so sensitive"; "You don't even look like a homo to me"; "It's the blatant ones that give the others a bad name." In vain did our hero try to explain that this was not what he had been asking for help about. His words were drowned in a flood of liberal acceptance and understanding. Years of empathetic flinching at veiled anti-semitic remarks and my summer with black authors fell into place.

With the aid of the man who had inadvertently become the gay focal point of that memorable encounter group, an experimental gay encounter group was set up for the following month in New York City. The idea was simply to provide an encounter group for men who had some concerns related to homosexuality where they need not spend time coping with prejudiced spectators or self-styled helpers. We did not invite gay women because we wanted to keep the group as uncomplicated as possible and just pay attention to male-male relationships.

Selecting people for the group proved to be educational. We had spoken of it as a gay group but the definition of *gay* began to fuzz when I spoke on the telephone with a man who said he did not want to come to my office for a screening interview and wondered if I would meet him in an out of the way diner for coffee because he was concerned about his wife or business associates discovering his homosexuality. He thought it might mean the end of his marriage and would certainly mean the end of his career. We began to use gay to describe anyone who was aware of erotic attraction to members of the same gender no matter how outwardly ungay in life style he appeared. But even that definition has not proved very useful since it describes such a large and varied population.

Undeterred by imprecise vocabulary, we held our first experimental group with eight men. It was dramatic and different. I had just finished a one-year study of the human potential movement and had participated in an unusually wide variety of group experiences around the country, but this group was different. All that I could verbalize at the time was a special feeling of support or closeness that lent dignity to words not easily spoken aloud.

In the years since 1969 the gay groups I have conducted

have developed some sameness in format from group to group. Usually the group meets for a weekend, starting Friday evening and ending Sunday afternoon. Often I have had huge posters of various well known men scattered around the walls and some music on the phonograph that has to do with being a man. For the hour or so during which members are arriving, each is instructed to find a comfortable place to sit, relax, and listen to the music. I suggest each one look frankly at the other men in the room and find what he thinks and feels about these unknown men without any verbal interaction. As soon as everyone has arrived and had a chance to get settled, there is a period of sensory awareness and relaxation exercises, some milling, and some loosening up, nonverbal games. Then the group sits together to hear each man say what he hopes and fears of the weekend and the impressions he has accumulated of the other men in the room.

After that the group becomes free form; a wide variety of techniques from the human potential movement are used as appropriate. Participants are discouraged from relying on habitual self-understanding when they say things like "I'm always somewhat aloof" or "I'm a big talker." They are reminded, "That was yesterday. This group is an artificial community, a new world where you can try new behavior on for fit."

There is usually a generous sprinkling of gay humor and some in-group camping, but the group soon becomes sensitive to symptoms of poor self-concept resulting from the incorporation of the cultural prejudice. The limp wrist and lisp may be thrown into the conversation at a seemingly appropriate moment, but someone will pick them up. "Hey, Tom, I think you just put yourself down and played nigger and it doesn't make me feel very good because that puts me down too. I don't have to play Miss Thing by letting my wrist go limp so Mr. Straight will give me permission to dig sex with other guys."

There is an impressive amount of fraternal support in the group but the group can come down hard on someone who is not trying to be a self-respecting man. There is a growing awareness that incorporated cultural prejudice can do serious damage to a relationship between gay males. "Where's your pride, Joe? You don't have to beg and grovel. You're a man, and you could be a good-looking man if you liked yourself more and stopped sneaking around dark alleys and copping quick gropes. How can we relate to one another as men when you think you're a receptacle who can be used by any stud with an urge? You see me as less than a man, too, when you act like that."

Time and again a member of the group will reveal, to his own surprise, how much of the prejudice against homosexuality he has incorporated. "Drag queens are okay, man. I mean everybody's got a right to do his own thing. But they give me the creeps and they make all of us look bad. Every time somebody finds out I'm gay I can almost see them flash a picture behind their eyes of one of those goddamn queens."

Someone on the other side of the room says, "Take off the hard hat and the combat boots and relax. Ain't nobody here but us. How about taking it easy on your brothers? Some of us learned to hide being gay by acting super butch all the time, but some of us picked up on the stereotyped picture of a queer and started wiggling hips and carrying purses. And who's to say whether queens act that way from cowardice or courage?"

A third man joins in. "I figure the drag queens are like the old slave who had the shit beat out of him until he learned to bow his head and say, 'Yassah, boss,' and think he liked it. Now you young bucks come along and kick him in the ass for acting that way. Feel sorry, man! If you want to kick somebody's ass, go get the guys with the whips in their hands who made that queen turn to drag in the first place."

A quiet, pipe-smoking fourth man says, "I put on a dress a few times, and I bet if we had not been so brainwashed everyone would try on different clothes at different times just like little kids do—to see how it feels to be the kind of person who wears that kind of clothing."

"Right on!" yells a bearded college student. "Drag can be liberating."

The search goes on. The group moves of its own momentum, rooting out internalized prejudice, offering support, exchanging information and experience, in search of identity and self-understanding. The group is reluctant to label someone sick because they are keenly aware of how destructive this simplistic equation of pathology and homosexuality has been.

In the first few groups I decreed a rule that there was to be no behavior that could be understood as sexual intercourse, though sexual arousal was permissible. My reasoning was that it would free participants to explore supposedly sexual attractions without feeling compelled to follow through with behavior leading to orgasm. This rule was helpful to some participants, but in the course of several lively discussions, I was helped to see that by making such a law I was contributing to feelings of guilty illegality when someone from the group had personal valid reasons for interacting sexually. I also was helped to see that I had no right to legislate other humans' sexual behavior when it did not directly involve me and that such a rule hinted at a hidden assumption held by many professionals that sex is bad unless proven otherwise.

I no longer use a no-sex rule but I do suggest that people consider whether such an individually self-imposed rule of thumb might not free a person to explore sexual feelings in a new way. I point out that, as with all other behavior during the weekend, each person must decide for himself what he wants and needs to do at any given moment and be responsible for that decision. I also ask that no behavior, sexual or otherwise, be kept secret from the group.

In most groups, sexual intercourse is discouraged by most of the participants as a possible distraction in the context of the group weekend. As one member said, "If you're looking for action, there's plenty of it at the baths and the bars. If you're looking to get your head together about being gay, this is the place. I've done a little cruising since we've been here but just for fun. If you and I go climb into that sleeping bag in the corner, it would probably be a groove—but later, baby. I want to spend as much time as I can with everybody here because I'm beginning to see we've all got something to offer one another and I need it."

While specific sexual behavior is underplayed, affection is not. Men lean against one another, give back rubs, hold hands, cuddle, and interact physically with one another in comfort that is astonishing to see, only because it makes one vividly aware of the wide range of possibilities and of how absent such skin contact between men is in our everyday world.

At about the same time I started conducting the gay groups, I began to offer general male groups (not restricted to gays) at various growth centers. These groups were titled *On Being a Man* or *Natural Man*. They were not attempts to immerse participants in consideration of homosexuality but were more an outgrowth of the early draft-dodger groups in the college. They were designed to facilitate a kind of male liberation, where a man could consider the difference between cultural definitions of various male roles and his own needs, expectations, and satisfactions in those roles. It was also a natural place to take a good here-and-now look at male-male relationships, and the inevitable talk of homosexuality performed its usual catalytic magic for the group.

With more experience in these groups, I became aware of how much damage is done to the average male by the fear of homosexuality and by the complex misunderstanding of the phenomenon in our culture. Many men who think of themselves as homosexual or bisexual are not liberated by their ability to make sexual contact with other men. They have been told repeatedly that they are abnormal, sick, depraved, wicked, perverted, handicapped, immature, disgusting, and generally not up to expected human standards. Some of this negativism is incorporated into self-concept and distorts relationships with other men and with women. Men are apt to be treated as sex objects and women as objects of fear and complex fantasy. (One man said, "My wife never knew she was sleeping with an enemy alien all those years.") But we have all been taught to expect anyone with admitted homosexual interests to be damaged, so these kinds of observations were not so surprising even when they emerged in the mixed (gay and straight) groups.

The big surprises came with clearer understanding of the straight or supposedly nonhomosexual men. With saddening regularity they described how much they wanted to have closer, more satisfying relationships with other men: "I'd settle for having one really close man friend. I supposedly have some close men friends now. We play golf or go for a drink. We complain about our jobs and our wives. I care about them and they care about me. We even have some physical contact—I mean, we may even give a hug on a big occasion. But it's not enough."

In one group, a huge, soft-spoken Texan who had described himself as a Little League father asked an aggressive middle-aged businessman if he could give him a back rub during the group break time. Half an hour later the businessman was sobbing loudly. When he had gotten to a point where he wanted to talk he told the rest of us that he had flashed a rapid set of mental pictures: his father giving him a nightly ritual back rub in bed that ended abruptly at about age ten with no explanation; a "you hold mine and I'll hold yours" sex play scene with a playmate at about age six; comforting a close Navy buddy in his arms a few hours after he had been wounded and a few days before he died; and sitting in the living room at home looking at his eleven-year-old son and not knowing how to touch him.

His face fell into a mask of mourning as he said, "I've pushed away the wanting because of a scared feeling that it was wrong. Now my dad's dead, my buddy's dead, I never even got to know that kid back home, and my son and I are afraid to touch each other." He started to cry again, turned to the Texan, and said, "If you don't think I'm crazy already, you sure will now, because all I want to say to you, Bill, is 'thanks.' Things may turn out different for my son."

An ex-star of college football turned long-hair dropout asked for six volunteers who would be willing to stand nude in a small circle around him. He said, "I want to shut my eyes and really get into it and see if there's any part of me that wants to get it on with men."

Later he was laughing and saying, "Far out! You know when I was playing ball there was always the locker room fooling around, but all we ever did was slap one another on the ass sometimes. For the last year I've gotten really close to some dudes and wondered what it would be like to make it with one of them—you know, just to give him pleasure because the vibes are good between us. But just now I flashed how important and at the same time absurdly unimportant it all is. I really got into touching you guys, and I didn't turn to stone, man. I got turned on once or twice and it was a groove. I didn't have to do anything and I didn't have to stop myself from doing anything. I could just be there and let the feelings flow back and forth."

He closed his eyes for a quiet moment and a smile spread on his face. "It's beautiful. I can be me with you, and with you, and with you, and whatever is between us is there and we can just let it be. That skin over tight muscle is a whole different trip than a chick. It's like with guys I've been walking around with my eyes tight shut with all kinds of 'should' and 'shouldn't' in my head because I was afraid that if I got into my feelings with dudes I'd find out I was queer or that I had no feelings at all. It's far out! I learned it so long ago with chicks—you know, that you only have to listen to what's there between you and flow with it and not hassle about it and nobody gets hurt."

The theme, sounded time after time, is: "A large segment of my feelings about other men are unknown or distorted because I am afraid they might have something to do with homosexuality. Now I'm lonely for other men and don't know how to find what I want with them."

The spectre of homosexuality seems to be the dragon at the gateway to self-awareness, understanding, and acceptance of male-male needs. If a man tries to pretend the dragon is not there by turning a blind eye to erotic feelings for all other males, he also blinds himself to the rich variety of feelings that are related. If he offers himself up as victim to the dragon by owning awareness and saying "therefore I am queer," he plunges into a type of homosexuality that may be physically gratifying but keeps him occupied with the dragon at the gate (usually compulsively searching for sexual contacts) and just as estranged from the self-awareness, understanding, and acceptance that await him on the other side of the gate.

The dragon need not be at the gate. It is a monster that has been created by our society. Homosexuality is a reality but it need not be a monster. Since it is firmly chained to the gate at this point in the evolution of our culture, however, a man has few choices. He can blind himself to the dragon and be blind to what lies beyond the gate. He can stand far back from the dragon and settle for awareness that there is a barrier between himself and the gate that he is unwilling to confront. He can compulsively interact with the dragon. Or he can confront the dragon—find strength to admit homoerotic impulses, admit that he is a beautiful and impressive dragon (valued along with other things life has to offer, in addition) and pass through the gateway to self-awareness, understanding, and acceptance. The man who has confronted the dragon and tamed him with honesty admits to the dragon's power and beauty and explains that he is also interested in the riches that lie beyond the gate.

Some professional colleagues with whom I have discussed these groups have asked about homosexual panic and the worrisome possibility of turning a latent homosexual into a screaming queen. These fears are developed in a vocabulary that may need revision. I have seen no homosexual panic and suspect that such a psychodynamic phenomenon is impossible in an atmosphere where homosexual awareness is valued and therefore genuinely accepted. Homosexual panic probably needs the catalytic fear of possible punitive reaction to expressed desire, much as a potential fire needs oxygen. Since the group provides no foundation for such fear, it would be an unusual man who could carry enough imagined foundation into the group to actually get his panic-fire going.

The notion of latent homosexuality no longer makes sense to me. My experience suggests that the average man has awareness of the erotic impulses and fantasies stirred by interaction with other males. To be sure, some men store this information in a side room of their awareness, but it is there and they know where to find it. The so-called latent homosexual, with his amazing total lack of awareness of the homoerotic desire that bubbles actively within him, must also have an unconscious warning device that steers him away from all-male encounter groups. At least I have not yet made his acquaintance. It may well be that he is an extremely rare species and that we have produced most latent homosexuals in the eye of the beholder with inaccurate theories of human sexuality. Or it may be that the men who sign up for all-male groups are unusually strong emotionally. Certainly no man is forced to join such a group or forced to participate in any particular activity in the group. But in my experience the fearsome results of opening Pandora's box have failed to materialize. What happens is more like admitting that the emperor has no special robes. It is commonplace for a man to become more sensitive to his homosexual interests during the course of the group experience, but I have seen no panic and no dramatic change of sexual identity.

For groups that I conduct privately, not assembled at growth centers, there is a brief screening interview designed to clarify expectations and the reality of the contract. History of psychotherapeutic experiences, permission to contact any current therapist, fantasied expectations of the weekend, and the fact that homosexual feelings will be directly confronted are ingredients of the interview, but less than 4 per cent of the men interested in an all-male group have been discouraged by the interview.

While there is overlap in format from gay group to mixed male group, they differ in emphasis. The mixed male group pays quite a lot of attention to homosexuality, but the focus is on the oppressive tyranny of male roles in our culture. The major task is to become more aware of differences between satisfying yourself and satisfying your culture in the ways you shape your male roles. The usual mixed male group gives fraternal support to the individual as he searches for his own truth. Aggression and competition are discouraged as part of the usual cultural oppression of males. Clear statements of vulnerability and need are supported.

The first evening session of the mixed group is an overture with themes of the weekend to come. As in the gay groups, each entering man is invited to silently find his feelings about each of the other men and review his expectations for the weekend. Sensory awareness and relaxation are followed by some attention to self-concepts through the creation of self masks with two faces. There is meditation, talk of expectations and fears, body contact that tends to elicit erotic feelings, and introduction to the use of "want ads."

One wall is usually designated the community bulletin

board, and there is a suggested ground rule that each man have at least one want displayed on the bulletin board at all times. When that want is invalidated by satisfaction or time, it must be replaced by at least one more want. Many ads have to do with physical contact, ranging from a foot massage to a request to be bathed and rocked. Many are as simple as a want to have someone to get an ice cream soda with. Much of the content has a remedial flavor, a catching up with things missed somewhere back along the way.

Saturday morning is a quiet time filled with silent focus on self, alone but in the presence of others. Many men make use of available art materials during this time. Some, to their own amazement, write poems or create admirable pictures. Afternoon is devoted to group remembering. People share memories of the past and there is bittersweet laughter about secret sore spots that seem less important in the light of sharing. This sharing can lead to an impromptu dance lesson, pillow fight, or Boy Scout initiation ceremony as long remembered past wishes float to the surface. The evening is focused on self-concept, starting with each man talking about his body and getting corrective feedback, where appropriate, from the entire group.

The final morning starts with review of what has happened for each man and the ways in which he is satisfied and dissatisfied with the weekend. The remainder of the morning offers an opportunity to satisfy wants in the context of here and now with awareness of feelings attached to risk-taking. Finally they talk of what parts of the weekend learning can be taken from the artificial group community back into the everyday world.

Scattered throughout the weekend are verbal sharing times with the asked or unasked question, "What does all this have to do with the man you want to be?" The group becomes sensitive to oppression and skillful at distinguishing the ways society imposes it and the ways it is self-imposed.

All-male groups, whether gay or mixed, question basic assumptions about masculinity. Each man is offered help in finding what he has to give and what he wants to receive from other men as a way of increasing his understanding and acceptance of self. He is offered support in tracking down his homosexual feelings and separating them from other masculine affectional feelings so that they can be experienced in perspective. To some men, a surprising by-product is more satisfying interaction with women and children. The most obvious probable reason is that he comes to each relationship less disguised in restrictive he-man roles and he is thereby less likely to encourage reaction in equally restrictive roles.

Apparently, homosexual self-understanding (which is accompanied by understanding of a wide spectrum of male-male affectional needs) is a necessary facet of male liberation. (My work in mixed groups of females and males leads me to suspect that the same is true for women.) It is a necessary step in throwing off the yoke of society's voice saying, "If you want to be a man you must . . . you should . . . you dare not." Such self-understanding is a necessary step toward manhood if that state implies having all parts of emotional self intact and available. Homosexual encounter is useful in any all-male growth group, and it would be a strange men's group in which it did not surface.

24

Ethnotherapy in Groups

Price M. Cobbs

For the past ten years I have gathered clinical evidence and studied mental functioning related to racial attitudes. These studies point to a clinical model capable of changing attitudes about race. To this model I have given the name *ethnotherapy*.

In my psychiatric practice I treat many black patients, the majority poor, and a few not so poor. Over the years in this broadly representative pool of patients I have noted a general shift in a specific attitude. At the beginning of the study I recorded that many blacks were either reluctant or psychologically unable to discuss in any depth the influence of skin color on their lives. The subject of race was usually introduced and stressed by the therapist rather than mentioned spontaneously by the patient. Then, as if a dam had collapsed, black patients began discussing its profound implications for them and their situations.

An important factor in the growing ability to talk about racial matters was the exploding social climate of the 1960s. Blacks in great numbers were emerging from a dormant period.

Many were marching, sitting-in, and protesting. The social turbulence resonated deep within individuals, and blacks far removed from active participation in demanding their rights openly responded. In homes, on street corners, in church—in short, everywhere—blacks began to shatter a previous silence and were eager not only to discuss race but often little else.

My patients began actively to initiate talk about "what it's like to be black," opening up new dimensions in their lives and also in the psychotherapeutic process. Patients who for years had talked unproductively about narrow aspects of their lives suddenly saw themselves against the background of American society. Many searched their own experiences with the excitement of adventurers, for the first time honestly weighing the color of their skin. For example, an individual would finally recognize and confront his self-hatred (the gravest psychological wound inflicted upon the oppressed). This dissection, painful to the patient and requiring great skill of the therapist, formerly had taken protracted months and years. Now it was anticipated eagerly by both with the knowledge that the person might quickly undo years of self-depreciation and crippling inhibitions. Another would report a casual discussion with a friend concerning discrimination in securing a job, and in the recounting, random thoughts coupled with newly released feelings and a fresh insight would appear.

I should state categorically here that extensive and deeply felt changes were noted and recorded. I am not suggesting superficial shifts in behavior or transient alterations in thoughts stimulated by a compelling social event. I cross-checked incessantly, studied extensive background material, and followed up my patients. In this explosive social area the stakes are high, and I wanted to be dead certain that the results could withstand the most rigorous scrutiny. Thus, my clinical data give more than ample evidence of the long-lasting nature of these changes.

Most importantly, whatever their presenting problems, at some point in the treatment process most patients for the first time became acutely aware of constant anger and rage, not directed at a specific person, but at white America. This emerging black rage exerted a healing effect on many a tortured psyche. Tightly held in by chronic depression and self-hatred, an enormous reservoir of psychic energy was turned outward and directed toward society. Daily many blacks improved their emotional state by no longer rationalizing and passively adjusting to a society which they had always known hated them.

I reached the conclusion that with therapist and patient attacking problems along the axis of blackness in America, a catalytic effect occurred. Moreover, in reflecting on these findings I ventured the thought that blacks in this country share common factors in their view of the world which gives their psychological lives a uniquely different cast.

When a child is born into a society which daily offers the view that he is inferior by virtue of inheriting more melanin, kinky hair, or thick lips, a distorted self-image is too often the outcome. This characterological scarring occurs to some degree in the psychological growth and development of all non-white Americans. The malignancy of white racism exerts its effect regardless of how benign the early family and social atmosphere. The clinical work leading to *Black Rage* (Grier and Cobbs, 1968) showed that if enough of these negative perceptions about self are explored and understood by the patient they can be transformed into a powerful, constructive force for positive change in the personality.

As one result of success with black patients, I was encouraged to initiate more discussions of race with white patients. During the turbulent sixties, they too were increasingly preoccupied with race in America, as the civil rights period highlighted the strivings of black people and focused on various aspects of racism. Whatever else occurred, for the first time many white people were forced to think about blacks.

Introducing race into the therapeutic process adds a drive and intensity which melts resistance and permits a much fuller view into the recesses of the psyche. I have long believed that many personal problems of both blacks and whites are at bottom related to race. When racial conflict is personally experienced or even thought about, an individual is more likely to take a critical look at himself. Another insight derived from dealing with race in therapy is that *all* blacks store abundant memories of how their color negatively influences their life in America. These stored memories contain terrible pain, and as a matter of psychic economy, most blacks suppress them and hold them away from view. My findings also suggest that whites increasingly have their own memory bank about what it's like to be black. But while blacks acquire their memories in confrontations with a hostile, white-dominated society, whites gather their conclusions by observation and generally in the absence of any interaction.

What the majority of white people do is to define and describe blacks as the opposite of whites in every way. Having so defined them, they unknowingly measure everything blacks say or do against a white standard rigged to make blacks appear inferior. This comparison is made universally by white Americans. Its universality and its importance belie the myths stating that racial prejudice is inversely related to education, social class, or emotional maturity.

As a result of these and other conclusions, I was forced to look beyond the immediate lives of my patients and search deep into history. I can only conclude that in a distant time when the fortunes of war left the white European to contemplate his victories and to write his history, white thoughts and acts came to be considered civilized while those of dark-skinned people were dimissed as primitive. In the ineluctable march of history white supremacy became a permanent fixture. Thoughts were created to account for it and Christianity was bent to justify it. Feelings of superiority and inferiority based on color were accepted by societies and each generation they were driven deeper and deeper into the unconscious of individuals. Customs and conventions were erected, and where race entered, fact became fiction and fantasy became truth.

An interface was formed which separated not only races of men but man from himself. This cleavage allowed conquerors and colonizers to exploit, plunder, and exterminate darker people without the slightest remorse. A critical cornerstone of racial hatred was imported to America by the first white emigrants. It became permanent first in individual whites and then in the

national character with the massacre of native American Indians and the brutal enslavement of Africans. It remains in the
gentlest of Americans and is now called white racism.

The malignant disease of bigotry does not yield to the
passage of time, the enactment of laws, or the effects of education. Racism is rarely openly expressed; it is not *openly* taught
by parents or teachers and is not identifiable by geographic
regions. More often than not, Americans acquire attitudes about
blacks which are the result of a twisted and distorted group
logic, a logic rarely examined critically. Racism comes at white
Americans from so many directions that education affords no
barrier. The most educated man may be the most bigoted.

In those the disease attacks, many normal physiological
and psychological processes are interrupted and made deviant:
For people of color there is scarcely a pathological process of
body or mind which is not adversely affected by white racism.
For those harboring the disease, it creates a faulty mental set,
affecting the functions of thinking and feeling. If, in the young
science of psychiatry, we can poorly understand the etiology
of schizophrenia and yet label it a mental disease, surely white
racism with its more known vectors can be called a disease.

In *Black Rage* and *The Jesus Bag* (Grier and Cobbs,
1971), we use case histories to document the effects of racial
prejudice on the psychological life of blacks in America. It
creates a surging anger which if not understood and corrected
will surely see this country destroy its ethical aspirations in
racial warfare. Because my experience told me that the rage of
blacks is in response to the hatred of whites, and because I am
convinced that there must be a rapid reduction of both, I have
made this interaction my primary clinical and theoretical challenge.

A few studies and books in the past century (notably
The Authoritarian Personality, Adorno and others, 1950) raised
black hopes by pointing out that individuals with psychological
insight about their own mental functioning had greater capacity
to develop insights about the society in which they lived. This
deduction suggested that a significant number of people would
better understand prejudice in society and hopefully be moved

to eliminate it if they better understood their inner lives. But since 1950 as a greater number of individuals have sought relief for emotional problems, this understanding has not occurred. Few patients *or* therapists have recognized the cultural pact existing between individuals and their society to hide the flaw of racial hatred. Even fewer have considered racial prejudice a mental disease to be diagnosed and treated.

More recent studies purporting to demonstrate that in small groups an increase in an individual's self-acceptance leads to reduction in racial prejudice contain little rigor. There is to me scientific naivete in the assumption that an individual can identify and understand a malignant disease and one endemic to his society and yet never directly attack the disease in himself or in his society.

One bleak result of the scarcity of accurate information about racial pressure is evident to those few of us occupied scientifically with the final eradication of this disease. There are no reproducible models or techniques with which individuals, groups, and institutions can wage war on racial hatred with any reasonable confidence of success. When I had worked with enough individual patients to be satisfied with my findings, I set out to create such a model.

Since the etiology of racism is so much a group phenomenon, a small group seemed a logical place to test my findings and try to start the process of correction. The obvious attraction of group work for the therapist is the opportunity to influence many more people. As a black psychiatrist, attempting to cure racial prejudice, I found this attraction paramount. I felt the interaction between group members, black and white, would bring out the more dangerous problems. Also, at the minimum, a group would be an excellent setting to help individuals share the mounting volume of information about blacks.

I was aware that during the past forty years there have been other attempts to resolve social problems by group actions. But I also knew these attempts had rarely involved the specific study of the dynamics of prejudice. A clinical model used in certain of these attempts was the T-group and laboratory method. Some of the great work of Kurt Lewin, whose field theory included action research in producing social change, made this model possible.

Although social action was a primary concern of those founding the T-group movement in 1946, this concern has faded over the years. Since that time, training and encounter groups have proliferated in schools and industry, but prejudice has seldom been the focus of this work. Personal growth and an awareness of the senses are stressed, and these groups have been led by skilled professionals or, at times, amateurs. The object is to persuade an individual to observe both his own behavior and that of others in the group. Though the distinction is hazy, the difference between the groups described here and group therapy is that the latter treats the emotionally disturbed, while the former tries to improve the interpersonal relations of normal people. For my work, perhaps the most important function served by encounter and sensitivity groups is that they have encouraged "normals" to participate in groups without fear of being labeled medically sick. This factor was tremendously important when I began to use small groups for treating racial prejudice.

The first psychotherapy groups written about took place in the early 1900s in this country and consisted of people who shared the same problem, the then dreaded and frequently fatal disease of tuberculosis. At that time theoretical awareness of the group process was limited; however, clear parallels were suggested in the use of a group setting to attack a disease shared by all participants. In later years Alcoholics Anonymous and more recently the treatment of drug abuse has demonstrated the same principle. The success of these examples indicated that people suffering from similar problems, problems caused in part by society, find a strengthened ability to solve them when the problems are seen in concert rather than singly.

Are not black people suffering from problems caused by their society? Is the prejudice heaped upon them not a disease every bit as virulent as tuberculosis and as socially disabling as alcoholism or drug addiction? Are not their personalities crippled in ways which make it likely they can help each other? Such an examination of the black experience strongly suggested that a group format held promise as an effective instrument for treating certain aspects and consequences of racial prejudice. With honestly motivated whites as participants, trying to discover how they acquired racial prejudice and probing its usually unseen pathological effect on their personal lives, at the minimum a microcosm of cause and effect could be constructed.

And so the first experimental group using techniques directed at racial differences was held in July 1967 (brilliantly described by George Leonard in *Education and Ecstasy*, 1967). In this group more than a third of the participants were black, and included were a young Nisei and an immigrated Chinese-American. The initial group was not intended primarily as psychotherapy; rather our aim was to conduct a small group consisting of individuals of different backgrounds in an honest examination of attitudes and feelings.

Overwhelmingly, the whites in the first group considered themselves educated and tolerant, if not avant-garde, in their attitudes concerning racial matters. Yet, once the group began, it was apparent that whites almost to a person came less to gain greater understanding of themselves and their own prejudices than to place blacks once again under the microscope of "interracial understanding." It was also clear that the blacks were there for more compelling emotional reasons. Of high priority was the need to vent rage, first at each other and then at the whites present.

Techniques for leading this type of group were in an early stage of development, but we were determined to go much beyond the usual process of blacks explaining themselves and whites either indicting or exculpating themselves. We wanted to make certain that this and subsequent groups did not deteriorate into frivolous exercises.

The departure point and theme were the participants' thoughts, attitudes, and feelings regarding race. The task of the two leaders was to make certain that communications were clear, that clarification and interpretations were timely, and that in the end the group's processes were therapeutic and growth-producing for all.

People sat in a circle so that each could see the others,

and everything said was confidential. Participants were encouraged to interact vigorously and honestly in pointing out inconsistencies and falsehoods in the communications of fellow participants. They were instructed to strive for honesty and openness, to give personal history only when it related to how they came to the group. For the life of the group, ritualized politeness and reserve were suspended in an effort to achieve maximum group interaction.

Finally, I was eager to try the specific methods of direct inquiry about race which had proven so valuable an adjunct to individual therapy. Information would be challenged, examined, and discarded if necessary. The leaders would be active in describing inconsistencies and use all their knowledge of personality dynamics and group functioning to help the participants understand their words and actions on the subject of race.

Even with the newness of the technique, intellectual vigor and emotional intensity—usually long coming in other small groups—were noted very early. Ideas exploded and strong feelings quickly sprang forth. We immediately realized that we did not need to "soup-up" the group with gimmicks or parlor games.

We decided to have the techniques of group leadership flow from a black life style, rather than from the standard, more restrained clinical models. This decision immediately allowed the group to be more open and direct and, above all, to be more comfortable in expressing feelings. I wanted to contribute the sensitivity and thoughtfulness of traditional individual and group therapy. This approach, I reasoned, would allow a faster and deeper entry into the hidden vaults of the psyche, while adhering to professional ethics which respected all participants.

After the first effort, a group of mental health professionals, black and white, came together to regularly hold what we at first called racial confrontation groups and then later ethnotherapy. Under laboratory conditions, new leadership methods were tried and constantly refined. After each group, leaders exchanged information covering all aspects of the process. In order to effectively develop this exciting new group format, these seasoned clinicians drew from all previous training and experience. Early in our discussions I became convinced that we were indeed creating a specific treatment method capable of definitively altering the effects—on victim and victimizer alike—of racial prejudice.

Each session was dissected minutely. A weekend group would last twenty hours, over two days. Afterward, the known individual history, method of participation in the group, and personality characteristics of each participant were studied in detail. Lengthy analyses containing all available information were written on every participant.

When the subject of racial prejudice was first introduced in the group, why did some whites sit in total silence while others engaged in non-stop talking? What were the underlying psychological dynamics of a young, aggressive black man who verbally would viciously attack a quiet black woman and yet blatantly ignore a racial slight by a white woman? Could we correctly identify and subsequently predict some of the family interactions and social forces which shaped individual responses made in a group?

We probed the deeper reasons why people—black or white—came to the ethnotherapy groups, an intense and fatiguing two days, all the while protesting that they were free of racial prejudice. After spending considerable time in conducting groups, study, and discussion, we began to see a form and shape emerge for our groups.

Under the present format, groups are held over a two-day period, usually a weekend. They last from ten to twelve hours each day. Experience told us that these sessions were long enough for each person present to interact with the group in sufficient depth to achieve the desired level of intensity. The ideal group size is between twelve and fourteen with an equal division of men and women and at least six blacks. We often include members of other oppressed American minorities as participants and as leaders. Participation is always voluntary.

The basic rules of our ethnotherapy groups are very simple. The here and now is stressed, but participants are encouraged to supply enough details from their life history so that each may be understood in depth by the others. This personalization minimizes the tendency of group members to draw and respond to stereotyped conclusions. Also, the confidential nature of the group is underlined at the beginning and repeated throughout. The groups are a dynamic and intense experience and breaches of confidentiality have proven no more a problem than they are in any form of therapy. In discussing racial matters, however, many people want reassurance that their words have no destructive aftermath.

This work was given a tremendous boost when a research grant was secured to conduct a Racial Confrontation Group Project with participants drawn from the University of California at San Francisco, a widely renowned medical center. We therefore had access to an educationally diverse and racially mixed population of more than 10,000 people; we hoped people from this setting would resist acknowledging racial prejudice as a mental disease less than does the general population. We were able to hold groups regularly and scientifically match samples for outcome. In over two and a half years, more than one hundred groups and fourteen hundred individuals have been seen and followed up. The exciting results of this crucial study will be published at the end of 1972.

A study of racial prejudice in the United States provided a rationale for some of the techniques we developed and used. Since the most cursory look reveals that blacks are really not listened to by most whites, in the groups blacks are encouraged to speak up and talk louder if necessary. Eliminated is the usual cultural surgery of brutally laying bare the innards of the victim while blithely ignoring the victimizer. We deliberately create a climate where those who are usually ignored can be heard. And, as in all effective psychological interchanges, we do not discourage language which reflects the life people live; obscenities are heard with equanimity. Such acceptance of varying life styles and their modes of expression permits an acceleration of intense interaction.

We stress active participation by each person, rather than merely passive learning. Individuals must react and respond to real people in a real-life situation instead of play acting. The cutting edge of the instrument which facilitates the process and makes therapeutic change possible is the ability of the leaders to help participants jar loose, dissect, and examine in fine detail the usual information about race which our society makes certain we all receive and too often incorporate. What comes out is an astonishing variety of biases, fears, and appalling lack of knowledge.

Most of this misinformation is held by the majority of white Americans, but as it is antithetical to the expressed democratic ethos it is deliberately kept from awareness. Such misguided feelings and attitudes are available, nonetheless, and intelligent and skillful prodding brings them into the open. Where many are resistant, if not ashamed, to acknowledge these fears and lies in isolation, the presence of others facilitates this self-observation. A relaxation of shame occurs when they realize that others share the same thoughts.

Although each group has a life of its own, our hypothesis and methods provide a definite pattern of several stages. First, there is the initial explanation of the purpose and format of the group. All participants are told they must make a commitment to remain until the end of the group, and unlike members of other groups, our participants rarely break this pledge. It is explained in detail that all communications will be verbal. Feelings about race are too explosive to flirt with the danger of physical retaliation. Participants are encouraged to be open and honest in whatever they say. Although instructions are given to try to let only one person speak at a time, in the beginning interruptions are frequent. Then, as the group coalesces, the right of individuals to not be interrupted is rigidly respected.

A starting point might be to ask each participant to tell something about himself and why he came. This request brings forth various biographical details such as age and occupation, and occasionally a person is interrupted by the nervous laughter of a self-conscious joke. This early in the group, participants engage in the social jockeying which people have developed to express one thought while thinking another.

Participants are invited to discuss what being black or

white means to them personally and then what it means against the backdrop of the American social milieu. How does the fact of skin color influence daily decisions? What thoughts and feelings are stimulated when the person examines himself in light of social definitions of who is acceptable and nonacceptable in this country. Further, what discussions, recent and remote, has an individual had about the reality of skin color, both for himself and for others.

This invitation leads to a certain amount of verbal sparring seen in most groups and generally attributable to anxiety. One group might first discuss "race relations." During this period (and leaders keep it as brief as possible) every worn cliche from past decades of cocktail conversation is tentatively offered up for discussion. "Is Stokely Carmichael really as militant as H. Rap Brown?" "Martin Luther King was really a great man, but . . ." And then someone, invariably an earnest, well-scrubbed white young man with short hair and no sideburns, begins a soliloquy with "If only Malcolm X lived!"

During this stage, called racial and personal exploration, the leaders use their utmost powers of intelligent observation to make an accurate early assessment of each participant. What are the characteristics of individuals in the group? What are their expectations? Leaders must be skillful in quickly evaluating the personality patterns, intellectual capacity, and verbal facility of each person. In their early words and actions, who seems sensitive and who is insensitive? Does someone appear depressed, and is another unusually nervous? What is the racial and sexual composition of the group, and how might this affect the process of the group? Who immediately begins talking and why, and who shrinks into a corner? Is the anxiety level of the group too high for effective interaction, and, if so, how can it be lowered? Hours of discussions, supervision, and previous experience must now crystallize into a thought-out plan of action. Who needs prodding and who needs support? There are always those who soon reveal their emotional fragility and need the therapeutic protection of the leaders.

Leaders actively help individuals and then the group to set goals. With racial conflict everywhere so close to breaking point, our thinking is that each participant must be urged to immediately convert new information and fresh insights into vigorous action outside the group.

Close to the beginning, a black may launch an attack on a white, and two factors are immediately clear. The black is very angry and the white is very hurt by the attack. My findings suggest that this peculiar sensitivity of most whites is born of denial; they take on a defensive, self-righteous posture, all the while professing ignorance of the reason for the attack and what it means. They hear angry words and immediately speak of morality and propriety. Then someone may give a lengthy discourse on how the "race problem" will remain unsolved until blacks stop ruffling people's feelings. Surprisingly—and this occurence is so consistent as to constitute a rule—they do not at this stage mention the content of the attack, only the form. This leads to a necessarily frank discussion of common stereotypes about blacks spoken aloud and discussed here for the first time in a racially mixed group. As the depth of the hostility and contempt is called to view, whites deny that they hold such attitudes.

In response, black participants counterattack, first with disbelief, then anger. It is as if they say to themselves, "How can you take us to be such fools?" Aloud, they say, "We know from long and bitter experience with whites that all are foes, that you in this room have the very same thoughts as the rest of the bastards. Why don't you own up to it. We already know. We know not by the words you speak, but by your actions toward us." The blacks are stunned as they realize that whites really believe the lies they tell themselves—and that blacks share belief in many of those lies.

Then, voices lose a bit of stridency, words become less frequent, and the room is quiet. People sit and stare at each other with a look of disbelief. They know without a word being spoken that in this incredible gulf of difference lies the sickness of racial prejudice.

As we gained more experience we began to note a point in each group where no obscure interpretation was required. Two men, one black and the other white, argue violently over whether a grown man should feel offended if called "boy." After an obscenity slips out unexpectedly, a strained silence hangs over the group. Then the argument resumes, voices lower, and the words spoken are carefully chosen; a condescending tone creeps in which is familiar to every black in the room. White participants demonstrate repeatedly by word and deed that even though their attitude is hidden, they come to the group convinced of their superiority over blacks.

The next distinct stage of the group is labeled the period of black exploration. Black participants probe their lives against a backdrop of social issues of the day. They try to define black identity or to identify how the word *black* came into use. Whites are silent during this period, which generally lasts at least several hours. The blacks continue talking until someone mutters self-consciously that she is revealing too much of herself and whites should not be around. Another chimes in that certain issues should never be discussed in front of whites because "you can't trust them."

With this, they turn to the black leader. Can he be trusted? There follows a barrage of questions on specifics of the black experience. "Is he together?" "Can we really let our hair down here?" "Are you really black or are you another cop-out Negro?" "What do you know about Malcolm?" "How do you stand on Black Nationhood?" Subtly the blacks have formed an alliance.

A few of the whites fidget and whisper. Finally, the questions—"Is this why we came?" "Are we here for two days just to listen to blacks?" "What about us?" There is an accusation that the assembled blacks are not really as angry and therefore as real as a "genuine" militant known to a white participant.

The next stage, black-white confrontation, is a natural, orderly consequence of allowing, even encouraging, the group to polarize. American society has done so thorough a job that only a nudge is necessary. The whites, now apart, turn inward to question themselves rather than querying blacks.

"Don't attack me, I've been for colored people all my life." There is a nervous shift of topics, and the dialogue turns to white guilt. One leader describes the nature of guilt and its effect when it is in ascendancy. Such cannot describe the white treatment of blacks. It is vital that the world perceived by blacks be seen clearly so that it can be distinguished from the world of white perception. If a white man interprets the world for a black, he shoves the black into a disastrous misapprehension. We stress that difference, gross and subtle, between the perceptions of blacks and whites.

At such a point in the group the leaders must be especially skillful in pointing up mindless stereotypes, lack of reasoning, and flights into rhetoric. One notion triggers the next, and there seems no end to the demeaning, dehumanizing thoughts of people when they speak of race.

In time the statements come to have a less arrogant ring. A participant tells a most private thing, obviously not intended for public consumption, and after a pause a head shakes in disbelief. There is a questing, amorphous quality to the group. With each passing hour facades slip away and more is revealed. Superficial meanderings suddenly stop in midsentence. Finally a white participant says, "I don't know." From then on a difference is felt in the group. We are now at the stage of ethnotherapy.

Feelings and thoughts surface quickly and are expressed flinchingly. The material is now often of a most intimate quality having little to do with race, or at least seeming so. Private miseries of marriage and family come to the fore. The mood of the group is intense. Pain is shared. A few pioneers expose long-buried secrets and are astonished at finding support in twelve other people. With our technique, without exception, each group has an electrifying moment when a participant grits his teeth and tells a "shameful" secret. The alchemy of the small-group setting frees these previously bound emotions. In the process they are intensified, and the group adds to them a contagious quality.

The ability of a group to stimulate emotions was first described by group therapist S. R. Slavson. Where the prevailing mood of a group is tense, hostile feelings can be released and elevated to an intense, even unbearable pitch by the group process. Inherent in this setting is the potential for mutual induction and intensification of all psychic processes. These powerful possibilities call for trained and sensitive group leaders.

Such insights compelled us to refine our techniques still further, since no other issue of our time has greater capacity than race for arousing tension and hostility. With such potent material as the crucial variable in this carefully worked out technique, the groups have a predictable essence. The leaders come to recognize and expect certain maneuvers and defense mechanisms which are repeated in each group.

The most predictable response is an expression of strong, deeply felt negative attitudes about blacks. The manner of a friendly young white man, too effusive and cheerful, is paradigmatic. He arrives early, grins at everyone, and shakes hands. He announces that he is free of prejudice and loves all races. But as the group begins he sits between two whites and stares at the floor. In time the reason for his anxiety and protestations becomes clear. He has many racist attitudes.

There is generally a participant, white or black, who comes to the group seeking only information. His statement is taken at face value, until time reveals that whenever anything is offered as information he already knows the answer. Such investigators find it particularly difficult to accept information from a black leader.

As noted earlier, we turned early to the question of why people wanted to attend groups. Several predispositions were common to most of our participants. Many whites voiced a belief, apparently honestly felt, that they were free of prejudice and therefore came to learn more about themselves. As an afterthought, a few added that they also came to help other whites become prejudice-free. Some whites, the overwhelming majority being mental health professionals or teachers, refined this statement and expressed a desire to learn the technique. With this desire they sought to exempt themselves from examination. As in any small group, a number of people came to satisfy curiosity. A handful of whites openly stated a desire to understand and change their own prejudice, and hopefully their number is increasing. With the wide distribution and discussion of the Kerner Commission Report a rising number of whites are now moved to ask themselves: "Am I a white racist?"

Then we finally discovered whether we were in fact identifying and treating a mental disease that affected all Americans. We noted that whatever the increment of racial prejudice possessed by people who came to the group, they shared a vague sense of some missing ingredient in their lives. Among other things, the alienation and rebellion of white youth is an important symptom of this society-wide phenomenon.

In searching deeper for reasons for this consistent finding we came to other conclusions. In a country historically ordered to demonstrate the notion that white is superior to black, most individuals are affected in ways they scarcely know. As long as social groupings are not examined for their root causes, those on top (whites) can function as if everything is fine. But an examination has been occurring, and the gut feelings of the rightness of things is beginning to crumble. This country has now had a generation of blacks pointing out not only the malignant effects on them of the social order but, and this is just as important, gradually demonstrating something about their own lives and culture. As blacks actively reclaim their history, many whites, too, are forced to examine American history.

This process has served to make blacks more proud and assertive, in addition to giving their lives more meaning and direction. In many whites we have observed the opposite effect. To the extent that most white Americans have incorporated being an American as part of their personal identity, certain psychological issues accrue that cannot be avoided. If a person lives in a society which has always taken great pains to deny and distort a basic value system of white supremacy, then that same society creates the conditions under which most individuals will develop and mirror the same value system.

The mere fact of being an American has heretofore allowed any white to favorably compare his life to that of a black. But now, as the examination goes deeper and information is shared more rapidly and more completely, something goes wrong. Where blacks seem to have a vitality and a joie de vivre, many whites feel an emptiness in their lives. And in their most secret hours the scars of white racism whisper to them that blacks, whatever their labeled deficiencies, possess a vital element of the human spirit which they themselves are lacking. And now a few know that if they are to reclaim this element blacks must serve as therapists and teachers.

With blacks, motivation for attending the group is more directly related to seeking relief. Whatever reason is stated openly, the need to ventilate frustration and hostility is foremost. Guiding and regulating the expression of rage tests the skill of the group leaders, and the absence of such skills is a major factor in the failure of most so-called racial encounter groups. They become mere exercises in catharsis.

While we acknowledge that ventilation is an absolute necessity in a group with the aim of releasing suppressed feelings, leaders must have the training and experience to accomplish this without damage to any individual. The explosiveness of the groups is impressive, and the potential dangers quite early led us to see the need for serious leaders with a passionate commitment to healing.

Each of our groups has a black and a white leader and we use both men and women. This pairing has proven of inestimable value and allows us to plan actions based on predictions of behavior in the group. For example, we are certain that in each group someone will use the word *primitive* in describing something said by the black leader. It matters not what it is. Likewise, the black leader is expected to show more feelings (soul) and possess less intelligence than does the white leader. On the other hand, early in each group, some participant will use the word *weak* to describe the white leader. In the absence of facts, a soliloquy begins which leads to: "How else can a white person work on equal par with blacks?"

The white leader is assumed to have more technical competence and intellectual skill but at the same time is thought professionally inadequate, or else why is he there? These consistent differences in perceiving the leaders are of great help, not only in further perfecting our instrument but also as a living demonstration to the group of the many ways that Americans, black and white, have from birth incorporated racist ideas.

A primary task of the leaders is to create for the group a supportive climate of trust and confidence. They must guide the group expertly and know when to evoke feelings, when to search for buried thoughts, and when to leave them alone. Most importantly, they must help all participants develop a sense of relating to real human beings in order to put an end to the American tradition of dehumanization.

All the leaders are mental health professionals with group experience, and before leading an ethnotherapy group they undergo at least eighty to one hundred hours of direct training in this technique. They also participate in and observe many groups before actually leading a group. They must demonstrate a high order of sensitivity to the experience of oppressed people, have specific skills in group leadership, and cover an extensive reading list. These leaders must be equipped with a rare blend of passion, intelligence, and specific training.

We train and use associate leaders. They are individuals who possess the intuitive gifts of insight and empathy and who instinctively take to the group process. After a lengthy training period they work under the supervision of the leaders. An associate leader might be a young black undergraduate, a welfare mother of little formal education, or an older housewife with previous group training. We also frequently inject a specialist in the group, such as a teacher with an extensive knowledge of black history.

All participants are rigorously screened prior to the group to weed out those with obvious psychological maladies which might make the experience harmful. We have found the labels liberal and conservative to have little validity in our groups. By using trained leaders and judicious screening we have been able to avoid the group casualties both described and whispered about following other forms of group encounter. Also, there is an open follow-up for any individual who desires to bring up something in a more intimate setting or to get a referral for treatment.

Many observations from groups have provided further

evidence for an expansion of the views offered in *Black Rage* and *The Jesus Bag*. I say that the black man in America has had to develop certain personality characteristics and psychic defenses which are separate and distinct from those of white Americans. He has done this in order to survive both physically and psychologically. The first case in point is the black norm, an explicit wariness and suspiciousness which is a necessary part of the armor of blackness. While such traits might in whites be labeled as pathology, I view them as necessary for black survival and by definition healthy. And I see these traits demonstrated repeatedly in groups. When whites refer to blacks as having "a chip on the shoulder," it means that certain defenses are working. The individual is protecting himself from danger, and a hostile manner is many times a part of defense. Blacks must base their functioning on the fact that racial attack can always occur, and in order to survive they must be ready.

A high price is paid when the total personality must maintain constant vigilance, standing ready for flight or fight. Protection from danger of all kinds takes highest priority, and it is rarely absent from any human transaction. Such people are adroit at reacting and responding, but their personalities may interlock with the oppressive society to inhibit initiative. Worst of all they may come to view themselves as natural victims. In response to pressure they develop a personal and a group identity which gives them the role of victim. They assume that they deserve it.

Carried to a logical conclusion, this self-view indicates the existence of a psychology of the oppressed separate and distinct from that of the oppressor. Individuals facing a society in which they are victimized may never develop even a conception of being able to master that society. Our studies tell us that a person only needs to be black in America for this perception to be true. The society never pays off for him. All the rules, the institutions, and structures have a payoff for the oppressors and not the victims. In the explosive interaction of victim confronting oppressor this attitude now *must* be changed, and I think one way is to apply the process of ethnotherapy.

Bibliography

ADLER, A. *Understanding Human Nature*. New York: Fawcett World, 1968.

ADORNO, T. W., FRENKEL-BRUNSWICK, E., LEVINSON, D. J., and SANFORD, R. M. *The Authoritarian Personality*. New York: Harper, 1950.

AMERICAN PSYCHIATRIC ASSOCIATION. *Diagnostic and Statistical Manual of Mental Disorders*. (2nd ed.) Washington, D.C., 1968.

AMERICAN PSYCHIATRIC ASSOCIATION. *Encounter Groups and Psychiatry*. Task Force Report 1. Washington, D.C., 1970.

AMERICAN PSYCHOLOGICAL ASSOCIATION. *Casebook on Ethical Standards of Psychologists*. Washington, D.C., 1967.

ANONYMOUS. "The Great Escape." *Wall Street Journal*, 1971, *84* (35), 1.

ARGYRIS, C. "On the Future of Laboratory Education." *Journal of Applied Behavioral Science*, 1967, *3*, 153–183.

ASCH, S. E. "Interpersonal Influence: Effects of Group Pressure upon the Modification and Distortion of Judgments." In E. E. Maccoby, T. M. Newcomb, and E. L. Hartley (Eds.), *Readings in Social Psychology*. New York: Holt, Rinehart and Winston, 1958.

AUERSWALD, E. "Interdisciplinary Versus Ecological Approach." *Family Process*, 1968, *7*, 202–215.

AXLINE, V. M. *Play Therapy*. Boston: Houghton Mifflin, 1947.

BACH, G. R. *Intensive Group Therapy*. New York: Ronald, 1954.

BACH, G. R. "The Marathon Group: Intensive Practice of Intimate, Interaction." *Psychological Reports*, 1966, *18*, 995–1002.

BACH, G. R. "Marathon Group Dynamics: II. Dimensions of Helpfulness: Therapeutic Aggression." *Psychological Reports*, 1967, *20*, 1147–1158.

BACH, G. R. "Discussion." *International Journal of Group Psychotherapy*, 1968, *18*, 244–249.

BACK, K. *Sensitivity Training and the Search for Salvation.* New York: Russell Sage Foundation, 1972.

BALINT, M. "The Concepts of Subject and Object in Psychoanalysis." *British Journal of Medical Psychology*, 1958, *31*, 83–91.

BARRETT-LENNARD, G. "The Relationship Inventory: Revision Process." Mimeographed paper. Ontario, Canada: University of Waterloo, 1970.

BATCHELDER, R. L., and HARDY, J. M. *Using Sensitivity Training and the Laboratory Method: An Organizational Case Study in the Development of Human Resources.* New York: Association Press, 1968.

BATESON, G., JACKSON, D., HALEY, J., and WEAKLAND, J. "Toward a Theory of Schizophrenia." *Behavioral Science*, 1956, *1*, 251–264.

BENNE, K. D. "History of the T-Group in the Laboratory Setting." In L. P. Bradford, J. R. Gibb, and K. D. Benne (Eds.), *T-Group Theory and Laboratory Method.* New York: Wiley, 1964.

BENNIS, W. G. "Goals and Meta-Goals of Laboratory Training." *Journal of Applied Behavioral Science*, 1965, *1*, 131–148.

BENNIS, W. G. "Patterns and Vicissitudes in T-Group Development." In L. P. Bradford, J. R. Gibb, and K. D. Benne (Eds.), *T-Group Theory and Laboratory Method.* New York: Wiley, 1964.

BENNIS, W. G., and SCHEIN, E. *Personal and Organizational Change Through Group Methods.* New York: Wiley, 1965.

BENNIS, W. G., and SLATER, P. *The Temporary Society.* New York: Harper and Row, 1968.

BERLIN, J. I. "Program Learning for Personal and Interpersonal Improvement." *Acta Psychologia*, 1964, *13*, 321–335.

BERZON, B., PIOUS, C., and FARSON, R. E. "The Therapeutic Event in Group Psychotherapy: A Study of Subjective Reports by Group Members." *Journal of Individual Psychology*, Fall, 1963.

BERZON, B., and SOLOMON, L. N. "The Self-Directed Therapeutic Group: An Exploratory Study." *International Journal of Group Psychotherapy*, 1964, *14*, 366–369.

BESSELL, H., and PALOMARES, O. H. *Methods in Human Development.* San Diego, Calif.: Human Development Training Institute, 1967.

BLAKE, R. R., and MOUTON, J. S. "Some Effects of Managerial Grid Seminar Training on Union and Management Attitudes Toward Supervision." *Journal of Applied Behavioral Science,* 1966, *2,* 387–400.

BLANCHARD, W. H. "Intellectual Inhibition and the Search for Scientific Truth." *Journal of Social Psychology,* 1958, *47,* 55–70.

BLANCHARD, W. H. "Ecstasy Without Agony Is Baloney." *Psychology Today,* 1970, *3,* 64.

BLOOM, B. S. (Ed.) *Taxonomy of Educational Objectives.* New York: McKay, 1956.

BRADFORD, L., GIBB, J. R., and BENNE, K. *T-Group Theory and the Laboratory Method.* New York: Wiley, 1964.

BUBER, M. *I and Thou.* (2nd ed.) New York: Scribner's 1958.

BUHLER, C. *Values in Psychotherapy.* New York: Free Press, 1962, pp. 108–109 and 165.

BUHLER, C., and MASSARIK, F. (Eds.) *The Course of Human Life.* New York: Springer, 1969.

BUNKER, D. "Individual Applications of Laboratory Training." *Journal of Applied Behavioral Science,* 1965, *1,* 131–148.

BURTON, A. "The Psychotherapy of a Non-Diseased Person." In A. Burton (Ed.), *Modern Psychotherapeutic Practice.* Palo Alto, Calif.: Science and Behavior, 1965.

BUTLER, J. M., and HAIGH, G. "Changes in the Relation Between Self-Concepts and Ideal-Concepts." In C. R. Rogers and R. Dymond (Eds.), *Psychotherapy and Personality Change.* Chicago: University of Chicago Press, 1964.

BUTLER, J. M., RICE, L. N., and WAGSTAFF, A. K. *Quantitative Naturalistic Research.* Englewood Cliffs, N. J.: Prentice-Hall, 1963.

CADDEN, J. J., FLACH, F. F., BLAKESLEE, S., CHARLTON, JR., J. "Growth in Medical Students Through Group Process." *American Journal of Psychiatry,* 1969, *126,* 862–867.

CAMUS, A. *The Myth of Sisyphus.* New York: Knopf, 1955.

CARKHUFF, R., and BERENSEN, B. *Beyond Counseling and Therapy.* New York: Holt, Rinehart and Winston, 1968.

CARSON, R. *Interaction Concepts of Personality.* Chicago: Aldine, 1969.

CHAMPNEY, H. "The Measurement of Parent Behavior." *Child Development,* 1941, *12*(2), 131–168.

CLARK, I., and CLARK, F. "Notes on the Conduct of Married Couples

Groups." *Human Relations Training News*, 1968, *12*, 3.

CORNELISON, JR., F. S., and ARSENIAN, J. M. "A Study of the Responses of Psychotic Patients to Photographic Self-Image Experience." *Psychiatric Quarterly*, 1960, *34*, 1–8.

CORSINI, R. J. *Methods of Group Psychotherapy*. New York: McGraw-Hill, 1957.

COUTU, W. "Role-Playing Versus Role-Taking." *American Sociological Review*, 1951, *16*, 180–187.

DARWIN, C. *The Descent of Man*. New York: Appleton-Century-Crofts, 1871.

DAVIS, S. A. "Building More Effective Teams." *Innovations Magazine*, 1970, *15*, 31–41.

DOLL, R. C. (Ed.) *Individualizing Instruction*. Washington, D.C.: Association for Supervision and Curriculum Development, 1964.

DREXLER, A. B. Personal communication with W. B. Reddy, 1971.

DRURY, S. "The Effects of Structured Exercises on Encounter Groups." Doctoral dissertation. Chicago: University of Chicago, Department of Psychology, December, 1971.

DYMOND, R. "Interpersonal Perception and Marital Happiness." *Canadian Journal of Psychology*, 1954, 8, 164–171.

EGAN, G. *Encounter: Group Processes for Interpersonal Growth*. Monterey, Calif.: Brooks/Cole, 1970.

ELLIS, A. "Symposium on Neurotic Interaction in Marriage Counseling." *Journal of Counseling Psychology*, 1958, 5, 24–33.

ENRIGHT, J. "Awareness Training in the Mental Health Professions." In J. Fagan and I. L. Shepherd (Eds.), *Gestalt Therapy Now*. Palo Alto, Calif.: Science and Behavior, 1970.

FAGAN, J., and SHEPHERD, I. L. (Eds.) *Gestalt Therapy Now*. Palo Alto, Calif.: Science and Behavior, 1970.

FEDERN, P. *Ego Psychology and the Psychoses*. New York: Basic Books, 1952.

FERENCZI, S. *Final Contributions to the Problems and Methods of Psycho-Analysis*. New York: Basic Books, 1955.

FITTS, W. H. *Manual, The Tennessee Self-Concept Scale*. Nashville, Tenn.: Department of Mental Health, 1965.

FORDYCE, J. K., and WEIL, R. *Managing with People*. Reading, Mass.: Addison-Wesley, 1971.

FORER, B. R. "Group Psychotherapy with Outpatient Schizophrenics." *International Journal of Group Psychotherapy*, 1961a, *11*, 188–195.

FORER, B. R. "Schizophrenia: The Narcissistic Retreat." *Journal of*

Projective Techniques, 1961b, *25,* 422–430.

FORER, B. R. "The Therapeutic Value of Crisis." *Psychological Reports,* 1963, *13,* 275–281.

FORER, B. R. "The Vicissitudes of Human Development as Exemplified by the Life of a Clinical Psychologist." *Indian Psychological Review,* 1965, *1,* 150–153.

FORER, B. R. "The Taboo Against Touching in Psychotherapy." *Psychotherapy: Theory, Research and Practice,* 1969a, *6,* 229–231.

FORER, B. R. "Therapeutic Relationships in Groups." In A. Burton (Ed.), *Encounter: Theory and Practice of Encounter Groups.* San Francisco: Jossey-Bass, 1969b.

FOULDS, M. L. "Effects of a Personal Growth Group on a Measure of Self-Actualization." *Journal of Humanistic Psychology,* 1970, *10,* 33–38.

FOULDS, M. L. "Measured Changes in Self-Actualization as a Result of a Growth Group Experience." In *Psychotherapy: Theory, Research and Practice,* in press.

FREEDMAN, L. Z., and ROE, A. "Evolution and Human Behavior." In A. Roe and G. G. Simpson (Eds.), *Behavior and Evolution.* New Haven: Yale University Press, 1958.

FREUD, A. *Introduction to Psychoanalysis for Teachers and Parents.* New York: Emerson Books, 1935.

FREUD, S. *Three Essays on the Theory of Sexuality.* London: Imago, 1949.

FREUD, S. "Further Recommendations in the Technique of Psychoanalysis." In *Collected Papers.* London: Hogarth, 1950.

FREUD, S. *The Ego and the Id.* New York: Norton, 1961.

FRIEDRICHS, R. W. *A Sociology of Sociology.* New York: Free Press, 1970.

FROMM, E. *The Art of Loving.* New York: Harper and Row, 1956.

FROMM-REICHMANN, F. "Notes on Personal and Professional Requirements of a Psychotherapist." In D. M. Bullard (Ed.), *Psychoanalysis and Psychotherapy: Selected Papers of Frieda Fromm-Reichmann.* Chicago: University of Chicago Press, 1959.

FULLER, F. F., BROWN, O. H., and PECK, R. F. *Creating Climates for Growth.* Austin: Hogg Foundation, University of Texas.

GEERTSMA, R. H., and REIVICH, R. S. "Repetitive Self-Observation by Video-Tape Playback." *Journal of Nervous and Mental Disorders,* 1965, *141,* 29–41.

GIBB, J. R. "Factors Producing Defensive Behavior Within Groups."

Final Technical Report, Contract Nonr-3088(00), Office of Naval Research, 1962.

GIBB, J. R. "Effects of Human Relations Training." In A. E. Bergin and S. L. Garfield (Eds.), *Handbook of Psychotherapy and Behavior Change*. New York: Wiley, 1971a.

GIBB, J. R. "Sensitivity Training as a Medium for Personal Growth and Improved Interpersonal Relationship." In G. Egan (Ed.), *Encounter Groups: Basic Readings*. Belmont, Calif.: Wadsworth, 1971b.

GIBB, J. R., and GIBB, L. M. "Role Freedom in a TORI Group." In A. Burton (Ed.), *Encounter: Theory and Practice of Encounter Groups*. San Francisco: Jossey-Bass, 1970.

GOFFMAN, E. *The Presentation of Self in Everyday Life*. New York: Doubleday, 1959.

GOLDSTEIN, A. P., HELLER, K., and SECHREST, L. B. *Psychotherapy and the Psychology of Behavior Change*. New York: Wiley, 1966.

GOLEMBIEWSKI, R., and BLUMBERG, A. *Sensitivity Training and the Laboratory Approach*. Atasca, Ill.: Peacock, 1970.

GOODALL, K. "Tie Line." *Psychology Today*, July 28, 1971.

GOTTSCHALK, L. A., and PATTISON, E. M. "Psychiatric Perspectives on T-Groups and the Laboratory Movement: An Overview." *American Journal of Psychiatry*, 1969, *126*, 823–839.

GRIER, W. H., and COBBS, P. M. *Black Rage*. New York: Basic Books, 1968.

GRIER, W. H., and COBBS, P. M. *The Jesus Bag*. New York: McGraw-Hill, 1971.

GRIVER, J., ROBINSON, M., and FRANKLIN, R. Personal communication with F. Stoller, 1965.

HAIGH, G. V. "Letter to the Editor." *Psychology Today*, 1969, *3*, 4.

HALEY, J. *The Power Tactics of Jesus Christ and Other Essays*. New York: Avon (Discus), 1971.

HALL, E. T. *The Silent Language*. New York: Doubleday, 1959.

HALLECK, S. *The Politics of Therapy*. New York: Science House, 1971.

HAMPDEN-TURNER, C. *Radical Man*. Cambridge, Mass.: Schenkman, 1970.

HARLOW, H. "The Nature of Love." *American Psychologist*, 1958, *13*, 673–685.

HARLOW, H., and ZIMMERMAN, R. R. "Affectional Responses in the Infant Monkey." *Science*, 1959, *130*, 421–432.

HARRISON, R. "The Impact of Laboratory on Perception of Others by the Experimental Group." In C. Argyris (Ed.), *Interpersonal*

Competence and Organizational Effectiveness. Homewood, Ill.: Irwin, 1962.

HARRISON, R. "Group Composition Models for Laboratory Design." *Journal of Applied Behavioral Science,* 1965, *1,* 409–423.

HARRISON, R., and LUBIN, B. "Personal Style, Group Composition, and Learning." Part I. *Journal of Applied Behavioral Science,* 1965a, *1,* 286–294.

HARRISON, R., and LUBIN, B. "Personal Style, Group Composition, and Learning." Part II. *Journal of Applied Behavioral Science,* 1965b, *1,* 294–301.

HENDIN, H., GAYLIN, W., and CARR, A. *Psychoanalysis and Social Research: The Psychoanalytic Study of the Non-Patient.* Garden City, N. Y.: Doubleday, 1965.

HOFFMAN, L. R., and MAIER, N. R. F. "An Experimental Reexamination of the Similarity-Attraction Hypothesis." *Journal of Personality and Social Psychology,* 1966, *3,* 145–152.

HORA, T. "Tao, Zen, and Existential Psychotherapy." *Psychologia,* 1959, *2,* 236–242.

HORNEY, K. *Neurosis and Human Growth.* New York: Norton, 1950.

IGEL, G. J., and CALVIN, A. D. "The Development of Affectional Responses in Infant Dogs." *Journal of Comparative and Physiological Psychology,* 1960, *53,* 302–305.

JACKSON, D. "The Study of the Family." *Family Process,* 1965a, *4,* 1–20.

JACKSON, D. "Family Rules: Marital Quid Pro Quo." *Archives of General Psychiatry,* 1965b, *12,* 589–594.

JAFFE, S. L., and SCHERL, D. J. "Acute Psychosis Precipitated by the T-Group Experience." *Archives of General Psychiatry,* 1969, *21,* 443–448.

JOHNSON, F. C., and others. "An Investigation of Motion Picture Film and the Program Analyzer Feedback to Improve Television Teacher Training." U. S. Office of Education Project 374. Athens, Ohio: Ohio University, 1960.

JOURARD, S. *The Transparent Self.* New York: Van Nostrand, 1964.

JOWETT, R. (Ed.) *Plato: The Republic.* New York: Everyman, 1946, pp. 425–434.

JUNG, C. *Memories, Dreams, Reflections.* New York: Vintage, 1963.

KADIS, A. "A New Approach to Marital Therapy." *International Journal of Social Psychiatry,* 1964, *10,* 261–265.

KASSARJIAN, H. H. "Social Character and Sensitivity Training." *Journal of Applied Behavioral Science,* 1965, *1,* 433–440.

KATZ, M. "Agreement on Connotative Meaning in Marriage." *Family Process*, 1965, *4*, 64–74.

KEEN, S., and RASER, J. "A Conversation with Herbert Marcuse." *Psychology Today*, 1971, *4*, 35–40, 60–66.

KENISTON, K. *The Uncommitted*. New York: Harcourt, Brace, Jovanovich, 1965.

KERNAN, J. P. "Laboratory Human Relations Training: Its Effect on the 'Personality' of Supervisory Engineers." Doctoral dissertation. New York University, 1963.

KNAPP, R. R. *The Measurement of Self-Actualization and Its Theoretical Implications*. San Diego, Calif.: Educational and Industrial Testing Service, 1971.

KOCH, S. "Psychology Cannot Be a Coherent Science." *Psychology Today*, 1969, *3*, 14, 64, 66–68.

KOGAN, N., KRATHWOHL, D. R., and MILLER, R. "Stimulated Recall in Therapy Using Videotape: A Case Study." *Journal of Counseling Psychology*, 1963, *10*, 237–243.

KRUSCHKE, D., and STOLLER, F. H. "Face to Face with the Drug Addict: An Account of an Intensive Group Experience." *Federal Probation*, 1967, *31*(2), 47–52.

KUEHN, J. L., and CRINELLA, F. M. "Sensitivity Training: Interpersonal 'Overkill' and Other Problems." *American Journal of Psychiatry*, 1969, *126*, 840–845.

LAING, R. *The Politics of Experience*. New York: Ballantine, 1967.

LAKIN, M. "Some Ethical Issues in Sensitivity Training." *American Psychologist*, 1969, *24*, 923–928.

LENNARD, H. L., and BERNSTEIN, A. *The Anatomy of Psychotherapy*. New York: Columbia, 1960.

LEONARD, G. *Education and Ecstasy*. New York: Dell, 1967.

LEONARD, G. "The Man and Woman Thing." *Look*, December 24, 1968.

LEVITSKY, A., and PERLS, F. S. "The Rules and Games of Gestalt Therapy." In J. Fagan and I. L. Shepherd (Eds.), *Gestalt Therapy Now*. Palto Alto, Calif.: Science and Behavior, 1970.

LIEBERMAN, M. A., YALOM, I. D., and MILES, M. B. "The Group Experience Project: A Comparison of Ten Encounter Technologies." In L. Blank, G. B. Gottsegen, and M. G. Gottsegen (Eds.), *Encounter: Confrontations in Self and Interpersonal Awareness*. New York: Macmillan, 1971.

LIEBERMAN, M. A., YALOM, I. D., and MILES, M. B. *Encounter Groups: First Facts*. New York: Basic Books, 1972.

LUBIN, B., and EDDY, W. B. "The Laboratory Training Model: Rationale, Method, and Some Thoughts for the Future." *International Journal of Group Psychotherapy*, 1970, *20*, 305–339.

LUBIN, B., and ZUCKERMAN, M. "Level of Emotional Arousal in Laboratory Training." *Journal of Applied Behavioral Science*, 1969, *5*, 483–490.

LUNDGREN, D., and MILLER, D. "Identity and Behavioral Changes in Training Groups." *Human Relations Training News*, Spring, 1965.

MC CLOSKY, H., and SCHAAR, J. H. "Psychological Dimensions of Anomie." *American Sociological Review*, 1965, *30*(1), 14–40.

MAHLER, M. "On Child Psychosis and Schizophrenia: Autistic and Symbiotic Infantile Psychoses." *Psychoanalytic Study of the Child*, 1952, *7*, 286–305.

MARCUSE, H. *One-Dimensional Man.* Boston: Beacon, 1968.

MASLOW, A. H. *Toward a Psychology of Being.* New York: Van Nostrand, 1958.

MATSON, F. W., and MONTAGUE, A. (Eds.) *The Human Dialogue.* New York: Free Press, 1967.

MEAD, G. H. *Mind, Self, and Society.* Chicago: University of Chicago Press, 1934.

MILES, J. "Changes During and Following Laboratory Training: A Clinical Experimental Study." *Journal of Applied Behavioral Science*, 1965, *2*, 215–242.

MILES, M. B. "Organizational Development in Schools: The Effects of Alternative Strategies of Change." Mimeographed research proposal. New York: Horace Mann-Lincoln Institute of School Experimentation, Teachers College, 1963.

MINTZ, E. E. "Marathon Groups: A Preliminary Evaluation." *Journal of Contemporary Psychotherapy*, 1969, *1*, 91–94.

MOOR, F. J., CHERVELL, E., and WEST, M. J. "Television as a Therapeutic Tool." *Archives of General Psychiatry*, 1965, *12*, 217–220.

MORENO, J. L. *Who Shall Survive?* New York: Beacon House, 1953.

MORTON, R. B. "The Organization Training Laboratory: Some Individual and Organizational Effects." *Journal of Advanced Management*, 1965, *30*, 58–67.

NATIONAL INDUSTRIAL CONFERENCE BOARD. "Behavioral Science Concepts and Management." Report #206. Washington, D.C., 1969.

NATIONAL TRAINING LABORATORIES. *News and Reports*, 1969a, *3*, 4.

NATIONAL TRAINING LABORATORIES. *Standards for the Use of Laboratory Method.* Washington, D. C., 1969.

NATIONAL TRAINING LABORATORIES. "Proposal for Division of Accreditation." Memo to Network Members. Washington, D. C., October 7, 1970.

NAVRAN, L. "Communication and Adjustment in Marriage." *Family Process,* 1967, *6,* 173–184.

PARLOFF, M. B. "Group Therapy and the Small-Group Field: An Encounter." *International Journal of Group Psychotherapy,* 1970, *20,* 263–304.

PERLS, F. S. "Workshop vs. Individual Therapy." *Journal of the Long Island Consultation Center,* 1967, 5(2), 13–17.

PERLS, F. S. *Ego, Hunger and Aggression.* New York: Random House, 1969a.

PERLS, F. S. *Gestalt Therapy Verbatim.* Lafayette, Calif.: Real People Press, 1969b.

PERLS, F. S., HEFFERLINE, R. F., and GOODMAN, P. *Gestalt Therapy.* New York: Dell, 1965.

PERLS, L. "One Gestalt Therapist's Approach." In J. Fagan and I. L. Shepherd (Eds.), *Gestalt Therapy Now.* Palo Alto, Calif.: Science and Behavior Books, 1970.

PHILLIPS, E. L., and WIENER, D. N. *Short-Term Psychotherapy and Structured Behavior Change.* New York: McGraw-Hill, 1966.

POSTMAN, N., and WEINGARTNER, C. *Teaching as a Subversive Activity.* New York: Delacorte, 1969.

REDDY, W. B. "Sensitivity Training or Group Psychotherapy: The Need for Adequate Screening." *International Journal of Group Psychotherapy,* 1970, *20,* 366–371.

REDDY, W. B. "Interpersonal Compatibility and Self-Actualization in Sensitivity Training." *Journal of Applied Behavioral Science,* 1971a.

REDDY, W. B. "On Affection, Group Composition and Self-Actualization in Sensitivity Training." *Journal of Consulting and Clinical Psychology,* 1971b.

REICH, W. *Character Analysis.* New York: Orgone Institute, 1949.

ROGERS, C. R. *Counseling and Psychotherapy.* Boston: Houghton Mifflin, 1942.

ROGERS, C. R. *On Becoming a Person.* Boston: Houghton Mifflin, 1961.

ROGERS, C. R. "A Plan for Self-Directed Change in an Educational System." *Educational Leadership,* 1967a.

ROGERS, C. R. "The Process of the Basic Encounter Group." In J. F. G.

Bugental (Ed.), *Challenges of Humanistic Psychology*. New York: McGraw-Hill, 1967b.

ROGERS, C. R. "Interpersonal Relationships: U.S.A. 2000." *Journal of Applied Behavioral Science*, 1968, *4*(3), 265–280.

ROGERS, C. R. "The Group Comes of Age." *Psychology Today*, 1969, *3*, 27, 29–31, 58, 60–61.

ROGERS, C. R. *On Encounter Groups*. New York: Harper and Row, 1970.

ROGERS, R. *Coming into Existence*. New York: World Publishing, 1967.

ROSENBERG, M. *Society and the Adolescent Self-Image*. Princeton, N. J.: Princeton University Press, 1965.

SATIR, V. *Conjoint Family Therapy*. Palo Alto, Calif.: Science and Behavior, 1964.

SCHACHTER, S. "Deviation, Rejection, and Communication." *Journal of Abnormal and Social Psychology*, 1951, *46*, 190–207.

SCHIFF, S. B., and REIVICH, R. S. "Use of Television as Aid to Psychotherapy Supervision." *Archives of General Psychiatry*, 1964, *10*, 84–88.

SCHMUCK, R. A., and MILES, M. B. *Organizational Development in Schools*. Palo Alto, Calif.: National Press Books, 1971.

SCHOFIELD, W. *Psychotherapy: The Purchase of Friendship*. Englewood Cliffs, N. J.: Prentice-Hall, 1964.

SCHUTZ, W. C. *FIRO: A Three-Dimensional Theory of Interpersonal Behavior*. New York: Holt, Rinehart and Winston, 1958.

SCHUTZ, W. C. *The Interpersonal Underworld*. Palo Alto, Calif.: Science and Behavior, 1966.

SCHUTZ, W. C. *Joy*. New York: Grove, 1967.

SCHUTZ, W. C. *Here Comes Everybody*. New York: Harper and Row, 1971.

SHERIF, M. "Group Influence upon the Formation of Norms and Attitudes." In E. E. Maccoby, T. M. Newcomb, and E. L. Hartley (Eds.), *Readings in Social Psychology*. New York: Holt, Rinehart and Winston, 1958.

SHIBUTANI, T. *Society and Personality*. Englewood Cliffs, N. J.: Prentice-Hall, 1961.

SHLIEN, J. M. "Toward What Level of Abstraction in Criteria?" In H. H. Strapp and L. Luborsky (Eds.), *Second Research Conference in Psychotherapy*. Washington, D. C.: American Psychological Association, 1961.

SHOSTROM, E. L. *The Personal Orientation Inventory*. San Diego:

Educational and Industrial Testing Service, 1963.

SHOSTROM, E. L. *The Caring Relationship Inventory.* San Diego: Educational and Industrial Testing, 1966a.

SHOSTROM, E. L. *Manual for the Personal Orientation Inventory: An Inventory for the Measure of Self-Actualization.* San Diego: Educational and Industrial Testing Service, 1966b.

SHOSTROM, E. L. "Group Therapy: Let the Buyer Beware." *Psychology Today,* 1969, *4,* 37–40.

SHOSTROM, E. L. *Pair Attraction Inventory.* San Diego: Educational and Industrial Testing, 1970.

SHOSTROM, E. L., and KAVANAUGH, J. *Between Man and Woman.* Los Angeles: Nash, 1971.

SIMKIN, J. S. *Individual Gestalt Therapy: Interview with Dr. Frederick Perls.* Audio-tape recording. Philadelphia: Association for the Advancement of Psychotherapy Tape Library, No. 31, 1967.

SIMKIN, J. S. *In the Now.* A training film. Beverly Hills, 1969.

SIMKIN, J. S. "Mini-Lectures on Gestalt Therapy." Unpublished manuscript, 1971.

SKINNER, B. F., and FERSTER, C. B. *Schedules of Reinforcement.* New York: Appleton-Century-Crofts, 1957.

SLATER, P. E. *Microcosm: Structural, Psychological and Religious Evolution in Groups.* New York: Wiley, 1966.

SLAVSON, S. R. "General Principles and Dynamics." In S. R. Slavson (Ed.), *The Practice of Group Therapy.* New York: International Universities Press, 1947, pp. 19–39.

SMITH, G. B. "Design for Change." Final Report, Model Treatment Program, Institute for the Study of Crime and Delinquency. Sacramento, Calif., 1968.

SOHL, J. *The Lemon Eaters.* New York: Dell, 1968.

SOLOMON, L. N., and BERZON, B. "The Self-Directed Group: A New Direction in Personal Growth Learning." In J. T. Hart and T. M. Tomlinson (Eds.), *New Directions in Client-Centered Therapy.* Boston: Houghton Mifflin, 1970, pp. 314–347.

SOLOMON, L. N., BERZON, B., and DAVIS, D. "A Personal Growth Program for Self-Directed Groups." *Journal of Applied Behavioral Science,* 1970, *6,* 427–451.

SOLOMON, L. N., BERZON, B., and WEEDMAN, C. W. "The Self-Directed Therapeutic Group: A New Rehabilitation Resource." *International Journal of Group Psychotherapy,* 1968, *18,* 199–219.

SORRELLS, J., and FORD, F. "Toward an Integrated Theory of Families and Family Therapy." *Psychotherapy*, 1969, *6*, 150–160.

SPITZ, R. "Anaclitic Depression." *Psychoanalytic Study of the Child*, 1946, *2*, 313–342.

SROLE, L. "Social Integration and Certain Corollaries." *American Sociological Review*, 1956, *21*, 709–716.

STEPHENSON, W. *The Study of Behavior*. Chicago: University of Chicago Press, 1953.

STIMSON, A. "Marital Interaction Patterns, Effective Communication and Satisfaction: An Exploration of Problem-Solving Behavior." (Doctoral dissertation, New York University.) Ann Arbor, Mich.: University Microfilms, 1966, No. 66–8584.

STOLLER, F. H. "TV and the Patient's Self-Image." *Frontiers of Hospital Psychiatry*, 1965, *2*(7).

STOLLER, F. H. "The Long Weekend." *Psychology Today*, 1967, *1*(7), 28–33.

STOLLER, F. H. "Accelerated Interaction: A Time-Limited Approach Based on the Brief, Intensive Group. *International Journal of Group Psychotherapy*, 1968a, *18*, 220–235.

STOLLER, F. H. "Marathon Group Therapy." In G. M. Gazda (Ed.), *Innovations to Group Psychotherapy*. Springfield, Ill.: Thomas, 1968b, pp. 42–95.

STOLLER, F. H. "A Stage for Trust." In A. Burton (Ed.) *Encounter: Theory and Practice of Encounter Groups*. San Francisco: Jossey-Bass, 1969.

STONE, W. N., and TIEGER, M. E. "Screening for T-Groups: The Myth of Healthy Candidates." Paper presented at the American Psychiatric Association Meeting, San Francisco, 1970.

STRASSBURGER, F. "Ethical Guidelines for Encounter Groups." *APA Monitor*, 1971, *2*, 7.

STRUPP, H. S., and BERGIN, A. E. "Some Empirical and Conceptual Bases for Coordinated Research in Psychotherapy." *International Journal of Psychiatry*. 1969, *72*, 18–90.

SULLIVAN, H. S. *Conceptions of Modern Psychiatry*. (2nd ed.) Washington, D. C.: William Alanson White Foundation, 1947.

TOFFLER, A. *Future Shock*. New York: Random House, 1970.

TRYON, R. C., and BAILEY, D. S. *Cluster Analysis*. New York: McGraw-Hill, 1970.

VALIQUET, I. "Contribution to the Evaluation of a Management Development Program." Unpublished master's thesis. Massachusetts Institute of Technology, 1964.

VAN DER VEEN, F. "Client Perception of Therapist Conditions as a

Factor in Psychotherapy." In J. T. Hart and T. M. Tomlinson (Eds.), *New Directions in Client-Centered Therapy*. Boston: Houghton Mifflin, 1970.

VAN KAAM, A. *The Art of Existential Counseling*. Wilkes-Barre, Penna.: Dimension Books, 1966.

VONNEGUT, JR., K. *Cat's Cradle*. New York: Dell, 1963.

WATTS, A. *Psychotherapy East and West*. New York: Ballantine, 1969.

WATZLAWICK, P. *An Anthology of Human Communication*. Palo Alto, Calif.: Science and Behavior, 1964.

WATZLAWICK, P. "A Structured Family Interview." *Family Process*, 1966, 5, 256–271.

WATZLAWICK, P., BEAVIN, J., and JACKSON, D. *Pragmatics of Human Communication*. New York: Norton, 1967.

WECHSLER, I. R., MASSARIK, F., and TANNENBAUM, R. "The Self in Process: A Sensitivity Training Emphasis." In I. R. Wechsler and E. H. Schein (Eds.), *Issues in Training*. Washington, D. C.: National Education Association, National Training Laboratories, 1962.

WEDEL, C. C. "A Study of Measurement in Group Dynamics Laboratories." Doctoral dissertation. George Washington University, 1957.

WHITING, B. B., *Six Cultures: Studies of Child Rearing*. New York: Wiley, 1963.

WILMOTH, J. "A Gestalt Premarital Interviewing Model for Use by Pastoral Counselors." Master's thesis. Berkeley, Calif.: Pacific School of Religion, 1971.

WILLEMS, E. P., and RAUSH, H. L. (Eds.) *Naturalistic Viewpoints in Psychological Research*. New York: Holt, Rinehart and Winston, 1969.

WINTHROP, H. "Humanistic Psychology and Intentional Community." In A. J. Sutich and M. Vich (Eds.), *Readings in Humanistic Psychology*. New York: Free Press, 1969, pp. 280–298.

YALOM, I. D. *The Theory and Practice of Group Psychotherapy*. New York: Basic Books, 1970.

YALOM, I. D., FIDLER, J. W., FRANK, J., MANN, J., and SATA, L. *Encounter Groups and Psychiatry*. Task Force Report 1. Washington, D. C.: American Psychiatric Association, 1970.

YALOM, I. D., and LIEBERMAN, M. A. "A Study of Encounter Group Casualties." *Archives of General Psychiatry*, 1971, 25, 16–30.

Index